W9-BVE-088

Fodor's

E X P L O R I N G

PARIS

FODOR'S TRAVEL PUBLICATIONS, INC.

NEW YORK • TORONTO • LONDON • SYDNEY • AUCKLAND

HTTP://WWW.FODORS.COM/

While every care has been taken to ensure the accuracy of the information in this guide, time brings change, and consequently the publisher cannot accept responsibility for errors that may occur. Prudent travelers will therefore want to call ahead to verify prices and other "perishable" information.

Copyright © 1996 by The Automobile Association.
Maps copyright © 1996 by The Automobile Association.

All rights reserved under International and Pan-American Copyright Conventions. Distributed by Random House, Inc., New York. No maps, illustrations, or other portions of this book may be reproduced in any form without written permission from the publishers.

Published in the United States by Fodor's Travel Publications, Inc.
Published in the United Kingdom by AA Publishing.

Fodor's and Fodor's Exploring Guides are trademarks of Fodor's Travel Publications, Inc.

ISBN 0–679–03211–8
Third Edition

Fodor's Exploring Paris

Author: **Fiona Dunlop**
Revision Verifier: **Teresa Fisher**
Cover Design: **Louise Fili, Fabrizio La Rocca**
Front Cover Silhouette: **David W. Hamilton/Image Bank**

Special Sales

Fodor's Travel Publications are available at special discounts for bulk purchases (100 copies or more) for sales promotions or premiums. Special editions, including personalized covers, excerpts of existing guides, and corporate imprints, can be created in large quantities for special needs. For more information write to Special Marketing, Fodor's Travel Publications, 201 East 50th St., New York, NY 10022.

Manufactured in Italy by Printers Trento S.R.L.
10 9 8 7 6 5 4 3 2 1

Fiona Dunlop lives in Paris where she has reported on the city's cultural life for newspapers and magazines such as *The Times*, the *Sunday Times*, the *European, Art International, Vogue Décoration*, and *Elle Décoration*. She is author of the *Paris Art Guide*, and of *Mexico* and *Singapore & Malaysia* in both Fodor's Exploring series and the AA Essential Explorer series. She has contributed to several other guides including the *Time Out Guide to Paris*.

Gustave Eiffel's world-famous construction has become the emblem of Paris

Elegant bronze statues guard the Palais de Chaillot

About this book
This book is divided into three principal sections.

The first part of the book discusses aspects of life today and in the past. The second part covers places to visit, including drives and walks. The Focus On features, also in this section, look at subjects in greater detail. The final part is made up of Travel Facts, giving practical information for the traveler, and the Hotels and Restaurants section, which is a selective list of accommodations and places to eat.

Some of the places described in this book have been given a special rating:

▶▶▶   Do not miss

▶▶   Highly recommended

▶   See if you can

General Contents

French telephone numbers
As of October 18, 1996, all French telephone numbers will change from the current eight-digit format to ten-figure numbers. See pages 270–1 for details.

6

Walks

Drive

My Paris

by Annabel Buffet

Annabel Buffet
Annabel Buffet has been a model, a singer, and a writer. Her books include *Daily Love, Good Manners, Beautiful Lies,* and *St. Tropez, Today and Yesterday.* She married the artist Bernard Buffet in 1958; they have three children: Virginie, Danielle, and Nicolas.

Why is Paris still the city of everyone's dreams? What makes it the highlight of any itinerary? No one can deny the city's beauty. Its sights and walks are overwhelming, whether you are strolling along the banks of the Seine, or admiring the perspective that follows a magnificent straight line from the Arc de Triomphe to the Louvre, or walking in Montmartre or St.-Germain-des-Prés along streets that keep alive the shadows of the past. Then, of course, there is the world-famous Paris cuisine. And when you have satisfied your gastronomic desires you will face another temptation: window-shopping. The avenue Montaigne, the Faubourg St.-Honoré, the delightful place des Victoires, all combine to form a stunning tableau of elegance and taste.

On the other hand, Paris can be something very different from haute-couture shopping or meals in three-star restaurants. I remember my emotions when, after the war that had exiled me to the South of France, I returned to Paris for the first time. I was 17 years old; in my purse I had scarcely enough for the bare necessities of life. I came out of the Gare de Lyon, deafened by the noise and disorientated by the soft Ile de France light, so different from the sun of Provence. The intense life of the capital gripped me, and scared me a little. A day or two later, that anxiety had disappeared. A week later, I had fallen in love with Paris for good. It was on foot and (when money permitted) by bus that I learned to love the city, area by area. Each quartier is a self-contained village; each has its churches, its cafés; and yet each breathes something that is the very essence of Paris: liberty.

Paris is, and will remain, a jewel case in which one diamond will always sparkle: respect for the human being. Tenderhearted Paris, irrepressible Paris: this is where life is truly free and unconstrained.

Life in Montmartre: the place du Tertre

My Paris
by Maurice Raimbeaux

When I first arrived in Paris, I stayed in a small hotel not far from the Etoile. Every morning I would walk to the metro, mesmerized by the giant Arc de Triomphe. Later, as I rose in the bank hierarchy, I didn't have to get up so early—but I still have fond memories of the morning light reflecting off the stone. Strangely, I've never been to the top of the Arc: I'm convinced it's only for tourists!

In the early days I also reveled in the Tuileries gardens; instead of having lunch in the bank cafeteria, I'd buy a sandwich and head for a sunny park bench.

Only for tourists? The towering Arc de Triomphe

Since then I've lived in five different arrondissements and discovered that Etoile was probably the most mundane. It's impossible to pick a favorite area: each quartier has its own personality. I loved Pigalle, where as a young bachelor I lived in an artist's studio; many of my neighbors were painters and sculptors. There was a strong village atmosphere, and on warm summer evenings we'd walk up the butte Montmartre looking for a cool breeze.

When I got married, my wife and I moved to the rather bourgeois fifth arrondissement, right behind the Panthéon. Our apartment building had two entrances: on one side was a maze of narrow silent streets, on the other the rue Mouffetard, with its cheap restaurants, colorful market, and crowds of students. On Sundays we'd often go for a walk in the Luxembourg gardens—later taking the baby—and watch the old men playing chess by the Orangerie. But that apartment became too small for us, so we moved to the Marais, where high-ceilinged apartments in former aristocratic townhouses were still relatively cheap.

It was the beginning of an enormous upheaval in that neighborhood, with gentrification transforming its character fast. We still live there, but we miss the early days, when there were fewer art galleries, restaurants, and yuppies—although I suppose I must admit I'm one of them!

Maurice Raimbeaux
Maurice Raimbeaux is a banker who has lived in Paris for almost 20 years. He was born in a mountain village in the Pyrénées and went to the university in Toulouse, before moving to Paris as a bank trainee.

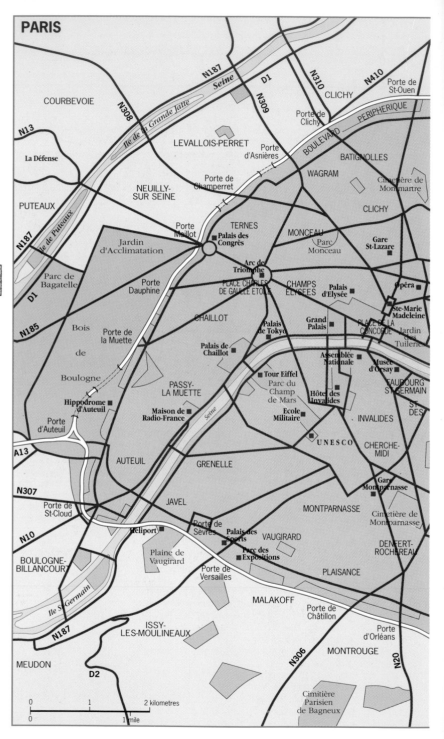

PARIS

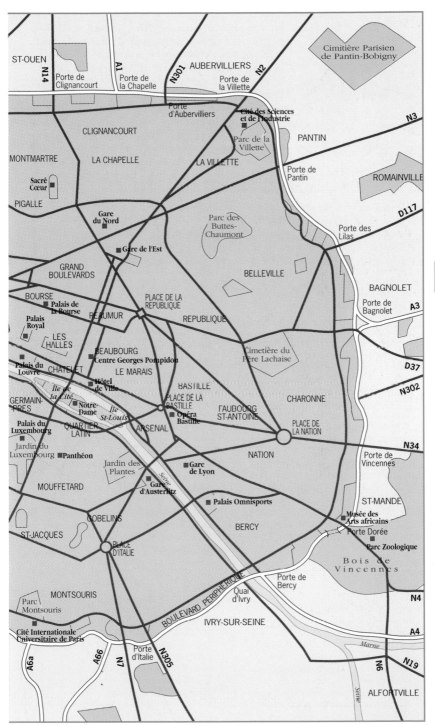

■ **Paris is one of the most densely populated cities in the world. Not only that: it is perhaps the capital most talked about, most written about, most hyped, most dreamed about.** A vacation spent there leaves indelible memories—whether of the clear spring light on the Seine, a gastronomic fantasy, an exhausting string of masterpieces at the Louvre, or a short-tempered waiter serving a tray of delectable oysters. Full of contrasts, thick with history, it is also a city on the move, looking to the future ...■

Parisians themselves remain a mystery. Their general love of the good things in life—food, sex, and fashion (not necessarily in that order)—is accompanied by a strong intellectual streak. TV programs regularly feature groups of writers chatting about their books, ideas, and projects, while newspapers contain long columns written by philosophers. This interest in abstraction spins off into conversations in which heated arguments are commonplace and a necessary part of any friendship. For some, such a strong emphasis on abstract thought stops action, or at least postpones it, and the business world suffers directly.

Defining a typical Parisian means taking into account not only the many provincials who flock to the city but also a traditional foreign influx, whether from Central Africa, North Africa, Vietnam, or Europe. Communities form rapidly, from the African and Arab quarters in Belleville to the Chinese and Vietnamese in the 13th arrondissement. Racism is disturbingly on the increase, particularly in the soulless suburbs bereft of social life and structure, and continues the traditional French xenophobia. In contrast, the prosperous and sacrosanct 16th arrondissement remains intact with its breed of bourgeoisie sprinkled with the odd princess, sheikh or retired Hollywood diva. In between the extremes lies the heart of French business and social trends.

Paris Style Ever since the heady days of the 1920s, Paris has harbored a hotbed of foreign artists, thinkers, and political refugees, all of whom have contributed to the clichés of bohemianism. Glamour is never far: Paris is a city where enjoyment costs little, as it is always on display. Appearances are paramount, and the impeccably groomed businessman or woman, totally at ease drinking a champagne cocktail in the latest trendy restaurant, may well turn out to live in a minute studio apartment in a distant arrondissement. Money is worn on the back, or on the plate, and this can also be interpreted as a sheeplike trait. Fashion is not invented, it is followed; woe betide the pretender who misses the season's mark. Yet this apparent conformism is peppered with strong anarchistic qualities, as traffic policemen and tourists well know. The notion of queueing (although originally from a French word) still seems to escape the Gallic consciousness; individualism wins hands down over any civic conscience or community sense.

Changing city The Paris of the 1990s has a radically different face to that of only 15 years ago. Fourteen years of a president who, to some, seems to mold himself on predecessors such as Louis XIV or Napoleon III, have left their distinctive mark. *Grands projets* hit the skyline, new quartiers are created, and Paris is gradually undergoing total gentrification. An obsession with history and their role in the continuum is another characteristic of French rulers, and former President Mitterrand was no exception. Which other world capital has invested so much in cultural structures as a national trademark?

❏ The population of Paris (intra-muros, or within the ring road) stabilized in 1990 at 2,152,400 after 30 years of dropping. Each residence/apartment/house has 1.92 inhabitants, compared with 2.35 in 1954. Ten percent of lodgings are empty, rising to 18 percent in the center. ❏

Mind and body If the Parisians love culture and abstract ideals, they are equally preoccupied with sex, from the hot spots of Pigalle to advertisements whose blatancy makes Anglo-Saxon feminists blanch. Parisian women somehow manage to retain an ambivalence: supremely elegant, they are increasingly prominent in French business and politics.

Thus a renovated Paris, its sense of pride (and sometimes superiority) intact, faces a new Europe. Times have changed and a non-French-speaking visitor is no longer ostracized. A new generation eagerly attempts to bridge the language barrier. And remember that however reserved a Parisian exterior may be, humor will always permeate it. The Parisian character lies somewhere in between Latin demonstrativeness (they would kiss their worst enemy on the cheek, left and right) and bourgeois restraint. Underneath is a *bon viveur* who, whatever his faults, helped coin the phrase *savoir vivre*.

All life is here: café society still flourishes in Paris, despite many other changes in the city

■ France has at last attained political stability and is now regarded as one of the most powerful Western democracies. In the last two centuries, it has been ruled by no fewer than 16 constitutions, and only a few decades ago, in the immediate postwar period, government after government failed in their attempts to rule an ebullient nation undergoing profound socioeconomic changes. Then came de Gaulle and the Fifth Republic. And then, after the dramatic events of 1968 and two intermediary presidents, came "the quiet strength" of the late President Mitterrand ...■

14

Modern French history reached its lowest ebb with the national disgrace of Pétain's Vichy Régime. In 1945, the Fourth Republic was accepted by referendum and women were at last given the vote. But inherent constitutional weaknesses led to 30 successive governments, often rocky coalitions. The Algerian War of Independence finally brought down this Republic: under threat of a military coup d'état, the National

Assembly admitted defeat in 1958 and called on de Gaulle to bail his country out.

Although a national referendum ratified the new constitution, many doubted that the Fifth Republic would survive the general's departure. Yet, although severely shaken by the events of 1968

The National Assembly, where presidents dare not tread

(student revolts and national strikes brought the country to a standstill), it still survives today.

Political structure At the head of the government stands the president, elected every seven years by universal suffrage. Far from being a mere figurehead, as in many other European republics, he is head of the army, responsible for nuclear defense, nominates the prime minister, can call referendums or dissolve Parliament. Based in the Elysée Palace, the president is not allowed to set foot in the National Assembly at the Palais Bourbon. He is answerable to the Conseil Constitutionnel, an independent body, and arbiter of the constitution.

Nominated by the president and often changed at his whim, the prime minister heads the government and ensures execution of the laws. Based at the Hôtel Matignon, he nominates ministers in collaboration with the president, but owes his authority to the confidence of the National Assembly. The government can be censured by Parliament with a vote of absolute majority. Government's inner core, the cabinet, meets every Wednesday at the Elysée for a working meeting chaired by the president.

Parliament is composed of two chambers: the National Assembly, with 577 deputies elected every five years, and its upper body, the Senate, with 318 senators elected by local representatives every nine years. The differences in duration of power between the president (still seven years, despite various proposals to shorten the term) and the Assembly (five years) has led to potentially divisive situations. In 1986, when Mitterrand was already five years into his first mandate, new legislative elections produced a right-wing parliamentary majority. This led to the paradoxical and thorny situation of a Socialist president ruling with a right-wing (Gaullist) prime minister— Chirac—and the term "cohabitation" was coined. A repeat situation was produced in 1993 when RPR Edouard Balladur was appointed

prime minister under the then still-reigning Mitterrand.

Quick changes Chameleon-like, French political parties are constantly changing initials, allegiances, and coalitions. Divided roughly equally between right- and left-wing, there are currently six main parties: the PS (Parti Socialiste), RPR (Gaullist), UDF (center-right), PC (Communist), MRG (a coalition of left-wing groups including ecologists) and FN (Front National, extreme right). The latter, led by Le Pen, has seen an ominous increase in support, particularly in the south, but maverick Bernard Tapie, the working-class hero, has recently managed to swing some of these votes into the left-wing camp.

Technocracy As a nation, the French are not strongly unionized, and members are diminishing in number: only 13 percent of the workforce are now registered. But the area in which the French maintain overwhelming numbers is the army of civil servants. The traditionally heavyweight state administration dates back to the 17th century, was perfected by Napoleon, and assured a legal and technical continuity throughout the turmoil of French

15

> ❏ In all, 2,600,000 French men and women work for the state. ❏

political history. Exemplary in many fields, it has some of the best training grounds for top-ranking administrators. Yet it is also stifling, encumbering the nation with an excessive bureaucracy. It also ensures that governmental power is far-reaching and all-encompassing: not always a healthy situation.

Above all, France is a technocracy in which civil servants play often dominant roles in economic or technical development. But when the traffic policeman, one of the millions of civil servants, has handed out your parking ticket, remember that a new president always gives an amnesty for recalcitrants: so hold on!

■ **Frenetic is the only word to describe architectural activity in Paris over the last decade. Cranes groan on the horizon, while other machinery burrows away underground. Little remains untouched and, as a result, Paris has undergone a major facelift, with entire quartiers like Le Marais restored to their former gleaming glory and countless sheets of glass lovingly installed into the modernist facades of Paris's new landmarks ...■**

16

The key building is the **Centre Pompidou**, more commonly known as **Beaubourg**, completed in 1977 and now attracting more visitors than the Eiffel Tower. Controversially high tech, in marked contrast to the surrounding 18th- and 19th-century townhouses, it set the tone for a new generation of architects and a new attitude toward public building. Although instigated by President Georges Pompidou, it was finished under Giscard d'Estaing—who had attempted to ax the plan—and was soon followed by more ambitious projects such as the **Parc de la Villette**, a kind of glorified urban playground, still under development, and the transformation of a former railway station and hotel into the **Musée d'Orsay**. Politics and architecture have always gone hand in hand, and the 1980s saw a particularly complex wrangle, with the then Gaullist mayor of Paris, Jacques Chirac, countering the grandiose, some say megalomaniac, projects of Socialist President Mitterrand. Many were bulldozed, and huge budgets scrapped, but quite a lot were built.

Grand finale With Mitterrand's 14 years of presidency over, so his *grands projets* are approaching completion. The last one on the board is Dominique Perrault's national library, nicknamed the **TGB** (Très Grande Bibliothèque), whose four 328-foot glass towers imitate the form of open books.
The cement mixers will not leave when the TGB is completed, as the Mairie de Paris has since instigated

❏ The new Bibliothèque de France, being built at a cost of about 5.2 billion francs, will provide 248 miles of shelves to take some of the strain off the Bibliothèque Nationale. ❏

an ambitious plan to overhaul this rather neglected quarter in the southeast of Paris. Immediately north across the river, in Bercy, there has already been a transformation, with Chemetov's one-legged **Ministry of Finance** limping into the Seine, a state-of-the-art American Center designed by Frank Gehry, and numerous office and apartment buildings jostling for a view over the newly landscaped **Parc de Bercy**.

New look Louvre Most close to the Parisian heart has been the creation of the *Grand Louvre* with I. M. Pei's metal and glass pyramid personally chosen by the president. When the whole project is completed in 1997, the Louvre will be the world's largest museum (although it seems like that anyway), at a cost of over $1 billion. The pyramid's symbolic position on the east-west axis marks a straight line from the **Opéra Bastille** in the east to the **Grande Arche**, far to the west at La Défense, with the **Tuileries, Concorde, Champs-Elysées**, and **Arc de Triomphe** in between. Apart from pleasing a Cartesian sense of logic and geometry and bowing to a tradition of French rulers from Catherine de Médicis onward, it also makes life easier for the landmark-seeking visitor.

The Louvre: I. M. Pei's modern-day pyramid

La Grande Arche crowns the new business district of La Défense and has created a desperately needed focal point for what was previously a mass of tower buildings left over from the 1960s and '70s. Von Spreckelsen's gateway design leaves the axis open for development and the city without limits.

Completed just in time for the 1989 Bicentenary celebrations, the Grande Arche had a warmer reception than Mitterrand's other pet project, the "people's" opera house at the Bastille. The design was by unknown Canadian architect Carlos Ott. Plans were radically modified, but it eventually opened in 1990. Although overpowering the rest of the place, the **Opéra Bastille** improves inside and would seem to have overcome its teething problems.

Nouvel architecture Paris in the 1990s cannot be discussed without mentioning the enfant terrible of architecture, Jean Nouvel. His much-praised **Institut du Monde Arabe**, completed in 1986, is a masterpiece of sculptural purity and was followed in 1994 by the equally intriguing new **Fondation Cartier**.

The city's architectural renaissance has added to its unique style, not only in status-symbol monuments, but also in the far-flung arrondissements and the suburbs.

ORA GRAY DUNCAN

12 AVRIL 1922

■ **There are more than enough stars and wannabes in Paris to launch another galaxy. Below is a checklist of prominent characters who have been part of Paris life during recent years—though not all have been worthy of gracing the cover of the gossip rag** *Paris Match* **...**■

Azzadine Alaïa Of Tunisian origin, Alaïa was adopted by the French fashion world when he worked from his living room in the early 1980s, selling clinging dresses in black leather and slinky jerseys. He opened a boutique in the Marais and is now an international fashion name.

Isabelle Adjani Born in Paris of a German mother and Turkish father, Adjani started acting at age 14 and later joined the Comédie Française. She became famous with Truffaut's *Adèle H* in 1975. In 1981, she won the Cannes prize for best actress for her role in James Ivory's *Quartet*.

Pierre Boulez The great classical composer was born in 1925 and studied music at the Paris Conservatoire under Messïaen. He worked as a conductor in London and New York before directing acoustic research at IRCAM.

Daniel Buren France's most controversial contemporary artist, Buren was born in 1938 near Paris. Since the 1960s he has specialized in scandals and in taking intellectual stands in the art world. Stripes are a constant theme—see his columns in the Palais-Royal.

Henri Cartier-Bresson This world-famous globe-trotting photographer was a founding member of the Magnum photo-reporters' agency, and now lives on the rue de Rivoli. His images have become icons of the 20th century.

César A diminutive, bearded figure from the south of France, César's pop art sculptures astonished the public in the early 1960s; he is particularly famous for his giant bronze thumbs. See his *Centaur* at the Carrefour de la Croix Rouge in St.-Germain.

Patrice Chéreau Theater and film director Chéreau first achieved international fame in the 1970s, with a revolutionary production of Wagner's *Ring Cycle* in Bayreuth and Berg's *Lulu* in Paris. After successfully directing the Théâtre des Amandiers in Nanterre, Chéreau recently resigned to concentrate more on personal work.

Catherine Deneuve A blonde beauty propulsed to fame by director Roger Vadim in the 1960s, Deneuve's destiny was sealed by Jacques Démy's *Les Parapluies de Cherbourg* and Polanski's *Repulsion*. Her face was a model for every town hall statue of *Marianne*.

Gérard Départieu His bulky, muscular frame is now world-famous, following major roles in films by Wajda, Truffaut, Ferreri, Pialat, and Resnais. Départieu recently turned to directing, with *Tartuffe*. He divides his time between tending his Burgundy vines and his Parisian apartment.

Marguerite Duras The late author and film director Duras' entire output expresses the incommunicability of love in a tense, lonely world. She became famous in the 1950s, sealing her status with her film *India Song* and by writing the screenplay for Resnais' *Hiroshima mon amour*. Her bestseller *L'Amant* (1984) was based on her childhood in Indochina.

Serge Gainsbourg Although he died aged 62 in 1990, Gainsbourg's influence on French rock music and youth culture continues. Iconoclastic, with a sardonic humor inspired by

18

Face of France: Catherine Deneuve

Surrealism, he revolutionized French *chanson*, changing the writing and sonority of sung French. He was married to Jane Birkin, and their daughter Charlotte Gainsbourg is now a talented young actress.

Jean-Paul Gaultier The ultimate French fashion designer of the 1980s, this recognized enfant terrible introduced the androgynous look, baroque caricatures, and extraordinary fabrics. He started designing at Cardin's and created his own label in 1976.

Jean Nouvel One of a new generation of architects who put French design on the map. Nouvel's first major Parisian project was the Institut du Monde Arabe (1986). His designs make sophisticated use of high-tech materials and are often technical feats. His *Tour sans fin* design for La Défense, a 1,312-foot tower, is proving difficult. Nouvel is often spotted at Les Bains nightclub.

Christine Ockrent Came to fame in the 1980s as a TV newscaster, leading to clones on every other channel. Her "superwoman" legend grew when she had her first child at the age of 40. She worked for CBS in the U.S. and the BBC in the U.K., and now occasionally still presents Edition Le Soir for France 3.

Joël Robuchon This creator of everyone's dream cuisine is based in his 16th-arrondissement restaurant. A leading nouvelle cuisine chef, he started at the ovens at age 15 and worked his way up to cook under André Moreau at the age of 21.

Yves Saint-Laurent Born in Algeria in 1936, YSL divides his time between Marrakesh and Paris. He designed for Christian Dior from 1957 to 1960 and founded his own fashion house in 1962. The first couturier to introduce *prêt-à-porter*, he developed licensing for accessories, thus revolutionizing the fashion business. He invented the trouser suit in the 1970s.

■ **When all is said and done, what remains of a civilization is its culture, and this the French understood long ago. The electricity of Parisian cultural life has always attracted foreign artists, and today the capital is a stage for top international figures. Stimulated by a healthy rivalry between theaters and encouraged by generous state subsidies, the situation for the arts is enviable ...■**

The all-powerful minister of culture does not only cover traditional forms; he is also minister for rock music and comic strips, while guiding the destiny of the fashion industry. But this paternalistic umbrella has its negative effects, creating a climate of dependency. The hard edge— a will to succeed and survive—is sometimes lacking.

Picture palace Living up to its role as nation-inventor of the cinema, France's capital offers over 300 different films weekly. Since the heyday of the *nouvelle vague*, new blood has appeared (Beineix, Léo

Théâtre des Champs-Elysées

Carax, Bertrand Blier, Coline Serreau, Luc Besson, Chantal Akermann, Jean-Jacques Annaud, Alain Corneau) while the older intimist generation of **Rivette,**

❑ In 1955, admissions to movie theaters in France numbered 385 million. In 1989, they numbered 118 million. ❑

Chabrol, Rohmer, Resnais, or **Tavernier** have not said their last words. The third largest producer of films in the world, much of France's cinema is filmed in the studios of Billancourt in west Paris, while once a year all eyes are on the Cannes Film Festival. Yet cinema audiences are dropping.

Music Whether jazz, rock, or classical, sounds emerge from clubs, theaters, hotels, churches, or concert halls all over the capital. Maintaining its pivotal role as the European jazz center, Paris has attracted a stream of top American musicians since **Sydney Bechet's** days. Jazz clubs abound; traditionalists vie with experimentalists; **Miles Davis** would appear for a lightning set; and local musicians create their own syntheses.
   Rock music, on the other hand, remains the black sheep of French culture—despite desperate state support. Exceptions such as the **Gypsy Kings** or **Les Négresses Vertes** bend the rule, but ultimately creative rock escapes the French character and language, possibly too analytical for such basic rhythms.

Cinema lines are on the decline

The recent explosion of "world music" has given black Africans and North Africans (mainly Algerians and notably Khaled) a chance to express new sounds, amalgamations of native harmonies with westernized arrangements.

Opera and classical music are centralized fields in France: 75 percent of French composers over 40 studied at the Paris Conservatoire, and the sophisticated new Conservatoire at La Villette will no doubt maintain this status quo. **Pierre Boulez, Henri Dutilleux, Edgar Varèse**, and the Greek-born **Iannis Xenakis**, with **Olivier Messïaen** (who died in 1992) as a strong background influence, are France's contemporary masters who, although sometimes open to electro-acoustic innovation, avoid minimalist American models.

Dance has progressed by leaps and bounds throughout the 1980s and, unlike music, has found its place in the regions. The companies of young choreographers such as **Jean-Claude Gallotta** (Grenoble), the late **Dominique Bagouet** (Montpellier), **Karine Saporta** (Caen), and **Angelin Prelocaj** (Chambéry) still have to perform in Paris, usually at the Théâtre de la Ville, to confront the capital's sophisticated audiences and critics. The Opéra de Paris ballet company, now directed by the brilliant young dancer **Patrick Dupond** after years of Rudolf Nureyev's vagaries, wavers between the classics and occasional avant-garde choreography.

Theater covers traditional boulevard farce, **Molière** or **Racine**, **Brecht, Beckett**, or **Koltès** and includes that uniquely Parisian institution, café-théâtre. As in other fields, injections of foreign talent are welcome and the theater scene would not be the same without **Ariane Mnouchkine's** theater complex in Vincennes, La Cartoucherie, or **Peter Brook's** company based at Les Bouffes du Nord. Director **Patrice Chéreau** remains the enfant chéri of both public and critics and mounts his innovative productions all over Europe. A vital motor is the Festival d'Automne, which, every autumn, invites foreign directors from **Luc Bondy** to **Heiner Müller** or **Robert Wilson**, giving Paris an enviable and dynamic window on world theater.

Art Parallel to the performing arts is a lively visual art scene. Currently suffering from world recession, private and public galleries have been aided by government subsidies and purchases. But state aid does not create talent, and French artists still look too closely at their American or German contemporaries, although exceptions such as **Boltanski, César**, or **Buren** have international status.

Paris is still a magnet for creative talent and culture vultures alike; and with three weekly book programs on TV, France is unlikely to lose touch with its literary roots.

■ **Despite repeated offensives from Milan, New York, London, and Tokyo, the uncontested center of fashion remains Paris. With an arrogant, relentless hold on women's wardrobes worldwide, its high fashion dictates are unashamedly copied in countless sweatshops from Hong Kong to Taiwan to Paris itself. Haute couture may be having a hard time, but the new generation of *prêt-à-porter* designers are flourishing and keeping the tricolor flag flying. Fashion and its accessories are France's best ambassadors ...■**

Paris quite simply breathes fashion. No central street is complete without its chic boutique and no woman rightfully self-assured without her designer accessory. Non-French designers, models, and photographers flock to Paris for essential training and, more than anything else, sensitizing to a general spirit of fashion awareness. It is a bitchy, backbiting business but it is also glamorous and/or outrageous: no self-respecting fashion professional can ignore it.

Big business In the 1990s, haute couture and fashion creators together represent a several billion franc industry, 67 percent of which is exported. It is hardly surprising that most of the 3,000 or so private haute couture clients are foreigners: prices range from 25,000 to 50,000 francs, a level more accessible to wives of sheikhs or Hollywood film moguls. Fashion Creators (Créateurs de Mode) is the name given to upmarket *prêt-à-porter* designers (**Chloé, Kenzo, Sonia Rykiel, Thierry Mugler**, etc.) whose fame is often as great as their elders, and who officially joined forces with the couturiers' federation in 1975.

Strangely anachronistic, the *grands couturiers* have to follow a rigid set of rules in order to be allowed into the hallowed, legally protected circle, currently numbering 21. These include presenting twice-yearly collections of at least 75 models to the press and at least 45 times to

clients inside the couture house. January and July are the big months for, respectively, the Spring-Summer and the Autumn-Winter collections. Carefully juxtaposed, the fashion creators show their new designs in early October and March (when Parisian hotels are full to the brim). The Cour Carrée in the Louvre has been a major venue for presenting these fashion shows, but a new custom-designed area beneath the Tuileries opened in late 1993.

Invention and tradition Dreaming up innovative garments for a wide public has been a Parisian tradition since the first couturiers started up earlier this century. In the 1910s and '20s, the master was **Paul Poiret**, the man who declared the corset undesirable and swathed his customers in Arabian Nights gear but later admitted "I freed the bust but enslaved the legs." **Chanel** first recognized a new direction for women after World War I and created soft, loose boyish-looking cuts as well as the famous "little black dress." Much to her annoyance, the exuberant personality of **Elsa Schiaperelli** soon stepped in with humor, a clever antidote during the 1930s depression. She was the one to introduce the padded shoulders that remained fashionable until World War II. When **Dior** stunned the postwar world with his New Look, women were ready to return to a more feminine line and be extravagant with yards of cloth: this carried on throughout the 1950s.

Since then, couturiers like **Courrèges** (1960s space-age), **Saint-Laurent** (1970s retro influences), and the latest to be admitted to the inner circle with a flamenco flounce, **Christian Lacroix**, have influenced and reflected the spirit of the time.

Rule-breaking is part and parcel of Parisian fashion extremism. Waists are clinched or forgotten, skirt lengths short or long, trousers baggy or drainpipes, dresses clinging or billowing. Certain younger designers have led the way: **Thierry Mugler** (luxury Hollywood kitsch), **Jean-Paul Gaultier** (outrageous humorous designs), and **Claude Montana** (for moody science fiction heroines), while **Alaïa** was the man to bring back the feminine figure. Foreign designers such as **Karl Lagerfeld**, the Japanese contingent (from the precursor **Kenzo** to **Miyake**, **Yamamoto** and **Rei Kawakubo** of Comme des Garçons) have all gravitated to Paris, confirming the city's dual role as respected guardian and juvenile tearaway.

French fashion on display

■ **Of all the countries in the world, France is the most closely associated with food, with gourmets and gourmandize. Food is a subject taken seriously, and has at least 15 national magazines devoted to it. Fortunes are spent on ingredients, let alone on restaurants. But food combines both science and pleasure, and so corresponds perfectly to the dual French psyche ...■**

Although this "science" has been the nation's prerogative since the days of Rabelais, most French choose to forget that it was the dreaded Catherine de Médicis who brought chefs from Italy to introduce new dishes in the 16th century. But the advent and spread of public restaurants and cafés in Paris did not happen till the Revolutionary period. Before the Revolution, Paris boasted about 2,000 cafés; by the early 1800s, they had doubled in number. Ancien régime cuisine was known for being elaborate, rich and heavy, with diners often struggling through 20 courses. In 1783, the first grandiose *dîner philosophique* was launched, creating that link between literature and gastronomy that is so much a part of France.

Change of diet World War I ended the gourmet golden age of the 19th

Simple and stylish: poulet à l'estragon *(chicken with tarragon), originally a Lyonnais dish*

century, bringing a sense of measure and even, in some cases, frugality. With the spread of motoring, a new accent was put on regional cuisine, echoed by the famous Guide Michelin, and when, in 1936, annual paid vacations became law, restaurants were at last democratized. The gastronomic variety of the provinces was soon discovered with a vengeance by crowds of foreign tourists armed, as always, with the little red book. Culinary dynasties in family inns scattered throughout France, from the Bocuse at Collonges to the Daguin at Auch, soon gained national and international status.

Culinary revolution A new consciousness of ecology, macrobiotics, and dietary considerations influenced the cuisine of the 1960-70s, culminating in **Michel Guérard**'s famous *cuisine minceur*. Its emphasis on balanced nutrition and adventurous experiments created the subversive nouvelle cuisine. A new generation of chefs looked beyond France for inspiration. Partly due to the innovation of apprentice Japanese chefs in Paris, aesthetic presentation became paramount and classic table service vanished.

However, by the late 1980s the tide was turning. Too many

❏ The crêpe suzette was invented by mistake in Monte Carlo at the turn of the century. Chef Henri Charpentier was preparing some crêpes for the Prince of Wales and set fire to the alcohol he was imbibing them with. Delighted with the result, the Prince suggested naming them after his young companion. ❏

---

unworthy chefs jumped on the two-carrot nouvelle cuisine bandwagon, leaving customers unsatisfied and hungry. As a result, wholesome, old-fashioned bourgeois cooking is back in fashion. Yet Guérard's techniques, applied to traditional recipes, now

inspire a lighter cuisine, which satisfies both sophisticated and hungry appetites.

Great Chefs

Antoine Beauvilliers opened a famous restaurant in Palais-Royal in 1790 and wrote *L'Art du Cuisiner* in 1814, analyzing cooking with a clear, scientific approach.

Paul Bocuse Descendant of a line of chefs since 1765 and an apprentice at Lucas-Carton and Lapérouse, Bocuse returned to his family restaurant outside Lyon in 1959 and very soon became known as France's unofficial gastronomic ambassador.

Auguste Escoffier The creator of the peach melba started in the kitchens at the age of 13 in 1859 and lived to be 90, mainly working in London's Savoy and Carlton hotels.

Michel Guérard started as a pastry chef at the Crillon. In 1972, he opened his famous restaurant at Eugénie-le-Bains in the southwest, where he created imaginative, light, aromatic food with the accent on fish, fowl, and veal.

Joël Robuchon continues Guérard's tradition with intensely flavored combinations (cauliflower and caviar, lobster and artichoke). Recently his restaurant moved to a magnificent art-nouveau mansion.

Guy Savoy As unpredictable in his repertoire as Robuchon, Savoy experiments with textures and flavors and has a restaurant in the 17th arrondissement.

Taillevent Cook to 14th-century kings including Philippe VI, Taillevent wrote the oldest known treatise on cooking, Le Viandier.

François Vatel The 17th-century inventor of *crème chantilly* was chef to Fouquet, then the Prince de Condé. He committed suicide because the fish was not up to standard at a banquet in honor of Louis XIV.

■ **Children's Paris is not all puppet shows. Specially designed facilities are installed all over the city and keep the whole age range of children, from toddlers upward, out of mischief. Almost every arrondissement has public squares equipped with sandboxes and/or swings and slides. Although you may think that this diminutive section of the population seems thin on the ground, it emerges visibly on Wednesdays, Saturdays, and Sundays. Avoid most destinations mentioned below on these days ...■**

If museum visiting is your priority, the Atelier des Enfants at the **Centre Pompidou** is a possible solution. Any child aged 6 to 12 can be booked in immediately prior to sessions on Wednesday and Saturday afternoons. There are extra sessions during school vacation times. Nearby is another supervised playground, this one an open-air labyrinth full of slides, swings, and tunnels. The **Jardin d'Enfants** accepts children aged 7 to 11, but check exact opening hours (105 rue Rambuteau, tel: 45 08 07 18).

Puppets and parks The infamous puppets (*guignols*), whose squeaky language won't mean much to a non-French child, are still good value. All function afternoons only on Wednesdays and on weekends. The following parks provide shows: **Montsouris, Rond-point des Champs-Elysées, Champ de Mars, Luxembourg, Buttes-Chaumont**, and **Jardins du Ranelagh**. Best of all is the **Jardin d'Acclimatation** in the Bois de Boulogne (*open:* daily, 10–5, 6 in summer; metro: Sablons), where Parisian children revel in pleasure trains, donkey rides, and boat trips. A children's zoo, a hall of mirrors, a *guignol* theater, and an educational **Musée en Herbe** complete the package. At the eastern end of Paris, the Bois de Vincennes has an equivalent area, the **Parc Floral,** which features a miniature train, a games area, and a mini-golf course.

Museums Top of the list of museums catering for children comes the **Inventorium** at the Cité des Sciences et de l'Industrie (metro: Porte de la Villette), where children are encouraged to crack the mysteries of science: the computer games are as instructive as the keyboard experiments. (See pages 175 and 183.) In the same scientific vein but less high-tech is the **Palais**

de la Découverte, part of the Grand Palais (see page 124). Stargazers shouldn't miss its planetarium.

Children with budding creative talents can participate in the artistic activities at the Atelier des Enfants in the **Centre Pompidou** (see page 26). They are often related to the main exhibition. Otherwise, there is a library with a large selection of books, comics, and videos (some in English). The waxworks at the Musée Grévin (see page 124) never fail to provoke thrilled squeals.

Circuses For chilly or rainy days, the heated **Cirque Diana Moreno** in the Jardin d'Acclimatation is ideal and boasts breathtaking acrobats (sessions on Wednesday, Saturday, and Sunday afternoons). The famous national **Cirque Alexis Grüss** is now based at 41 avenue Corentin Cariou 75019 (tel: 40.36.08.00). Children are thrilled by the equestrian pantomimes and a team of clowns.

Outside Paris the field widens, from the **Parc Astérix** to **Thoiry** and **Disneyland Paris** (see pages 196–7).

None is more than 25 miles away, and Thoiry can be reached by train from Montparnasse (go to Beynes, then take a taxi). Astérix, of course, has more meaning if your children have spent time perusing the comic-strip hero's life. Whatever, the park makes a lively outing.

Thoiry (*open:* daily, 10–6) is, however, the star here, as between the 800 wild-ish animals, the Renaissance château, and the Museum of Gastronomy, few tastes are neglected. The interest of the château and its gardens, landscaped by Le Nôtre, will fade into insignificance once your children know that this is the largest safari park in Europe. To the southwest of Paris, in Elancourt, is **France Miniature**. Children can pretend they are giants in this "mini France" where 200 French monuments have been scaled down to a 30th of their original size.

Open: Mid-March to mid-November, 10–7.

Concentration: being entertained is a serious business

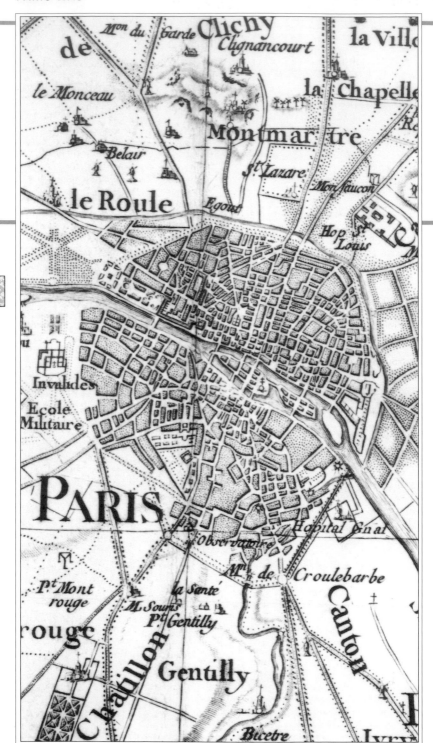

■ **Paris's first occupants were a Celtic tribe called the Parisii, who settled on the Ile de la Cité. Strategically located at the confluence of three rivers, the Seine, the Marne, and the Oise, they flourished on trade until Caesar's Gallic Wars engulfed them in 52 BC ...■**

Renaming the settlement *Lutetia*, the Romans soon set about creating their own structures, which continued to thrive for almost 500 years. After rebuilding the Ile de la Cité, the Romans moved across the Seine to the Left (south) Bank, where some monuments still stand today. The amphitheater (now called les Arènes) on the Montagne Ste.-Geneviève could hold up to 15,000 people and became the backdrop for gladiator fights as well as more sober and less bloody entertainment.

Growing needs The rapidly expanding population demanded baths, and of the three sites uncovered (Collège de France, rue Gay-Lussac, and Cluny), the latter, built around AD 200, remains remarkably well preserved. In true Roman style, no fewer than 10 miles of richly decorated aqueduct were built to supply water to these establishments. The central forum was located in the rue Soufflot (now below ground), while the adjacent Montagne Ste.-Geneviève became the main residential quarter.

Roman roads Although nothing remains of the Imperial palace (apparently on the site of the present Palais de Justice) or the theater (on boulevard Saint-Michel), the Romans left a network of firmly traced roads. Their north-south axes form the basis of Paris's main arteries, such as the rue St.-Martin, which cuts straight as a die across the Seine to the rue St.-Jacques, or the parallel boulevard Saint-Michel, the east-west rue des Ecoles, or the rue de la Montagne Ste.-Geneviève, which steadfastly climbs the slope to become the rue Mouffetard.

End of an era River and road trade assured a peaceful prosperity until around AD 275, when increasingly frequent Barbarian attacks eventually destroyed most of the Left Bank, forcing the inhabitants to withdraw onto the Ile de la Cité. This soon became a walled enclave, its ramparts built with the ruins of the Left Bank. Although a fragile peace was restored and the population spread to the Right Bank, the northerners eventually won the day in 486 when Clovis, chief of the Franks, conquered the Roman ruler Syagrius at the battle of Soissons.

The frigidarium from the Roman baths, at the Musée de Cluny

■ Although the courageous Geneviève had saved Paris from Attila's Huns in the 5th century, later becoming the city's patron saint, the Ile de France soon fell under the rule of a series of Frankish kings. Power fell into the hands of rulers with the exotic names of Clovis, Childebert, and Dagobert, but when Charlemagne moved the capital of his powerful empire to Aix la Chapelle in the early 9th century, Paris went into a dramatic decline ...■

Concentrated on the Ile de la Cité, the only signs of the city's former prosperity and importance were now at the neighboring abbey of St.-Denis, the royal graveyard since Dagobert. Only in the 10th century, with the rise to power of the Capetians, dukes of France and counts of Paris, did the city regain its luster. The development of agriculture and trade in the Middle Ages ensured new growth and wealth. For the first time, the Right Bank was settled and the swamp to the east, the Marais, was drained and cultivated. A port was established on place de la Grève (now l'Hôtel-de-Ville) opposite the Cité, and a central market appeared at the end of the road from St.-Denis, named after its wooden pavilions: Les Halles.

Financial pulse The Right Bank soon became the city's commercial heart. Its streets were still exceedingly narrow (the smallest a yard wide) and filthy. Muddy, badly lit, congested, and a haven for nocturnal thieves, they remained the terror of the visitor well into the 19th century. The houses were plain and narrow, made of wood beams and plastered rubble, with high pitched gables. They took up every available space within the city walls and even piled up onto the town's four bridges, notable chiefly for the frequency with which they collapsed into the River Seine.
   A few buildings, like the royal palace (now the Palais de Justice), with its flamboyant Gothic chapel (**Sainte-Chapelle**), the splendid new

cathedral of **Notre-Dame**, or the fortress guarding the city's western gates, the **Louvre**, provided a note of distinction in this otherwise crowded, unplanned, and smelly city.

Scholarly city In the late 12th century, under Philippe-Auguste, the **University of Paris** was founded and trades and crafts came under the control of tightly organized, prosperous guilds. The University, which gave its name to the Latin

France emerged from the Middle Ages under the reign of François I

Quarter on the Left Bank, soon became one of the most renowned in Europe, boasting scholars like Guillaume de Champeaux and Peter Abélard.

Abélard and Héloïse Two of the most colorful and tragic figures of medieval Paris were the great scholar and theologian Abélard and his beloved Héloïse, daughter of a Notre-Dame canon, Fulbert. After a passionate love affair they had a child and secretly married. Fulbert wrought a terrible revenge: tied up by three hired thugs, Abélard was castrated. Further pursued by the Church for alleged heresy in his writings, Abélard wandered from monastery to monastery until he found refuge at the abbey of Cluny. He died in 1142. Eight poignant letters survive to this day, exchanged by Abélard and Héloïse after their separation. They are buried together in the Père-Lachaise cemetery, and at 9 Quai aux Fleurs you can see their sculpted heads.

Big city By the reign of Philippe Auguste's famous grandson, Saint-Louis (1226–70), Paris was already a major European capital and, with its 200,000 inhabitants, the most populous city on the continent.

A memorable moment for the city came in 1263, when the Parisian

Charles VII's reign saw the end of the Hundred Years' War: here he enters Paris in 1436

merchants elected their first representative, the Prévot des Marchands.

At war The Hundred Years' War (from the mid-14th to mid-15th centuries) plunged the city back into turbulence, bringing medieval peace and prosperity to a violent end. Paris was at times ruled by the English, who defended the city successfully against Jeanne d'Arc. Violence also returned in the form of a rebellion in 1358, led by the Prévot, Etienne Marcel, against the sovereign, the Dauphin Charles; unable to bear numerous humiliations, the dauphin was forced to escape to the south of France to rally the nobles to his cause. Marcel was eventually murdered, enabling the dauphin to return to Paris. Yet this first act of rebellion gave birth to the distrust that existed between the rulers of France and their capital city well into modern times. Abandoning the central Cité palace in favor of mansions closer to the city wall, the kings increasingly favored provincial châteaus—a trend taken up to the full by the king who in many ways characterized late medieval France: François I.

■ **Despotic and capricious, yet also a refined Renaissance gentleman, François I epitomized the contradictory aspects of French society in the 16th century. Still based on feudalism, this society nevertheless felt the increasing weight of royal authority as François I centralized power from his capital, Paris, seat of the Treasury, the Mint, and the law courts ...■**

The court diligently followed him from one splendid Loire château to the next, in Paris settling in the Louvre, rebuilt by the king in the brand new Renaissance style imported from Italy. Elaborate costumed balls, ballets, and ceremonies kept the courtiers amused, and the title of Majesty, previously reserved for the Holy Roman emperor, was now applied to the French king.

Age of rebirth The breath of the Renaissance swept France in the wake of Italian artists imported to decorate Fontainebleau. The new passion for antiquity, poetry, literature, and philosophy culminated in the founding of the Collège de France (1530), the kingdom's first secular educational institution. This was the age of Rabelais, Montaigne, the Humanist publisher Robert Estienne, and of noble patrons of the arts and humanities, notably François I's sister, Marguerite de Navarre, and Henri II's mistress, Diane de Poitiers.

Massacre and war This enlightenment was brought to an abrupt end by the Wars of Religion that swept through France in the latter half of the century (1562–98), a period dominated by the cunning Catherine de Médicis, wife of Henri II and domineering mother of the last three Valois kings (François II, Charles IX, Henri III). Its darkest episode occurred on Saint Bartholomew's Day (August 24, 1572) when, pressed by his mother, the vacillating Charles IX ordered the massacre of Protestant nobles gathered at the Louvre to celebrate the wedding of Henri de Bourbon

(the future Henri IV) to the king's sister. Three thousand strangled and knifed Protestant corpses were thrown into the Seine on that fateful day, and for over 20 years civil war raged throughout France.

"Paris is well worth a mass" are the famous words uttered by Henri IV, the first Bourbon king, before abjuring his Protestant faith, last obstacle to his accession to the throne of France. His triumphal entry into a devastated and hungry Paris in 1594 spelled the temporary end to the wars of religion.

New era A pleasure-loving man, with as many mistresses as his predecessors, Henri IV was nevertheless the king who seriously set to reorganizing the kingdom and notably its capital, Paris. Completing the great gallery of the Louvre, the Hôtel de Ville started by François I, and endowing the city with new squares (place des Vosges, place Dauphine), bridges (Pont-Neuf), and a hospital for plague victims (St.-Louis), Henri began the process that would transform the still largely medieval city of the 16th century into the classical capital of the 17th and 18th centuries.

The first half of the 17th century (the Grand Siècle) was dominated by foreign and civil wars and the anxious personality of the chronically ill homosexual, Louis XIII, who was sustained by the efforts of his brilliant but equally hypochondriac minister, Cardinal Richelieu. This was the Paris of Alexandre Dumas' *Three Musketeers*, teeming with intrigue and the ongoing rivalry between the cardinal and the queen, the willful and very Catholic Anne of

Henri IV pictured with his friend, Gabrielle d'Estrées

Austria, who was forever conspiring with the English and the Spanish against French interests.

Middle classes Amid court conspiracies and religious turmoil, there emerged a Parisian class composed of the new civil servants, financiers, and wealthy merchants, who provided the backbone of a great religious and cultural revival in the capital. Among the new churches and convents rose the sober, well-proportioned mansions of the Marais, in which cultivated women of taste, the hostesses, presided over the first Parisian salons. The most celebrated of all was the Marquise de Rambouillet, in her rue St. Honoré house, who received all the great luminaries of her day from La Rochefoucauld to Corneille. Molière, whose theater troupe settled in Paris in 1658, satirized the new manners in his great play, *Les Précieuses Ridicules*.

The Fronde (1648–52) was the last great civil disturbance experienced

> ❏ "People of quality know everything without ever having been taught"—Molière, *Les Précieuses Ridicules*. ❏

by Paris before the French Revolution. The victory of the regent, Anne of Austria, and her wily prime minister, Cardinal Mazarin, over the rebellious Paris bourgeoisie and the nobility paved the way to the absolute power of Louis XIV.

■ **When, at the death of his mother's old prime minister, the Cardinal Mazarin, in 1661, Louis XIV announced he would govern on his own, his ministers and the court were stupefied.** Yet *l'Etat c'est Moi* perfectly describes the spirit of the later 17th century, a time when all the energies and resources of the kingdom were harnessed into the service and glorification of one single being and symbol: the Sun King ...■

Though refusing to name a new prime minister, Louis XIV would have been unable to carry through his ambitious projects without the help and administrative talent of his finance minister, the dour, workaholic Colbert. Colbert's dream, a great palace for the king in Paris—the Louvre—was abandoned (literally without finishing the roof) in favor of Versailles, yet other of his projects were carried through. Royal academies were established to control every facet of French cultural and intellectual life, and a great Royal factory, the Gobelins, was set up to produce the furniture, silver, and tapestries needed to fill Versailles.

Cultural capital By the end of the century, the talents of architects, painters, cabinet makers, musicians, and playwrights trained to serve the king were already turning Paris and Versailles into the artistic and cultural center of Europe. Nor did the removal of the court into the glittering and tightly controlled environment of Versailles mean that Paris was neglected. New squares, hospitals, bridges, churches, and monumental avenues (Champs-Elysées, the Grands Boulevards), and better policing and lighting

transformed the flowering city more than ever before.

Much of the vitality of the great king's reign was, however, extinguished long before his actual death (1715). The removal of the five-year-old Louis XV to the Tuileries palace by the regent signaled a renewal for the capital. Bored with the rigidity, etiquette, and dusty grandeur of the Sun King, the court and nobility returned to Paris to throw themselves enthusiastically into a life entirely devoted to pleasure and dalliance.

Frivolity and flowers Thus sensual, frivolous rococo was born in the aristocratic mansions of the Faubourg St.-Germain and the bankers' houses of the quartier St.-Honoré. Watteau's flirting couples in romantic parks, Boucher's rosy mythological posteriors, shells, flowers, and tendrils interpreted in chair legs and sofas, all provided the decorative background to the first half of Louis XV's reign.

Yet this is also the period of the revival of the literary salon. As the century wears on, touches of intellectual curiosity, moralism, and pedantry invade the witty, polished atmosphere of the salons of Mesdames du Deffand or Epinay. Beginning with Voltaire, this libertarian spirit, alternately flirting with and defying royal authority, was enshrined in the circle of the new philosophers and encyclopédistes, the compilers of the world's first dictionary—Diderot, Buffon, Condorcet, Rousseau, D'Alembert, Helvétius.

❏ "You are going to be a great king. Do not copy me in my love of building or in my love of warfare; on the contrary, try to live peacefully with your neighbors."—Louis XIV to the future Louis XV. ❏

❏ "In an aristocracy, honors, pleasures, power, and money are easily obtainable. Great discretion, however, is necessary. If abuse is flagrant, revolution will be the consequence."—Voltaire, *Philosophical Dictionary.* ❏

Shift of focus Though the court returned to Versailles in 1724, it would never again be the focus of French life as it was under Louis XIV. It was to Paris that the aristocrats, even the king, now escaped for their fun, to the masked balls, the opera and, the latest rage, the first public art exhibitions, the salons held every other year in the Louvre.

This spirit of reform found its first visual outlet in the city's architecture. Though still elegant, from 1750 a sobriety and studious historical allusion pervaded the neoclassical style, with its Corinthian columns, swags, and triangular pediments spreading across Paris from the place Louis XV (Concorde) to the Eglise Ste.-Geneviève (Panthéon) and the new Royal Mint, La Monnaie.

By the middle of the reign of Louis XVI (1774–93) and his beautiful, frivolous, unpopular queen, Marie Antoinette, the still polite reformist mood of the earlier half of the century had turned into a flood of open sedition. Malicious printed jokes openly circulated at the Palais-Royal and ended up beneath the queen's plate at Versailles. The well-intentioned but indecisive Louis XVI, unable to control the situation any longer, called for the representatives of all classes, the *Etats Généraux*, to meet in Versailles in May 1789. No one dreamed it, but that fateful spring was the end of the ancient régime.

The Water Gardens at Versailles: under Louis XIV's reign, Versailles became the focus of court life

■ **The Revolution signaled the end of royal excesses and the rise of popular democracy in a momentum that continued throughout the uprisings of the 19th century. Long before the gathering in Versailles of the *Etats Généraux*, which brought together the clergy, nobility, and the Commons, trouble was afoot and the air rife with political agitation. Much of this was fermented at the Palais-Royal, residence of the dukes of Orléans, the rival branch of the royal family ...■**

The Palais-Royal, though open to the public, was out of bounds to the police; so speechmaking and the distribution of antigovernment pamphlets went on unhindered. It was here, in July 1789, that a young journalist, Camille Desmoulins, gave the battle cry *aux armes!* to defend the city from a rumored attack by the king's army. A great mob invaded the city hall and raided the Invalides barracks for muskets. Next morning, July 14, the same mob presented itself at a fortress on the eastern edge of the city, the Bastille. A four-hour battle, the first violent act of the Revolution, led to the fall of the fortress, the liberation of six prisoners (mostly counterfeiters), and the beheading of the governor. From here on, events moved at a breath-taking pace until the Revolution finally ran out of steam in July 1794.

Royal prisoners A new mayor was nominated and the city organized its own national guard, headed by the Marquis de Lafayette. In October, the royal family was forcibly brought back from Versailles and installed in the Tuileries palace, virtual prisoners of the people and the new National Assembly. A period of relative calm, in which a constitution and new laws were promulgated, ended abruptly with the king's failed attempt to escape on June 21, 1791.

Now the antimonarchist and left-wing forces in the city, radicalized by the outbreak of war, gained the upper hand. On August 10, 1792, the Paris mob attacked the Tuileries palace, massacring 600 of the king's Swiss Guards and a few unlucky cooks and servants. A terrified royal family fled to the Assembly and the next day were locked up in the old medieval tower of the Temple.

Soon the new Assembly, the Convention, abolished the monarchy and proclaimed the First Republic, along with a new calendar: 1792 became Year I of the new era. The king was tried, found guilty of high treason, and guillotined on January 21, 1793. This was the year that opened the most violent period of the Revolution: the Reign of Terror. Nobles who had failed to emigrate, priests, the queen, and ordinary citizens were whisked to the Conciergerie prison on the Ile de la Cité. Judged by a mock court, they were then sent by the cartload, their hands tied and napes shaved, rattling along the rue St.-Honoré to the guillotine on place de la Revolution (Concorde). As the stench of blood on the square led to complaints from the neighbors, the guillotine was moved for a brief period to place de

❏ Originally a revolutionary song, next a chant for the Republicans confronting the monarchists, the *Marseillaise* became the national anthem in 1880. It was written in 1792 by Rouget de Lisle and became known as the *Marseillaise* when Parisians heard troops from the south of France singing it as they entered the capital. ❏

la Nation, but soon returned to the central and convenient Concorde.

Political power was now concentrated in the hands of the misnamed Committee of Public Safety, led by a former lawyer, the calculating Robespierre. By now, the Revolution was devouring her own children. Beginning with the mayor of Paris, a stream of moderate deputies was led to the blade. In March 1794, Robespierre eliminated the left wing and hit the center, including the revolutionary leaders Desmoulins and Danton.

Robespierre now stood alone, but he had gone too far. The remaining deputies in the Convention, sensing their own short life expectancy, finally found the courage to gang up against him. In July, Robespierre was arrested. He escaped and called the Paris citizens to his defense, but for the first time since 1789, the Paris mob, tired and dispirited, did not respond. Robespierre was guillotined on July 28, 1794. The Terror and the Revolution were over.

A social system on trial: Louis XVI comes before the people's court in 1792 (above) and (below) the march to Versailles, 1789

■ Following the bloody days of the Terror and before France's first emperor arrived on the scene with due pomp and ceremony, France was ruled by an intermediary government, known as the Directoire (1795–1799). This was a time of winding down of tensions and of gradual economic recovery, despite the continuing social and political instability ...■

With the old nobility and Church decimated by revolutionary fervor, the bourgeoisie now controlled all political and financial power. The selling off of confiscated religious and noble properties during the Revolution further ensured that the new class of profiteers and property owners, no matter how

conservative, would never accept a return to the old status quo.

Defeat and caution The Paris municipality, last stronghold of the left wing and the working classes, the *sans-culottes* ("without breeches," that is, not aristocratic) was suppressed in 1795. From Napoleon's era on, the city fell under the authority of the Prefect of the Seine, appointed by the government. So wary had the government become of the Parisians' seemingly endless potential for rebellion (borne out by the events of 1830, 1848, 1871, 1936, and 1968) that it took two centuries for Paris to be allowed a freely elected mayor, in 1977.

Reaction and release Three years of revolutionary terror and patriotic fervor were succeeded by a mood of frivolity and unprecedented sexual liberation. Long-haired dandies and ladies in Greek hairdos and see-through dresses, known as *incroyables* and *merveilleuses*, danced the night away at the Café Frascati on the Grands Boulevards. Among the fashionable accessories of the day was a red ribbon worn around the neck, a discreet allusion to the past ravages and excitement of the guillotine.

One of the smartest Parisiennes of the period was the widow of a guillotined aristocrat, now mistress of the most powerful directeur, **Joséphine de Beauharnais**. In 1796 she fell into the arms of an ardent,

Napoleon at the peak of his career: as the conquering general, portrayed by David...

rising young general, **Napoleon Bonaparte**. Eight years later, already owner of the most ravishing country house near Paris, Malmaison, she was crowned in Notre-Dame as empress of the French.

The Napoleonic age Napoleon's lightning rise and fall from power and glory, though brief (1800–14), left an indelible imprint on France and its capital city. Named First Consul of the Republic after the 1799 coup d'état, the ambitious young general soon proclaimed himself emperor of the French. A new nobility, composed of princes and barons (as opposed to the old dukes and counts) was invented. Most European territories conquered in the 1806–10 campaigns were carved out into kingdoms and principalities for the rest of the family and in-laws such as Murat, named king of Naples. Paris was now capital of the greatest European empire since Charlemagne.

Reconstruction A far-reaching program of renovation and building was drawn up by the two official architects of the reign, **Percier** and **Fontaine**, whose object was to turn the city into a monumental New Rome. The result was an unprecedented proliferation of columns and "temples" (the new **Assembly**, the **Bourse**, the **Madeleine**), Roman military monuments (**Colonne Vendôme, Arc du Carrousel, Arc de Triomphe**) and straight streets (**Castiglione, Rivoli**). Just as notable were the practical improvements in the city's infrastructure, the first signs in Paris of the dawning of an industrial age: the building of canals, the new stock exchange, an improved water supply and sewerage, modern cemeteries, a new meat market, even an iron bridge. The odd and even numbering system for the city's streets, with the low numbers beginning closest to the Seine, also dates from Napoleon I.

Napoleon's most permanent legacy to France and Paris was, however, the great national

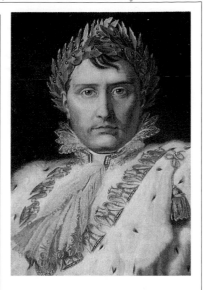

...and as self-styled Emperor Napoleon I of France, shown here wearing his coronation robes in a tapestry by Gérard

institutions in the fields of culture, education, and law that he intitiated or reformed. The Louvre **Museum**, inaugurated during the Revolution, was greatly enriched by the artistic booty hauled in from all corners of the new empire. The prestigious **Grandes Ecoles**, still the training ground for France's ruling élite, the **Polytechnique, Ecole des Mines, Ponts et Chaussées, Ecole Normale Supérieure**, and the **Natural History Museum** date from Napoleon, as does the first national legal system in France, inspired by Roman Law, the Code Civil.

Capital city The concentration of the country's culture, government, education, financial, and political power in the capital, begun by the Bourbons and pursued by the Revolution, was brought to a climax by Napoleon. His ambitious plans for France brought added status to the city. The preeminence of Paris in France would now remain unchallenged by every succeeding régime until the election in 1981 of François Mitterrand.

39

■ **Nineteenth-century Paris can largely be characterized by a tapestry of weak rulers, violent social conflicts, rising liberal intellectualism, and a new, monied bourgeoisie. Beyond the barricades and banks, the arts flourished and foreign artists flocked to contribute to the capital's movements, but even greater designs were afoot. Symbolic of a will and need to change the fabric of society, Haussmann's mid-century urban transformations were a turning point for a new industrialized society ...■**

40

Before Napoleon III maneuvered into place, France underwent the last convulsions of its luckless monarchy during the Restoration. Under Louis XVIII and Charles X, a new romantic spirit developed in the arts (spearheaded by Delacroix, Géricault, Victor Hugo, Balzac, Berlioz, Baudelaire, Rimbaud), partly inspired by the philosophy of Rousseau and a nostalgia for the "purity" of the Middle Ages—and controversially practiced by the architect Viollet-le-Duc.

Rebels and royalty The 1830 uprising, which rapidly turned to a bloody insurrection, ended the Bourbons' lineage and brought to power the "citizen-king" Louis-Philippe of Orléans, more acceptable to the populace. But beneath a superficial self-satisfaction ("France is a nation which is bored," wrote Lamartine in 1839), the country was in ferment: strikes, spreading Republicanism, assassinations, and a dropping standard of living, accompanied by the rising power of a corrupt monied class, all combined to make an explosive situation.

The year 1848 signaled the end of the July Monarchy. Blood and barricades soon heralded victory for the Republicans and elections brought to power Louis-Napoléon, nephew of Bonaparte, described by de Toqueville as "an enigmatic, somber, insignificant numbskull." Yet, inspired by the parks of his London exile and determined to end the overcrowded conditions of the capital (as well as its potential for

another revolution), Napoleon III immediately implemented an urban shake-up. And onto the stage now stepped the Protestant administrator Baron Haussmann, who in 18 years managed to transform the face of the capital and prepare it for the 20th century.

❏ "Paris is the heart of France. Let's put all our efforts into embellishing this big city. Let's open new roads, make the populous neighborhoods which lack air and daylight healthy, and may charitable light penetrate everywhere in our walls."– Napoleon III. ❏

City facelift Between 1800 and 1850, the population of Paris had doubled to over a million; in 1832 a cholera epidemic claimed 19,000 victims. Housing and proper sanitation were thus desperately needed. Conscious of the imbalance in activities between the east and west, north and south of the capital, as well as the imminent asphyxiation of its narrow, overcrowded streets, Haussmann traced an urban web of wide boulevards and avenues. Against a backdrop of sparkling social gatherings, operettas by Offenbach, and haute couture by Worth, he set about tearing down 20,000 houses, building 40,000, constructing 56 miles of roads, 348 miles of sewers, and two reservoirs and landscaping two woods, three parks, two gardens, and 19 squares.

The final jewel in Napoleon III's crown was Charles Garnier's ostentatious Opera House, the only real symbol of Second Empire architecture.

Wholesale clearance The emperor's approach was romantic, that of Haussmann more inclined to straight lines. For 15 years, Paris was one gigantic building site, as Haussmann, with little consideration for preservation, swept away entire quartiers such as the Ile de la Cité, where only Notre-Dame, its immediate vicinity, and the western tip were spared. Many of the Faubourg St.-Germain's finest mansions crumbled to make way for the rue de Rennes and the boulevard St.-Germain, and much of the picturesque medieval Latin Quarter succumbed to demolition.

New conflict Modern sewerage, abattoirs (La Villette), a hygienic central marketplace (Les Halles), a public bus company, squares, and parks completed this metamorphosis. However, the drums were rolling again with the Franco-Prussian War of 1870; the ensuing siege of Paris, when Parisians ate anything from rats to inmates of the zoo, finally culminated in the last of the great revolutionary movements of the 19th century, the Paris Commune. Parisian radicals, disgusted with the terms of the peace treaty negotiated with Bismarck a year later, had taken up arms and controlled the city, declaring it a free commune. After a week of desperate fighting, when the Hôtel de Ville and the Tuileries Palace went up in smoke, the Communards massacred priests, and government troops shot on sight, the last stand took place at the Père-Lachaise cemetery. In that one week over 20,000 people died. It was the 19th century's last lesson in civil uprising.

Charles Garnier's Opera House, a Second Empire symbol

The Belle Epoque

■ **The shaky régime installed in France after the humiliating defeat inflicted by Bismarck's Prussia proved in the end to be the longest lasting since the Revolution. Paris hosted three Universal Exhibitions (1878, 1889, and 1900), which helped restore French morale and promote the prestige of the Third Republic ...■**

The Eiffel Tower illuminated, 1889

As well as boosting morale, the Universal Exhibitions left several new landmarks on the horizon: the Palais de Chaillot (later rebuilt); the Eiffel Tower, built for the first centenary of the Revolution, and the Pont Alexandre III. The Grand and Petit Palais appeared in 1900, the year when Paris was consecrated as World Capital and France recognized as one of the great industrial and colonial empires.

Nostalgia The Belle Epoque refers to the period between 1885 and the outbreak of World War I in 1914. Industrial squalor, labor strikes, and anarchist assassinations (like that in 1894 of President Sadi Carnot) were forgotten in favor of the good life at the Opera, new boulevard cafés, music and dance halls (Folies-Bergère, Moulin Rouge).

Middle-class weekends spent boating and picnicking in the country or the suburbs (now accessible by train) became the subject matter for a new generation of painters, the Impressionists: Monet, Renoir, Degas, Caillebotte, Sisley. The artists themselves lived in the new Batignolles district, north of St.-Lazare station, and met in the cafés of Pigalle and Clichy.

Change of mood By the 1880s, the sunny insouciance of '70s Impressionism gave way to a more imaginative but also pessimistic mood. In poetry this was expounded by the Decadents, later the Symbolists, inspired by the writings of the explosive lovers, Verlaine and Rimbaud. The leading fin de siècle Symbolist was undoubtedly Mallarmé, whose enigmatic verses best convey the melancholy that overcame his generation.

The late 1880s were marked by modern art's first martyrs: Gauguin and Van Gogh, the latter's style having developed in the Bohemian atmosphere of the still, half rural Montmartre. By the '90s, a new intricate decorative style, art nouveau, blossomed on the apartment buildings of Guimard, the new metro, and department stores (Galeries Lafayette). This was also the city of Proust and Toulouse-Lautrec—a teeming cosmopolitan Paris, where an overindulged high society rubbed shoulders in a frisson of pleasure with the alcoholics,

A dance capturing the exuberance of the Belle Epoque: the can-can

43

morphine addicts, prostitutes, can-can dancers, and singers at the Moulin Rouge and the new cabarets of Montmartre. The Bohemian life, epitomized by low dives like Montmartre's *Lapin Agile*, gradually shifted into a more sophisticated gear as artists and poets moved to the new Montparnasse cafés, the Dôme and the Rotonde. This was when Derain, Matisse, Picasso, Braque, Delaunay, and Léger laid the foundations of 20th-century art.

The Banquet In 1908, Picasso threw a dinner party at his Montmartre studio that later became one of the legends of early Modernism. Guest of honor was Henri Rousseau, the great "naïve" painter. Other guests included the poets Max Jacob, André Salmon, and Apollinaire, the American collectors Leo and Gertrude Stein, and the painters Vlaminck, Braque, and Marie Laurencin. Marie Laurencin danced, while her lover Apollinaire, unperturbed, caught up with his correspondence in a corner of the room. Frédé, owner of the *Lapin Agile*, wandered in with his donkey Lolo, who consumed the last of the food. To crown the evening, two of the poets faked an attack of delirium, frothing (chewed soap) at the mouth, which sent the smartly dressed American guests scurrying home.

This mix of exaltation and buffoonery perfectly conveys the atmosphere of Parisian Bohemia before the Great War—a certain innocence and joie de vivre later lost in the more worldly ambience of 1920s Montparnasse. In the same years Eric Satie, Stravinsky, Alfred Jarry, Proust, and Diaghilev revolutionized modern music, theater, literature, and ballet. Rarely had so much innovative talent in all the arts gathered in the same place at the same time as in the Paris of 1900 to 1914.

❏ The Bateau Lavoir was a ramshackle wooden piano factory below the Moulin de la Galette, used as a studio by Picasso and his contemporaries —the city's poorest painters and poets. It was so named because of its resemblance to the laundry boats on the Seine, adorned with sheets and trousers hanging out to dry. ❏

■ **Paris between the wars was described as "a magnificent and well-equipped showcase." Its frenetic cultural pleasures attracted a stream of foreign artists, firstly political refugees from Eastern Europe and then, as the 1920s gained momentum and became *les années folles*, an influx of Americans living high on their dollars. Jazz was the rhythm, Chanel the fashion, Charleston the step, art deco the style, Surrealism the art, and Montparnasse the quartier that epitomized the cultural climate of this period ...■**

44

Profoundly marked by World War I, in which 1.4 million Frenchmen had died and over a million were disabled, the nation licked her wounds and embarked on an energetic and creative commitment. Victory celebrations were held in an attempt to wipe out memories of Big Bertha, the huge German cannon that had bombarded Paris, and national pride was restored by the return of Alsace-Lorraine from German annexation. But could France after 1914 ever know another Belle Epoque?

Shock value Although Apollinaire, the inventor of the term Surrealism, died in 1918, it was only after the war that Tristan Tzara brought the Dada movement from Zürich to Paris. "Art is nonsense," cried its protagonists, the poets Breton, Eluard, and Aragon, rejecting traditional values and aiming to shock, as did Duchamp by exhibiting his "ready-made" urinal. However, they soon realized the limitations of negativity and by the time art students ceremonially drowned a Dada effigy in the Seine in 1921, the movement was dead.

Drawn to Freud's discoveries, Breton and his band, joined by the German Max Ernst, turned to free association, to the power of the subconscious and to images generated by dreams. In 1924 their influential Surrealist Manifesto announced a Parisian movement that was to infiltrate much of European creativity (art, literature, film) right up to World War II and beyond.

Although their political affiliations were largely pro-Communist, it was on this point that the group eventually broke up. Nevertheless, artists such as Dalí, de Chirico, and

❏ "Pure automatism"— André Breton, describing the Surrealist movement. ❏

the filmmaker Buñuel, despite disputes with the authoritarian leader Breton, spread its images throughout the world. Magazines were used to spread Surrealist ideas, starting with *La Révolution Surréaliste* in 1924. Other magazines brought the gospel to Belgium, England, and New York.

Kiki and co. Alongside these purveyors of fantasy, other creative individuals gathered around the tables of the famous Montparnasse cafés, Le Dôme, La Rotonde, and La Coupole. These included Russian and Polish émigrés (Chagall, Lempicka), Léger, Soutine, the

❏ "Handpainted dream photographs"—Salvador Dalí, describing his own work. ❏

stylish Foujita, and the vivacious Kiki de Montparnasse, dancer and model, who lived with photographer Man

Ray. Montparnasse meant cheap accommodations and meals, freedom and congenial company, but this foreign influx sometimes encountered French xenophobia from supporters of the fascist *Action Française*, steadily gaining popularity.

The U.S. factor Less integrated was a growing American community, steeped in dreams of Paris and busily penning some of the 20th century's most innovative literature. At the center of this web was Sylvia Beach's bookshop in the rue de l'Odéon, Shakespeare and Company, which attracted expatriate scribes such as Hemingway, Ezra Pound, Henry Miller, F. Scott Fitzgerald, and Gertrude Stein. Beach's devotion to James Joyce stretched to typing his illegible manuscripts and actually publishing *Ulysses*, a feat that nearly bankrupted her bookshop but left the world with a masterpiece. The Wall Street crash in 1929 announced the end of high living for many of the American expatriates, although the economy of France itself had a delayed reaction.

With the advent of the talkies, American films dominated Paris—but there was soon another, hotter import: that of jazz and black culture. The Bal Nègre, in the 5th arrondissement, was packed nightly with elegant women shaking to the new dance rhythms in the arms of West Indians or Africans. But the climax came in 1925, when the *Revue Nègre* hit town. Josephine Baker, attired in Poiret, Sonia Delaunay, or Schiaparelli, outshone homegrown star Mistinguette.

Meanwhile, three World Fairs proved to the world that native French culture was far from dead. In 1925, the Exposition des Arts Décoratifs marked, in Le Corbusier's words, "the decisive turning point in the quarrel between the old and the new." Art deco was acknowledged king, with the modernist designs of Ruhlmann, Dunand, Mallet-Stevens, and Chareau reinforcing Le Corbusier's *Esprit Nouveau*. The 1931 Exposition Coloniale, symbolizing France's strong colonial power, bequeathed the city with the striking Musée des Arts Africains; but it was the 1937 Universal Exhibition that left the strongest architectural mark, in Trocadéro's Palais de Chaillot and the Palais de Tokyo. It also exhibited Picasso's *Guernica*—an anguished sign of what was to come.

The Palais de Chaillot, built for the Exposition Universelle in 1937

■ **When the bells of liberation finally tolled at Notre-Dame on August 26, 1944, Paris emerged from 50 months of German occupation. Humiliated by the all-powerful German army that had taken over the capital, some Parisians had escaped, others turned a blind eye, some collaborated, and some resisted. Hundreds of thousands died. Miraculously, the city itself survived and even General Von Cholitz disobeyed Hitler's final desperate orders to blow it up ...■**

46

At the outbreak of war in September 1939, little changed for Paris, but by May 1940, when the German army crossed the French borders, the capital woke up. Traumatized by memories of the Great War, the French army was by then in disarray: 100,000 escaped via Dunkirk but thousands more were taken prisoner, and others fled to the south of France. Refugees poured in, including herds of abandoned cattle, and a frenzied exodus southward from the capital saw government ministries, the press, the civil service, and the contents of the Louvre taking to the road. When the German tanks finally rolled in on June 14, they were greeted with an eerie, deserted city; only a quarter of its inhabitants had remained.

France divided Soon Paris adopted a different rhythm. Four days after de Gaulle's impassioned though unheeded radio message from London, an armistice was signed between the aging French president, Marshal Pétain, and Hitler, allowing the Germans to occupy and use Paris "temporarily" as its military headquarters for the occupied zone. Free France kept 40 percent of the country, with its government based

in Vichy. For many, relieved to see the end of war and disorder, Pétain was seen as a savior despite disastrously unfavorable peace clauses and the reality that France had become a colonized country.

Occupied city In Paris, clocks were changed to central European time, all luxury hotels and public buildings were requisitioned, swastikas fluttered from their roofs, road signs appeared in German, and the changing of the guard goose-stepped down the Champs-Elysées daily at 12:30PM. Commerce was stimulated by the big-spending habits of the occupiers, who could pay in Deutschemarks.

For the average Parisian, shortages and rationing became part of daily life as the cost of living rose dramatically along with the mortality rate. Soon a flourishing black market was controlled by criminal gangs making vast fortunes. Gasoline was unobtainable and Paris fell silent. Meanwhile, Jews had to wear yellow stars, 30,000 Communists were arrested, trade unions were

German troops in Paris

abolished, and the left wing banned.

In July 1942, 13,000 Jews were rounded up in abominable conditions at a sports stadium before being deported to concentration camps. This was the turning point, and the silent majority began to form an underground resistance movement. From all classes and ages, their only common purpose was a desire to rid France of its invaders.

Initially operating through individual acts of sabotage, the Resistance achieved a unity when **Jean Moulin**

❏ At the Mémorial de la Déportation, 200,000 quartz pebbles line the tunnel of a crypt that commemorates the same number of French who died during the Holocaust. Buried at the eastern tip of the Ile de la Cité, this monument was built in 1962 to a stark and effective design by G.H. Pingusson. ❏

was parachuted in to coordinate all regional networks. Perturbed by Resistance activities, the Germans and the Vichy police reacted violently, arresting, assassinating, and deporting. Moulin himself was arrested and executed in June 1943, but by then the *maquis* were riding high on de Gaulle's momentum from Algiers, where he set up a government in exile.

The tide turns Strikes and demonstrations grew, clandestine newspapers boosted morale, and by the time the Allies disembarked in June 1944, posters and tracts called for an insurrection. Between August 19 and 24, Paris resumed its street-fighting. Trees were felled, paving-stones dug up, barricades erected, ambushes laid, and sharpshooters installed. When General Leclerc's tanks rolled in, it was to an accompaniment of ringing bells, ecstatic crowds, and the refrain of the Marseillaise. The next day Von Cholitz capitulated, and on August 26 de Gaulle led the emotional liberation celebrations down the Champs-Elysées to Notre-Dame.

47

■ **A city is characterized by its architecture and monuments, but a less definable spirit is created by its culture, a product of personalities from all epochs. Below are some of the famous Parisians who have left their mark …■**

Apollinaire (1880–1918) Of Polish descent; one of the early 20th-century intelligentsia who led the schools of Cubism and Futurism, and France's first modern poet. *Alcools* and *Calligrammes* abandoned punctuation and experimented with typographical patterns.

Baudelaire (1821–67) Poet, critic, translator of Edgar Allan Poe. Introduced a modern sensibility and explored the musicality of the French language. With his mulatto mistress, he led a debauched life of opium and alcohol, haunted by a sense of his own damnation. Many poems in *Les Fleurs du Mal* were banned for offending public morals. He died of syphilis.

Simone de Beauvoir (1908–86) Sartre's lifelong companion, and a novelist and essayist in her own right. *Le Deuxième Sexe* (1949) and *Les Mandarins* (1954) became handbooks for French feminists. Contributed to the existentialist review *Les Temps Modernes*.

Brassai (1899–1984) Of Hungarian origin but Parisian by adoption, Brassai was a photographer who became "the eye of Paris," chronicling the nightlife and streetlife of the city in the 1920s and '30s.

André Breton (1896–1966) Founder and theorist of Surrealism, an art collector and mentor for many painters. Breton was a poet and writer; *Nadja* was his semi-autobiographical novel.

Coco Chanel (1883–1971) The first truly modern couturier introduced jersey, short skirts, simple box jackets, and "the little black dress" in the 1920s. She started a vogue for costume jewelry and aimed to democratize fashion.

❑ "Each frill discarded makes one look younger"—Coco Chanel. ❑

Colette (1873–1954) The first woman to preside over the Académie Goncourt. Her writing was supple, sensuous, and intuitive,

Colette poses for a 1909 magazine

often exploring more perverse sides of human nature.

Le Corbusier (1887–1965) Of Swiss origin, Le Corbusier settled in Paris in 1917 as a painter, then became an architect who propagated the use of reinforced concrete. His rigid style revolutionized architecture.

Claude Debussy (1862–1918) Debussy entered the Paris Conservatoire at age 10. His music used mood and suggestion in works such as *Prélude à l'après-midi d'un faune* (1894) and *Pelléas et Mélisande* (1902).

Anatole France (1844–1924) Parisian novelist, critic, and essayist. France was elected to the Académie Française, and won the Nobel Prize for literature in 1921. He confessed to finding Proust unreadable. His erudite work emulated 18th-century Classicism with an ironic style.

Léon Gambetta (1838–82) Gambetta was a lawyer before entering politics, a brilliant orator who opposed the Second Empire. He became a deputy but left Paris by balloon during the 1870 Prussian siege to organize resistance from Tours. With Thiers, he was instrumental in forming the Third Republic in 1875.

André Gide (1869–1951) Critic, essayist, novelist, and founder of the influential *Nouvelle Revue Française* in 1908. *La Porte Etroite* was his first major public success. Gide's questioning of moral dilemmas included his own homosexuality.

Victor Hugo (1802–85) Champion of Romanticism in poetry, drama, and novels, famous for *Notre-Dame de Paris*. Hugo was politically active as a Royalist and then a Republican; he exiled himself in Guernsey after Napoleon III's coup d'état. After his death, his body lay in state under the Arc de Triomphe before being transported to the Panthéon.

André Malraux (1901–1976) A charismatic idealist, aesthete,

Debussy, master of mood music

novelist, essayist, traveler, and Minister of Culture. He wrote *La Condition Humaine*, based on his days in Indochina. During the Spanish Civil War, Malraux organized Republican volunteers. Called upon by de Gaulle to "change the color of Paris," he renovated the center and took culture to the suburbs.

Jean-Paul Sartre (1905–80) Paris-born philosopher, novelist, dramatist, and exponent of Existentialism, starting with the novel *La Nausée*. He wrote prolifically during the war and in the 1950s, and was active in the Communist Party. Sartre refused to accept the Nobel Prize for Literature in 1964.

François Truffaut (1932–84) Film director of the postwar *Nouvelle Vague* movement, who started as a critic in the influential *Cahiers du Cinéma*. In a series of five films, starting with *Les Quatre Cent Coups* (1959), Truffaut explored the dreamy personality of Antoine Doinel.

Emile Zola (1840–1902) A novelist of the Realist school, conveying the tumultuous life of Paris and grim details of a growing industrial society. He defended Dreyfus with a celebrated open letter *J'accuse*, accusing the government of a miscarriage of justice.

PARIS

Musée de Montmartre

Station Pont Cardinet · Square des Batignolles · Cimetière de Montmartre

Bal du Moulin Rouge · PLACE DU TERTRE

BLVD BERTHIER

BLVD DE CLICHY

AVE DE LA PORTE DE CHAMPERRET · AVENUE DE VILLIERS · 17

BOULEVARD DES BATIGNOLLES

RUE DE CHATEAUDUN

Porte des Ternes · **Palais des Congrès** · Parc de Monceau · St-Augustin · **Gare St-Lazare** · 9

AVENUE DE WAGRAM · BLVD DE COURCELLES

Musée Jacquemart André

RUE DE LA PEPINIERE · BOULEVARD HAUSSMANN

Porte Maillot · AVENUE DE LA GRANDE ARMÉE · AVE DE FRIEDLAND

Arc de Triomphe · **Lido** · PLACE CHARLES DE GAULLE ETOILE · **Office du Tourisme** · **Palais de l'Elysée** · PLACE DE LA MADELEINE · **Opéra** · BLVD DES ITALIENS · **Palais de la Bourse**

AVENUE FOCH · AVENUE DES CHAMPS ELYSÉES · **Ste-Marie Madeleine** · BLVD DES CAPUCINES · RUE DU 4 SEPTEMBRE · **Bibliothèque Nationale**

AVENUE HUGO · 16 · AVENUE MARCEAU · PLACE VENDOME · **Jeu de Paume** · PL DES VICTOIRES

AVENUE D'IENA · **Grand Palais** · **Petit Palais** · PLACE DE LA CONCORDE · **St-Roch** · **Palais Royal** · 1

Palais Galliera · COURS ALBERT 1 ER · **Orangerie** · RUE DE RIVOLI · **Comédie Française** · **Bourse du Commerce**

Palais de Chaillot · **Palais de Tokyo** · NEW YORK · COURS LA REINE · **Jardin des Tuileries** · RUE DE RIVOLI · **Palais du Louvre**

Seine

Jardins de Trocadéro · QUAI D'ORSAY · QUAI D'ORSAY · QUAI DES TUILERIES · **Musée du Louvre** · QUAI DU LOUVRE

Tour Eiffel · Esplanade des Invalides · **Palais Bourbon-Assemblée Nationale** · **Musée d'Orsay** · QUAI VOLTAIRE · **Conciergerie**

Parc du Champ de Mars · 7 · **Hôtel des Invalides** · **Musée Rodin** · **Ecole des Beaux-Arts** · **Institut de France** · **St-Germain des Prés**

AVE DE TOURVILLE · RUE DE VARENNE · **Hôtel Matignon** · RUE DE BABYLONE · BOULEVARD SAINT-GERMAIN

Ecole Militaire · **St-Sulpice** · **Palais du Luxembourg**

UNESCO · 6

AVENUE EMILE ZOLA · BLVD GARIBALDI · Jardin du Luxembourg

15 · RUE LECOURBE · BLVD PASTEUR

RUE DE VAUGIRARD · BLVD DE VAUGIRARD · **Tour Montparnasse** · BOULEVARD DU MONTPARNASSE

RUE LEBLANC · **Gare Montparnasse** · Cimetière du Montparnasse · BOULEVARD DI

Porte de Sèvres · BOULEVARD VICTOR · **Parc des Expositions** · BOULEVARD LEFEBVRE · 14 · **Observatoire**

Porte de la Plaine · PERIPHERIQUE · BLVD ST-JACQUES

Basilique du
Sacré-Cœur

18

RUE MARX DORMOY

RUE DE FLANDRE

QUAI DE LA SEINE

Bassin de la Villette

BOULEVARD BARBÈS

BOULEVARD DE LA CHAPELLE

ROCHECHOUART

Gare
du Nord

RUE DU FAUBOURG ST-DENIS

QUAI DE LA VILLETTE

AVENUE JEAN JAURÈS

19

RUE LA FAYETTE

JE DU MAUBEUGE

BOULEVARD DE MAGENTA

RUE LA FAYETTE

Gare
de l'Est

FAUBOURG SAINT-MARTIN

10

Canal Saint-Martin

AVENUE DE VILLETTE

BLVD DE LA VILLETTE

Parc des
Buttes
Chaumont

Folies
Bergère

usée
révin

BLVD BONNE NOUVELLE

BOULEVARD
POISSONNIÈRE

2

RUE RÉAUMUR

BOULEVARD DE STRASBOURG

RUE DU TEMPLE

BOULEVARD DE MAGENTA

BLVD
ST-MARTIN

RUE ST-MARTIN

Hôpital
St-Louis

20

BLVD DE BELLEVILLE

Hôtel des Postes
St-Eustache

BOULEVARD DE SÉBASTOPOL

Conservatoire
National des
Arts et Métiers

RUE RÉAUMUR

RUE
BEAUBOURG

3

PLACE
DE LA
RÉPUBLIQUE

AVENUE DE LA RÉPUBLIQUE

Les Halles

Forum

RUE DU RENARD

BLVD DU TEMPLE

BOULEVARD VOLTAIRE

11

Tour
St-Jacques

Beaubourg/Centre Georges
Pompidou - Centre National
d'Art et de Culture

Archives
Nationales

BVD BEAUMARCHAIS

BOULEVARD RICHARD LENOIR

Théâtre du
Châtelet

QUAI DE LA
GISSERIE

Théâtre de
la Ville

Musée
Carnavalet

Musée
Picasso

Hôtel
de Ville

QUAI DE GESVRES

VOIE GEORGES

HÔTEL DE VILLE

PLACE DES
VOSGES

RUE DE RIVOLI

RUE ST-ANTOINE

4

Île
de la
Cité

BLVD DU PALAIS

Préf. de
Police

Hôtel
Dieu

Cathédrale
Notre-Dame

QUAI DE L'

Q DE POMPIDOU

QUAI DES CÉLESTINS

QUAI DE
BLVD HENRI IV

PLACE
DE LA
BASTILLE

RUE DU FAUBOURG
ST-ANTOINE

Île
St-Louis

QUAI DE LA

PONT DE SULLY

QUAI HENRI IV

Opéra
Bastille

Musée de
Cluny

BLVD
MONTEBELLO TOURNELLE

BLVD
SAINT-GERMAIN

PONT MORLAND

AVE LEDRU ROLLIN

RUE DE LYON

AVENUE DIDEROT

12

Sorbonne

Panthéon

Institut du
Monde Arabe

QUAI ST-BERNARD

Seine

QUAI DE LA RAPÉE

AVENUE DAUMESNIL

BOULEVARD

Gare
de Lyon

Jardin
des
Plantes

PONT D'AUSTERLITZ

5

Mosquée

ôpital
al de Grâce

Muséum National
d'Histoire Naturelle

Gare
d'Austerlitz

QUAI D'AUSTERLITZ

BLVD DE BERCY

Palais
Omnisports
de Bercy

PORT-ROYAL

Manufacture
des Gobelins

BLVD ST-MARCEL

AVE DES GOBELINS

RUE DE L'HÔPITAL

13

PONT DE BERCY

QUAI DE LA GARE

QUAI DE BERCY

BLVD AUGUSTE
BLANQUI

PLACE
D'ITALIE

BOULEVARD VINCENT AURIOL

0   ½   1 km

0   ½ mile

LE CAFÉ DU
COMMERCE

THE LEFT BANK

A new Paris skyline
A huge redevelopment project in the 13th *arrondissement* will have as its skyline symbol four glass towers—part of the new Bibliothèque de France (National Library), a vast and ambitious operation that will close former President Mitterrand's 14-year reign of *grands projets*. Meanwhile, the entire surrounding *quartier* of Tolbiac, which runs east along the Seine from the Gare d'Austerlitz, will be restructured at a projected cost of 25 billion francs: all part of a massive boost for the Left Bank image.

It is impossible to tire of Paris's central Left Bank area. Its narrow streets, lined with shops and restaurants, combine with breathtaking monuments and Parisian chic to create a unique atmosphere. However the city may develop, nothing can change the historic streets and buildings of the **Quartier Latin**, the **Montagne Ste.-Geneviève**, and **St.-Germain-des-Prés**.

Transformations There have, however, been changes further afield. **Montparnasse**, the quarter famous for its literary and artistic connotations in prewar Paris, is a flagrant example. Today, the main boulevard presents a rather artificial, plastic face. The architectural faux pas of the 685-foot **Tour Montparnasse**, part of Pompidou's heritage, is so extraordinarily out of place that it almost assumes a perverted monumental glory. The urban developments behind the city's most confusing station (Montparnasse) are best ignored. Many Left Bank residents claim that they hardly ever cross the Seine. They have their Roman ruins, their cinemas, galleries, literary cafés, and halls of learning. They also have France's government, concentrated in the **Faubourg St.-Germain**, once the height of bourgeois fashion. Between the **rue du Bac** and **Les Invalides** is yet another world: hidden ministry gardens and embassies housed in superb 18th-century mansions. Immediately to the west are the stately residential avenues of the 7th arrondissement leading south to the heavily populated 15th. Apart from the **Eiffel Tower** and **Les Invalides**, this area is devoid of "tourist attractions"; all the more reason to give it some attention.

In the southern 13th arrondissement, Southeast Asian immigrants have created a firmly identifiable **Chinatown**. Here you can celebrate Chinese New Year or sample ethnic cuisine. Towering over you are high-rise blocks, a far cry from the historic townhouses and middle-class apartments nearby, and proof that even the Left Bank of Paris is still evolving.

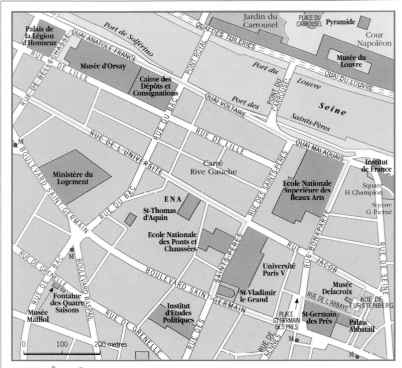

Walk Exploring the Rive Gauche

Starting at the 12th-century church of St.-Germain-des-Prés, walk down the rue Bonaparte and turn right immediately after the corner garden into the rue de l'Abbaye. Turn left into the rue de Furstenberg.
Here you cross the lovely square once inhabited by painter Delacroix, before coming to the rue Jacob.

Follow rue Jacob to the left.
This street has numerous antiques and interior decoration shops.

At the rue Bonaparte, follow this fascinating shopping street to the right.
On your left you will pass the grand entrance to the **Beaux-Arts.**

Having reached the Seine, walk along the Quai Malaquais, which leads directly into the Quai Voltaire and the Quai Anatole-France.
From here there is a good view of the Louvre across the Seine. The quais themselves are lined with upscale antiques shops and the odd restaurant. At **19 Quai Malaquais** stands a literary landmark; Anatole France was born here, and it was previously the home of George Sand, who was deeply involved with Alfred de Musset.

Cross the rue du Bac.
Pass the courtyard of the **Caisse des Dépôts**, dominated by a sculpture by Dubuffet, before coming to the almighty Musée d'Orsay.

Circle around to the left, following the chic rue de Bellechasse to the rue de l'Université. Turn left.
The route continues past more antiques shops and galleries.

At the rue des Saints-Pères, turn right to rejoin the boulevard St.-Germain, with the church along to the left.

53

THE RIGHT BANK

A horseman looks out over the 17th-century place des Victoires, now a focus for 20th-century fashions

Place des Victoires
The imposing place des Victoires was developed in 1685 by the Dauphine's tutor, Maréchal de la Feuillade. Laid out by architects Hardouin-Mansart and Prado, it continued a century-old Parisian tradition of majestic squares, started by Henri IV. Although many of the facades have since altered, this circle of elegant mansions has lost none of its original grandeur, housing the chic boutiques of Kenzo, Cacharel, and other leading fashion names.

Look at a map of Paris. Notice how the Seine gently curves around the Left Bank, almost enclosing it, leaving the Right Bank more open and more extensive. Covering a much greater area, it governs the north, east, and west of Paris, and over the centuries has suffered for it. The Baron Haussmann created his wide arteries here; kings built their palaces here; and every ruler left at least one monument. Less intimate in scale, more disparate in style, its atmosphere can be stately or decidedly tacky, and is certainly less easy to define. This is also the banking and business center, and its rhythm is fast: those notorious long Paris lunches are here generally replaced by a quick sandwich.

Changing pace This is contemporary Paris. It also boasts two opera houses, two museums of contemporary art, the Louvre, countless other monuments and museums, and a dense concentration of gastronomic halts and nocturnal haunts. Cushioning the grandeur are burgeoning new quartiers, rebuilt or redeveloped. The most obvious is the **Marais,** which over the last 15 years has undergone intensive renovation and is now a hive of avant-garde art galleries and trendy restaurants. Historic buildings have become museums, like the **Musée Picasso**, while at the eastern end the **Bastille** is developing along similar lines. Towering over the central square is a mammoth and prestigious new opera house, while in the backstreets flourishes a mass of tiny boutiques, shady bars, and experimental galleries.

Les Halles The central area of the Right Bank is monopolized by another renovated area, **Les Halles,** the hub of Paris that kicks off the arrondissement system (this curls outward snail-like from here). The **Centre Pompidou** remains a controversial landmark, offering hot culture and panoramic views, while just a few streets away is the infamous **rue St.-Denis**, thick with sex shops and prostitutes. Unfortunate in the spectacular and protracted bulldozing of its past, Les Halles has taken on a peculiar identity, closely linked with a vast underground shopping center and the RER station, which speeds in suburban teenagers for their nights on the town.

Once again, things change radically only a few streets away. Here you enter the realm of fashion victims and ultra-chic designer clothes shops, which revolve around the superb 17th-century **place des Victoires**. Continuing the paradox, this area skates around the **Banque de France** and the **Bourse** before, deep in the 2nd arrondissement, becoming a maze of wholesale rag-traders and basement sweatshops. Punctuating all the above are the main press offices and news agencies of the capital.

Nightlife For the visitor, the Right Bank also means glamour and glitter. While the avenue **Montaigne** and the **Faubourg St.-Honoré** maintain their monopoly on haute couture and related boutiques, the **Champs-Elysées** has seen better days. However, many of Paris's luxury hotels and exclusive nightclubs cluster around this major axis, and the temples of its top chefs are generously sprinkled between the 8th and the adjoining 17th arrondissements.

Meanwhile, the 16th arrondissement maintains its discreetly chic residential atmosphere, at the same time displaying some of France's most innovative architecture from the turn of the century, as well as monumental relics from various Expositions Universelles that are now Parisian landmarks.

Montmartre Few come to Paris without the obligatory pilgrimage to Montmartre, which, although still attracting residents from the world of film and media, has turned over many of its charms to the tourist masses. At the bottom of the hill in **Pigalle**, tourist buses line the boulevard while sex shops and clubs ply their trade, but in the streets running downhill through the 9th arrondissement you will find some of the city's more genuine nightlife. This village-like area runs down to the *grands boulevards*, once a social hub, now following the same fate as the Champs-Elysées.

New developments are legion on this side of the Seine, from the mega development of **La Défense**, ongoing since 1958, to (marginally) more modest projects such as **La Villette** and **Bercy**, both of which should soon be completed. This policy of injecting life and facilities into neglected outlying areas attempts to combine the latest architectural styles harmoniously with historical features and structures. But traditionally working-class districts such as **Belleville** or the **Bastille** are both suffering at the hands of property developers. Nothing is built without controversy: all the more fuel for Parisian polemics; all the more coffees to accompany the endless debate and discussion. At least those essential Parisian characteristics are saved.

A view across the Seine of the 8th arrondissement on the Right Bank—a bustling district dominated by the Champs-Elysées and the rue St.-Honoré

Happily floating midstream in the Seine, the **Ile de la Cité** and the **Ile St.-Louis** are as different in character as the two banks they separate. One is the site of the first (pre-Roman) settlement of the Parisii tribe; the other is the symbol of a successful 17th-century property development. Linked by a fragile footbridge, both are surrounded by extensive water-level quais, favorites with anglers, sunbathers, young couples, book readers, and a cross section of the Parisian gay community.

Ile St.-Louis Densely inhabited by successful literati and a cosmopolitan breed of wealthy business people, the Ile St.-Louis has become an exclusive residential area inevitably frequented by tourists. One long street that runs from end to end is a mass of restaurants and shops more geared to foreigners than to locals, although many residents swear by the quality of the food shops. Locally produced, world-famous ice cream is a strong attraction, but the architectural unity and beauty of Le Vau's 17th-century townhouses and the elegant comfort they exude make neck-craning the favorite pastime here. One of Paris's best views is from the western tip of the island along the Seine.

Ile de la Cité Historically the heart of Paris, the Ile de la Cité boasts three major monuments: **Notre-Dame**, **Sainte-Chapelle**, and the **Conciergerie**. Also strong on government buildings such as the **Palais de Justice**, the **Hôtel-Dieu** (a hospital), and the **Préfecture**, the result is a bizarre mixture of the sublime and the banal. Some residents manage to squeeze in between the medieval monuments, living along the quais or on the delightful **place Dauphine**, while the flower market occupies a square behind the Préfecture, constantly passed by police cars and ambulances that, sirens wailing, tear past the soaring Gothic towers of Notre-Dame. This relaxed eclecticism is perhaps symbolic of the entire city: nothing is sacred, but every area eventually has its monument.

Famous food stores
Two of Paris's most famous food institutions are on the Ile St.-Louis. The tiny bakery of Haupois in rue Deux Ponts produces some of the best baguettes in Paris in its wood-fired ovens. However, the biggest lines are always outside Berthillon in rue St.-Louis-en-Ille, reputedly one of the best ice-cream shops of Europe, with over 30 delicious flavors including bestsellers *marron glacé* and wild strawberry.

56

Sainte-Chapelle and the gates to the Palais de Justice, Ile de la Cité

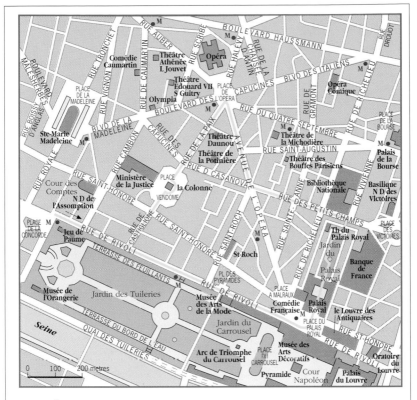

Walk **Exploring the Rive Droite**

From the place de la Concorde, cross to the Tuileries gardens beside the Jeu de Paume.
From here you can either walk along the **Terrasse des Feuillants**, set up by Le Nôtre in the 1660s, and enjoy the view across the garden or follow the arcaded **rue de Rivoli** and its tourist shops.

After an underpass, walk beside the Musée des Arts de la Mode, soon followed by the Musée des Arts Décoratifs, before reaching the Louvre itself. At the place du Palais-Royal, turn sharp left, cross the rue St.-Honoré to the Comédie Française and enter the Palais-Royal through a discreet arch.
Here you confront the controversial art installation by Daniel Buren, before entering the gardens proper. Walk to the end, leaving on the left

side past the historic restaurant **Le Grand Véfour.**

Go up to the rue des Petits Champs. Turn left here, passing the Bibliothèque Nationale on your right, and go on to the avenue de l'Opéra.
Japanese restaurants in the side-streets indicate the proximity of Paris's "Little Tokyo."

Turn right toward the opera house, cross the avenue, then turn left and walk down the rue de la Paix.
This is Paris's high-class jewelry street, which leads to the no less classy **place Vendôme.** The legendary **Ritz Hotel** occupies the right half of the square.

Go straight on down the rue de Castiglione, until you reach the rue de Rivoli and the Concorde.

57

■ **As dawn breaks over Les Halles, clusters of bleary-eyed, home-bound night-hawks cross paths with the first wave of workmen. The rue Montorgueil, one of the main market streets when Les Halles was really Les Halles, still has many classic suppliers and services intact …■**

Little has changed here, except that in 1992 most of this lengthy street was transformed into a pedestrian precinct. The first café to open its doors, at 5:30AM—the **Pointe Sainte-Eustache**—is also the first on the street at the Les Halles end. Not overly boisterous when they arrive, local workers in their *bleus* (traditional blue overalls) soon warm up with *un petit coup de blanc sec* or even manage a quick cognac. Employed in the market or on local building sites, they face a long day, generally out of doors; hence their winter alcohol requirements.

Early risers Also starting the day early are the municipal workers, emptying trash cans into their poison-green wagons. When Paris regained its first mayor since the Revolution, in 1977, it also gained an army of street-cleaning machinery, including motorized "poopscoopers." Streets are cleaned in the early mornings by streams of water gushing through the gutters, channeled by strategically positioned lumpy rags. In the wake of the sanitation truck, concierges soon emerge to pull in their cans and restore order to the buildings in their care. Their net-curtained *loges* still exist and concierges continue to fulfill an important social role in Parisian residential life.

By 8AM a few white-collar workers start appearing, some hurrying straight to the metro, others taking time to stop for a coffee and croissant as they peruse the morning paper. By now the market is getting into its swing, although officially most stalls and shops open at 9AM. Boulangeries are an exception, opening at around 7:30, when the baguette is often at its optimum. Queen of the pâtissiers in the rue Montorgueil is **Stohrer**, founded by Louis XV's chef pâtissier at No. 51 in 1730.

Cosmopolitan tastes Montorgueil literally means "proud mount," a poetic way of describing the road's gentle slope up to the Grands Boulevards. The southern end was once the central oyster and seafood market where produce from the northern ports ended up. This explains the proximity of the all-night seafood counters on the adjoining **rue de la Coquillière**. Today, cosmopolitan tastes have moved in and the choice is more eclectic: an oriental grocer sells manioc, lychees, and sweet potatoes; a North African wholesaler displays buckets and barrels of olives, grains, dates, and nuts; further up, a pungent Greek grocery offers hummus or stuffed vine leaves, while the windows of two Italian delicatessens are full of fresh pasta and strings of salamis. As you wander through the crowds you will hear Spanish, Arabic, or even English and German. The

Royal pastries
Pâtisserie Stolier, one of the oldest and finest in Paris, was opened in 1730 by a Polish pastry cook who had moved to Versailles, following the marriage of Marie Leszczynska to Louis XV. The interior of the shop is decorated with 19th-century wall paintings: one shows La Renommée carrying a tray of "Puits d'Amour" (Wells of Love), an 18th-century specialty still sold today.

fresh fruit and vegetable stalls attract every nationality, generation, and status, as do the prices, which are a fraction of those at neighborhood grocery stores.

Lunch break Bistros abound in this street. At the traditional **Le Brin de Zinc et Madame** at No. 50, you can eat a wholesome dish of pork and lentils, **L'Escargot** at No. 38 was the first restaurant in Paris to serve snails. They're still a specialty. Shoppers gradually disappear as 1PM approaches: this is closing time for the fish, meat, fruit, and vegetable shops, which take a rest till 4PM. With its new pedestrian status, rue Montorgueil has blossomed into a favorite lunchtime haunt for fashion victims from nearby boutiques.

The afternoon session closes again at around 7:30, though some late-opening stores benefit from the last few office workers hurrying home with a baguette and a bottle of wine to catch the 8PM TV news.

Twilight zone Although ostensibly quiet in the evenings, the rue Montorgueil is far from dead. There are several popular restaurants, including the famous **Au Pied du Cochon**, which stays open till the early hours. But the side streets are where it is all happening: the rue **Tiquetonne** boasts Thai transvestite bars or an all-night African restaurant, and the **rue Marie-Stuart** an equally eccentric selection, covering ethnic flavors from Spain to the Cameroons, all of which keeps the locals going until the 24-hour cycle starts again.

Tour de Jean Sans Peur
Near the junction of rue Montorgueil and rue Etienne-Marcel lies a rare example of a domestic Gothic tower, the Tour de Jean "Sans Peur" (without fear). Despite his name, Jean, Duc de Bourgogne, feared retaliation following the assassination of the Duc d'Orléans in 1408 on his orders, so he added a massive square 88-foot stone tower to his home and slept at the very top, as far as possible from his would-be attackers.

59

Business as usual in the rue Montorgueil, all that remains of the original Les Halles Market, once the center of Paris's oyster trade

ACADEMIE FRANÇAISE

60

The Institut de France, home of the Académie Française

R.E.CARD.BASILICAM.ET.GYMNAS.F.C.

Rue Montorgueil
Three-and-a-half miles of streets around the rue Montorgueil have been repaved to create Europe's largest pedestrian area, using a total volume of granite cobblestones equivalent to that of the Eiffel Tower.

▶ **Académie Française**
Institut de France, 23 Quai de Conti, 75006
metro: Pont-Neuf

This venerable institution, although somewhat dusty at the edges, remains a heeded voice in certain French circles, its 40 members occasionally emitting dictums that just have to be obeyed. Founded by Richelieu in 1635, the Académie's rule over the standards of the French language, which includes a high level of protectionism, is embodied in the *Dictionnaire de la Langue Française*, a 10-tome affair that is periodically revised and published, volume by hefty volume.

The Académie's weekly meetings, which once a year become solemn occasions in the famous domed hall, are held at the **Institut de France**, an edifice that you cannot fail to spot in its prime Left Bank position overlooking the Pont des Arts. The building itself was designed in 1663 by Le Vau, one of the architects of the Louvre, and was financed by a generous donation from Cardinal Mazarin to found a college for choice provincial students. By 1790 it had lost this function to the vagaries of the Directoire, and five years later the five academies of the Institut de France were moved in.

Elected only when a seat is liberated by a member's death, the average age of *académicien* is consequently elevated. Today the Académie Française is a concerted voice of historians, writers, doctors, and representatives of the Church, army, and diplomatic circles.

Although the Institut is not open to individual visits, which means nobody can pay homage to Mazarin's tomb, you can enter the courtyard to have a closer look.

▶ **Angleterre, Hôtel d'**
44 rue Jacob, 6e

This elegant, 18th-century townhouse in the heart of the antiques district once housed the British Embassy, whence its name. This generated a diplomatic incident when Benjamin Franklin refused to set foot on "British soil" to sign the U.S. Declaration of Independence. More recently, Hemingway lived here (modestly) and it is now a charming and discreet hotel preserving many of its historic features, including a flowery courtyard.

Aquariums

Apart from the small aquariums squeezed between cages of rabbits in the shops along the Quai de la Mégisserie, underwater enthusiasts can also see no fewer than eight aquariums at the **Centre de la Mer et des Eaux**, 195 rue St.-Jacques, 5e (tel: 46 33 08 61). Set up by Jacques Cousteau, it explains his ambitious underwater projects undertaken since the 1960s. However, Paris's largest liquid universe and the second largest in Europe is housed nearby at the **Musée des Arts Africains et Océaniens** (see page 63).

▶▶▶ **Arc de Triomphe**

Along with the Eiffel Tower, the Arc de Triomphe remains the great Paris landmark, dominating the axis leading east down the Champs-Elysées and west down the avenue de la Grande Armée toward Porte Maillot and La Défense. The central point of a web of 12

61

avenues constantly swirling with traffic, this major cross-roads is known as the Etoile (star). The Arc's conception goes back to Napoleon, who in 1806 commissioned an awesome memorial to be built for the French army, but it was not until 1836, under Louis-Philippe, that the monument was completed. By the time Haussmann had finished with redesigning Paris, the Etoile had assumed the form it has today, and its symbolic role was confirmed after World War I with parades of victorious troops marching through and the burial of the unknown soldier beneath. Over 70 years later, a ceremony takes place every November 11 (Armistice Day), and the flame is lit daily at 6:30PM.

The sculpted facade is actually the work of three different sculptors, and the 30 shields studding the crown of the arch each bear the name of a Revolutionary or Imperial victory (Waterloo does not figure). The Arc stands 165 feet high, and it is worth braving the long lines to take the elevator, or laboring up the steps—the view is superb and gives a clear vision of Haussmann's urban layout. Access is via the underpasses beneath the chaos of the traffic.

Open: daily, 10–5:30; 9:30–6:30 in summer.

Symbol of military victory and power, and a long-lasting landmark: the Arc de Triomphe

Archives Nationales

The bureaucratic personality of France is well symbolized by its Archives Nationales, which fill 217 miles of shelves in the Marais. Napoleon was responsible for housing them in the remarkable Hôtel de Soubise (see page 126), but they have since spilled over into adjacent mansions and in 1988 a new center was built in the rue des Quatre Fils.

Open: Wednesday to Monday, 2–5.

Walk From the Etoile and along the avenues

Start at the Etoile metro and walk down the Champs-Elysées.
Stop at the famous **Fouquets** at No. 99, an exclusive restaurant declared a historic monument.

Continue to Rond-Point and turn right into the avenue Montaigne.
This is the mecca of French haute couture. You will pass Louis Vuitton, Chanel, Cartier, Givenchy, *et al.*, as well as the luxurious Plaza-Athénée hotel, and, at No. 15, the **Théâtre des Champs-Elysées**. Designed in 1911–3 by Auguste Perret, it saw the first scandalous performance of Stravinsky's *Le Sacre du Printemps*, choreographed by Nijinsky. The marble facade and the interior were recently restored and crowned by a controversial restaurant.

Cross the place de l'Alma and take the avenue du Président-Wilson.

Pass the mammoth colonnaded 1937 buildings of the **Musée d'Art Moderne** and the **Palais de Tokyo**, both important exhibition centers. On the other side of the avenue rises the imposing **Palais Galliera**.

Turn right onto the avenue Pierre Ier de Serbie, from the place d'Iéna.
The entrance to the Palais Galliera is on this avenue.

Walk straight on, crossing the avenue Marceau with the church of St.-Pierre-de-Chaillot on your left, until you come to the avenue George V.
A short detour to the right takes you to the neo-Gothic **American Cathedral**.

Turn left and pass the prestigious hotels George V and Prince de Galles before returning to the Champs-Elysées.

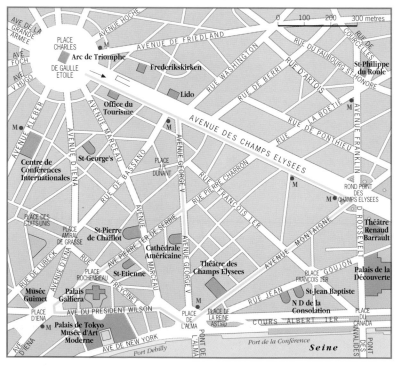

►► **Arts Africains et Océaniens, Musée des**
293 avenue Daumesnil, 12e
metro: Porte Dorée

This museum is a perennial favorite for children. The basement aquariums are a constant draw: leopard sharks swim in the company of a fish named Grace Kelly, yellow-tailed Picasso balistas, bewhiskered catfish or a mound of slow-motion turtles all circulate eternally. Apart from these attractions, the museum is

63

yet another Parisian monument to the aesthetics of art deco. Built for the 1931 Exposition Coloniale in reinforced concrete, its colonnaded facade is backed by an extraordinary stone bas-relief by Alfred Janniot depicting the glories of the French colonies. Inside, two floors of galleries open onto an enormous ballroom with a superb "pagoda" ceiling, mosaic floors, and murals by Ducos de la Haille. More astonishing examples of art deco are found in two circular rooms leading off the main entrance hall: both boast murals, this time by Lemaître and Louis Bouquet, and are respectively decorated by Printz and by Ruhlmann.

The actual collections cover parts of the Pacific (Melanesia, New Hebrides, Australia), Central and West Africa, and finally, on the top floor, the arts of the Maghreb (Algeria, Tunisia, and Morocco). The latter displays silver jewelry, ceramics, Koranic tablets, arms, and textiles as well as architectural features. However, the main riches of the museum lie in the African department on the first floor: here the tone is set by Dogon masks, rings, and statues, reflecting a fascination for the coexistence of life and death. Other tribes such as the Bambaras, Lobi, Akan, Benin, and Kongo are represented by items ranging from basic to sacred.

The Pacific islands are represented on the ground floor by masks, carved wooden statues, and a collection of Australian aboriginal art. Bark painting represents the aborigines' approach to their natural world.

Open: Wednesday to Monday, 10–noon, 1:30–5:30; weekends, 12:30–6.

The popular Musée des Arts Africains et Océaniens, set in splendid isolation on the edge of the Bois de Vincennes

A memorable avenue
Originally an unpaved track across swampy ground, the avenue des Champs-Elysées, almost 2 miles long and 232 feet wide, is today one of the world's most famous thoroughfares, full of cinemas, clubs, and shops. From the top of the Arc de Triomphe, with its breath-taking views toward La Défense and place de la Concorde, it is easy to imagine the numerous grand processions through the arch over the centuries.

Fashion museums
The Musée des Arts Décoratifs rivals the adjacent Musée de la Mode et de la Costume for the best collections dedicated to the great couturiers of Paris, largely as a result of its exceptional Jeanne Lanvin display, which includes unique fashion accessories and historical designs from the inter-war Parisian fashion boom, within the context of Lanvin's reconstructed apartment.

 **Arts Décoratifs, Musée des**
107 rue de Rivoli, 1e
metro: Palais-Royal
For art-nouveau and art-deco fanatics, this is the place to go. The museum was founded by the Union Centrale des Arts Décoratifs in a wing of the Louvre at the beginning of this century to collect and exhibit "beauty in function." Its didactic role reached its zenith in the 1920s and '30s, with internationally renowned designers such as Le Corbusier, Charlotte Perriand, and Mallet-Stevens contributing to its influence.

The museum itself still possesses the charm and drawbacks of its early years: despite some renovation it remains a labyrinth, awaiting expansion into an adjoining wing of the Louvre, scheduled for 1996. In the meantime, its tricky access and itinerary make it a tranquil haven of reconstructed salons of the 18th century or ornate oak-paneled halls, thick with tapestries. Pick up a plan of the four floors when you buy your ticket; it is sorely lacking in signs or logic.

Floor by floor On the top floor (Level 5) you can see two precious collections only open to the public on Thursday afternoons. One is a collection of glass that skips through the centuries and countries, from Roman times through ornate Dutch and Bohemian pieces of the 17th and 18th centuries to the inventive finesse of Murano, along with the sober forms and clear colors of Chinese pieces. Gallé, Daum, and Tiffany are well represented. The other treasure here is a collection of wallpaper from its

handpainted 17th-century origins to early 20th-century samples.

The lower floors are organized according to periods, so here you can make your choice between medieval/Gothic and Renaissance (Level 2) or the fabulously rich 1900–25 gallery (Level 1), which includes a room entirely faced in art nouveau woodwork (Georges Hoentschell) with furniture by Hector Guimard (famous for his metro entrances). Much of the 1920s collection was donated by the couturier Jeanne Lanvin. Of the many stunning reconstructed interiors from her 7th arrondissement apartment, don't miss Rateau's remarkable bathroom design.

Levels 3 and 4 are devoted to the 17th- to early 19th-century collections, and here you can focus on porcelain, vast panels of wallpaper depicting exotic landscapes, or marquetry masterpieces by Boulle. Again, entire rooms are reconstructed in the style of different periods, while the corridors are lined with watercolors.

State of the art Finally, don't miss the contemporary design section back on Level 1, which displays furniture and objects by today's stars: designers such as Jean-Michel Wilmotte, Philippe Starck, or Andrée Putman. After a quiet period, French decorative arts have come back into their own, and this is a good place to get a quick overview of what the last decade has produced. On the same level, apparently an anomaly in this museum, is the Dubuffet donation that the painter gave the museum in 1967 in thanks for arranging his first retrospective. Jean Dubuffet, the master of *art brut*, died in Paris in 1985. Temporary exhibitions of crafts or design complete the cycle.

There is a bookshop on the ground floor and a gift shop opposite that sells copies and a good range of contemporary design—glass, jewelry, ceramics, and other items. *Open*: Wednesday to Saturday, 12:30–6; Sunday, noon–6.

▶▶ **Arts de la Mode, Musée des**
107 rue de Rivoli, 1e
Part of the same umbrella structure as the above, the Musée des Arts de la Mode was opened in 1986 in the far corner of the Musée des Arts Décoratifs. Following the same fate, it awaits a major extension so that it will at last be able to accommodate its permanent collections. For the moment, after a dynamic program of temporary exhibitions ranging from St. Laurent to theater designs by Tirelli or the history of French perfume, it is a museum keeping a low profile, open only during exhibitions. Despite spectacular renovation that gives some fabulous vistas east over the Tuileries, administrative problems have left it unfinished.

In 1991, the government finally earmarked 175 million francs for the entire restructuring and modernization of both these museums, which now also incorporates the **Musée de la Publicité**. In 1996, this exceptional Parisian showcase spanning the history of design, advertising, and fashion will present a refreshed face to the public. *Open:* Wednesday to Saturday, 12:30–6; Sunday, noon–6 during exhibitions only.

Hector Guimard
Hector Guimard (1867–1934), one of the leading lights in the French art nouveau movement, initially made his mark on Paris with his Castel Béranger, a spectacular apartment block of stained glass, mosaics, and elegant wrought ironwork at 14 rue La Fontaine in the Autenil district. He then went on to design the entrances for the Paris metro. Today only a few remain, including the striking Porte Dauphine and the Abbesses metro with its unusual amber lights and green iron arches.

65

■ **Reveling in its historic reputation, the Paris art scene is, in the mid-1990s, reeling from the shock of recession. After experiencing a rather low ebb with international attention firmly focused on New York throughout the 1960s and 1970s, Paris has nevertheless reemerged as a contemporary art crossroads ...■**

Purchasing arts and antiques
There seems to be a limitless choice of arts and antiques, ranging from the famous galleries around the rue du Faubourg-St.-Honoré to the avant-garde galleries of the Marais and Bastille, or even one of the many flea markets. To export designated *objet's d'art* worth more than 1,000,000 francs you need a certificate of authenticity available from the Centre Français de Commerce Extérieur (tel: 40 73 30 00).

The late 1980s saw an unprecedented boom in the art market worldwide, and Paris reaped the rewards with galleries monopolizing areas such as the Marais, their scale often directly proportional to the conceptual nature of the work shown. The Bastille, too, had its renaissance, and many younger gallery owners turned to this booming quarter as an alternative to the high-flying rents now common in the Marais. But since then, economic reality bit and many have closed their doors.

Left Bank But what about the traditional hotbed of art in St.-Germain-des-Prés? The rue de Seine, rue Mazarine, and adjoining characteristic streets have put their avant-garde days behind them. Today this area has its own distinct flavor, nothing to do with what is going on across the Seine. Antiques, art deco furniture, prints, ethnographical wonders, and 1950s abstract paintings are the mainstay of hundreds of small galleries lining a well-defined territory between the rue Bonaparte, rue Guénégaud, and the rue de Seine. High-quality antiques

shops are concentrated further west in what is known as the *Carré Rive Gauche*, a grid of streets running between the Quai Voltaire, the rue du Bac, the rue de l'Université, and the rue des Saints-Pères, including the famous rue de Beaune.

Back in the epicenter of the Left Bank galleries, head for the eclectic atmosphere of the rue des Beaux-Arts. Beautiful objects abound while galleries such as **Albert Loeb** and **Claude Bernard** still promote the figurative style that made their reputations a few decades ago. The rue de Seine offers anything from floral prints to Jean Cocteau originals, while the **Galerie Isy Brachot**, on the corner of the rue Guénégaud and the rue Mazarine, has two galleries showing relatively avant-garde work. The **Galerie Montenay** at 31 rue Mazarine concentrates on young European and American artists and is worth checking out. For contemporary sculpture, go to **JGM** in the short but sweet rue Jacques-Callot.

Meanwhile, there is no shortage of prospective painters in the area: the **Ecole des Beaux-Arts** in the rue Bonaparte regorges flocks of portfolio-lugging students, and the eternal café meeting point, **La Palette**, remains a favorite for gallery owners and artists alike.

Right Bank chic For strictly high-price brackets, head for another traditional gallery agglomeration over on the Right Bank. Here, between the avenue Matignon, the Faubourg St.-Honoré, and (further north) the boulevard Haussmann, you can track down works by artists, dead or alive, who have hit the heights. The **Galerie Lelong▶** at 13/14 rue de Téhéran, founded by the illustrious art

Bargain hunting
For anyone unconcerned with the latest volatile trends of the art world, Paris has an unbeatable selection of backstreet galleries showing classical paintings and drawings, both old and new. If you like the object, you can buy it; but unless you have real flair, don't think you're making an investment—only dealers govern that domain and the last few years have proved how wrong even they can be.

67

A spacious converted workshop is the setting for European and American art in the Galerie Yvon Lambert's collection (see page 68)

Auction houses

The leading Paris auction center is Drouot-Richelieu at 9 rue Drouot, named after the Comte de Drouot, Napoleon's aide-de-camp, and founded in 1858. Viewing is from 11AM to 6PM the day before the sale. The auction takes place in French and a 10–15 percent buyers' premium is added to the purchase price. Sale details are available in La Gazette de l'Hôtel Drouot.

The Galerie Maeght, run by Yoyo, granddaughter of artistic talent scout Aimé Maeght

dealer Aimé Maeght, still shows artists such as Magnelli, Alechinsky, Francis Bacon, or Tapiès, as well as younger names such as James Brown or Garcià-Sevilla. Nearby, the prestigious **Galerie Louis Carré** could be exhibiting anything from Delaunay to Hartung or a French contemporary such as Jean-Pierre Raynaud. For more accessible purchases, go to **Artcurial**, the art department store at 9 avenue Matignon, which specializes in multiples (prints, jewelry, carpets) and boasts one of the best art bookshops in town.

On a very different note, clustered around Beaubourg and spreading east through the Marais, are hundreds of contemporary galleries promoting today's avant-garde. From the narrow rue Quincampoix, parallel to the boulevard Sébastopol, to the labyrinth circling around the Musée Picasso and over toward the place des Vosges, galleries exhibit installations, large format paintings, or photographs and occasionally words. To find your way in this circuit, pick up one of the specialized listing maps, *Rive Gauche Rive Droite*, that are distributed free in the galleries. This itinerary is strictly for the initiated, the state of art today often being generally inaccessible.

Architecturally speaking, it is an opportunity to look at some remarkable renovations of mansions or factories—ceilings are high and often skylit, courtyards are commonplace, and floors are bleached wood or painted concrete. In the rue St.-Merri, the **Galerie Maeght** now occupies a generous 2,400 square yards inside 17th-century walls. The **Galerie Yvon Lambert** in the rue Vieille du Temple (showing top European and American names from Kiefer to Barcelo or Richard Serra) glows in the natural light of a converted workshop while underneath, around, and above it a Greek dealer, Renos Xippas, has designed a labyrinthine gallery space for exhibiting contemporary talents.

The youthful Bastille For unknown talent, the Bastille is perhaps the best bet. Although the area between the rue de Charonne, rue de Lappe, and rue Keller has experienced a gallery invasion lately, quality is not always the common denominator, so don't be fooled. An exception is the impressive **Galerie Durand-Dessert** at 28 rue de Lappe, which occupies four floors of former factory space and exhibits highly regarded international work by the likes of Mario Merz, Kounellis, William Wegman, Barry Flanagan, as well as Gérard Garouste and Bertrand Lavier. However, you're unlikely to find a bargain here.

Juggling hard to become Europe's art capital, Paris thus covers the gamut of periods, prices, and styles with specialized geographical concentrations. And outside the gallery circuit there still exist numerous "salons," a harkback to the 19th-century tradition, although their participants are unlikely to cause ripples, as did their forerunners, the Impressionists. The **Grand Palais** hosts many of these salons, but the art affair of the year is the **FIAC**, a contemporary art fair that attracts galleries and collectors from all over the world every October. Its opening (*vernissage*) is the epitome of the Parisian art world: international, elegant, and pretentious.

►► **Art Moderne de la Ville de Paris, Musée d'**
11 avenue du Président-Wilson, 75016
metro: Iéna

This monumental, colonnaded construction standing high above the Seine was designed by Aubert, Dondel, and Viard for the 1937 International Exhibition. It was intended to celebrate the progress of technology, but labor disputes meant that when the day of its official opening arrived, little was complete and the president was rushed around an unfinished site. However, one brilliant survivor of this harrowed period is Dufy's 197-foot by 33-foot mural dedicated to *La Fée électricité*, colorfully intact and covering the walls of a mezzanine room. Another great mural, Matisse's *La Danse* (1932), together with four major paintings, *Rhythmes* (1938) by Robert Delaunay, dynamize the lofty main hall downstairs.

After years of neglect the museum has now come into its own, guided by a new team of curators. The permanent collection built up over the years from private donations gives the flavor of a museum of 20th-century *Ecole de Paris*, yet a lively contemporary department consistently produces temporary exhibitions of outstanding quality and ambition, which help keep this museum within an international sphere.

The core collection Start your visit downstairs, where the permanent collection kicks off with Utrillo, Rouault, Valadon, Bonnard, and Vuillard. Don't miss the latter's exquisite portraits of his contemporaries, Bonnard,

Modern art is still a going concern: a display at the Musée d'Art Moderne (left) and on the gates of a Paris school (above)

Summer on the terrace
Both the museum bookshop (limited in space but well stocked) and the snack bar on the lower floor are worth investigation. The latter is particularly enticing in the summer months, when tables move outside onto the terrace dotted with Bourdelle's statues overlooking the river—but as always, avoid peak lunch hours when the lines are usually long.

69

Maurice Denis, Roussel, and Maillol. The next step is Fauvism (Matisse, Derain), Cubism (Braque, Picasso) and related contemporaries Metzinger, Lhote, Léger, Gromaire, Robert and Sonia Delaunay. Two works by R. Delaunay in particular are worth stopping at: his *Ville de Paris* (1911) and his *Rugby Players*. This burgeoning pre-war period, when Paris was an international hub, also encompasses Modigliani, Szenes, Foujita, Chagall, Soutine, all immigrant artists who contributed to creating the first *Ecole de Paris*. Less strong on Surrealism, the collection moves into abstraction (Arp, Domela, Magnelli, Fautrier) and *nouveau réalisme*, a 1960s return to figuration and France's version of Pop Art.

Recent renovations to the museum mean that the exceptional collection of art deco furniture has, sadly, vanished from the exhibitions. At the moment there are no plans to show it again. The Musée des Enfants, which was behind the art deco room, has also been lost in the reorganization, but the galleries for temporary exhibtions are now much improved.

The spacious galleries on the street level and first floor are reserved for temporary exhibitions, usually keeping a historical 20th-century figure parallel with avant-garde work by young artists of today.

Open: Tuesday to Friday, 10–5.30, till 7 on weekends.

▶ **Astérix, Parc** see page 27

 Avaux, Hôtel d'
71 rue du Temple, 3e
metro: Arts et Métiers
Built by Le Muet in 1650 for the Comte d'Avaux, this mansion in the heart of the Marias is immediately memorable for its imaginative facade. Pushing open its imposing gate decorated with sculpted heads, you enter a vast, ordered courtyard of massive Corinthian pilasters. The left wing facade is actually a trompe-l'oeil, designed to hide part of Philippe Auguste's peripheral wall. The mansion now belongs to the government and is partly used for storing archives.

▶ **Bac, Rue du**
This mainly 18th-century street winds south from the Pont-Royal and crosses the boulevard St.-Germain before narrowing into a classy shopping street, ending at the almighty department store **Au Bon Marché**—Paris's oldest. The name Bac goes back to the days when the Louvre palace was under construction and a boat (*bac*) ferried stone across the river to the site.

As you wander southward from the bridge, you pass some of Paris's most prestigious antiques shops, as well as the **Galerie Maeght**, which, at No. 42, occupies the former Hôtel de Boulogne, built in 1744 for a gentleman who died nine years later, completely bankrupt from fast living. One of his financial victims was Voltaire. Another literary association with the rue du Bac is the memory of Alexandre Dumas' three celebrated sword-thrusting musketeers, who were based in barracks in this street.

South of St.-Germain, the rue du Bac boasts anything from shoes to fine wines, furniture, or a branch of

Paris's oldest house
The oldest house in Paris is at 51 rue de Montmorency, 3e and was built by Nicolas Flamel in 1407. The house in nearby rue du Volta, reputed to be older, is in fact a 16th-century reconstruction. The smallest house, at 38 rue du Château d'Eau, has a facade measuring 3½ feet wide and is 16 feet high.

American in Paris
American-born James Whistler was just one of many American and English artists who moved to Paris seeking inspiration from the French Impressionists, in particular Claude Monet at his last home in Giverny, a small village on the Seine (see page 200–1). Their works can be seen in Giverny's striking modern gallery, the Musée d'Art Américain.

Hédiard. Its houses once sheltered literary salons and members of the 19th-century intelligentsia such as Chateaubriand (at No. 118–120), who was buried a few doors away from his home at the chapel of the **Missions Etrangères**.

After making a nice little profit selling a painting to the French government in 1893, the American painter James Whistler installed himself at No. 110. Cohorts such as Degas, Toulouse-Lautrec, Manet, and the writers Mallarmé and Henry James dropped by for animated discussions, while his child models scandalized the concierge by frolicking naked in the garden.

At No. 136–140, the **Hôtel de la Vallière** houses the Chapel of the Filles de la Charité where, in 1830, a nun named Catherine Labouré experienced repeated visions of the Virgin Mary. As is the way with such things, a considerable furor was created, but in the end the nun was canonized. Even now, a million or so pilgrims come by every year to see her relics.

The garden of the Maison de Balzac (left), where Honoré de Balzac (below) went into hiding from his debtors

▶ Balzac, Maison de
47 rue Raynouard, 16e
metro: Passy

Pursued by debtors, the writer Honoré de Balzac laid low in this pretty Passy house from 1840 until 1847, using an assumed name but nevertheless managing to pen *La Cousine Bette* and *Le Cousin Pons* in a creative flow that happened from midnight onward. This intimate museum contains portraits and caricatures of the writer and of his favorite mistress, alongside other memorabilia. A library devoted to his works and critical reviews of them completes the Balzacien picture.
Open: Tuesday to Sunday, 10–5:40.

▶▶ Banque de France
rue Croix-des-Petits-Champs, 2e

A Napoleonic initiative, the Bank of France was founded in 1800 and soon moved to its present imposing quarters, conveniently down the road from the Bourse (stock exchange). Although the mansion was built in 1635 by François Mansart, much was rebuilt in the 19th century. It is not open to visits.

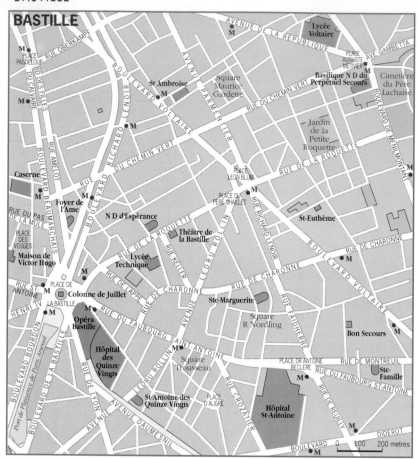

BASTILLE

Place de la Bastille
Nothing remains of the Bastille St.-Antoine except a line of paving stones in the modern square marking the original site of Charles V's 1380s fortress, built to guard the eastern entrance to the city. During the reign of Louis XIII it housed political prisoners, including Voltaire and the Marquis de Sade, precipitating the storming of the Bastille on July 14, 1789—today celebrated as French National Day.

▶▶ **Bastille**
metro: Bastille
Forever linked with the storming of its prison in 1789—the first violent uprising of the French Revolution—today's Bastille area is just as lively, though more dedicated to a hedonistic way of life. Designer bars, nightclubs, white-walled art galleries, a marina, and ethnic restaurants create its 1990s character while its new symbol, the "people's" opera house, towers over the main square.

A new look Only 15 years ago this was still a resolutely working-class district, full of specialized crafts workshops often located in verdant courtyards or hidden passages. Artists were the first to move in, transforming derelict industrial spaces into spacious studios and homes. And where artists go, galleries follow, soon chased by appropriate watering holes. The **marina** terminating the Canal St.-Martin was redeveloped in the early 1980s, and soon after that the **opera house** rose from the ground, vying for attention with the central column, the **Colonne de Juillet**, erected in 1840 to commemorate victims of the 1830 uprising. Beneath the

Looking to the future and commemorating the past: the Opéra de la Bastille (left) and the Colonne de Juillet (below)

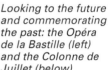

traffic circulating wildly around it are buried hundreds of revolutionary-era citizens.

Unique streets Today's main artery running northeast from the square is the **rue de la Roquette**: here you have your choice of hip bars, trendy clothes shops, and the adventurous **Théâtre de la Bastille**. The perpendicular **rue de Lappe** has maintained a nocturnal reputation since the 1930s when the Balajo dance hall attracted the likes of Mistinguett, Arletty, and Piaf. This street also has traditional connections with the Auvergne: a specialized grocery shop and a restaurant roofed with wooden clogs remain—but who knows for how long?

Other lively streets worth investigating are the **rue Amelot**, **rue de Charonne**, and **rue Keller**, while the **Faubourg St.-Antoine** is traditionally lined with furniture shops, from kitsch to contemporary, part of its long-standing crafts tradition. To alleviate the tedium of this stretch, go into No. 56, the **Cour du Bel Air**, where you will discover a paradisical ivy-clad courtyard with a rare charm and the odd gallery.

Meeting of worlds North of the Faubourg you feel the strangely schizophrenic character of this area, still undergoing transformation. Street water pumps used by African immigrants stand in front of art galleries selling paintings for thousands of francs. Carpenters knock back their breakfast stimulants at a bar next to sleek young advertising executives. Many worlds meet at the Bastille but their universe is still without definition.

■ **The Seine and its banks give as much flavor to the city as any monument. It runs a 482-mile course from Burgundy to the Channel and joins both the Oise and the Marne just outside Paris. Named by Julius Caesar, it was described in 1862 by Verlaine as a "muddy old snake" with its cargoes of "wood, coal, and corpses." Today the river boasts cleaner water (much appreciated by local anglers), new cargoes of sightseers, houseboats, and riverside expressways speeding traffic along this essential artery ...■**

Boating on the Seine

The *bateaux-mouches*, which sail along the Seine night and day, can be boarded at the Pont de l'Alma and during summer run every half hour from 10AM–11PM (tel: 42 25 96 10). At the Pont d'Iéna, you can catch a *bateau parisien* (tel: 44 11 33 44), traveling east to the Ile St.-Louis and west as far as the scaled-down version of the Statue of Liberty. All trips provide a multilingual commentary and last about an hour. For trips on smaller rivercraft, go to the tip of the Ile de la Cité at Pont-Neuf for the Vedettes du Pont-Neuf (tel: 46 33 98 38).

With the city divided between Rive Gauche (Left Bank) and Rive Droite (Right Bank) and monuments lining both banks, the Seine can never be ignored. Sensitive to winter rain, it often reaches menacing levels, leading to the closure of its lower banks (*berges*) and creating ensuing havoc in the Parisian traffic flow. However, the Seine blossoms into its own in the warmer months, sprouting contented anglers, rows of *bouquinistes*, idle students, snoozing tramps, star-struck lovers, and various forms of sun worshipers. When you tire of retracing Parisian history, chasing the latest architectural feats, or fox-trotting through the traffic, this should be your destination.

River history Until the 14th century, the banks of the Seine remained a web of towpaths and specialized ports. The first quai to be structured was the **Quai des Grands-Augustins** in 1313, but it was the Rive Droite that developed fastest under Henri IV, soon becoming a continuous stretch from the **Tuileries** to the **Quai des Célestins**. Louis XVI was the savior of the Rive Gauche and built up the embankment leading from the **Quai St.-Bernard** through **St.-Michel** and the **Quai des Grands-Augustins** as far as the **Invalides**. Following the pattern set by the construction of the **Pont-Neuf** in 1607 (now the oldest bridge in Paris), other bridges were gradually cleared of houses and shops, and under Napoleon the last water mills disappeared, leaving an unimpeded view along the river. Haussmann is once again to be thanked for the trees that line long stretches of the quais and provide essential summer shade.

River road Scandal broke out in the 1960s when part of the precious Rive Droite was developed into an expressway; public outcry was such that the equivalent Rive Gauche project was abandoned. However, one of the great Parisian nocturnal experiences is speeding through the Rive Droite tunnel from Concorde and emerging at river level with a glittering view across to the **Ile de la Cité** and the floodlit turrets of the **Conciergerie**.

River walks For a historic riverside promenade, you could do a lot worse than choose the central Rive Droite stretch, accessible from beside the **Pont des Arts**, which runs as far as the **Pont Alexandre** next to the **Grand Palais**. A leisurely walk here will take you past a string of monuments across the river (**Institut de France, Beaux-Arts, Musée d'Orsay, Assemblée Nationale**), as well as some imaginatively decked out houseboats and, in summer, an inevitable army of bronzing bodies.

For pure romanticism nothing can beat the quais of the **Ile St.-Louis**, while, on the Rive Gauche, you can now walk unimpeded from the **Pont-Royal** (beside the Musée d'Orsay) right through the center as far as the **Pont d'Austerlitz** in the east, emerging at the **Jardin des Plantes**. At **St.-Michel** there is a section frequented by down-and-outs.

Down by the river again, in front of **Notre-Dame**, the route moves into a more upscale stretch with houseboats and a contemporary sculpture garden. This part is also characterized by joggers and amateur painters having a shot at the backview of Notre-Dame: it provides a superb view of the elegant mansions lining the **Ile St.-Louis** opposite.

Riverside reading If you want to dig out obscure magazines, secondhand and antiquarian books, prints, or postcards, don't forget to investigate the *bouquinistes*. Most are concentrated on the Rive Gauche between the **Quai de la Tournelle** and the **Quai Malaquais** (opposite the islands); their wooden stalls are an inimitable fixture of the riverside landscape.

Two ways to see the river: by bateau-mouche *or just by sitting on the banks*

■ **Thirty-five bridges span the Seine along its 8-mile flow through Paris; the oldest, dating back to 1607, is the Pont-Neuf. Tramps sleep below them, lovers are entwined atop them, suicides throw themselves off them, and poetry is written about them. From the two-tiered Pont du Bir-Hakeim, with its art-nouveau pillars and metros rattling across the top, to the idyllic planked footbridge, the Pont des Arts, idolized in the songs of Georges Brassens, the bridges of Paris are all part of the city's cultural and physical landscape ...■**

76

For centuries the city had only two bridges: the **Grand Pont** and the **Petit Pont**, which linked the Ile de la Cité with both banks. It was only in the late Middle Ages that three more wooden bridges appeared, the **Pont Notre-Dame**, the **Pont au Change**, and the **Pont St.-Michel**, none of which were solid constructions, and so frequently bowed to high waters, ice, fires, or collisions by rivercraft. However, their commercial viability was underlined in 1414 by a letter from Charles VI that authorized the building of houses on the Pont Notre-Dame "for the good, the decoration, and the increased revenue of the town." **The Pont au Change** (opposite Châtelet) was so named for its continuous rows of money changers' shops, and when

the **Pont Marie** was built in 1635, it still carried an overload of real estate.

Bridges boom Things changed with the farsighted minister Colbert who, in 1716, created an official institution, the **Ponts et Chaussées**, which led to the feverish construction of 21 new bridges. Existing bridges were being cleared of their cumbersome houses, and by the time Napoleon came along, new materials such as cast iron created the uncluttered spans that we see today. Building has started on Paris's 36th bridge, the **Pont Charles-de-Gaulle**, which will grow into place by 1997 to link the fast-developing 12th and 13th arrondissements in eastern Paris.

Pont-Neuf Paris's oldest bridge, the Pont-Neuf, is also its most famous. Built to facilitate the king's journey between the Louvre Palace and the abbey of St.-Germain-des-Prés, its innovative, houseless design was controversial. Flamboyant as ever, Henri IV inaugurated it in 1607 by galloping across on his charger; and today his equestrian statue still dominates the stretch (an 1818 replacement of an earlier statue, melted down during the Revolution). For years this was the site of a permanent funfair, attracting jugglers, acrobats, and street sellers; painted by Turner, the Pont-Neuf was also ceremoniously wrapped up by the artist Christo in 1985.

Pont-Neuf, the city's oldest bridge

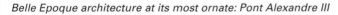

Belle Epoque architecture at its most ornate: Pont Alexandre III

Pont Marie The 1635 Pont Marie joins the Ile St.-Louis with the Right Bank. Named after the property developer of the Ile St.-Louis, a certain Mr. Marie, this bridge nearly had a very short 20-year life. It was top-heavy with four-story houses (all the more *écus* to the developer), until the spring thaw of 1658 caused a powerful flood, and half of these homes, shops, and their occupants toppled into the Seine.

Pont-Royal Slightly more youthful, the Pont-Royal, which joins the Tuileries to the rue du Bac, was entirely financed by Louis XIV and built in 1689 by Gabriel after Mansart's design. This time the object was to make life easier for

nobles visiting the palace from the exclusive Faubourg St.-Germain. The pure classical style of its graceful stone arches has never been modified, and on each end pillar there is a hydrographic scale showing historic high-water levels.

Pont Alexandre III In complete contrast, the wildly ornate Pont Alexandre III flashes its gilt and bronzed cupids in the setting sun. Symbolic of the optimism of the Belle Epoque, it was built for the 1900 Exposition Universelle and dedicated to a new alliance between Russia and France. The first stone was laid by the tsar in 1896, and the facades bear coats of arms of the two countries. Over 15 artists worked on this wedding-cake bridge to create winged horses, gilded cupids, garlands, and various other Greco-Roman artifices on every available ramp, balustrade, or corner.

Pont de l'Alma Commemorating a victory over the Russians by the Franco-British alliance in the Crimean War, the Pont de l'Alma was originally built in 1856 and replaced in 1974. Of the four symbolic statues of the participating armies only the Zouave soldier remains, acting as an official high-water marker.

> ❏ A bridge you may not discover easily is the romantically curved footbridge from which Arletty murmured *"Atmosphères, atmosphères"* in Marcel Carné's classic film, *Hôtel du Nord*. This is no figment of cinematographic imagination but actually spans the Canal St.-Martin, a 2.8-mile canal running from the Bastille to the Canal de l'Ourcq. ❏

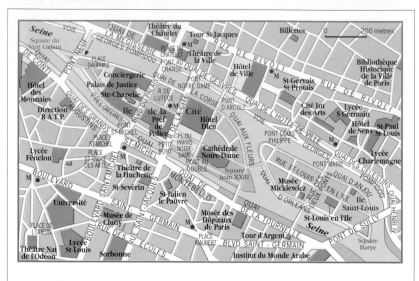

Walk Exploring the city's islands

Start at Pont-Neuf. Cross to the statue of Henri IV, where steps lead down to the island tip.
Here you can circle around the island tip, or take a boat trip.

Back up on the bridge, cross to enter the place Dauphine.
The **place Dauphine** is where Yves Montand and Simone Signoret both used to live.

In front of the Palais de Justice, turn right, then left along the Quai des Orfèvres to the Pont St.-Michel. Turn left here.
The route now takes you past the courtyard of the **Palais de Justice**.

Immediately after the Préfecture, turn right onto the rue de Lutèce.
The **rue de Lutèce** leads through the flower market to the **rue de la Cité**.

Go left at the rue de la Cité and turn right along the Quai de la Corse.
The **Quai de la Corse** continues into the **Quai aux Fleurs** and has a view north of the **Hôtel de Ville** and east toward the **Ile St.-Louis**.

Circle around back to Notre-Dame.
At this point you are walking among Paris's oldest medieval streets.

Walk around Notre-Dame and through the gardens on the south side; cross the little bridge onto the Ile St.-Louis.
Once the home of wealthy financiers and magistrates, the island remains remarkably conserved; keep an eye open for superb courtyards, wrought-iron details, and sculpted heads.

Follow the Quai d'Orléans past some magnificent 17th-century town-houses to the rue des Deux Ponts. Turn left here, then right into the rue St.-Louis-en-l'Ile.
Pass Paris's best ice-cream maker, **Berthillon**, and the island's richly decorated church. The corner **Hôtel Lambert**, at No. 2, is reputed to be the finest mansion of this period in Paris, designed by Le Vau in 1640.

Turn left along the Quai d'Anjou.
At **17 Quai d'Anjou** is a house with a fine balcony, where both Baudelaire and Théophile Gauthier once lived. At **No.19** is the mansion where Camille Claudel lived and worked.

Cross the Pont Louis-Philippe, with its stunning view along the Seine.

► Baccarat, Musée

30 bis rue de Paradis, 10e
metro: Château d'Eaux
A visit to this glass museum and showroom will take you into a street packed with porcelain and crystal outlets. The best example has got to be the wonderful 1900s ceramic facade of No. 18. Baccarat, however, has remained the king here ever since 1828, when he became supplier to royalty and heads of state and subsequently moved his company to the present site. The museum exhibits anything from chandeliers to perfume bottles.
Open: Monday to Saturday, 10–6.

Beaubourg see pages 80–1.

► Beaux-Arts, Ecole Nationale Supérieure

14 rue Bonaparte
metro: St.-Germain
Once a convent, now Paris's art school, built between 1820 and 1862, this imposing facade glowering across the river at the Louvre is the hub for Parisian art students. Its entrance at 14 rue Bonaparte leads into the main courtyard, which still contains a selection of architectural features salvaged by the archeologist Lenoir from destructive revolutionary fervor. Look inside at the rather dilapidated central hall and galleries, feel the dust, then compare the recently restored Chapelle des Petits-Augustins (1608), in which plaster casts, Renaissance reproductions, and the real thing nonchalantly rub shoulders. The exhibition halls opening onto the quai sometimes hold interesting shows and may be worth a look.
Open: Monday to Friday, 8–8; library, 1–6.

►► Belleville

metro: Belleville, Ménilmontant
Rising almost as high above central Paris as Montmartre, and with corresponding panoramic views, the northeastern quarter of Belleville is a colorful, eclectic mixture. Its traditional working-class character combines with an immigrant population and errant artists to animate its streets, bars, and restaurants, though real estate promoters have already wrought patchy havoc.

Throwing the light on glassware: the Musée Baccarat boasts over 1,200 masterpieces, including entire services designed for royal courts of Europe

Backstreets of Belleville
If you explore the side-streets leading off the rue de Belleville, rue de Ménilmontant, and the rue des Pyrénées, you'll come across some surprises: look for the Passage de la Duée (3-foot wide) or the atmospheric Passage des Soupirs. And if you yearn for a vast choice of Asiatic or North African cuisine, this is where to head.

MUSEE NATIONAL D'ART MODERNE

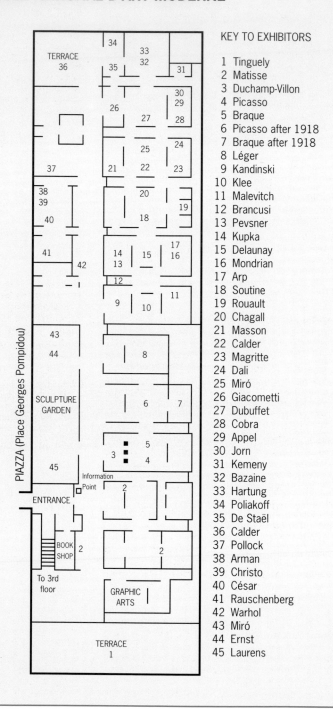

TERRACE 36

34

33
32

35

31

26

30
29

27

28

25

24

37

21

22

23

38
39

20

40

18

19

41

14
13

15

17
16

42

12

9

10

11

43

44

8

SCULPTURE
GARDEN

6

7

45

5

3

4

Information
Point

2

ENTRANCE

BOOK
SHOP

2

2

To 3rd
floor

GRAPHIC
ARTS

TERRACE
1

PIAZZA (Place Georges Pompidou)

KEY TO EXHIBITORS

1 Tinguely
2 Matisse
3 Duchamp-Villon
4 Picasso
5 Braque
6 Picasso after 1918
7 Braque after 1918
8 Léger
9 Kandinski
10 Klee
11 Malevitch
12 Brancusi
13 Pevsner
14 Kupka
15 Delaunay
16 Mondrian
17 Arp
18 Soutine
19 Rouault
20 Chagall
21 Masson
22 Calder
23 Magritte
24 Dali
25 Miró
26 Giacometti
27 Dubuffet
28 Cobra
29 Appel
30 Jorn
31 Kemeny
32 Bazaine
33 Hartung
34 Poliakoff
35 De Staël
36 Calder
37 Pollock
38 Arman
39 Christo
40 César
41 Rauschenberg
42 Warhol
43 Miró
44 Ernst
45 Laurens

▶▶▶ Beaubourg

Centre Georges Pompidou place, Beaubourg 75004
metro: Rambuteau, Hôtel de Ville, Châtelet
This factory-like museum and freewheeling cultural center stands out as a landmark of high-tech style in the middle of historic Paris, as well as being a symbol of democratized culture.

MNAM▶▶▶ For many visitors, the priority is the national collection of modern art (MNAM) on the fourth floor. Inside the glass walls, major movements and/or artists are displayed chronologically in partitioned spaces. The collection continues on the third floor, where works covering the last 25 years are exhibited. Starting with the **Fauves** (1905), a remarkable itinerary leads you through **Cubism, Dada, Surrealism, abstraction, pop art, minimalism,** and today's **conceptualism.** Matisse is extremely well represented; Cubist works by **Picasso, Braque,** and **Juan Gris** are shown with **Picabia,** followed by **Léger's** visions of the mechanized world. One of the most successful rooms combines **Calder's** ethereal mobiles with paintings by **Miró,** including the vast, luminous *Bleu II.* The most striking piece as you leave this floor is an early example of conceptual art, **Beuys'** *Infiltration homogène* (1966), a grand piano neatly encased in felt with its empty double (*La Peau*) hanging on a wall nearby.

Grandes Galeries Above the museum, on the fifth floor, are the Grandes Galeries, where major temporary exhibitions of 20th-century art are held. Next door is a cinema showing films relevant to these blockbuster exhibitions and a large, but somewhat uninspiring cafeteria that has seen better days, as has its notion of cuisine. The panoramic view from the terrace is nevertheless the destination for a daily average of 25,000 visitors.

Other attractions Part of the second floor is occupied by an enormous, well-equipped, and very popular **reference library.** Back on the ground floor, activities start buzzing again around the **Forum,** a central hole used for unusually scaled exhibitions. The spaces tucked below the surrounding mezzanine structures include a cinema, the **Salle Garance,** which has daily programs of rarely shown films in thematic festivals, and a packed **bookshop.** Another active department is the **CCI** (industrial design), with a documentation center and two galleries used for temporary exhibitions ranging from architecture to furniture design. The mezzanine **Galeries contemporaines** are used for works by contemporary artists.

Children's choice If you have children in tow, you could drop them off at the **Atelier des Enfants** while you check the program of concerts and/or dance, held in the basement halls, which concentrate on international avant-garde performers. Related debates and lectures are often worth following here.
Open: Wednesday to Monday, noon–10; weekends, 10–10.

A popular venue
Decried by many, Beaubourg's worst failing is in fact its great popularity, unimagined by architects Piano and Rogers when it opened in 1977. In its first 14 years of existence, over 90 million visitors crossed the threshold—so expect long lines in the summer.

The show goes on, inside and outside the Beaubourg, ranging from street theater to Surrealism and caricature artists to Cubism

The Seasons

■ **As the city's face changes with the transience of the seasons, so does its fun. Numerous events are held year in, year out at the same date, the most famous being Bastille Day on July 14, a great opportunity to witness boisterous street partying. The Office de Tourisme (127 Champs-Elysées, 8e; tel: 49 52 53 54) publishes an annual guide every October; below are some of the regular highlights ...■**

Paris in the springtime
Paris has always had strong associations with spring. A surprisingly large percentage of Paris's annual 20 million visitors come during springtime when blossoms flourish and the streetside cafés come alive after the long winter. Spring is the season of fairs, concerts, and flower shows, particularly spectacular at the Bagatelle Gardens and the Parc Floral. As an added incentive, many hotels offer special spring weekend packages.

Celebrations for Bastille Day, July 14, a national holiday throughout France

Winter
Epiphany: the Russian Orthodox version of Christmas on January 6 and 7 is celebrated at the **Saint Alexandre Nievsky Cathedral** (12 rue Daru, 8e). For the French, January 6 becomes the **Fête des Rois**, memorable for its pâtisserie *galette du Roi*, an almond cake ring containing a hidden bean. The cruncher of the bean dons a gold foil crown and chooses his consort.

Chinese New Year: between late January and early February, Chinatown comes into its own. Make sure you are in the 13th arrondissement between the avenue d'Ivry and the avenue de Choisy for this colorful event (for information, tel: 45 20 74 09).

Spring
Foire du Trône: France's largest funfair sets up from March to May at the **Porte Dorée**, next to the Bois de Vincennes. Cotton candy and bumper cars replace what was originally a medieval fair during Holy Week.

May Day: May 1 is Labor Day, still taken very seriously, with marches organized by most trade unions, shops and museums closed, and no newspapers. Buy a bouquet of symbolic lily of the valley from a street seller and join the crowds.

The month of May includes **Ascension** and **Whitsun**, which add two further opportunities to join a midweek holiday to a weekend for four or five days' break.

Roland-Garros: the French Tennis Open is held from late May to early June and is now a fashionable place to be seen.

Theoretically, tickets for outside courts can be bought on the day, but black marketeers have wrapped up this trade. Otherwise, apply in writing to Stade Roland-Garros, 2 avenue Gordon Bennett, 75016 Paris (tel: 47 43 48 00).

Summer

Exposition de roses: against the bucolic background of the **Jardin de Bagatelle** in the Bois de Boulogne, an international rose competition is held on June 21 and the rose garden remains open till October. The Trianon also hosts the **Chopin Festival**, which is held from late June to July (tel: FNAC 40 41 40 00).

Fête de la Musique: midsummer night is now loudly celebrated all over Paris with free concerts. Key sites (including the **Palais-Royal**, the **Bastille**, **place de la République**) resound to amplified rock or world music into the small hours.

Course des Garçons de Café: over 500 professional waiters and waitresses career around the streets of Paris, each bearing aloft a tray laden with bottle and glasses. The fastest nonspilling participant wins. Starting and finishing at the **Hôtel de Ville**, this unusual race takes place in late June.

Bastille Day: the action really takes place on the evening of July 13 with *bals populaires* pulling in pulsating crowds to every square or fire station. Beware of firecrackers, which are freely tossed around. Fireworks and the ubiquitous *merguez* (barbecued spicy sausages) complete the ambience. On July 14, a surprisingly pompous military parade passes down the **Champs-Elysées**, accompanied by an impressive fighter-jet flyby.

Tour de France: the grand finale of this wildly popular bike race pedals manically along the quais of the Rive Droite before crossing the finishing line in the **Champs-Elysées** during the third week in July.

Autumn

Festival d'Automne: the city's most avant-garde cultural festival sets the ball rolling after the long summer break. Held in various venues over Paris, its dance, theater, and music events are always worth investigating (tel: 42 96 96 94).

Fête des Vendanges à Montmartre: Montmartre's biggest yearly splash takes place for the harvesting of its tiny vineyard on the first Saturday in October.

Prix de l'Arc de Triomphe: This is *the* equestrian event of the year, opening the racing season in early October at the **Hippodrome de Longchamp**.

FIAC: a social event thinly disguised as an international art festival, the FIAC (Faire International d'Art Contemporain) opens the art season in late October under the spectacular webbed iron domes of the **Grand Palais**.

A new wine

On the third Thursday in November, the race is on to get the first bottles of the year's Beaujolais Nouveau to Paris. Never regarded as a serious wine, it can be over-acid or fruity, but the tradition of who gets there first has spread all over the world. On that revered Thursday afternoon, Paris stops work, bars spill out into the street, and endless vociferous opinions on this year's vintage float away into the night air.

BERCY

The National Library
The Bibliothèque Nationale contains 11 million printed books, 15 million prints and photos, 1 million records, 600,000 maps, 800,000 coins and medals, and 350,000 periodicals. Every year a further 80,000 books are added to the collection.

► **Bercy**
metro: Bercy
Once nostalgically known for its wine warehouses, which formed a self-sufficient village of their own in eastern Paris, Bercy is now an area undergoing intensive development. Already the site for the **Palais Omnisports** (which plays a double act of accommodating sports activities and rock concerts) and the mammoth **Ministry of Finance**, Bercy spreads east from the **Gare de Lyon** through a maze of new office and apartment buildings. Another new arrival, the **American Center**, daringly designed by Frank Gehry, opened in 1994 as a lively pole for American culture, counterbalancing the Mickey Mouses of Euro Disney outside Paris. However, not all is concrete in Bercy. At the heart of these sites lies a freshly landscaped park, the **Parc de Bercy**, which has preserved some of the old wine warehouses from the bulldozers, allowing some remnants of its past to linger on.

► **Berryer, Cité**
25 rue Royale, 75008
metro: Madeleine
Once an open-air market, this alleyway leading off the rue Royale recently attained the distinction of historical monument. In fact, it's more of a lunchtime haunt for local businessmen, and it is at its best in the summer months, when the restaurants and wine bars invade the pavement.

► **Bibliothèque Nationale**
58 rue de Richelieu, 75002
metro: Bourse, Palais-Royal
Nearly 12 million books are stored in this sprawling symbol of French literacy, which has evolved since the 17th century as a combination of the royal library with that of Cardinal Mazarin. A copy of every publication made in France has to be deposited here. The original Hôtel Tubeuf gradually accumulated adjacent annexes, culminating in the Galerie Colbert, which exhibits prints and photographs. All this will be moved in 1997, but for now take a look at the soaring glass-domed reading room in the main building, designed by Labrouste (1873), or the sumptuous Galerie Mazarine, designed by François Mansart: here Romanelli's mythological ceiling paintings vie with Grimaldi's landscapes for splendor.
   The **Cabinet des Médailles et Antiques►** (*open:* Monday to Saturday, 9–5) has a remarkable display built up from royal collections and confiscations made during the Revolution. From Greek and Roman antiques to thousands of medals and coins or Dagobert's throne, it makes a curious mixture.

►► **Bois de Boulogne**
metro: Pointe Dauphine, Maillot, d'Auteuil
Nearly 2,000 acres of park and playground make up western Paris's lungs, well frequented on weekends by the better-heeled inhabitants from nearby Neuilly and the 16th arrondissement. A favorite medieval hunting ground, in the 18th century it became an aristocratic leisure ground. Finally, Napoleon III and Baron

The Bibliothèque Nationale contains records of all French publications in a magnificent setting

Landscaped romance from the 18th century: the Jardin de Bagatelle in the Bois de Boulogne

Haussmann gave the park the form it has today and made it public. It is awash with lakes, waterfalls, follies, winding paths, and open spaces, with two racetracks: Auteuil and Longchamp. Its nocturnal users (transvestites, prostitutes) are a very different race from the jogging businessmen of the morning hours.

Make for one of the high spots, the **Jardin de Bagatelle**►, where a small château (built in 1775) overlooks a romantic park originally laid out by the landscape gardener Thomas Blaikie. Rose bushes abound (over 700 varieties) and a restaurant with open terrace overflows on summer nights. Further south, the **Pré Catalan** is another well laid out garden, with a gigantic copper beech as its main feature. Here there is another upscale gastronomic halt overlooking a small lake. The **Jardin Shakespeare** adjoins it, so-called because of its open-air theater and vegetation inspired by the bard's botanical references.

Children's pursuits If your children-in-tow are tiring, head for the **Jardin d'Acclimatation**► on the far north edge (metro: Les Sablons) where amusements await them—from toy trains to puppet shows, an "enchanted river," and a small zoo. This section of the park is open daily, 10–6, with special events on Wednesdays and on the weekends.

● **Stroll** *For a dream and a stroll, go to the* **Serres d'Auteuil** *at the southern point of the Bois (metro: Porte d'Auteuil). Here the tropics await you in some superb 19th-century greenhouses. If you are here in late May, walk a little farther and you'll come to* **Roland-Garros**, *where the famous French Tennis Open takes place.*

Jogging in the park
The best jogging track in the Bois de Boulogne surrounds the Lac Inférieur, an idyllic expanse of water punctuated by two islands, where you can rent rowboats or bicycles.

BOULEVARD SAINT-MICHEL

Shakespeare & Co.
At 93 place Edmond-Rostand, next to the Luxembourg metro station, is the house that sheltered the American bookshop owner, Sylvia Beach (founder of Shakespeare & Co., an American literary landmark in prewar Paris) from the Nazis for two years.

▶ **Boulevard Saint-Michel**

Traditionally thick with students and tourists, the boulevard Saint-Michel had its heyday during the 1968 student riots, when barricades outnumbered cafés and confrontations with the forces of order carried on deep into the night. In Roman times, it was one of the two roads leading south from the Ile de la Cité, lined with baths, a theater, and the forum.

Today its bookshops and cinemas are interjected with an increasing number of cheap clothes stores and fast-food joints. Although it is the symbolic heart of the Latin Quarter, the boulevard is really only of passing interest, as the architectural and historical high points lie in its side streets.

Nightlife At its northern starting point by the Seine, the Fontaine St.-Michel, designed by Davioud in 1860, is a favorite nocturnal gathering point for street artists, entertainers, and other hangers-out. The nearby metro entrance is one of the few remaining Hector Guimard art nouveau originals. Cafés and cinemas are buzzing into the early hours, and if you're short of reading matter or cigarettes at this time, here is where to go. In the daytime you are more likely to see students escaping to the cafés from long lectures at the Sorbonne or the Ecole de Médecine.

● **Stroll** *If you take a stroll starting on the corner of the boulevard St.-Germain, you cannot miss the superb* Musée de Cluny▶▶▶, *floodlit at night, a forceful presence by day. As you head uphill you pass the* **place de la Sorbonne,** *a small square lined with trees and café-terrasses, even at chillier times of the year. The* **place Edmond-Rostand,** *crowned by an inevitable fountain, ends the slope and the animated section of the boulevard, opening out onto the* **Jardin du Luxembourg** *to the west and with an impressive vista of the* **Panthéon** *to the east.*

▶ **Bourbon, Palais**
33 Quai d'Orsay, 75007
metro: Assemblée Nationale
Hiding behind the imposing facade of this 18th-century mansion are the halls of French power: its central parliament, the Assemblée Nationale. Elected every four years, its 577 deputies come and go, and are usually more absent than politically present, a habit that has led to some scolding in recent times from the powers above.

Delacroix's masterpiece
A tour of the Palais Bourbon includes the sumptuous library ceiling painted by Delacroix in 1838–47 with his version of the history of civilization. Tours take place every Saturday at 10, 2, and 3 unless the National Assembly is sitting. The first 10 visitors to arrive each day are allowed in to watch the debates.

The mansion's history Originally constructed for the Duchess of Bourbon in 1722, the building passed through the hands of the Condé family and Louis XV before revolutionary confiscation. In 1807 Napoleon, with an astute eye for aesthetics, insisted on a new neo-classical facade (by Poyet) to mirror that of the Madeleine, directly opposite across the Seine and the place de la Concorde.

Today visitors (in limited numbers) can observe heated debates from the gallery overlooking the vast crimson and gold embellished chamber.

Bourse du Commerce

Palais de la Bourse, rue Vivienne, 75002
metro: Bourse
Every major city has its money-spinning hub and in Paris
it all happens at the Bourse, another neoclassical
Napoleonic invention. Once the Corn Exchange, the
circular building is the only relic still left from Les Halles.
It was built on the site of a convent in 1826 and was
then remodeled in 1888. It is now the marketplace for
commodity traders, setting the tone for the surrounding
streets, which are full of money changers and
restaurants called *L'Ecu* or the *Stock Exchange
Luncheon Bar* (1878).

Inside the Bourse, you can watch brokers haggle and
bonds change hands at a frenetic pace from the visitors'
gallery overlooking the den.

The fluted column adjoining the building was once part
of Catherine de Médicis' Hôtel de la Reine, built in 1572,
and apparently the home of her personal astrologer,
Ruggieri.

Open: Monday to Friday, tours at 1:30; 2; 2:30, and 3.
Reservations in advance (tel: 42 33 99 83).

Bricard de la Serrure, Musée

1 rue de la Perle, 75003
metro: Saint-Paul
An eccentric collection of door decorations—locks, keys,
knockers, handles, and plaques—dating back to Roman
time is housed in a magnificent 1685 mansion, built by
the architect of the Hôtel des Invalides, Libéral Bruant,
for his own personal use.

Eugène Bricard was the 19th-century man hellbent on
gathering these unusual objects from all periods and
countries, displayed in six lofty rooms. Bricard still exists
as a lock manufacturer.

Open: Monday to Friday, 10–noon and 2–5.

*Money and security:
the Bourse du
Commerce (above)
and the Musée
Bricard de la Serrure
(below)*

■ **Paris has for a century rested on the green laurels of Haussmann's two woods (Vincennes and Boulogne), three parks (Montsouris, Monceau, and Buttes Chaumont) and two gardens. There are few other real breathing spaces ...■**

The Jardin du Luxembourg, at the heart of the Rive Gauche, is the most popular park in Paris

Birth of the Forum des Halles
Developers were presented with a gaping hole when the 19th-century Baltard pavilions, site of the central fruit and vegetable market, were demolished. The hole remained for years, until one bright spark thought of filling it with a shopping center. Thus the Forum des Halles was born and an adjacent garden laid out. Today, locals cower under a sparse sprinkling of trees, trip over concrete steps, or squeeze onto one of the few triangles of grass to fight with litter or tramps.

The architectural renaissance of the 1980s has, however, woken up to arboreal needs and seen a renewal of the garden tradition, previously buried under a will to kill anything green in the urban mosaic. The **Parc de la Villette**, on the northeastern perimeter, whatever its overall design shortcomings, provides canals and vast lawns—good for local Frisbee experts— as well as "conceptual" gardens.

But gone are the 19th-century days of romantic artificial lakes and hills, exemplified by the Buttes Chaumont, a fantastic project that transformed a city rubbish dump into a hillocked miniparadise complete with grotto, waterfall, and colonnaded temple. Today, architects and landscape gardeners have to impose their abstract concepts on available structures, missing out completely on escapist naturalism.

Of the new park projects, the **Parc Citroën** is perhaps the most ambitious. On the site of the old Citroën factories in southwestern Paris, nearly 35 acres of land have been landscaped to lead directly down to the river, burying embankment traffic in their wake. Two gigantic high-tech greenhouses reign over a garden with more geometric precision than a Swiss watch. If this Cartesian approach touches your soul, don't miss the still emerging **Parc de Bercy** (see page 84), which follows a more classical pattern to match the layout of its former village of warehouses. A lucky bonus here is the existence of centennial trees—otherwise, parks take decades to assume any form.

Parks of the past Step back a century or so and you can rest in relative bucolic peace in any one of Paris's classic parks. The **Jardin du Luxembourg**, saved from Haussmann's ambitions by a petition of 12,000 signatures, remains a symbolic expanse. Creating a natural northern limit to the Latin Quarter and its itinerant students, it is also a favorite haunt for chic Montparnasse residents and their offspring. Its fountains, statues, kiosks, tennis courts, chess or card-players, and book-reading habitués give it an unchanging atmosphere, strengthened by endless literary and celluloid links. Remember the struggling Hemingway, who at low points would drop by the park to pick up a pigeon for dinner, or numerous *Nouvelle Vague* scenes with existentially oriented actors staring morosely into the pond.

Arty park Further to the south, the **Parc Montsouris** belies its granite quarry past and instead lives up to its 1920–30s arty character, the days when the nearby artists' studios were actually inhabited by brush or pen-

wielding luminaries (Braque, Derain, Salvador Dalí, and Henry Miller were all neighbors). Today swans, joggers, and child-minders are by and large the chief users of the park, joined by a brass band during the summer months (see page 151). Back on the Right Bank, the revamped **Tuileries,** conveniently laid out between the Seine and the rue de Rivoli, remain a centuries-old favorite. Otherwise, a great park classic is the **Parc Monceau,** originally planted in English style by Thomas Blaikie in 1783. Picturesque ruins of columns, a pyramid, tombs, Ledoux's rotunda, and statues complete a peaceful setting perfect for local nannies and their wards.

Over in Boulogne (metro: Porte de St.-Cloud), a curious and little-known garden gives an overview of different botanical styles, from a Japanese garden to a Vosges-type forest. The **Jardins Albert-Kahn** were laid out at the beginning of the century by a horticulturally obsessed philanthropist, who also founded a rare documentation center about nature all over the planet. Ultimately, though, you cannot beat the **Bois de Boulogne** (see pages 84–5) or the **Bois de Vincennes** (see pages 184–5) for bucolic escapism.

Relaxation among the flowers in the Parc Monceau— small, peaceful, and elegant

José-Maria Sert's 1925 ballroom in the Musée Carnavalet—a magnificent room in this, the first privately owned Renaissance mansion in Paris

The Marquise de Sévigné
The famous writer Marie de Rabutin, Marquise de Sévigné, leased the Hôtel Carnavalet from 1677 until her death in 1696. Here she wrote a collection of 1,500 letters to her daughter, today considered one of the great chronicles of 17th-century high society Paris.

▶▶▶ **Carnavalet, Musée**
23 rue de Sévigné, 75003
metro: St.-Paul

Two adjoining mansions in the Marais house the museum of the history of Paris from prehistory through to the 20th century. Exemplary in its presentation, it juxtaposes visions of Paris through the eyes of painters, documents, the decorative arts, and period rooms. Descriptive panels are in French only.

Entrance is through a beautifully sculpted courtyard of the 16th-century Hôtel Carnavalet, much transformed in 1660 by François Mansart before the arrival of its most celebrated resident, the writer Madame de Sévigné. The collections exhibited here take you from the origins of Paris through to the Middle Ages. The splendors of the Renaissance are evoked in four vast ground-floor rooms, while Madame de Sévigné's possessions and furnishings on the first floor give a rounded view of Louis XIV's era. Sizzling heights of decoration from under Louis XV's and XVI's reigns are displayed in paneled interiors, while the richly painted and gilded woodwork (1656) from the Hôtel Colbert de Villacerf is a superb example of Louis XIV ornateness.

Next door, the collections installed in the sleekly renovated Hôtel Le Peletier de Saint-Fargeau (1690) take you on through the Revolution to the 19th century and finish in the early 20th century. Look for the keys of the Bastille prison, Hubert Robert's paintings, made in and out of prison in the 1790s, and Le Sueur's unusual comic-strip account of this period. Anything and everything was decorated with revolutionary slogans—fans, plates, clocks, furniture. Napoleon's favorite campaign picnic case (110 pieces) introduces you to the Empire and the elaborate cradle of the imperial prince (1856) to the Second Empire. Reconstructed interiors include Proust's corklined bedroom and brass bed, Henri Sauvage's Café de Paris, and the ballroom from the Hôtel de Wendel, painted by José-Maria Sert in 1925.
Open: Tuesday to Sunday, 10–5:40.

► Cartier, Fondation
261 boulevard Raspail, 75014
(see page 122)

► Catacombes
1 place Denfert-Rochereau, 75014
metro: Denfert-Rochereau
Over 6 million slumbering skeletons hide out in the world's largest deposit of human bones. During World War II, this underground network of 102 miles of tunnels was used as a secret meeting place for Resistance fighters; today urban potholers regularly slip into them for chilly and chilling explorations. Visitors tour in groups to view the macabre remains. Bring a flashlight and sweater and be prepared to climb hundreds of steps.
Open: Tuesday to Friday, 2–4; Saturday and Sunday, 9–11 and 2–4.

►►► Chaillot, Palais de
place du Trocadéro, 75016
metro: Trocadéro
No fewer than four museums, a theater, and a cinema are housed in this colonnaded mammoth, which commands a stunning perspective of the Eiffel Tower and the Champ de Mars, directly across the Seine. Built for the Exposition Universelle in 1937, its curved wings are dotted with glittering bronze statues and the wide terraces overlook a fountain-ridden garden.

In the basement is the Théâtre National de Chaillot, whose postwar director, Jean Vilar, democratized theater and later founded the Festival D'Avignon. On the same level, but with access from behind in the avenue Albert de Mun, is the **Cinémathèque Française►**, founded in 1936 by Henri Langlois, a former hotbed of postwar New Wave film directors. Today it shows a fantastic schedule of film classics, changing daily—a cinephile's paradise.

Continued on page 94

The Catacombes
The Catacombes were originally channeled out in Roman times to provide stone and plaster; it was only after a campaign orchestrated by Voltaire in 1785 that the occupants of the pestilential cemeteries above ground were moved to these chambers below.

The impressive colonnaded wings of the 1937 Palais de Chaillot, a vast cultural center, frame the Eiffel Tower perfectly

■ Mountains of fruit and vegetables, hundreds of varieties of cheese, strings of saucisson, perfumed herbs: food markets are part and parcel of Paris life. Then there are books, stamps, flowers, birds; and antiques and bric-à-brac change hands as if industrialization had never existed ...■

Flea markets
The Paris flea market was first set up in a no-man's land in northeastern Paris around 1880. In 1920 Romain Vernaison, a property owner, installed stalls and let them to antiques dealers (Marché Vernaison), and the Marché Biron soon followed suit, in 1925. Today, the famous flea market at the Porte de Clignancourt covers 74 acres and has over 1,500 shops and 1,400 licensed stalls.

92

A stroll around a French food market is a gastronomical education in itself. When you see a stall holder squeezing camemberts, pressing avocados, or pinching melons you'll be witnessing a precise and incontestable philosophy in action. Parisians shop daily, as produce is fresh and the timing of its consumption must be perfect. Keep that camembert too long and it will walk off the table; eat it too soon and you miss its essence.

Apart from the circulating markets, which set up on sites and days all over the city, there are permanent daily street markets such as the **Marché d'Aligre**, the **rue Poncelet, rue Montorgueil, rue Mouffetard**, or the **rue de Buci**. These unveil their wares around nine in the morning and pack up toward seven, not forgetting a very provincial lunch break between one and four. Sunday afternoons and Mondays finally give market workers time to recuperate from the weekend onslaught, when even the most ardent restaurant-goers indulge in a serious return to their culinary sources.

Of over 80 permanent markets in Paris, the daily market at rue Mouffetard is one of the oldest and most popular

The art of shopping Every market has its historic boulangerie or cheese shop—often with fantastically ornate interiors worthy of a château—that proves the level of attention and pride bestowed on mere foodstuff. Amid the sea of outdoor stalls, these five-star landmarks can usually be spotted by their lengthy lines—Parisians are tremendously faithful, gastronomically at least. Cafés

are, of course, another integral part of market shopping. The market operation being a lengthy and concentrated business (each purchase requires at least five minutes, depending on the stall's popularity or the holder's garrulousness), it merits a drink and quick exchange of wit at halftime.

One of the most picturesque street markets, the **rue Mouffetard**, has also, unfortunately, become one of the most well known to tourists. It still has its charm, however, as does the **rue de Buci** in St.-Germain-des-Prés, expensive but another crowd-puller, due to its convenient central location.

But make sure you go to a typical local market such as the **rue Poncelet** (17th arrondissement), the **place d'Aligre** (12th), which doubles up as a bric-à-brac market and is also strong on North African specialties, or the **rue du Poteau** (18th), high on the slopes of Montmartre, with its inimitable "old Paris" character.

Famous fleas Flea markets (*marché aux puces*), are judiciously sited around the city perimeter. Their eclectic and often dusty and/or exotic goods never lose their pull, whether for well-heeled tourists and residents or for the poorer inhabitants of the metropolis. The world-famous **Porte de Clignancourt** flea market is rightly known as a tourist trap, yet its alleyways, covered markets, and stalls always come up with something for everyone—the sheer bulk of goods plus the laws of probability see to that. From old buttons to recycled clothes to Louis XV mirrors to 1950s coffeepots—it's very difficult not to find your own particular joy among these offerings.

Diametrically opposite the Porte de Clignancourt on the Paris map, the flea market at the **Porte de Vanves** has recently become a favorite with young trendies; there is little of great value but plenty of eccentricities, art-deco and 1950s furniture, a smattering of exotica, and quite a wide selection of old prints.

Not as popular nor as interesting as it used to be, the **Marché de Montreuil** in the east of Paris is gradually being taken over by bargain household goods stalls, leaving little space for the junk; however, secondhand clothes remain a specialty and Saint-Laurent jackets have been known to be found in perfect condition, so keep looking.

For secondhand books, if the *bouquinistes* (dealers) don't suffice, spend your weekend hours at the **Parc Georges Brassens** (15th), where you will find an unrivaled array of antiquarian and secondhand books.

Birds and flowers
For a market with color, go to the Marché aux fleurs (held daily on the Ile de la Cité in front of the Préfecture), replaced on Sundays by a bird market. Or try the stamp market held on Thursdays and weekends in the Cour Marigny, off the Champs-Elysées. The Marché St.-Pierre in Montmartre, famous for its cheap fabrics, is a good place to spot professional designers.

CHAILLOT, PALAIS DE

Musée de l'Homme
There is an excellent bookshop in the Musée de l'Homme, as well as the ultimate restaurant-with-a-view, the Totem.

Musée du Cinéma
In the basement below the palace, the Musée du Cinéma displays over 3,000 relevant items going back to the origins of photography. The Lumière brothers' photorama and Edison's kinetoscope of 1894 are included alongside set models by Eisenstein, photographs, costumes (worn by the likes of Valentino and Garbo), and actual sets from *Metropolis*. Entrance is only with guided tours (10, 11, 2, 3, and 4; closed Monday and Tuesday).

Continued from page 91

The east wing of Chaillot houses a rather extraordinary museum, created in 1882 by the architect Viollet-le-Duc. The **Musée des Monuments Français** (closed Tuesday) is a museum of full-scale copies of French architectural features from pre-Roman times to the 19th century. It is a good opportunity to see a succinct panorama of this field in one fell swoop. Reproductions of frescos, church facades, fountains, and sarcophagi all create an unreal atmosphere in a much-neglected museum.

Back above ground in Chaillot's west wing, you have the choice of two valiant museums, the **Musée de l'Homme** or the **Musée de la Marine▶** (both closed Tuesday). Predictably, the Musée de la Marine, one of the largest maritime museums in the world, set up by Charles X in 1827, concentrates on French naval history and is packed with ship models, marine instruments, paintings (including 13 of Vernet's *Ports de France*, executed between 1754 and 1765), and sculpture. Don't miss the emperor's barge (built in 1811 for Napoleon) or a cross-section model of the glittering transatlantic liner *Normandie*, the floating 1932 palace of decorative arts destroyed by fire during World War II.

The **Musée de l'Homme**, although a little shabby round the edges, houses fascinating anthropological and ethnographical displays. Mental travel is possible from the Pacific to Africa with detours around Asia and, particularly strong, South America. Watch out for the life-size "shark man," King Béhanzin, and the medieval frescos from Abyssinia, both in the very rich African section. On the top floor, in the Salon de la Musique, 500 or so world instruments are displayed with background sound. Live concerts are a regular feature.

94

An exhibit from the Palais de Chaillot's Musée de la Marine, portraying French maritime history from the 18th century to the present day

Cyclists in the Tour de France speed along the Champs-Elysées. The avenue is guarded by the Cheveaux de Marly (below)—but only by copies; the originals are in the Louvre

95

►► Champs-Elysées

The broad pavements and wide expanse of this avenue, which sweeps majestically down from the Arc de Triomphe to the place de la Concorde, no longer exude the glamour of times gone by. Although one of the places dreamed about by visitors to Paris, it proves a disappointment in today's age of fast food and shopping malls. Its best feature remains a string of large-scale cinemas showing the latest releases, hard to beat for their comfort (or their long lines).

You can thank Marie de Médicis, wife of Henri IV, for turning it into a fashionable driveway in 1616. Then thank the landscape designer, Le Nôtre, for the gracious alleys of trees and gardens leading from the Concorde that, by 1707, had earned the avenue its name: Elysian Fields. It was in 1824 that the avenue became structured with pavements and fountains, soon crowded with cafés and restaurants and a very swish clientele. Various Universal Exhibitions helped to increase its popularity, particularly in 1900, when the **Grand Palais** and **Petit Palais** sidled up together.

Center of ceremony Despite its tackiness, the Champs-Elysées remains the central Parisian stretch for official processions and celebrations. Catch it on July 14 (Bastille Day) and most of the French army rolls past with a jet accompaniment flying exceedingly low overhead. Later in July you may find yourself here for the last leg of the Tour de France bicycle race, an event deeply rooted in the French psyche, which pulls in thousands of spectators. You can catch the setting at its best around Christmas, when every tree glitters with festoons of elegant white lights—then try on New Year's Eve for size.

The lower half of the avenue boasts a few select restaurants nestling in the chestnut trees: **Ledoyen, Jardins de Lenôtre,** or **Le Pavillon du Gouverneur**—all have astronomical prices but make a nice indulgence with their garden terraces. Otherwise, avoid any eating establishment on this avenue—everything is geared toward unsuspecting tourists.

Great processions
In 1989, the Bicentenary celebrations culminated in Jean-Paul Goude's spectacular procession moving and dancing down to the Concorde, with Jessye Norman singing at its head. De Gaulle's triumphal Liberation march took place here in 1944, as did the silent procession in 1970 paying tribute to him after his death; and Victor Hugo's funeral parade made its way along the avenue in 1885.

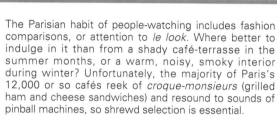

■ Where else did Lenin, Sartre, Picasso, Modigliani, Apollinaire, James Joyce, and Trotsky cultivate their genius but in Parisian cafés? Not to speak of the intellectuals of the Revolution, who plotted France's future in the watering holes of the Palais-Royal. The café tradition lives on, and Parisian thinkers still hatch ideas or chew the cultural cud in public rather than in their often minuscule abodes. Time was when the cafés were also part of the Great French Pickup tradition, but lone women are nowadays as much at ease here as they are at home ...■

The Parisian habit of people-watching includes fashion comparisons, or attention to *le look*. Where better to indulge in it than from a shady café-terrasse in the summer months, or a warm, noisy, smoky interior during winter? Unfortunately, the majority of Paris's 12,000 or so cafés reek of *croque-monsieurs* (grilled ham and cheese sandwiches) and resound to sounds of pinball machines, so shrewd selection is essential.

Many of the favorites are in upscale Saint-Germain, number one being the **Café de Flore**, which rose to fame when Sartre and Simone de Beauvoir set up literary shop there during World War II. Its 19th-century wood-paneled interior is as inviting as the terrace, which is glassed in during the winter, and if you get tired of the constant visual appraisal, go upstairs, where you can read *Le Monde* in peace. Clientele still includes philosophers, writers, artists, and, of course, a smattering of chic tourists. But, as in all historic cafés, watch out for the prices!

Historic haunts A few doors along is the equally famous **Aux Deux Magots**, named after the statues of two corpulent Chinamen astride their strongboxes. *Magot* also means a hoard of money, and this is what you'll spend if you succumb to the menu of 25 different brands of whisky. But think of the ghosts of Mallarmé, André Breton, Hemingway, André Gide, and Sartre and stick to a pot of their excellent espresso coffee. Tourists and Middle Eastern businessmen abound, and the odd native publisher or movie star still slips in.

For a more down-to-earth café, head down to the corner of the rue de Seine and the rue Jacques-Callot. Here you can plunge into the less monied and eccentric **La Palette**, with its comfortable and noisy back room or idyllic summer terrace. La Palette is a favorite with art students, artists, and gallery owners. Its walls are plastered with good and bad art, and its headwaiter-cum-proprietor is a classic: quick-witted or scowling, he's unforgettable.

Back in an increasingly characterless Montparnasse, an institution not to miss is **La Coupole**. Built in 1926 by an astute waiter working at Le Dôme across the street, its

Sartre and Simone de Beauvoir were regulars at the Café de Flore

majestic art-deco splendor is hard to rival, despite recent remodeling. The main hall is a world-famous brasserie whose ghosts include prewar Americans in Paris such as Hemingway (he went everywhere), Man Ray, and Henry Miller, backed up by locals Matisse and Kiki de Montparnasse. Across the road, the rival **Le Sélect** dates from the same period and still attracts a heterogeneous crowd late into the night.

Right Bank landmarks In the heart of the Rive Droite's commercial quarter, Opéra, stands another Parisian landmark café, the **Café de la Paix**. Although mainly frequented by exhausted tourists, its interior demands a visit. Designed by Charles Garnier, responsible for the neighboring opera house, the murals, moldings, and chandeliers are a shrine to the glorious excesses of mid-19th-century décor.

However many famous cafés litter the center of Paris, you will doubtless come across your own finds, rich in local characters and decorative idiosyncrasies. And don't miss out on the latest fin de siècle cafés, kicking off with the **Café Costes** and the **Café Beaubourg**. Both are in Les Halles, both owned by the same family, both designed by star architects, but there familiarity ends. The Costes, which opens onto the place des Innocents, has become a favorite hangout for suburban teenagers. The superb design and furniture by Philippe Starck are pure 1980s, and the innovatory downstairs toilets demand a detour. More inviting, however, is the Café Beaubourg on the square outside the Centre Pompidou. Here, in Christian de Portzamparc's postmodernist setting, you can watch Rive Droite intellectuals go by.

La Procope
The first café to open its doors in Paris was Le Procope (which still exists but as a restaurant), in 1686, run by a Sicilian who soon attracted most of the political and literary élite to his tables. Voltaire had a daily habit of drinking 40 cups of mixed coffee and chocolate there, and the young artillery officer Napoleon Bonaparte once had to leave his hat as a deposit while he went off to search for funds.

Café Marly
The latest designer café, the Café Marly, was conceived by Olivier Gagnère to slip effortlessly into a wing of the Louvre. It attracts an elegant crowd and in summer offers unbeatable views of the pyramid.

A teenage favorite: the Café Costes

■ In the early days, brasseries sold only beer. Today, high ceilings echo with clattering plates and chattering voices, mirrors double the people-watching scope, carved wood and etched glass partitions protect your privacy, and waiters in full-length white aprons swing trays of oysters or *choucroute* between the tables ...■

In search of oysters
For the best oysters, try Le Bar à Huîtres in the Marais, L'Huîtrier in the Chaillot quarter, the cheerful Bistrot du Dôme in Montparnasse, or nearby La Cagouille, which boasts one of the finest shellfish platters in town.

La Coupole, one of the celebrated Flo chain of brasseries, frequented by artists and intellectuals since it opened in 1927

An invention that arrived from Alsace in eastern France, brasseries offer wholesome fare that usually includes sausages piled high on *choucroute* (sauerkraut), ham, cassoulet, and anything else that can be concocted from a pig—all drowned in pitchers of beer. Many specialize in seafood, so if you're in Paris during September to April, when oysters are at their optimum, indulge yourself. Brasseries are mostly open on Sundays and last orders carry on well after midnight, making them an ideal choice for late eaters.

The world-famous brasserie **Flo** chain, which includes **Flo, Julien**, and **Terminus Nord** in the 10th, the **Vaudeville** in the 2nd, and, most recently, **La Coupole** in the 14th, is hard to beat for atmosphere, value, and spectacular settings. The **Brasserie Flo** itself remains a Parisian favorite, tucked away in a courtyard and inevitably packed, whereas **Julien**, more visible on the Faubourg, has a higher tourist concentration. Just opposite the Stock Exchange, the patronizing

Vaudeville waiters serve traders sweating over the *Financial Times* at lunchtime and a mixed glamorous bunch in the evening. The elegant **Terminus Nord**, the only jewel in the ambivalent quartier of the Gare du Nord, has an easygoing atmosphere.

La Coupole is, of course, La Coupole. Josephine Baker and her pet lion cub are not the only celebrities to have sat on its brown velvet seats under its soaring art-deco ceiling. Despite its recent, much criticized renovation, the famous pillars painted by artists (in exchange for meals) such as Chagall, Léger, Juan Gris, Delaunay, and Soutine remain. Othon Friesz's dynamic murals have been restored and 600 seats are still available. Actors, artists, models, businessmen, and plain ordinary people all mix in to this nonstop party.

Paris's star brasserie, the **Lipp**, is centrally situated on the boulevard St.-Germain, where all celebrities seem to tread. Once ruled by a man with an iron glove, Roger Cazes, who was quick to decide whether you were worthy of a ground-floor table or were to be relegated upstairs, it now has a less disdainful management. Long a favorite with politicians (from de Gaulle to Pompidou and Mitterrand) it is also a great haunt for authors. Idiosyncrasies prevail: no soup on Sundays, roast pork on Monday, cassoulet on Thursday, and nonstop *choucroute*. No reservations; pot luck and the shape of your face decide your destiny.

First draughts One of Paris's oldest brasseries (1864), and apparently the first to serve draught beer, the **Bofinger** thrives in a side street off the Bastille. Blessed with an elaborate glass dome, extensive marquetry, and gracefully framed mirrors, it is a delight to dine in.

Less opulent but serving the same basic fare minus the shellfish, the **Brasserie de l'Ile Saint-Louis** boasts the best brasserie terrace in Paris. A south-facing view over the Seine, Notre-Dame a few yards away, and Berthillon ice creams: its credentials are impeccable. Inside, the stuffed stork perched on the bar is about the same age as the 1913 espresso machine, and the barman has pulled draught beer here since the 1950s. Crowded and cramped, its backroom restaurant remains a firm favorite with tourists and eccentric locals.

Pigalle, too, has its *choucroute* institution, namely the venerable **Brasserie Wepler** on the place Clichy. Better value than the central establishments and just as accommodating in size, its oyster bar is outstanding. The vast, brassy décor is not the most discreet, but its eclectic clientele fills out the corners comfortably.

A sign of good taste: the still flamboyant Bofinger serves excellent shellfish, grilled meats, and choucroute

Gabriel's imposing Ecole Militaire in the Champ de Mars, where Napoleon trained to become an officer

► **Champ de Mars**

Originally laid out for army maneuvers, whence the name, which refers to Mars, the Roman god of war, the green lawns of the Champ de Mars stretch from the Eiffel Tower down to the Ecole Militaire. It was the site where the Roman invaders battled it out with the Parisii in 52 BC to obtain supremacy over Paris and where the Parisians later beat off the Vikings. The Champ de Mars has witnessed many an official celebration, horse races, and ballooning experiments by the Montgolfier brothers. It is a favorite with children of chic local residents.

Dominating the area is the Ecole Militaire, designed as a military academy by Gabriel (also responsible for Versailles' Petit Trianon), who was commissioned by Louis XV and his mistress, Madame de Pompadour.

Chartres see pages 194– 5.

► **Chasse et Nature, Musée de la**

60 rue des Archives, 75003
metro: Rambuteau, Hôtel de Ville

Definitely one of Paris's more curious museums, this is also a great favorite with children, enthralled by rooms of hunting weapons and stuffed animals. Housed in a Marais mansion, the Hôtel Guénégaud, which was built in 1650 by François Mansart, it possesses a tiny yet perfectly manicured garden at the back, visible from the rue des Quatre Fils.

The museum collection itself covers hunting arms used from prehistory until the 19th century (knives, crossbows, swords, air guns, rifles). On the second floor big-game hunting comes to the fore with souvenirs of the museum's founder, Monsieur Sommer. A rich collection of relevant paintings and decorative arts include hunting and animal scenes depicted by François Desportes, the court artist employed by Louis XIV at Versailles, alongside Chardin, Oudry, and Carle Vernet.

Open: Wednesday to Monday, 10–12:30 and 1:30–5:30.

"An excellent sailor"
Thanks to a new tax on playing cards and the lottery, funds were found for the colonnaded and domed Ecole Militaire, completed in 1773 and considered to be Gabriel's masterpiece. Thus the 18th-century gamblers inadvertently financed the grooming of France's military cadets, one of whom was none other than Napoleon, who entered the academy at age 15, in 1784, considered fit "to be an excellent sailor."

■ **Since 1895, when Louis Lumière held his first movie projections in a basement room of Le Grand Café, at 14 boulevard des Capucines, Paris has remained the world capital of movies. Nearly a century later, there are over 300 films showing at any time of the day or evening, from old Hollywood classics to recently released European avant-garde efforts—and many foreign language films are shown in their original version (labeled VO) ...■**

City images Many French film-makers are inextricably linked with the atmosphere of Paris, not least being the directors of the 1930s and '40s. Born in Les Halles and a pupil of the famous Lycée Louis-le-Grand, René Clair showed Paris for the first time on screen in *Paris qui dort* (1923) and soon after in *Sous les toits de Paris*. Yet however authentic they look, his charming, animated old streets, rattling omnibuses, and smoking chimney pots were all studio-built.

A decade later, Marcel Carné, another Parisian born and bred in Batignolles, focused on the rough, industrial life of the faubourgs, encapsulating Montmartre and Jean Gabin in the *Quai des Brumes* and the Canal St.-Martin in *Hôtel du Nord*, which starred the legendary Arletty and Louis Jouvet. *Les Enfants du Paradis* poetically interpreted the street underworld around the Cour des Miracles in a classic Parisian fresco. The other side of the Parisian coin was reflected in Jean Renoir's *La Règle du Jeu* (1939). Here was the elegant, muted, bourgeois world of Proust and the 16th arrondissement, rife with barely disguised jealousies.

Classic venues To see such Parisian classics, go to the **Vidéothèque** (see page 183), the **Cinémathèque** (see page 91), the **Salle Garance** at Beaubourg (see pages 80–1) or the **Palais de Tokyo** (see page 62); all specialize in revivals, as do certain Rive Gauche cinemas. For these programs, which often change daily, check one of the weekly listings magazines (*Pariscope* and *L'Officiel des Spectacles*), published on Wednesdays. But for real audience comfort go to any of the following: **Kinopanorama** (15th), **Max Linder** (9th), **Forum Horizon THX** (1st), or **Rex** (2nd). Strangest of all is **La Pagode** (7th), built in 1896 as a private ballroom in the form of a pagoda, and a lavishly decorated "Chinoiserie" cinema since 1931.

101

Mass-release films are shown in a string of Champs-Elysées cinemas

At the crossroads: place du Châtelet sits over the largest metro station in the world, a veritable subterranean labyrinth

Tour St.-Jacques
Just north of the place du Châtelet lies a 175-foot-high tower in the Flamboyant Gothic style, all that remains of the 16th-century Church of St.-Jacques-la-Boucherie — once a meeting point for pilgrims setting out to St. Jacques' shrine at Compostela in Spain.

Dragons in the street
The best time of the year to visit Chinatown is during Chinese New Year (late January), when dragons and other revelers take to the streets.

Châtelet, Place du

A hectic central crossroads, the place du Châtelet lies between the Pont au Change, which crosses to the Ile de la Cité, and the boulevard de Sébastopol. Once the site of an imposing fortress, Châtelet is known today for its vast underground metro station, where all lines and all street performers seem to meet. Two important theaters flank the square and in its center the sphinx-endowed fountain, erected in 1808, commemorates yet another Napoleonic victory, the Egyptian campaign.

Both identical theaters were built by Davioud in 1862 but now lead separate and even rival existences. The **Châtelet** concentrates mainly on opera and classical music, with occasional ballet, and usually has a rich program of international performers. It recently acquired an annex in Les Halles, the Auditorium, where more unusual or obscure music is performed.

The modernized interior of the **Théâtre de la Ville**, previously named the Sarah Bernhardt, has preserved for posterity the diva's dressing room. Audiences flock here to see the top names of contemporary dance or innovative French theater. Early evening concerts of jazz or world music have recently been scheduled to give homebound office workers a chance to unwind.

► Chinatown

Following world tradition, Paris now has its very own Chinatown in the 13th arrondissement, spreading south from the place d'Italie through the rue de Tolbiac to the Porte de Choisy. Asians are now said to constitute 10 percent of the population of this arrondissement, and China is by no means the only country of origin. Squeezed between high-rises, pagoda-like shopfronts crammed with Chinese curios jostle with a fantastic variety of eateries on all scales, from Hong Kong-style canteens to more intimate Laotian, Cambodian, or Vietnamese places. Clubs, dance halls, and gambling dens also contribute to the atmosphere, but these are usually out of bounds to westerners, as the fortunes changing hands are illegal.

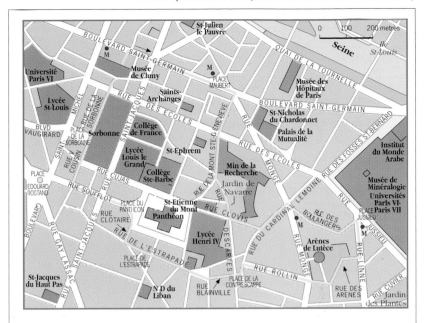

Walk A circular walk from the Musée de Cluny

Start in front of the Musée de Cluny. Walk east along boulevard St.-Germain to the place Maubert. Turn right behind the vast police station and walk up the steep rue de la Montagne Ste.-Geneviève.

Named after the patroness of Paris, the **rue de la Montagne Ste.-Geneviève** was part of the Roman road linking Lutetia with Italy, and for centuries was lined with colleges and schools. Some remain today.

At a fork, take the rue Descartes. The route now passes what was once the famous **Ecole Polytechnique** and is now a ministry (its delightful gardens are open to the public).

Turn left into the short rue Clovis. The **rue Clovis** was named after the king of the Franks who defeated the Romans and founded France. Near **No. 5** is a section of Philippe-Auguste's medieval city wall.

Walk downhill toward the place du Cardinal Lemoine and take the second narrow turning on your right down the rue des Boulangers, right up the rue Linné and right again into the rue des Arènes.

Here, you enter the ruined **Roman amphitheater**, now used for boules.

Exit onto the rue Monge, and take the rue Rollin opposite, which crosses the animated place de la Contrescarpe and becomes the rue Blainville.

The **rue Blainville** was the site of Paris's first public library.

Follow this street into the rue de l'Estrapade, turning right down the rue Clotaire to confront the illustrious Panthéon. Walk down the gracious rue Soufflot.

Below the **rue Soufflot** are the ruins of a Roman forum.

Turn right down rue V. Cousin, which leads to the rue de la Sorbonne, heart of French learning.

Pass **Ste.-Ursule-de-la-Sorbonne** (1642), where Richelieu is buried, before returning to the Cluny.

CLUNY, MUSEE DE (MUSEE DU MOYEN AGE)

Museum of the Middle Ages
Between 1500 and 1844, before it became a museum, the Hôtel de Cluny housed the likes of Mary Tudor; James V of Scotland, before his marriage to François I's daughter; and, in the 17th century, various cardinals including Mazarin.

► ► ► **Cluny, Musée de (Musée du Moyen Age)**
6 place Paul-Painlevé, 75005
metro: Cluny-La Sorbonne
Once a pied-à-terre for a wealthy order of Benedictine monks from Cluny in Burgundy, the former Hôtel de Cluny stands on and beside Paris's oldest Roman baths, the ruins of which can still be seen on the corner of boulevard Saint-Michel and the boulevard Saint-Germain. Built between 1485 and 1500, the mansion is one of France's finest examples of domestic Gothic architecture. Sold off after the Revolution to replenish government coffers, in 1833 it entered the hands of art collector Alexandre de Sommerard, whose rich finds form the basis of the museum today.

Although 8,000 Renaissance works were recently transferred to the museum at the Château d'Ecouen, the Cluny vaults contain another 20,000 objects, rarely displayed. However, those that are visible are superb. From the mutilated heads of statues from Notre-Dame (more revolutionary decapitation) unearthed in 1977 in a bank vault, to an incomparable series of 15th-century tapestries, to dazzling displays of jewelry, goldwork, medieval manuscripts, and stained glass, this is a collection of unfailing inspiration.

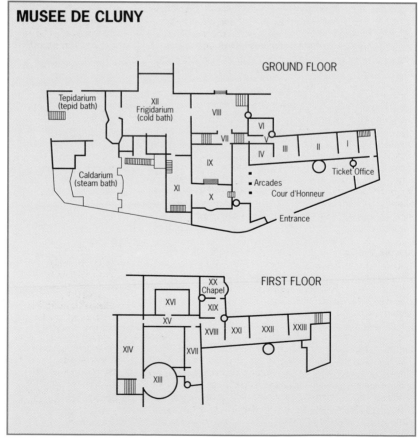

MUSEE DE CLUNY

La famille Jouvenel des Ursins (1445–1449), one of the tapestries in the Musée de Cluny—indisputably one of the finest collections of medieval art and crafts in the world

Roman baths On the lower floor, the late 2nd-century baths are a reminder of the strength of Roman architecture. The vaulted ceiling of the Frigidarium (cold bath) rises over 46 feet with 21-foot-thick walls. In one corner stands the *Pilier des nautes*, Paris's oldest sculpture. Leading off from here, a vast network of Roman vaults has recently been restored and can be toured.

Back on the ground floor, you enter the museum via displays of medieval costume and accessories; Byzantine, Coptic, and European textiles, and a series of tapestries. One series, *La Vie Seigneuriale*, shows the life of a noble household.

The first floor houses one of the museum's great splendors, the six allegorical tapestries of *La Dame à la Licorne*. Exquisitely woven, probably in the southern Netherlands for the Lyonnais family of Le Viste, their delicate tones represent flora and fauna as a graceful background to the central feminine figure. Each tapestry shows her acting out a sense—sight, touch, smell, taste, sound—while the enigmatic sixth work presents her in front of the motto *A mon seul désir* (to my only desire). Is this freedom from the senses or mastery of all five? Your guess is as good as anybody's over the last five centuries.

Jewels and crowns Room XVI presents a treasure trove of goldwork and jewelry: Gallic, Barbarian, and Merovingian examples include belts, buckles, bracelets, the sublimely fashioned Rose d'Or, six Visigoth crowns, and two 13th-century double gold crosses.

Apart from the stained-glass windows removed from Sainte-Chapelle and St.-Denis, the most striking church relic is the glittering gold altar frontal (1015) from Basel cathedral, made for the Emperor Heinrich II.

At the back of the top floor, don't miss the Abbot's Chapel with its flamboyant vaulting fanning out from a central pillar. Twelve niches contain statues of the Amboise family (Jacques Amboise rebuilt the mansion in 1500) and tapestries depicting the life of St.-Stephen carry on into adjoining rooms.

Open: Wednesday to Monday, 9:15–5:45.

Mistaken identity
The 21 mutilated heads from Notre-Dame, displayed in Room VIII, actually represented kings of Judea and Israel, but were assumed by the stampeding revolutionary mob to be kings of France—hence their sorry fate. These 13th-century heads, all without noses, were discovered during excavations at the Hôtel Moreau in 1977.

The guillotine
The guillotine is not such an anachronism: it was only abolished in 1961, after nearly 200 years of loyal service.

The Théâtre Français—home base of the Comédie Française, founded in 1681, and still Paris's most famous private theater company

An infamous criminal
One of Paris's most celebrated murderers was the infamous Landru, who recruited his victims through small advertisements suggesting marriage. He killed 11 women in total, using a gruesome assortment of weapons including a rolling pin and curling tongs. He was finally executed in 1922.

Collections Historiques de la Préfecture de Police, Musée des
1 bis rue des Carmes, 75005
metro: Maubert-Mutualité
If you feel like checking Charlotte Corday's statement about murdering Marat in his bathtub, this is where to go. Situated at the back of the 5th arrondissement commissariat (police station), this macabre little collection covers many of Paris's great criminal moments from the 16th century to the present. A particularly graphic representation shows the punishment meted out to the murderer of the Duc de Guise in 1563: he was tied to four horses and quartered. Other niceties include orders for the arrest of Docteur Guillotin in 1795 and a book splattered with the bloodstains of the assassinated President Paul Doumer. An array of weapons runs the gamut of brass knuckles, garrottes (strangling cords), variously concealed knives (one in a lady's fan), and a guillotine blade.
Open: Monday to Friday, 9–5; Saturday, 10–5.

► Comédie Française
2 rue de Richelieu, 75001
metro: Palais-Royal
A monument to French classical theater, the building named the Théâtre Français is actually a 1900 remodeling job of the original 1790 Doric-style edifice, mostly destroyed in a fire. It has been home since 1799 to the Comédie Française company, founded by Louis XIV with members of Molière's troupe. The playwright himself died on stage seven years earlier while performing in *Le Malade Imaginaire*; the armchair that cushioned his fall when illness struck can still be seen in the foyer along with busts and statues of dramatists: Carpeaux's Dumas, Rodin's Mirabeau, Clésinger's Georges Sand, and Houdon's sedentary Voltaire.

Although the basic repertoire of the Comédie Française remains a string of Molière, Racine, Corneille, and Marivaux classics, a recently appointed director has opened up the field. And nobody will forget the spirit of Sarah Bernhardt, the great tragic actress who played many of her finest roles here.

Phone 40 15 00 15 for information on the rare guided tours behind the scenes.

■ **French furniture and *objets d'art* design is well illustrated by the collection at the Musée des Arts Décoratifs, where much emphasis is put on the early 20th century. From the organic curves of art nouveau, French design moved effortlessly into a more sober art-deco style exemplified by the Exposition Internationale des Arts Décoratifs in 1925 ...■**

The great couturier **Poiret** bankrupted himself with his three converted barges decorated by Dufy; Parisian design then moved resolutely into geometric modernism. After **Dunand, Chareau, Ruhlmann,** and **Le Corbusier,** the next French designer to open up a new style was **Jean Prouvé,** master of 1950s curves.

New life After decades of remaining dormant, French design underwent a major renaissance in the 1980s. Stimulation came from the **Mobilier National,** which since 1964 had acted as an inspiring go-between for designers and furniture manufacturers and the newly created government agency **VIA,** which supported and promoted young designers. The **VIA** showroom, now in the Cour du Commerce St.-André, displays prototypes and manufactured items, all for sale, some more functional than others though standards have visibly dropped.

State style 1980s design became such a cultural symbol that even the president commissioned new furnishings for the Elysée, and some ministries have adopted a distinctly futuristic image. **Philippe Starck, Jean-Michel Wilmotte, Andrée Putman,** and **Garouste et Bonetti** are favorites in the official field, and their status is now firmly international.

Another wave carries with it the names of **Martin Szekely, Sylvain Dubuisson, Olivier Gagnère,** and **Marie-Christine Dorner.** A precursor in this field is the **Galerie Néotu** (25 rue du Renard, 4e; tel: 42 78 96 97), which regularly exhibits the latest in French avant-garde design.

The **Galerie Yves Gastou** (12 rue Bonaparte, 6e; tel: 46 34 72 17) exhibits designs by **Ettore Sottsass, Ron Arad,** and **Kuramata** while **En attendant les barbares** (50 rue Etienne-Marcel, 2e; tel: 42 33 37 87) is a hive of weird and wacky, multi-colored objects.

Décor of the day If you prefer to see examples of French design in situ, probably the most obvious relics of the 1980s in Paris are the interiors of the **Café Costes, Café Beaubourg** (see page 97), and **La Villa** (a hotel with a public bar and a jazz club at 29 rue Jacob, 6e, designed by **Dorner**). The more classical **Café Marly** (at the Louvre) leads the way for the 1990s.

Accessible design at the Café Costes—does it mark the end of an era, or simply a pause for thought?

Designs on the future? Although design is no longer the essential and magic password that it became in the 1980s, its importance has smoothly infiltrated daily life— whether sleekily renovated museums, dentists' waiting rooms, cinemas, or industrial objects. Possibly a saner approach on the way to the year 2000.

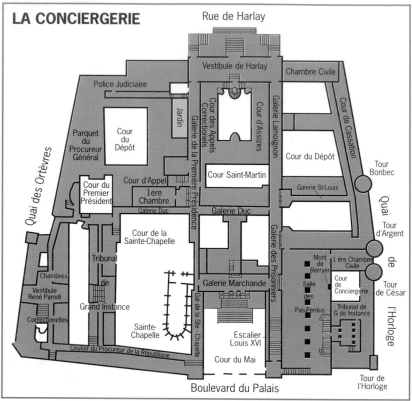

LA CONCIERGERIE

Rue de Harlay

Vestibule de Harlay

Chambre Civile

Police Judiciaire

Cour de Cassation

Cour des Appels Correctionels

Cour d'Assises

Galerie Lamoignon

Jardin

Galerie de la Première Présidence

Parquet du Procureur Général

Cour du Dépôt

Quai des Orfèvres

Cour du Dépôt

Tour Bonbec

Cour Saint-Martin

Cour du Premier Président

Galerie St-Louis

Cour d'Appel

1ere Chambre

Galerie Duc

Galerie Duc

Quai de

Tour d'Argent

Cour de la Sainte-Chapelle

Galerie des Prisonniers

Mont de Berryer

1ère Chambre Civile

Tribunal

Chambres

de

Galerie Marchande

Salle des Pas-Perdus

Cour de Conciergerie

Tour de César

Vestibule René Parodi

Correctionelles

Grand Instance

Ga. de la Ste-Chapelle

Tribunal de G de Instance

l'Horloge

Sainte-Chapelle

Escalier Louis XVI

Couloir du Procureur de la République

Cour du Mai

Boulevard du Palais

Tour de l'Horloge

"Madame Deficit"

The Conciergerie's most celebrated inmate, Marie-Antoinette, was not France's most popular queen. Nicknamed "Madame Veto," "Madame Deficit," or simply "the Austrian," she was renowned for her extravagance. Her millinery bills alone would have kept an average French family for its entire life, while her favorite hairdresser, Léonard, once accomplished the dubious exploit of weaving 18½ yards of ribbon into her hair. On her arrest in August 1792, legend goes that this same pampered hair turned gray overnight. The "simple" cell life had a disciplinary effect on her character and she behaved with dignity until her execution in October 1793.

Conciergerie, La

1 quai de l'Horloge, 75001
metro: Cité, Châtelet

Rising above the roofs of the Quai de l'Horloge on the Ile de la Cité, the twin towers of the Conciergerie struck horror into the hearts of thousands for over five centuries. Originally built to house Philippe-le-Bel's caretaker (concierge) and palace guards, by 1391 it was functioning as a prison and continued as such until 1914. Before entering, stop at the corner to look at the **Tour de l'Horloge**, which incorporates Paris's first public clock. Commissioned by Charles V in 1371, it is set against a constellation of gold fleur-de-lys; the surrounding sculptures of law and justice were added in the 16th century. A bell that rang for three days following the birth of any royal babe could not really toll for the revolutionaries, so in 1793 a new silver bell was installed.

Grim history The prisons of the Conciergerie are best known for their hospitable role during the Revolution, although they had already housed and tortured thousands, including Ravaillac, murderer of Henri IV. During the Terror, 4,164 citizens were held here, 2,278 of whom finished under the guillotine. The best remembered inmate is Marie-Antoinette, the extravagant Austrian wife of Louis XVI. Other guests

included Charlotte Corday, Marat's assassin; Madame du Barry, mistress of Louis XV; and, when the tide turned, Danton and Robespierre.

Entrance is through the Salles des Gardes, a vaulted stone chamber plunged into shadow by the construction of the embankment outside the windows. This opens onto the equally gloomy Salle des Gens d'Arme, an astonishing hall measuring 230 feet by 88½ feet. Said to be Europe's oldest surviving medieval hall, it was restored in the 19th century by Viollet-le-Duc. A spiral staircase at the back leads to the original kitchens. Four walk-in fireplaces big enough to roast a couple of sheep indicate the scale of medieval appetites.

Star-rated cells Back at the entrance to the Salle des Gens d'Arme, follow the rue de Paris, where less monied prisoners (*les pailleux*) snoozed on straw bedding. Three types of accommodation were available: the communal straw-strewn floor; a shared cell with beds; and for those with real pull and funds, a private cell complete with table for memoir-writing. From this corridor you reach what was once the prison's most animated crossroads, the Galerie des Prisonniers, where lawyers, visitors, and prisoners came and went. On the left was the barber's cell, where inmates were shorn before their trip to the guillotine (not for fashion—hair prevented the blade working properly).

A narrow staircase leads up to displays of objects related to the Conciergerie's bloody history. The first musty room is the most striking: wall panels list all the 2,780 guillotined victims of the Revolution.

Downstairs you reach the Chapelle des Girondins, named after the 22 condemned Girondins (left-wing members of the 1791 Legislative Assembly) who celebrated their last night with true revelry here. What is now the altar was the site of Marie-Antoinette's cell.

At the far end of the Galerie des Prisonniers, her cell has been recreated. None of its contents is authentic but the spartan furniture, peeling wallpaper, and models of card-playing guards behind a screen give the sorry feel of Marie-Antoinette's last sojourn.

Open: daily, April to September, 9:30–6; October to March, 10–4:30. (Closed on national holidays.)

Floodlights now shine on the grim facade of the Conciergerie

The city's first public clock, on the Tour de l'Horloge

Dr. Guillotin
Dr. Guillotin perfected his "philanthropic beheading machine" by trying it out on a miserable bunch of sheep in the courtyard of his home, No. 9, Cour de Rohan.

The Obelisk
The oldest monument in Paris, dating from the 13th century BC, was originally used as an astronomical instrument to measure the sun's shadow in the Temple of Thebes. Dragged from the desert to the Nile, loaded onto a special barge and towed to Rouen by paddlesteamer, it was then transported to Paris by French sailors and gunners. Its 19th-century pedestal illustrates the Obelisk's remarkable journey

The spacious, grandiose place de la Concorde, at the hub of Paris, is best viewed after rush hour

►►► Concorde, Place de la

Once a swamp, now Paris's largest square, throbbing with traffic and fumes, the Concorde was designed in 1775 chiefly to accommodate an equestrian statue of the reigning king, Louis XV. It soon changed name and function when the guillotine was trundled out. As the place de la Revolution it saw over 1,300 heads roll, including Louis XVI, Marie-Antoinette, Danton, and Robespierre. The architect, Jacques-Ange Gabriel, also designed the two properties flanking the rue Royale, one of which survived the Revolution in the hands of the Comte de Crillon, and is now the **Hôtel Crillon**.

With the cooling of revolutionary passions in 1795, the square was renamed Concorde and soon acquired Coustou's *Chevaux de Marly* at the entrance to the Champs-Elysées. The next transformation came in 1833 under Louis-Philippe, when he was presented with a 75-foot, 3,000-year-old obelisk by Mohammed Ali, viceroy of Egypt (see page 158). Gabriel's eight stone pavilions, each topped by a statue depicting a French town in human guise, still remain.

►► Cour du Commerce St.-André (Cour de Rohan)

59/61 rue St.-André-des-Arts, 75006
metro: Odéon
A shopping mall with atmosphere and history: it seems to be a contradiction in terms. However, Paris has 17 such places (see page 181) and the Cour du Commerce was the first. Built in 1776 on the site of a tennis court, it became a hive of revolutionary activity, with Marat printing his pamphlet *L'Ami du Peuple* at No. 8, Danton installed at No. 20, and the anatomy professor Dr. Guillotin at No. 9. At No. 4 you can see the remains of a 13th-century tower, part of the city wall, and the Renaissance courtyards of the Cour de Rohan are still picturesque. Today the passage houses restaurants and tearooms, and, at No. 4/8, the official window on French contemporary design, **VIA** (see page 107).

La Grande Arche, a window on new development in Paris, large enough to surround Notre-Dame—the centerpiece of a striking skyscraping business zone

▶▶ La Défense

RER: La Défense

Paris's new 300,000-ton white marble symbol, La Grande Arche, is the western gateway to the capital and reigns over an urban development first mooted in the 1930s. World War II put a brake on all urbanist projects, but by 1958 an astonishing edifice, the CNIT, had risen from the ground. Throughout the 1960s, wondrous and hideous architectural experiments sprouted in all directions, symbols of France's postwar mutation. Catastrophic in many cases, utopian in others, La Défense was intended as a new business and residential center. The oil crisis in 1973 slowed its momentum but had a positive effect, too, forcing architects and developers to look more closely at what was fast becoming a nightmare knot of viaducts, tunnels, and unrelated forms.

Three successive presidents examined three successive projects to complete *La Tête Défense* (head) and finally to provide this labyrinth with a focal point. An unknown Danish architect, Otto Von Spreckelsen, was finally selected by Mitterrand to build his marble "window on the world," the disemboweled cube that has become La Grande Arche. Its symbolic measurements (100 meters by 100 meters) echo those of the Cour Carrée in the Louvre. Completed in time (just) for the Bicentenary celebrations in 1989, its unfortunate architect had by then abandoned the whole project in a huff and died before its inauguration.

The wide esplanade of La Défense has now assumed its own identity, with office workers happily lunching by the fountains or on café terraces. Numerous contemporary sculptures punctuate this concrete landscape, one of the most striking being François Morellet's *La Défonce*, a fine geometric construction that topples into the recently opened underground storerooms of the national contemporary art collection.

La Grande Arche
Fast becoming a must on the tourist trail for its fantastic open-air panoramic views over Paris, La Grande Arche offers a ride to the roof in transparent elevators—vertigo sufferers beware! Beautifully designed galleries on the top floor house temporary exhibitions, as do the EPAD galleries buried beneath the forecourt outside (access to roof, daily 9–8 in summer; 9–7 in winter).

DELACROIX, MUSEE

Self-portrait, *by Eugène Delacroix— one of a collection of paintings, drawings, letters, and photographs in his modest former studio*

Eugène Delacroix
Although he yearned to be a pure classicist, Delacroix was the embodiment of romanticism. His wide knowledge of literature and his contact with the old masters of the Louvre gave him a rare imaginative breadth. The influence of classical legends and history is apparent in his early works: *Dante and Virgil Crossing the Styx, Death of Sardanapalus, The Capture of Constantinople* (all at the Louvre). But it was a trip to Morocco in 1832 that left an indelible mark on his style, foreshadowing Impressionism. Prolific and talented in every field, from portraits to wild beasts, Delacroix was also an accomplished decorator; you can see his vigorous style in the Chapelle des Anges of St.-Sulpice or the royal salon and library at the Palais Bourbon.

► ► **Delacroix, Musée**
6 place Furstenberg, 75006
metro: St.-Germain-des-Prés
The apartment and studio where the great romantic painter Eugène Delacroix (1798–1863) spent the last six years of his life is now a small but charming museum, which was renovated at the end of 1994. The place Furstenberg has hardly changed over the last century and still has a provincial atmosphere, with its flowering trees and decorative streetlights. Visiting this museum is more a chance to experience the calm and character of Delacroix's environment than to see his paintings; although a few are on view, most of them are safely and beautifully displayed in the Louvre.

Personal effects The first of the three rooms was his bedroom and still contains some furniture, as well as his treasured tobacco pot. The dining room displays his intricate painting table and the central salon his desk. Other memorabilia, etchings, sketches, watercolors, and letters are displayed throughout, but keep an eye out particularly for a recently acquired painting, *La Madeleine au désert*. Delacroix manages in this compelling image to convey the enigmatic strength and aura of the saint with a typically luminous yet ambiguous treatment.

Continue outside down a wrought-iron staircase across a tiny garden to Delacroix's studio, which he had built himself. The studio is a fairly ordinary building, though decorated with neoclassical bas-reliefs, and contains more studies, sketches, and a portrait of his redoubtable mistress, Jenny Le Guillou, who scared many a friend from his door in his later years. Lithography stones used to print his edition of Hamlet are presented, along with paintings by his disciples, Riesener and Andrieu.
Open: Wednesday to Monday, 9:45–5.

■ **There are signs that the high-flying days of "Gay Paris" are, if not over, at least dropping in altitude—despite a more liberal state approach in recent years. Encouraged by a government decision in 1981 to destroy secret service files on homosexuals, and by the lowering of the legal age for homosexual activity to 16 (as for heterosexuals), the gay population of Paris acquired a new identity virtually overnight ...■**

The headquarters of the gay community moved from the rather sleazy rue Ste.-Anne to the gentrified Marais, where certain locals still claim that "they've taken over." Since then, the tragic effect of AIDS has left its mark. The influential *Fréquence Gai*, Europe's only gay radio station, has disappeared: a telltale sign, perhaps, of the end of an era.

Changing attitudes AIDS has had an enormous influence on attitudes toward sexual life. Greater Paris has a population roughly equivalent to that of Greater London but twice as many AIDS cases. Unlike the United States, where cruising areas, saunas, and sex clubs were closed down, Paris has reacted more moderately, trying instead to change sexual behavior slowly, without putting a stop to it. However, the closing in early 1992 of the Bois de Boulogne, known for its nocturnal sexual activities, may be seen as a sign of major changes to come.

Areas known as gay meeting places include the Tuileries esplanade, overlooking the Seine, the riverbank opposite the Musée d'Orsay in the summer months, or the shady tranquility of the Père-Lachaise cemetery. Sunday afternoon dancing at **Le Palace**, a decade-old tradition, attracts hundreds of men (3 cité Bergère; 5–10). On other days of the week the hot spot is **Queen**, a predominantly gay disco (accepting women) with outrageous theme parties; 1970s disco on Mondays and house music on other nights (102 avenue des Champs-Elysées, open from midnight). For a more low-key evening, **Le Central**'s bar and coffee house in the Marais (corner of rue Vieille-du-Temple and rue Ste.-Croix-de-la-Brétonnerie) has become the epicenter. From here, it is a stone's throw to other popular bars such as the **Subway** (35 Ste.-Croix-de-la-Brétonnerie) and the very fashionable **Le Quetzal** (10 rue de la Verrerie).

An advice and information service is offered by Ecoute Gaie (tel: 48 06 19 11) or AIDES (tel: 44 52 00 00).

The gay community in Paris may be facing a more restrictive era

The Queen of Paris offers one of the most breathtaking views of the city, from its 905-foot viewing platform, and one of Paris's "top" restaurants

Tempting fate
The Eiffel Tower has inspired much idiosyncratic behavior. Those who have plummeted from its peak include a mustachioed Icarus who, in 1912, plunged to his death when his wings failed to open. He turned out to be a bankrupt tailor escaping from his debtors. In 1928, a watchmaker tried out a new parachute—too innovative: it didn't open either and he rapidly met his maker. A luckier performer cycled down the steps from top to bottom to win a bet, survived, but was arrested for provocative behavior.

►►► Eiffel, Tour

metro: Bir-Hakeim
RER: Champ de Mars
A hollow chandelier, staircase to infinity, tower of Babel, or aviary of the world, monstrosity or hallowed symbol of Paris, the Eiffel Tower has run the gamut of descriptions in its 100-odd years of existence. Built in a record two years by Gustave Eiffel for the 1889 Universal Exhibition, celebrating the French Revolution centenary, it was intended for demolition 20 years later. But by then it had as many artistic and intellectual fans as it had opponents when built, and it was saved for the utilitarian purposes of its broadcasting antennae. Thus the instincts of writers and artists such as Apollinaire, Dufy, Delaunay, Utrillo, and Pissarro were vindicated and

the scandalized agonies of Garnier, Verlaine, Leconte de Lisle, Maupassant, and Zola relegated to history.

Standing a regal 985 feet high, weighing over 7,000 tons and composed of 15,000 iron parts, the Queen of Paris (*dixit* Cocteau) sways no more than 5 inches in high winds and shrinks or grows 6 inches according to temperature. For 40 years it remained the highest structure in the world until it was usurped by New York's Chrysler Building, although it acquired an additional 65 feet in 1957 when television antennae were added to existing radio, telegraph, and meteorological apparatus. Mountaineers have scaled it, pilots have tried to fly through its pillars and, in 1909, the Comte de Lambert circled 300 feet above it in a flying machine.

Public spectacle About four million people visit this extraordinary construction annually, so be prepared for a long wait at the elevators. Go to the third floor (at 905 feet) for Paris's most spectacular view, which, on a clear day, extends 42 miles. Hardier folk can attempt the steps in the south pillar that lead up to the first and second platforms (at 185 feet and 375 feet respectively). Above all, don't dismiss its nocturnal transformation. Even if you are not dining in one of the tower's two restaurants, go to the top for a glittering visual feast or at least pass close by for an unforgettable vision of the 292,000-watt interior lighting system, illuminating the intricate structure against the night sky.

Towering figure The engineer Gustave Eiffel kept an office in his tower until his death in 1923. Although this was the ultimate symbol of his skill and imagination, Eiffel left hundreds of other constructions all over the world. Born in 1832 in Burgundy of German stock, he was already working on the famous Bordeaux bridge at the age of 26. Bridges soon became his specialty: iron and the hydraulic methods he used for installing their supports helped to build his reputation. Factories, churches, a synagogue (rue des Tournelles), shops (Le Bon Marché), banks, and, over a period of 18 years, 31 railway viaducts and 17 major bridges all came within his creative sphere. Egypt, Peru, Portugal, Hungary, Bolivia, and Indochina all have their Eiffel monuments, while the U.S. has its 150-foot Statue of Liberty—a mere stripling beside the tower.

Constructive contributions When his wife died at a young age in 1877, Eiffel threw himself heart and soul into his work, never remarrying. Shortly before the tower commission, he was involved in an embroglio over the Suez Canal and was sued for not respecting a deadline. He untied himself from these potentially uncomfortable knots with the help of fellow Freemasons, a powerful pressure group in those days. After his masterwork was built, he continued to produce marvels of engineering and contributed constructions to the 1900 Universal Exhibition. With the saving of the Tower from demolition in 1910, Gustave Eiffel must have been a satisfied man when he died at 91.
Open: daily, 9:30AM–11PM (July and August, 9AM–midnight).

Gustave Eiffel—the bridge engineer who startled the world with his Eiffel Tower in 1887

High jump
Three hundred seventy suicide victims chose this edifice to end their days. Protective shields, finally installed in 1971 on every outdoor platform, put an end to this tragic spinoff.

The "Magician of Iron"
The Eiffel Tower was without a doubt the pinnacle of Gustave Eiffel's lifetime achievements, for which he was nicknamed "magician of iron." He also used the tower for numerous aerodynamic experiments, working from Anteuil where he built the first aerodynamic laboratory.

l'Elysée, Palais de

55–7 rue du Faubourg St.-Honoré, 75008
metro: Miromesnil, Champs-Elysées-Clemenceau

This sumptuous residence has housed French presidents for over a century. Built in 1718, it was greatly altered in 1753 to suit the extravagant tastes of Madame de Pompadour. A radical volte-face came with the Revolution, when the Elysée turned into a public entertainment park, but under Napoleon it reverted to being a private residence—first for his sister, then for his wife Joséphine. Various other notables, including Wellington, Napoleon III (before becoming emperor), and Queen Victoria, passed through its courtyard, garden, and grand staircase before 1873, when it assumed its role as the president's official residence.

Already greatly modified, modernized, and enlarged, the Elysée continues to undergo the decorative whims of each president. Agam's op-art works, commissioned by Pompidou, have since been moved to the Musée d'Art Moderne. Valéry Giscard d'Estaing left his mark above all for inviting in the local street cleaners for a chat on his return from a radical night out. Mitterrand has had many of the salon ceilings painted in a neoclassical style by Gérard Garouste. So who's next?

Not open to the public.

Palais de l'Elysée, official residence of presidents since 1873 and the decision-making center of French politics. The French government meets here every Wednesday

116

A hidden corner in one of the courtyards of the Faubourg St.-Honoré, one of many reminders of bygone centuries here

Espace Salvador Dalí
11 rue Poulbot, 75018
metro: Abbesses
The 1,200-square-yard, black-walled Surrealist interior of the Espace Montmartre is a fitting backdrop for over 300 of Dalí's works (mainly sculptures and illustrations), some never seen in France before this fittingly weird exhibition opened in 1991.
Open: daily, 10–6.

Faubourgs
Inextricably linked with the urban development of Paris, the "faubourgs" still possess an identity of their own. Faubourg means "fake borough" and refers to the extension of inner streets beyond specific city boundaries. Paris's first suburbs have been integrated into the fabric of the city center for centuries, yet the word still has a pejorative ring: "he was born in the faubourgs" implies that someone's origins are not the most sophisticated. The queen of the faubourgs, Edith Piaf, nevertheless built her career on her modest beginnings in **Belleville**, making the faubourg accent chic in itself. Ironically, the oldest faubourg, the **Faubourg St.-Honoré**, which extended the central rue St.-Honoré, is now the hub of Parisian wealth while the **Faubourg St.-Germain** area is a haven for the discreet residences of the bourgeoisie.

Historically, the **Faubourg St.-Antoine**, running east from the Bastille to the place de la Nation, is "the crater from which revolutionary lava escaped most often." Today, more peaceful in spirit, its identity is still linked with the crafts of its former artisans.

The real atmosphere of the faubourgs is found in the area between the **Faubourgs Montmartre** and **Poissonière**. From the Grands Boulevards, the Faubourg Montmartre winds uphill toward Pigalle and Montmartre, carrying in its wake a colorful string of bars and cheap restaurants. Boasting some fine mansions but lacking in major sites, it is mistakenly overlooked by many visitors to Paris.

Le Général
A caricaturist's delight, with his towering height and unmistakable nose, Charles de Gaulle was to some a hero, to others a tyrant: without doubt he was a unique and outspoken French president. His escape to London in World War II and organization of the Free French movement made him a symbol of liberty, but after the war he fell from political favor. De Gaulle's comeback in 1958 led to a new constitution and a strengthened presidency. Age and narrow-mindedness brought his downfall; three years after the student riots and general strikes of 1968, he died at his home in Colombey-les-Deux-Eglises.

Poseurs' Paris

■ **There's no better place than Paris to play at being a jet-setter. Steeped in a tradition of ostentation, its temples of pretension and luxury are legion. An important feature of the Parisian psyche is the ability to flaunt style, which is often but not always necessarily linked with wealth. A fine line divides the BCBG (traditional chic) from the flashier and sometimes more imaginative displays of new money, but for outsiders this is not an essential factor. However, a thick wad of 500 franc notes or a collection of credit cards is ...■**

"Preppies" in Paris
Although a recently coined term, BCBG (*bon chic, bon genre*) has firmly stuck as a label for the Parisian equivalent of preppies. Its subjects hide out in the prosperous 16th arrondissement. Passy and Neuilly shelter hordes of this well-groomed species, clad in finely cut gray or navy suits (both sexes) and a touch of flamboyance symbolized by a Hermès scarf. Sleek discretion is the key. Weekend golf is the pastime.

Eating Glamorous gastronomy is no mean affair in Paris, and the moment you enter the three- and four-*toque* category of the Frenchman's bible, the *Gault Millau*, you are guaranteed not only an elegant setting and sublime victuals, but also a sophisticated array of dining companions. Try the historic monuments, such as **Lucas-Carton**, **Le Grand Véfour**, **La Tour d'Argent**, **Taillevent**, or **Ledoyen**. Allow yourself to be pampered by sycophantic waiters and relax in sensual comfort. And for the grand panacea of Parisian cuisine, book a table (months ahead) at **Robuchon**, where the lobster with artichoke will guarantee your elitist election to paradise.

Drinking Whatever your liquid tastes, Paris will provide the appropriate watering hole, from discreet *salons de thé* to shadowy nocturnal haunts. For the most elegant of breakfasts or teas, head for **Ladurée** in the rue Royale, where you'll wade through tote bags marked Lanvin or Chanel to get to a table. Savor the coffee while enjoying the ceiling fresco of a cherubic pastry chef. In the nearby rue de Rivoli reigns the historic **Angélina's**, also straight out of the Belle Epoque, as are some of its regulars. As day turns to night, head for **Le Forum** in the boulevard Malesherbes, where one of 150 cocktails should put you in the right mood; failing that, carry on to the bar of the **Hôtel George V**, where the champagne concoctions make up for the height of the bar stools. Still thirsty after midnight and on the Left Bank? Then go to Montparnasse's media mecca, **La Closerie des Lilas**, where tinkling piano music, polished wood, and a long history of illustrious drinkers combine to generate a special aura.

Shopping For chic shopping, stick to the Faubourg St.-Honoré, rue Royale, place Vendôme, and rue de la Paix. Have a shirt made to measure at **Charvet**, shoes at **Hermès** (by London bootmaker John Lobb), pick up a watch at **Van Cleef & Arpels**, indulge in a new haircut at **Carita's**, then stop for a snack at **Caviar Kaspia**. Short on household goods? **Lalique** in the rue Royale will supply a nice range of frosted crystal and **Christofle**, across the street, has the lobster forks. Need some new

asparagus dishes? Then head around the corner to **Au Bain Marie**, a haven for more imaginative BCBGs.

Sleeping For one of the world's best siestas, go to the sparkling **Crillon** and stretch out in a spacious suite with its terraced view over the Concorde. Or book in at Paris's first "grand hotel," the gilded and chandeliered **Meurice**, which dates from 1815. Then try the **Raphaël** on the avenue Kléber for a quick transposition to a country château atmosphere, increasingly appreciated by the film world. Or join the *crème de la crème* and ghosts of Proust and Chanel at the eternal **Ritz**.

Walking For a glamorous stroll you can definitely strike off the Champs-Elysées. Instead, keep to the streets of stylish shopping (above) or, for more bucolic surroundings, the shady paths of the **Parc Monceau**.

Dancing If you can talk your way in (no mean achievement), **Castel's** and **Régine's** remain Paris's glossiest nightspots, where a monied international set rubs shoulders on the dance floors. Or join the jet-setting businessmen and top models at **Olivia Valère** in the rue du Colisée.

119

Penniless Paris

■ **Paris is not solely reserved for the rich and famous, as many an impoverished writer or artist has found out. Its easygoing cafés make ideal focal points for struggling creators of all sorts and visitors on extra-low budgets. And you don't have to sleep under the bridges to survive ...■**

120

Tips for drinkers

For drinks and snacks, remember that prices are almost 50 percent cheaper if you stand at the bar. Beer drinkers should ask for *une pression* or *un demi*, signifying draught beer, as opposed to the pricier bottled variety. *Café au lait*, or *café crème* and tea are expensive customs—try and convert to black coffee, *un café*, the cheapest possible beverage.

A typical backstreet brasserie with its small tables and chairs overflowing onto the streets makes an ideal venue for a reasonably priced lunch

Locomotion Much of central Paris can be covered on foot, but there are moments when a metro or bus ride is unavoidable—and even welcome. Make sure you use either a carnet of 10 tickets (valid for all central Paris transportation) or a weekly *coupon jaune*, a better deal than the tourist-oriented Paris Visite, which provides unlimited transportation for three or five days. If you're really dug in for a longer stay, buy a *carte orange*, which whisks you around for a month. All season tickets are available at metro stations and are pretty reasonable for a reliable and efficient service.

Accommodations Give the faubourgs a go! Enjoy the colorful life of a less central quartier, hang out in local cafés, sample its bistros and markets, and you'll save yourself the price of a few more nights. One- and two-star hotels beyond the Bastille, around République, the Faubourg Montmartre or the Gare de l'Est, deep in Montparnasse, or as far south as Chinatown will come up with some surprisingly acceptable accommodations at (relatively) low prices.

Gastronomic survival If you're not developing the baguette-saucisson-and-cheap-wine-in-the-hotel-

bedroom technique, there are plenty of bistros that will supply you with a copious feed for 60 francs or so. Lunchtime fixed menus, even in classier areas, are invariably excellent value, as are the plats du jour in cafés and brasseries. Forget mineral water and order a free *carafe d'eau* or drink wine by the *pichet*.

Evening feeds prove more difficult, but not insoluble. Although much frequented by tourists, **Chartier** and its lesser known sibling, **Drouot**, provide good basic fare in extraordinary settings—but get there early. In the 5th arrondissement, a multitude of Greek, Italian, Vietnamese, and even French restaurants (try the **Bistrot de la Sorbonne**) cater to a vast student population. Head up the steep rue des Boulangers, where you can take your pick from a handful of bustling bistros. Alternatively, continue uphill to the rue Mouffetard, still a favorite despite being under touristic siege for a decade or so, and stop at **Le Pavé aux Herbes** for taramasalata and brochette.

In the 6th there is no shortage either: at the **Polidor** you eat with the spirits of Verlaine and James Joyce, while **Le Petit Saint-Benoît** offers bland but ancient décor and solid French cuisine. The popular **Restaurant des Beaux-Arts** is substantial and always fun. Off St.-Germain, the narrow rue Grégoire de Tours has a string of low-priced Greek and Italian haunts close to the action, and you can't go wrong for atmosphere and budget if you dive into the hub of streets surrounding rue de la Huchette: the odors of shish kebab announce an irresistible menu.

Don't forget Chinatown, in the 13th arrondissement, which feeds millions at low rates, while Belleville and La Goutte d'Or, although far from the madding crowd, have an insurpassable mixture of Asian, Arab, and African restaurants, all very reasonable. Couscous, served with meat or vegetables, makes an excellent cheap and balanced diet wherever you are in Paris.

Culture Entrance fees to museums mount up, so it may be worth investing in a *carte musée*, valid for one, three, or five consecutive days and providing unlimited entry to all monuments and museums, as well as avoiding the ticket lines.

Otherwise Sundays, although sometimes crowded, are often half price and in some cases free. Don't forget that private art galleries cost nothing (see pages 66–8), Parisian architecture and views are free, and street artists provide itinerant amusement.

Shopping Apart from the flea markets, Paris has a good line in cheap supermarkets and stores such as **Prisunic** and **Monoprix**, where you can pick up household gadgets or fashion accessories for unbeatable prices. Fashion victims should seek out the *dépôt-vente* shops, where little-worn designer and couture gear is sold at a fraction of its original price. Then there are the ubiquitous **TATI** branches (boulevard Rochechouart, rue de Rennes, République), where, if you fight through the crowds of concierges, you can dress yourself up for ridiculously small amounts, although no one's guaranteeing the quality.

121

For the cheapest lunch in Paris, look for the many stalls selling freshly-baked croissants, croque-monsieurs, and crusty baguettes

The Folies-Bergère, still going after all these years, is the oldest and best-known music hall in Paris

Gobelins tapestry center
Over 5,000 tapestries have been woven at the Manufacture des Gobelins, using a palette of almost 15,000 colors and including designs by Poussin, Boucher, Gromaire, Picasso, and Matisse.

Royal tapestries
When Jean Gobelin, a Flemish dyer, discovered the secret of making a scarlet dye and founded a small family business in 1440, he would never have imagined that one century later it would develop into the royal tapestry center. Today the internationally renowned factory is government-owned, with every item commissioned by the state. It is possible to watch the weavers only in natural light, as artificial illumination changes the appearance of the colors.

Folies-Bergère
32 rue Richer, 75009
metro: Cadet, Le Peletier
Tacky it may be, but the Folies-Bergère still stands after 125 years. Its bar has been immortalized on canvas by Manet, and this was where the likes of Mistinguett and Josephine Baker thrilled the audiences of the *années folles*, while the acrobatic Tiller Girls swung along astride their merry-go-round horses under its dome. The Folies-Bergère has today lost much of its sparkle and daring. Feathers, bare breasts, sequins, and plastic smiles seem a little systematic, as the army of dancers goes through its repertoire of *Bal à Versailles* or the Eiffel Tower can-can. Whatever, it is still the least pretentious of the Parisian cabarets and won't cost you an arm and a leg.

► Fondation Cartier
261 Boulevard Raspail, 75014
metro: Raspail
Ten years ago the Fondation Cartier (of jewelery and watches fame) began an experiment in corporate sponsorship by creating a sculpture park and contemporary art exhibition center in a lush park at Jouyen-Josas. In 1994, it took up residence in central Paris on the former site of the American Center. Its new building is the work of the architect Jean Nouvel (famed for the Institut du Monde Arabe). Huge glass windows open onto a garden landscaped by artist Lothar Baumgarten, making nature overobtrusive for the ground-floor exhibitions.

An impressive program of thematic exhibitions is planned (tel: 42 18 56 50 for details) to be shown parallel to selections from the foundation's permanent collection. Some 600 works by international contemporary artists cover disciplines ranging from video to painting, sculpture, installations, and design work.
Open: daily except Monday, noon–8; Thursday noon–10.

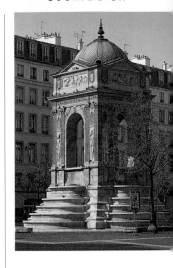

▶▶ Fontaine des Innocents

square des Innocents, 75001
metro: Châtelet, Les Halles

Sheets of water have gushed down three sides of this superb Renaissance fountain, designed by Pierre Lescot and sculpted by Jean Goujon, since it was erected in 1550. Now the focus of attention for the cruisers and bruisers of Les Halles, its cooling influence is even more necessary. For centuries this square was the site of a cemetery as well as a meeting place for the food merchants of Les Halles. In 1786, when not much available soil was left, it was decided to transfer the two million or so rotting skeletons to the Catacombs. The fountain, originally on the corner of the rue St.-Denis, was then shifted to its present central site and acquired its fourth side.

Fontainebleau see pages 198–9.

▶ Furstenberg, Place

metro: St.-Germain

Once the *cour d'honneur* of the abbot of St.-Germain's palace and named after Cardinal Furstenberg, who rebuilt it in 1699, this little square embodies everyone's dreams of Paris in the spring. Blessed with four perfumed magnolia trees, old-fashioned street lamps, and an unaffected architectural harmony, it makes a balmy evening's favorite for musicians and promenading couples. The corner houses, Nos. 6 and 8, which include Delacroix's former apartment and studio, were once the palace stables.

Giverny see pages 200–1.

Jean Goujon's 16th-century Fontaine des Innocents

▶ Gobelins, Manufacture des

42 avenue des Gobelins, 75013
metro: Gobelins

Not a factory churning out little creatures, but this has been the official tapestry factory since the heyday of Louis XIV. Originally a dyeworks set up by the Gobelin brothers, then taken over by Flemish weavers, it soon attracted royal attention through the eyes of Colbert, Louis XIV's astute minister. By 1662, it became the royal tapestry center and rapidly expanded to include furniture and carpet workshops. Much of the interior decoration of Versailles was woven, carved, or inlaid here and even Marie-Antoinette deigned to visit the workshops. You can still see the centuries-old looms clicking away today, guided by expert weavers who start their training at age 16. The interesting 1½-hour guided tour also takes in the famous Savonnerie carpet workshops.
Open: Tuesday, Wednesday, Thursday at 2PM and 2:45PM.

▶ Goutte d'Or

metro: Barbès-Rochechouart

Immediately east of Pigalle, the poetic-sounding Goutte d'Or (Drop of Gold) is a hive of cosmopolitan activity, where Arabs and Africans live, shop, lunch, dine, and hang out in an atmosphere straight out of Algiers or Abidjan. As with Belleville, the property developers are

123

A sudden death
One sunny day in 1610, Henri IV, traveling along the rue des Innocents, requested the coach's leather hood be lowered, despite earlier warnings from an astrologer that he would die that day. As he entered rue de la Ferronnerie, a lunatic called Ravaillac stabbed Henri and he died later that day.

Shedding its light across the river: the Grand Palais' massive roof, designed by Charles Girault

Captured on film
One permanent exhibition exists in the Grand Palais: the Jacques-Henri Lartigue donation, displaying the photographer's whimsical images of early 20th-century society.

moving in fast, while the city council is working hard at "cleaning up" an area also notorious for drug dealers and squatters. If you're seeking a friendly, low-priced couscous joint, go there on a summer evening when the locals congregate on doorsteps. This is not chic Paris—and unfortunately it won't last.

▶▶ Grand Palais
avenue Winston-Churchill, 75008
metro: Champs-Elysées–Clémenceau
Its soaring iron and glass domes visible from far along the river, the Grand Palais is another example of ambitious turn-of-the-century architecture. Built, together with the Petit Palais opposite, for the 1900 Universal Exhibition, it has since hosted hundreds of temporary fairs and art salons. Its west wing, which opens onto the avenue Franklin-Roosevelt, houses the Palais de la Découverte (*open*: Tuesday to Saturday, 9:30–6; Sunday, 10–7), a well-organized science museum that has a superb planetarium. The main halls on the east side exhibit art retrospectives and salons such as the FIAC, Paris's annual contemporary art fair.
Open: Thursday to Monday, 10–8; Wednesday, 10–10.

▶ Grand Véfour, Le
17 rue de Beaujolais, 75001
metro: Palais-Royal, Pyramides
Ornately mirrored, gilded, and painted, Le Grand Véfour restaurant is a living historic monument. Peep through the windows at its Restoration painted ceiling and glass-protected dancing walls: it is a seductive delight. Nestling in a neoclassical colonnade since the late 18th century, when the Palais-Royal was the heart of Parisian intellectual life, Le Grand Véfour has seen diners such as Napoleon, Victor Hugo, and Colette (who lived upstairs).

▶ Grévin, Musée
10 boulevard Montmartre, 75009
metro: rue Montmartre
Over a century old, the Musée Grévin is the Parisian answer to London's Madame Tussaud's. Throngs of immobile figures beckon you through the city's history, and blood and gore is assured in the Revolution section. Elsewhere, rock and film stars are aligned with presidents, and an annex in the Forum des Halles (*open*: Monday to Saturday, 10:30–6:45; Sunday, 1–6:30) displays scenes from the Belle Epoque.
Open: daily, 1–6 (school vacations, 10–7).

▶▶▶ Guimet, Musée (Musée Nationale d'Arts Asiatiques Guimet)

6 place d'Iéna, 75016
metro: Iéna, Boissière
This superb museum exhibits a remarkable display of oriental antiquities, built up from the industrialist Emile Guimet's 1879 collection. Much of the Louvre's Asiatic department has been transferred here to widen the panorama of sculptures, carvings, paintings, and artifacts from Indochina, China, Japan, Tibet, Afghanistan, Pakistan, and India.

Particularly stunning, the ground-floor halls contain Khmer art, which includes serene stone Buddhas and Hindu gods (6th- to 12th-century). In colorful contrast, the adjoining rooms display richly painted Tibetan and Nepalese tankas and intricate inlaid silverwork.

On the first floor, the Indian department includes early Mathura and Amarâvati carvings, south Indian bronze deities, and Moghul and Rajput miniatures. A rich Chinese department includes the Calmann collection, a wide-ranging display of porcelain. Both China and Japan are also represented in a separate collection at the museum annex (19 avenue d'Iéna), Le Panthéon Bouddhique, where Buddhas of all periods, mediums, and sizes meditate for eternity.
Open: Wednesday to Monday, 9:45–5:45.

▶▶ Les Halles

metro: Les Halles
RER: Châtelet–Les Halles
The "belly of Paris" (*dixit*, Emile Zola) has undergone multiple transformations since the great days of the food market that started around 1100. Neatly delineated by the rue Beaubourg in the east, the rue du Louvre in the west, the northern rue Réaumur, and southern rue de Rivoli, Les Halles functioned as a market until 1969. The grocers and butchers were then moved out to the suburb of Rungis and their superb 1860s Baltard pavilions were demolished (only one was preserved, now installed at Nogent-sur-Marne).

It took the city council and government 10 years of wrangling to decide how to fill the gaping hole: although the result is aesthetically disastrous, Les Halles has recovered its role as a central commercial and social hub. Venture below ground into the **Forum** for shopping, cinemas, swimming, billiards, videos, or concerts. Stay above ground for basic food and drink, hustlers, street artists, et al. The traditional 5AM onion soup can still be consumed at **Au Pied de Cochon**, but your fellow suppers will be tourists, not market vendors. Yet on a stroll through the surrounding streets you'll discover atmospheric bars and restaurants that haven't changed for a century.

▶ Hammam

La Mosquée, 19/39 rue Geoffroy-St.-Hilaire, 75005
metro: Censier–Daubenton
Sick of Parisian chic or lowlife? Then go to the Turkish baths at La Mosquée where, around a marble fountain sheltered by a tiled dome, you can mentally waft yourself to Marrakesh. The steam of the 90°C (194°F)

The Paris mosque
Hammam, home of the Grand Imam and spiritual center for the city's Muslim community, was built in Hispano-Moorish style during the 1920s. The grand patio was inspired by the Alhambra, with its decorative mosaics and fine cedar and eucalyptus woodwork. With an impressive 108-foot-high minaret and numerous ornately decorated domes, the mosque is considered to be a modern gem of European Islamic architecture.

Les Halles in its 20th-century guise—a traditional market venue for almost nine centuries, today Les Halles is one of the biggest shopping malls in Europe

*The Musée de
l'Histoire de France*

"Nothing"
At the Musée de l'Histoire de France, keep an eye out for Louis XVI's classic diary entry for July 14, 1789, the day the Revolution broke out: he quite simply inscribed *Rien* ("nothing").

Modern Arab architecture
The remarkable architecture of the Institut du Monde Arabe combines modern materials with the spirit of traditional Arab architecture. The south facade consists of 1,600 identical metal light screens that electronically filter the sunlight as it enters the building. Their design is taken from the carved wooden screens called moucharabiyahs, often found on buildings from Morocco to Southeast Asia.

sauna helps... allow three to four hours for the full relaxing benefit. Finish with a mint tea.
Open: for women: Monday, Wednesday, Thursday, Saturday; for men: Friday, Sunday.

▶▶▶ l'Histoire de France, Musée de
Hôtel de Soubise, 60 rue des Francs-Bourgeois, 75003
metro: Rambuteau, Hôtel de Ville
Although some of the historic documents displayed here are fascinating, the principal interest lies in the museum's sumptuous architecture. It was mostly built by Delamair in 1709 for the Princesse de Soubise, by extending a 14th-century manor (whose double-towered entrance on the rue des Archives remains intact), and the interiors were decorated in the 1730s by Boffrand. The richness of this period accompanies you from the majestic Cour d'Honneur into the ground-floor palace apartments, where Boffrand employed the talents of painters such as Boucher, Van Loo, and Natoire. The ornate decoration continues throughout the princess's first-floor apartments, where the museum documents are now displayed. Letters written by Charlemagne and Joan of Arc, the wills of Louis XIV and Napoleon, and Marie-Antoinette's last missive before the chop are worth a read.
Open: Wednesday to Monday, 1:45–5:45.

▶ Holographie, Musée de
Level 1, Forum-des-Halles, 75001; enter from the Porte Lescot
metro, RER: Châtelet–Les Halles
Buried in this central labyrinth is a museum favorite for children of all ages. Although invented in 1947, holography has only recently become known to the general public, mainly through the images on credit cards and beer taps. This small museum shows the use of laser technology for creating 3-D images of antiquities. Some of the holograms are fun, and even appear to move, but others are less inspiring.
Open: Monday to Saturday, 10–7; Sunday, 1–7.

▶ Huchette, Rue de la
metro, RER: St.-Michel
One of Paris's oldest streets, dating back to 1284, the rue de la Huchette is known today for its unadventurous gastronomy: it's souvlaki or souvlaki. At the heart of the Latin Quarter, students and tourists pile in here thinking they have discovered authentic Paris along its cobbled, narrow length. Two symbols remain of the 1950s, when this street experienced a real high: a minute theater and a basement jazz bar. Still running at the theater since the days when Ionesco first staged them are his plays *La Cantatrice Chauve* and *La Leçon*. Downstairs in the crowded *caveau* (cellar) at No. 5, bebop has hardly missed a note.

▶▶▶ Institut du Monde Arabe
1 rue des Fossés St.-Bernard, 75005
metro: Jussieu
Difficult to miss as you cross the Seine from the Ile St.-Louis, the Institut du Monde Arabe benefits both from

its strategic location on the Quai St.-Bernard and its sleek contemporary architecture. Founded in 1980, it moved into these custom-built premises in 1987, partly financed by the government and partly by 20 Arab states anxious to encourage cultural exchanges between Islam and the West. This aim is achieved through temporary exhibitions, a permanent museum collection, concerts, lectures, a library, and research facilities. Although budgets remain a thorny point—recent upheavals in the Middle East having stemmed the financial flow—and the museum is still sparsely filled, the institute is an attraction for anyone interested in the Arab world.

Before looking at anything else, notice the powerful aluminum and glass building designed by Jean Nouvel and the Architecture Studio. Apart from the light-sensitive diaphragm windows on the south facade, the transparent elevator shaft alone justifies the visit. Spirit yourself to the ninth-floor terrace, which provides magnificent views west along the river and north toward the Bastille. In the elegant, pricey restaurant you can enjoy the same views, along with baklava or shish kebab—or, more economically, enjoy a juice on the terrace.

Design priorities continue on the three floors of the museum, where astrolabs vie for attention with display systems. From Spain to India, spanning the 9th to 19th centuries, the ceramics, bronzes, ivories, and carpets of this collection reflect the brilliance of this civilization.
Open: daily (except Monday), 10–6 (library, 1–8).

The striking facade of the Institut du Monde Arabe, with its many Arab-Islamic treasures

■ Giving a definitive opinion about the best features in Paris is a hazardous enterprise. Seasons change, as do quality and popularity, all decisive factors in the enjoyment of certain rendezvous spots. Luckily, however, there are always unchangeable favorites and these include the places that are listed below ...■

Café bests The best café with a view is an outdoor terrace in central Paris, on the 10th floor of the department store **La Samaritaine**, overlooking Pont-Neuf. It is open only during the warmer months (generally May to October), and is a popular lunch spot for local office workers, but always has room at other times. The view due south and either way along the Seine of monuments within spitting distance is spectacular. A lookout point above displays an enameled "artist's impression" of Paris in 1900, and is good for comparing with today's horizon. A similarly central but more chic terrace with a view concentrating on the Ile St.-Louis and the Bastille, is on the ninth floor of the

Best for refreshments with a panoramic view—La Samaritaine department store

Institut du Monde Arabe. More a glorified tearoom, it is open 3–7 in spring and summer.

Antique bests If you are looking for top-class antiques, don't go to the **Marché de Vanves,** Paris's best junk market (*brocante* in French). Open Saturday and Sunday mornings at the Porte de Vanves, it has now established itself among young couples as the place to go for finding the ultimate item of battered yet stylish furniture. Sellers are full of witty banter and always ready to "discuss" a price. Rainy days, although not the most enjoyable, do lead to the best bargains.

Oyster bar bests Although difficult to pronounce, the best oyster bar, Le Bar à Huïtres (112 boulevard du Montparnasse) is without a doubt the most convenient. Oysters can be eaten in any quantity you like: on the sidewalk outside, or with more attention, seated at a bar stool inside. *Belons, fines de claires*, or *Marennes* are all superbly fresh and immaculately opened by friendly Bretons, and are best washed down with a pitcher of Sauvignon or a bottle of young Muscadet. **Montparnasse** is traditionally the seafood center of Paris because of its proximity to trains arriving directly from Brittany and Normandy. Remember that oysters are best consumed during the "r" months (September to April).

Tea break bests In winter months, *salons de thé* are easily the most accessible and comfortable places to recover from weary pavement- and museum-bashing, often graced with deep armchairs, reading matter, and classical music: they are an alternative to the bright, noisy atmosphere of bistros and cafés. A favorite in the Marais is **Les Enfants Gatés** (43 rue des Francs-Bourgeois). Convenient for the Musée Picasso, the Carnavalet, or the place des Vosges, it is a long-standing, unpretentious tearoom, which serves delicious cakes, savory tarts, and salads throughout the day (open 12:30–8).

Escapism bests If the slickness of central Paris restaurants and settings is becoming too much, head north of the center to the backstreets of the faubourgs. In the suitably dilapidated surroundings of the Passage Brady (metro: Château d'Eau, Strasbourg St.-Denis), you can indulge in Pakistani and Indian food in any of the countless budget restaurants that line this covered passageway. In summer, candlelit tables spill outside, spice levels run high, and the occasional errant rat only adds to the flavors of exoticism.

Studio bests For a fascinating view of how a late 19th-century artist lived, go to the best artist's studio-museum in Paris, the **Musée Gustave Moreau** (14 rue de La Rochefoucauld, 9e; tel: 48 74 38 50). Although the lower floors (his studio) have been open to the public for years, the upstairs apartment was only reconstructed and renovated in late 1991 and presents his rooms with the objects and decoration he chose. Moreau himself (1826–98) prepared the museum for posterity shortly before his death, and over 6,000 of his eery symbolist works are exhibited in this elegant townhouse. At last the artist's wish has been fully accomplished.

Bakery bests Parisians have been lamenting for several years the gradual disappearance of the good old baguette, with its crispy golden crust and soft white interior. Many boulangeries have turned to industrial baking methods, and that inimitable chewiness has given way to a bland, anonymous sponginess. But all is not lost. What has really taken Paris by storm over the last few years is a type of bread called **Pain Poilâne,** named after Lionel Poilâne and now airlifted to New York and Tokyo and sold all over Paris. For your first experience, go to the family bakery, 58 rue du Cherche-Midi, 6e, to savor this bread, which is made only with hand-ground French flour, yeast, and sea salt and cooked in a wood oven.

The Sun King's wounded soldiers were given a home at Les Invalides

The tomb of Marshall Foch in Les Invalides. Foch was overall commander of French, British, and American armies toward the end of World War I

► ► **Les Invalides**

metro: Latour–Maubourg, Invalides, Varenne

Pompous, severe, authoritarian, the 643-foot facade of the Hôtel des Invalides masks a masterpiece of French classical architecture. Designed by Libéral Bruand, it was completed in 1676 by Hardouin-Mansart, who later incorporated the impressive Eglise du Dôme (1705), a commission by Louis XIV to reflect the greatness of his reign. For once the Sun King was thinking of others, as Les Invalides was designed to house old soldiers, many disabled (hence the name) and reduced in their old age to dire straits. Six thousand once resided there; today under a hundred remain.

The main attraction for time-limited visitors is **Napoleon's tomb**, which presides gloriously over the crypt of the Dôme. Twenty years after his death on the distant island of Saint Helena, Napoleon's body was returned to France and, in 1861, like a Russian doll, it was encased in six layers of coffins crowning an immense granite base. Other military tombs fill the chapels of this superb baroque church, rich in painted cupolas, graceful arches, columns, sculptures, bas-reliefs, and inlaid marble floors. An ornate gilded, garlanded, and ribbed dome completes these glories.

Not to be confused with the Eglise du Dôme, the adjacent Eglise St.-Louis also concentrates on military memorabilia. Here numerous generals are buried, but more visible are the tattered remains of captured regimental banners hanging from the upper galleries.

On entering Les Invalides through its Cour d'Honneur you will be following in the footsteps of many a military hero, including de Gaulle and Churchill. For the ins and outs of military history, head straight to the **Musée de l'Armée►** (*open*: daily, 10–5). One of the world's largest in this field, its extensive collections of weapons, armor, flags, uniforms, and paintings trace the evolution of warfare from prehistoric days to World War II. Inevitably, Napoleonic relics abound (including his stuffed horse, Vizier), but other periods such as the Second Empire and both World Wars are equally well displayed. Nor is the Orient forgotten: one section specializes in the superbly crafted arms of the Middle and Far East.

In the **Musée des Plans-Reliefs** (*open:* daily, 10–6, winter till 5PM) scale models of fortresses in France and near her borders form a collection that originated under Louis XIV in 1668 and for years remained a military secret.

IRCAM
31 rue St.-Merri, 75004
metro: Hôtel de Ville
Behind the dancing, clanking sculptures of the Fontaine Stravinsky, in the shadow of Beaubourg, stands an understated entrance. It leads to one of France's most important cultural laboratories: below ground lies a high-technology music research center. The founder of IRCAM was composer and conductor Pierre Boulez; here, a team of electronic engineers and composers has unrivaled facilities for acoustic invention and experiment. Concerts and workshops are held in a futuristic auditorium, and visiting composers can try out the 4X, a digital sound processor that performs 220 million operations per second.

►► Jacob, Rue
metro: St.-Germain-des-Prés
Reeking of what everyone expects the Rive Gauche to be, the picturesque rue Jacob is crammed with galleries, antiques shops, bookshops, and interior-decoration shops. Stroll along this street, watching out for the shadows of former residents Racine, Wagner, Mérimée, and Stendhal, but keeping an eye open for ethnic jewelry, astrolabs, art-deco curios, Chinese porcelain, architectural prints, or swathes of sumptuous fabric. The choice is wide and quality generally reliable. Walk east and you'll end up in the Left Bank gallery mecca; go west and you'll eventually arrive at Les Invalides.

► Jacquemart-André, Musée
158 boulevard Haussmann, 75008
metro: St.-Phillipe-du-Roule
Once a prestigious private collection of 17th- to 18th-century European art and Italian Renaissance works, subsequently bequeathed to the nation, the Musée Jacquemart-André disappeared in a cloud of scandal when its curator was accused of appropriating funds. Result: the museum closed, but has now been renovated and reopened. This elegant 1870 mansion displays paintings and drawings by Rubens, Rembrandt, Frans Hals, Van Dyck, Chardin, Boucher, Watteau, and Lancret, alongside Savonnerie carpets and Gobelins tapestries.
Open: Tuesday to Sunday, 9:30–12:30, 1:30–6 by appointment only.

►► Jeu de Paume, Galerie Nationale du
place de la Concorde, 75001
metro: Concorde
Reopened in 1991 after five years of renovation and internal transformation, the Jeu de Paume now turns a rejuvenated face to the public. This is just another in a long string of mutations since its 1878 origins as an indoor tennis court. The Jeu de Paume saw its first exhibition in 1909 and by 1922 became a fully fledged

Place Igor Stravinsky
The charming place Igor Stravinsky, with its modern eccentric fountain and pond of psychedelic sculptures, pays tribute to the great Russian 20th-century composer who made Paris the center for his new style of music, abandoning conventional harmony, rhythm, and form. Indeed, the premier of his iconolastic *The Rite of Spring* in 1913 at the Théâtre des Champs-Elysées led to rioting in the audience. Where better for the innovative IRCAM music studios alongside this unique and extraordinary square?

Experimental music
"Listen to your century" is the slogan of the Ensemble InterContemporain, a group of contemporary instrumentalists based at IRCAM.

Galerie Nationale du Jeu de Paume, built by Napoleon III on the site of an orangery in the Tuileries Garden and famous for its exhibitions of contemporary art

museum, housing a number of outstanding exhibitions. Under the Occupation it was requisitioned by German troops for stocking works seized from Jewish art collectors and intended for transfer to German museums. Immediately after the war, it took on the cloak for which it is still remembered: that of the museum of the Impressionists. For 40 years it attracted millions of visitors (the highest density of any museum in the world) before closing its doors in 1986, after the exodus of its rich collection to the Musée d'Orsay.

Today, its successfully modernized interior contains several spacious galleries used for temporary exhibitions of international contemporary art.

Open: Wednesday to Friday, noon–7 (Tuesday till 9:30), Saturday to Sunday, 10–7.

▶ Justice, Palais de

2 boulevard du Palais, 75001
metro: Cité

"Liberté, Egalité, Fraternité" are the words inscribed above the entrance at the top of the grand marble steps leading into France's symbol of civil authority. It is only since the Revolution that the palace took on its present function. Before that it played royal palace, with many architectural transformations, from Roman times until 1358, when Charles V abandoned it completely. Turned over to the Parliament (the law court), it acquired a different aspect during the Revolution, when summary judgments were passed and over 2,500 prisoners left the Cour du Mai by the cartload, destined for the guillotine. The May trees have gone from the courtyard, as have the knitting gossips, but the main lobby (the 17th-century Salle des Pas-Perdus) is still thick with black-robed lawyers, judges, and plaintiffs. Don't miss the stunningly decorated blue and gold Première Chambre Civile, once possibly Louis IX's bedroom and later used by the Revolutionary Tribunal. It is possible to watch the action in most of the courts, but your French may not be up to the animated repartees.

Open: Monday to Friday, 9–5.

What's in a name?
The Jeu de Paume, meaning "game played with the palm of the hand," was originally built in 1851 as a real or "royal" tennis court at the west end of the Jardin des Tuileries. However, when lawn tennis became more popular than real tennis, the court was used to exhibit artworks.

▶▶▶ Louvre

rue de Rivoli, 75001
metro: Palais-Royal, Louvre

The Louvre represents an astonishing historical continuum of French rulers from the Middle Ages to the present day—and it is not over yet. Since 1981, this palatial museum has been in constant mutation, undergoing restoration and underground extension. Guiding these radical changes is the American architect I. M. Pei, whose transparent pyramid now crowns the Cour Napoléon. Nor have these transformations been without their archeological surprises: medieval fortifications have been thrown up in the wake of the bulldozers, along with thousands of other disparate objects, mundane or royal.

How to visit To do the museum and your intellect any kind of justice, several visits should be planned, bearing in mind the late opening hours on Mondays and Wednesdays when waits are distinctly shorter. High points of the collections are well signposted and regularly revised plans are available at the entrance. Between 1992 and autumn 1993 (bicentenary of the museum opening) 10,000 works were shuffled around; by 1997 at least the same number again will change place as renovations are gradually completed. For this reason, you may find certain sections closed.

History Its eventful background first took palatial form under Charles V who, in the late 14th century, transformed Philippe Auguste's fortress into a turreted medieval castle. It was not until the wily Renaissance king, François I, that the Louvre again hosted a royal presence. Considerable rebuilding was instigated, mostly designed by Pierre Lescot in 1546. François I, a man of taste, initiated the Louvre collection by looting Titians and Raphaels from Italy, and also brought the *Mona Lisa* and its creator, da Vinci, to France.

Consolation prize Strong-willed as ever, Catherine de Médicis had a completely new palace built in 1578 to compensate for her husband's accidental death in their Marais palace. It was here that she extorted from her hapless son the order for the Saint Bartholomew's Day massacre in 1572. The new royal residence, the Palais des Tuileries, was at the far end of the present Louvre, looking out across the Tuileries gardens.

Louis XIII set about extending the Cour Carrée, site of the original fortress, but abruptly stopped for financial reasons. Not so his son, Louis XIV, who brought in his pet architect Le Vau (conceiver of Versailles) to complete his father's project before the court transferred lock, stock, and barrel to Versailles. The Louvre's golden days were almost over, as the last king to live in the palace was Louis XV, and this was only while the Palais des Tuileries was being cleaned.

New role Meanwhile, other purposes were found for this vast building: concert hall, art gallery, and theater, it was also invaded by tenants, in particular a colony of artists, including Bouchardon and Boucher. Less socially acceptable were the squatters, "cabaret" artists, and

133

The Tour de l'Horloge
The extensive Palais de Justice complex decorates the quays of the River Seine with its many ornate ancient towers, including the unusual square 14th-century Tour de l'Horloge (see page 108), featuring the first public clock in the world. Beneath the clock face is the Latin inscription: "This clock which divides the day into twelve equal parts is a lesson that justice must be protected and the law defended."

Odd tradition
Louis XIV used the Salle des Caryatides for an unusual ceremony, when he annually washed the feet of 13 paupers.

LOUVRE

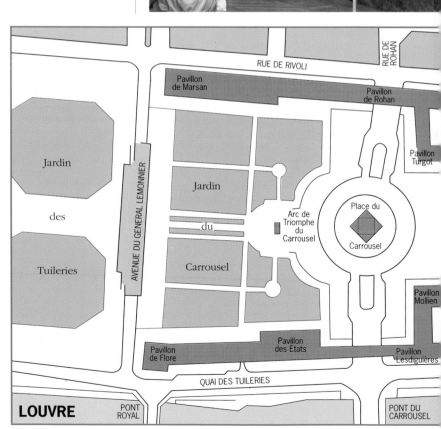

Did you know?
When the Louvre was opened to the public, the royal collection numbered over 2,500 works. Today there are over 30,000 exhibited. The Louvre's glass pyramid is cleaned monthly by eight professional mountaineers using 176 gallons of detergent.

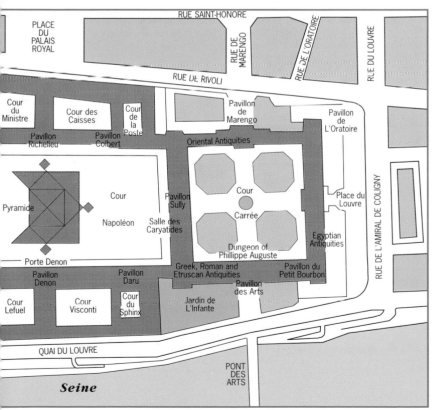

The Louvre—its old and new aspects. Its most recent addition, the glass pyramid entrance, was opened in 1989

The Future
By 1996, the Louvre will be the largest museum in the world, covering a mere 287,000 square yards (almost doubling its area).

whores who set up in and outside its walls, creating such a slum that in 1750 it narrowly escaped demolition. Another close shave came during the Revolution, when the Louvre was a tempting candidate for mob arson, but in 1793, a museum was opened to the public in the Grande Galerie—the Musée de la République.

Revival came with Napoleon, who moved into the Palais des Tuileries—severely ransacked by the mob—and celebrated his marriage to Marie-Louise in the Louvre. Always ready to leave his mark, Napoleon set about creating a central courtyard dominated by the Arc du Carrousel, building a northern wing, and adding floors. Equally important was Napoleon's contribution to the wealth of the museum, as at every one of his numerous victories, ransoms and looting increased the Louvre stock. Under Napoleon III, considerable extension finally united the Louvre and the Palais des Tuileries, although this union was short-lived: in 1871 the Tuileries palace was burnt to the ground by the Commune.

The Museum Entrance to the Louvre is through the unmistakable glass pyramid, which leads down into a gleaming marble underworld of further entrances for each wing. A gigantic bookshop, the *chalcographie* (print) department, a café, and restaurant all contribute to the animation of this crossroads, which also leads through to a vast shopping center beneath the Carrousel. The new area also contains the **Centre de la Mode** for professional fashion shows. On the east side of the Hall Napoléon, follow the Sully entrance to visit the impressive medieval remains of Philippe Auguste's

dungeons (c.1200) and galleries exhibiting pottery and royal artifacts found during excavations.

On the ground and first floor of the Sully wing are exhibited, at the far end, Egyptian antiquities, while the extensive Greek, Roman, and Etruscan collections are immediately to the right of the entrance. Here you will find the eternally serene *Venus de Milo* and, in the corner staircase of the Denon wing, the soaring *Victory of Samothrace*, one of whose mutilated hands is exhibited in a case nearby (it was excavated nearly a century later). In the southeastern corner of this wing is the **Salle des Caryatides**. This is the oldest surviving room of the palace built for Henri II and is named after the four monumental statues by Jean Goujon that support the end gallery.

The Orient On the north side, galleries of oriental antiquities are slowly being moved into place. A highlight of this section is the Cour Khorsabad, a skylit courtyard displaying the massive sculptural facades of crowned and winged bulls from the Assyrian Palace of Khorsabad (c.713 BC).

The paintings For many visitors, the Louvre means painting. Take the Denon entrance to the first floor, allowing a quick detour through the Italian sculpture section on the ground floor to look at, among the Bellinis, Della Robbias, and Donatellos, Michelangelo's

two formidable Slaves. Above is the Grande Galerie, where large-scale paintings by David, Gros, Géricault, and Delacroix still hang alongside Italian Renaissance masterpieces (da Vinci, Raphael, Titian); here, too, is the *Mona Lisa*, which is usually hidden from view by crowds of admirers.

French painting of the 18th and 19th centuries (Watteau, Boucher, Chardin, Fragonard, Robert, Ingres, Corot) is now concentrated on the second floor of the Cour Carrée, linking the Sully and Richelieu wings. Flemish, Dutch, and Northern schools complete the galleries of the magnificently renovated Richelieu wing on this floor while below, on the first floor, are exhibited the fabulous Trésor de St.-Denis and objets d'art.

Open: Wednesday to Monday, 9–6; Monday (Richelieu wing only) and Wednesday until 9:45PM.

Grand entrance
On either side of the entrance leading into the Louvre from the Palais-Royal, two immense glassed-in courtyards display monumental French sculpture, including the original *Chevaux de Marly*.

The Louvre galleries contain one of the world's greatest art collections including Venus de Milo *and* Leonardo da Vinci's Mona Lisa

The monumental 17th-century Palais du Luxembourg—the first palace built in Paris during "the century of palaces"—houses the Sénat, France's upper parliamentary house

► **Luxembourg, Palais du**
15 rue de Vaugirard, 75006
metro/RER: Luxembourg

Yet another symbol of the vagaries of French history, the Palais du Luxembourg and its famous gardens were originally commissioned by Marie de Médicis, the widow of the assassinated Henri IV. Bored with the Louvre, her idea was to build a palace that would remind her of her native Florence. After she had acquired the property from Duke Francis of Luxembourg, in 1612, the architect Salmon de Brosse was given plans of the Pitti Palace for inspiration and work started in 1615. However, by the time it was completed in 1631 she had twice been forced into exile: once by her own son, Louis XIII, and (following a reconciliation with the king) again by the powerful Cardinal Richelieu. She died penniless in exile in Cologne.

Many of the fabulous works of art commissioned for its interior have since been moved. The series of 24 allegorical paintings by Rubens depicting Marie de Médicis' life now hang in the Louvre's Galerie Médicis. Major renovation undertaken by Chalgrin (who later designed the Arc de Triomphe) was rudely interrupted by the Revolution, when the palace took on the role of prison (keeping out of trouble, among others, Danton, the De Noailles family, and Camille Desmoulins) before passing into the hands of the Directoire. Chalgrin's work resumed and by 1804 the palace was ready to receive the newly created Senate, which still meets here today. Delacroix added to the rich interior in 1847 by painting the library ceiling with homages to Virgil, Homer, and Dante, and the architect Alphonse de Gisors made major additions, including the fabulous Salle des Conférences.

War and peace After almost a century of relative calm, during World War II the Palais du Luxembourg was occupied by the head of the Luftwaffe for the western front, and its gardens were soon riddled with underground air-raid shelters. Today its political role and promenading popularity have regained the upper hand. Don't forget to pay homage to the instigator of this palace at the shady Fontaine Médicis. Set in one of the few original Italianate features, the fountain sculptures (added later) depict a bronze cyclops, Polyphemus, glaring downward at the innocent marble lovers, Acis and Galatea. Leaving no stone untouched, the reverse side, facing the rue de Médicis, boasts a bas-relief of Leda and the swan (1807). *Open*: to the public only one day a year—September 17, 9–6 (tel: 42 34 20 00).

Lycée Henri IV
23 rue Clovis, 75005
metro/RER: Luxembourg
In the heart of the intellectual 5th arrondissement, the Lycée Henri IV is one of France's most prestigious high schools and claims Jean-Paul Sartre among its former teachers. It was built in 1796 on the site of an abbey devoted to Ste.-Geneviève, the patron saint of Paris, and a former basilica founded by Clovis, the man who beat the Romans in AD 497. Once the Revolution had swept by, only the Gothic Tour de Clovis, the refectory, and some kitchens remained.
Closed to the public.

▶ Madeleine
place de la Madeleine, 75008
metro: Madeleine
Something of a white elephant, the Madeleine has had a checkered career, narrowly avoiding being transformed into a railway station, a stock exchange, a bank, a theater, and yet another temple to the emperor Napoleon. Although building started in 1764, many ups and downs ensued before the Madeleine at last regained its original function in 1842 and was completed as a church. The unmistakable Greek temple form, supported by 52 Corinthian pillars, commands a spectacular perspective down the rue Royale toward the Concorde and beyond. A classic site for society weddings and funerals, the rose marble interior has seen the coffins of Chopin, Josephine Baker, and, more recently, Marlene Dietrich.
Open: Monday to Sunday, 7AM–7PM. Closed at lunchtime on Sunday.

A church disguised as a Greek temple: the Madeleine

▶▶ Maison de Verre
31 rue St.-Guillaume, 75007
metro: rue du Bac
A temple to the purity of modernism, this extraordinary house was built between 1928 and 1931 by the art-deco architect Pierre Chareau, contemporary of Le Corbusier. Walls of glass bricks with steel frames and an airy geometric interior are the innovations that replaced a 17th-century townhouse. Only one thing remained: a stubborn tenant in her top-floor apartment.

Malmaison see pages 202–3.

Maison de Verre
The exterior of Pierre Chareau's Maison de Verre is visible from the courtyard, but written applications are necessary to tour inside (31 rue St.-Guillaume, 75007).

■ **"Paris is well worth a Mass,"** stated Henri IV before rapidly converting to Catholicism and bringing to an end the bloody Wars of Religion. Since then, the Catholic faith has dominated Paris and the main concentration of Protestants lies in the south of France. As a mere visitor to Paris you may think the same as Henri IV and, whether you are religious or not, may want to witness French church traditions for yourself. Or you may want to participate in the ceremonies of another faith. All is possible: Paris contains over a hundred parish churches and many a synagogue, temple, and mosque ...■

St.-Suplice
The 12th-century church of St.-Suplice, built for local peasants banned from the monastic church, is today considered to be the "cathedral" of the Faubourg St.-Germain.

St.-Etienne-du-Mont's arched rood screen forms one of Paris's most striking church interiors

Catholic Most churches are open from about 8AM to 7PM and hold morning, midday, and evening Masses, stepped up on Sundays to at least five throughout the day. For an atmospheric Catholic Mass, number one priority is **Notre-Dame**. Despite the hordes of fellow tourists, it's hard to find a more inspiring setting (see pages 154–7). **St.-Germain-des-Prés**, an ancient Benedictine abbey, offers a similarly historic context, while the nearby church of **St.-Sulpice** (see page 174) has the sounds of France's largest organ, as well as murals by Delacroix.

For diehards, **Sacré-Coeur** in Montmartre (see page 171) is a monumental basilica and has hourly services every morning, evening Mass at 6, and sung Mass at 11AM on Sundays.

140

Other options Although slightly off the main tourist beat, a handful of other Parisian churches will supply rare historic settings. Instead of Sacré-Coeur, for example, go around the corner to one of Paris's oldest churches, **St.-Pierre-de-Montmartre**, which has preserved much of its original 12th-century architecture. In central Paris, near Beaubourg, the **Eglise St.-Merri** is a superb example of Flamboyant Gothic, although it was not actually completed until 1612. A 1331 bell remains from the medieval chapel that previously occupied the site and, if you attend a midday service here, admire the superb 16th-century stained-glass windows and remarkable carved woodwork. The massive 17th-century organ was once played by Saint-Saëns and concerts are still held here (tel: 42 71 93 93 for details).

Another historic organ, one century older and particularly ornamental, remains in the church of **St.-Etienne-du-Mont**. The bizarre architectural mixture (Gothic, Renaissance, classical) is due to a long construction period stretching from 1492 to 1626. Don't miss the delicately fretted rood screen, unique in Paris, which forms an arch between the nave and the choir. Both Pascal and Racine were buried here, and Ste.-Geneviève's relics lie in the crypt.

Protestant There is a reasonable though more limited choice of Protestant churches. The neo-Gothic **American Church** on the Quai d'Orsay is a classic, particularly for the expatriate American community, which organizes all sorts of fundraising activities. Services are held at 11AM on Sundays. Not to be confused with this is the **American Cathedral** on the avenue Georges V, of Anglican leaning, which holds two Sunday morning services, one with a choir at 11AM. Paris's best reputed voices can be heard at **St. George's English Church** near the Etoile in their 10:30AM Sunday service. Presbyterians should make for the **Church of Scotland** on the rue Bayard or the Scots **Kirk Manse** on the rue Thimonnier.

Jewish At the heart of the Jewish quarter around the **rue des Rosiers**, there is a synagogue designed in 1913 by the art-nouveau architect Hector Guimard, although its facade is hard to see in the narrow rue Pavée. Farther north in the Marais, near another traditionally Jewish area, the Temple, is the synagogue on the **rue Notre-Dame-de-Nazareth** (tel: 42 78 00 30), while the 9th arrondissement, which bristles with kosher restaurants, has a large religious center on the rue St.-Georges and another synagogue, which can be found in the **rue de la Victoire**.

Islamic Despite the large percentage of Muslims in France, their worshiping needs are not the best catered to. The imposing central mosque's minaret rises over the **rue Geoffroy-St.-Hilaire** opposite the Jardin des Plantes (see page 151); note that Friday prayers at 12:30PM are reserved for Muslims.

See also **Travel Facts** pages 262–3.

St.-Roch
Creatively minded worshipers can head for the Eglise St.-Roch, which holds a special Sunday midday Mass in honor of artists and musicians. Some artists even have studios in the upper reaches of the church, and Corneille's tomb honors all writers. As with many of Paris's central historic churches, concerts are held regularly here.

St.-Eustache
For some of the best church music in Paris, visit the massive church of St.-Eustache, parish church of Les Halles, unusually combining Gothic structure with Renaissance decoration. St.-Eustache has had a long musical tradition: Liszt and Berlioz directed premiers of their work here and the choir, Les Chanteurs de St.-Eustache, are internationally acclaimed, especially for their concerts on Christmas Eve and St. Cecilia's Day.

141

LE MARAIS

Le Marais
The winding streets of the Marais boast what is considered to be the oldest house in Paris (c.1300), as well as a lively Jewish quarter dating from the 13th century.

▶▶▶ **Le Marais**
Only 15 years ago, the Marais was a dilapidated, neglected corner of central Paris, a far cry from the fashionable quartier it has now become. Its Cinderella-like transformation was mostly due to André Malraux who, in 1962, pointed out the historic value of numerous crumbling monuments, and a restoration program was slowly embarked upon, soon followed by an invasion of classy boutiques, restaurants, and art galleries.

The background Stretching west to east between Les Halles and the Bastille and north to south from the République to the Seine, the heart of the Marais remains immediately west of its lung, the place des Vosges. Before Henri IV commissioned this symmetrical "place Royale" in 1605, the nearby rue St.-Antoine was already

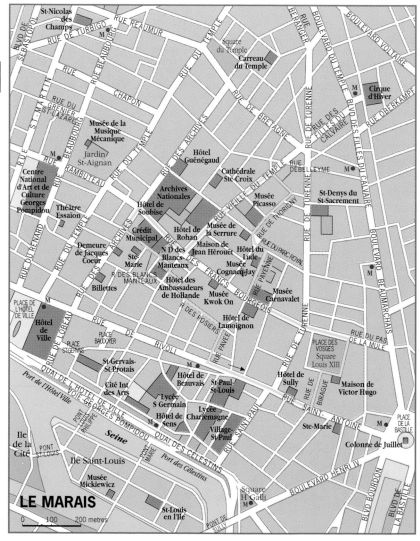

a popular axis for royal festivities, while for two centuries the northern section had been controlled by the powerful religious and military Ordre des Templiers (Knights Templar) until its brutal suppression in 1313. Even in Roman times, this low-lying area was called Le Marais (the marsh).

But it was the 17th and, to a lesser extent, the 18th centuries that propelled the Marais to its zenith, with aristocrats vying to create the most elegant mansion, the most imposing courtyard, or the most precious interior. Literary salons, philosophical debates, duels, love affairs, power struggles: the Marais rapidly became a hotbed for the likes of Madame de Sévigné, Voltaire, Molière, Racine, and Richelieu. With the Revolution, its aristocratic sun set and its glorious mansions were sold off to merchants and craftsmen.

Masterpieces It's impossible to wander around the Marais without stumbling across architectural masterpieces, even if you can only admire them from their courtyards. Don't miss the following: **Hôtel de Lamoignon**, 24 rue Pavée; **Hôtel de Sully**, 62 rue St.-Antoine (see page 178); **Hôtel de Rohan**, 87 rue Vieille-du-Temple; **Hôtel du Lude**, 13 rue Payenne; **Hôtel de Sens**, 1 rue du Figuier (see page 175); **Hôtel des Ambassadeurs de Hollande**, 47 rue Vieille-du-Temple; and the **Hôtel Salé**, housing the **Musée Picasso**, the **Hôtel Guénégaud** and its **Musée de la Chasse**, and the **Hôtel Libéral Bruand**, which houses the **Musée Bricard** (see pages 164, 100, and 87).

Between the restored facades you'll also find plenty of 20th-century temptations, in the form of hundreds of contemporary art galleries, restaurants, bars, clothes and antiques shops. Yuppies have moved in with a

Place Royal
Henri IV, founder of the place Royale, missed its inauguration ceremony: he had been assassinated two years earlier.

143

Architectural detail in Le Marais, one of the oldest areas of Paris, dotted with ornate 17th-century mansions

4ᵉ Arr
RUE DES FRANCS BOURGEOIS

Taking a break in the graceful place des Vosges—once the site of many jousting tournaments and duels

vengeance, yet there's a small **Chinatown** around the rue Chapon, where crowded backroom workshops churn out goods. The wholesale costume jewelry and rag trades still monopolize much of the **rue du Temple** and its side streets. A unique combination of history, function, and trendy chic makes this one of Paris's favorite strolling areas.

Place des Vosges▶ Since 1612, when 10,000 spectators watched the celebrations to inaugurate the "place Royale," a stream of famous characters has inhabited its mansions and apartments. Princesses, duchesses, official mistresses, Richelieu, Sully, Victor Hugo, Gautier, Daudet, Bossuet, and, more recently, painter Francis Bacon and architect Richard Rodgers (of Centre Pompidou) have gazed at its perfect symmetry.

Thirty-six houses faced with red brick and stone, with arcaded ground floors and steep pitched roofs, create the harmonious form of this square, which encloses a garden of fountains, plane trees, and gravel paths. Before the square was built it was the site of a royal palace, the Palais des Tournelles, abandoned and demolished by Catherine de Médicis when her husband Henri II was killed in a tournament here. The north and south facades retained the royal touch, as each has a larger, central house, respectively the queen's and the king's pavilions. In 1800 the name "place Royale" was replaced by "place des Vosges" in honor of the first French district to pay its new taxes.

Literary echo Although restaurants, chic clothes shops, antiques dealers, and art galleries now line the place des Vosges, there remains one remnant of the square's literary past in the **Maison de Victor Hugo** at No 6. Between 1832 and 1848, the great French writer penned many a manuscript here (see page 182). Maybe he witnessed one of the many duels that took place on the square, despite Richelieu's ban on them in the 17th century. This argumentative habit continued well into the 19th century, although the favorite dawn meeting place was transferred to the Bois de Boulogne.

Walk A tour of le Marais

See map page 142.

Starting from the metro St.-Paul, walk east along the rue St.-Antoine.
Pass the **church**, built in 1634, and on your left, at No. 62, the magnificent **Hôtel de Sully**.

Turn left onto the rue de Birague, which leads into the spectacular place des Vosges.
Notice that the facades are painted in trompe l'oeil to resemble brick. Commissioned by Henri IV, the square was completed in 1612 and became home to luminaries such as Richelieu, Molière, and, at No. 6, Victor Hugo, in a house now devoted to his museum. Continue around the square past restaurants, galleries, and some eccentric shops, look into the garden entrance of No. 28, the discreet hotel **Pavillon de la Reine**, and stop for a drink at No. 19, **Ma Bourgogne**, which in summer spreads its tables under the arcades.

Continue to the rue des Francs-Bourgeois.
Pass the **Musée Carnavalet**, built in 1540 and later home to the writer Madame de Sévigné.

Turn right along the rue Payenne.
The gardens on the right and courtyards on the left are typical of the 17th-century Marais style.

Follow the rue du Parc Royal to the left and turn right onto the rue de Thorigny.
Here you pass the **Hôtel Salé**, built in 1659, now the **Musée Picasso**.

At the end turn left along the rue Debelleyme, past some contemporary art galleries and left again down the rue Vieille-du-Temple.
Halfway down on your right at No. 87, you pass the carved gates of the **Hôtel Rohan** and, on the corner of the rue des Francs-Bourgeois, the picturesque 1510 turret of the

A boutique in le Marais

Maison de Jean Hérouët.

Turn right here, past more elegant mansions and the Crédit Municipal (municipal pawnshop) at No. 55 on your left.
On the right is the impressive 1709 courtyard of the **Hôtel de Soubise,** now the national archives.

A short distance down the rue des Archives, turn left again onto the rue des Blancs-Manteaux, which takes you back to the rue Vieille-du-Temple. Cut across to follow the rue des Rosiers.
This is the central Jewish quarter, full of specialist shops as far as the rue Pavée.

Turn right at the rue Pavée, past the synagogue designed by Guimard, to return to your starting point.

Musée Maillol
In the former house of 19th- century novelist Alfred de Musset, at 59 rue de Grenelle, 7e, is a small museum dedicated to Aristide Maillol (1864–1944), one of Paris's most influential turn-of-the-century sculptors. It contains a private collection of Maillol's works donated by his former model, Dina Vierny. Bronze figures by Maillol are also exhibited around the Jardin des Tuileries.

A fine collection of Monet's work is displayed at the Musée Marmottan, including Impression at Sunrise, *which gave its name to the Impressionist movement*

Marly, Chevaux de
Sculpted by Nicolas and Guillaume Coustou, these two groups of rearing white marble horses were salvaged from the Château de Marly (destroyed during the Revolution) and brought in 1795 to guard the entrance to the Champs-Elysées. Sixteen live horses were needed to pull their weighty mass. The originals are now preserved from pollution in the Louvre and copies stand in their place on the corner of the place de la Concorde.

► ► ► Marmottan, Musée
2 rue Louis-Boilly, 75016
metro: Muette
Located opposite the discreet charm of the Ranelagh gardens, which still boast a hand-cranked merry-go-round, the Musée Marmottan is another of the 16th arrondissement's hidden treasures. Although Paris's main concentration of Impressionist works is at the Musée d'Orsay, the Marmottan follows closely in the quality stakes.

The 19th-century townhouse originally contained a Renaissance and Empire collection bequeathed to the state by the historian Paul Marmottan, later extended by a generous Wildenstein donation of medieval manuscripts and finally by the magnificent Michel Monet donation. Son of the Impressionist Claude Monet, he left a collection of 65 of his father's works executed toward the end of his life at Giverny. Thus clouds of irises, wisteria, and water lilies fill much of an underground gallery, backed up with works by Monet's contemporaries such as Renoir, Pissarro, Sisley, Berthe Morisot, and Caillebotte. Another donation in 1987 extended this

remarkable collection to include Gauguin and Corot. Don't miss Monet's seminal painting, *Impression—soleil levant*, which gave the movement its name and was also one of a booty of nine paintings stolen from this museum in 1985 and recovered five years later in Corsica.
Open: Tuesday to Sunday, 10–5:30.

Marronniers, Hôtel des
21 rue Jacob, 75006
metro: Mabillon
Nature lovers should try to stay at this hotel in the heart of St.-Germain—its obsessive decorating style is nearly entirely based on vegetation, fruit, birds, and flowers, while two superb chestnut trees dominate the garden. Declared a national monument, the oak-beamed rooms and superb vaulted cellars (converted into lounges) combine to create an atmosphere of special charm.

▶ Memorial du Maréchal Leclerc de Hauteclocque et de la Liberation de Paris et Musee Jean Moulin
dalle-jardin Atlantique, 75015
metro: Montparnasse-Bienvenue
Two perspectives on World War II: one through the life and times of a great soldier, the other via the Resistance leader Jean Moulin. There is also an exhibition about the Liberation of Paris in this new museum.
Open: daily (except Monday), 10–5:40.

▶ Meurice, Hôtel
228 rue de Rivoli, 75001
metro: Tuileries
Once a favorite with the mustachioed artist Salvador Dalí, who made the Royal Suite his Paris base for 30-odd years, the Meurice still claims a good percentage of the world's rich and famous. Opened in 1816, it was Paris's first "grand hotel." During World War II, it had the doubtful honor of becoming Nazi headquarters and in August 1944 witnessed the surrender of Von Cholitz to the Allies. Retaining its aristocratic, old-world atmosphere, the Meurice makes an elegant setting for tea or cocktails.

▶ Monnaie, Hôtel et Musée de la
11 Quai de Conti, 75006
metro: Pont-Neuf
Another of the dignified facades lining the Left Bank of the Seine, La Monnaie was once the national mint. This elegant building was designed by Antoine in 1770 (he lived here until his death in 1801), replacing the 17th-century Hôtel de Conti. Today the workshops (*ateliers*) still make commemorative coins and guided tours explain the techniques (Tuesday and Friday only, 2:15–3).

At the front of the hotel, a series of lofty salons overlooking the Seine are used for temporary exhibitions; the main museum is situated at the back of the courtyard. Here the history of coins and medals is traced from 300 BC to the present. A museum shop opens onto the rue Guénégaud.
Open: Tuesday to Saturday, 10–1, 2–5:30; Wednesday, 1–9.

Ancient relics
The rue de Nevers, which runs parallel to the rue Guénégaud off the Quai de Conti, is one of Paris's oldest streets, and hasn't changed its skinny width since the 13th century. Once marking the boundary between a convent and a townhouse, it contains a section of the Philippe-Auguste city wall. The arch over the entrance (constructed at a later date) is engraved with part of Claude le Petit's 17th-century poem satirizing the Pont-Neuf (directly opposite) and its imminent collapse; the author finished at the stake.

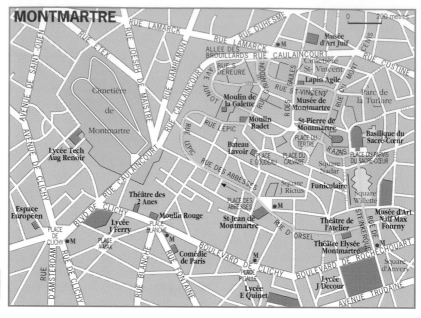

Le Moulin Rouge, opened in 1889 and made famous by Toulouse Lautrec with his many famous studies of cabaret artistes

▶▶▶ Montmartre

High on its northern hill overlooking Paris, Montmartre was long linked with the artistic community that scraped a living there. Toulouse Lautrec immortalized the can-can kicking Jane Avril, the Moulin Rouge, and singer-poet Aristide Bruant, and no doubt frequented the local hot cabaret, *Au Lapin Agile*. Meanwhile, Cubism was born in the draughty Bateau-Lavoir studios, which housed no lesser figures than Picasso, Juan Gris, and Braque. Today little is left of this burgeoning creative community: the "painters" on the place du Tertre can hardly swing a brush and real-estate values are high enough to keep any impoverished artist at bay. Yet as you wander through its backstreets, you can't help but be affected by the charm of this neighborhood, perfectly revealed in its romantic tree-lined steps, squares, gardens, and individually designed houses.

The Mill The landmark most associated with Montmartre is, of course, Le Moulin Rouge, located on the tacky boulevard de Clichy at the bottom of the hill in Pigalle, best known for its sex shops and hustlers. But why a mill? In fact, there were once over 30 windmills in Montmartre, which ground silex from the underground gypsum quarries riddling the hill, but by the early 19th century the quarrying and mills were abandoned to save the hill from collapse.

Following closely in the symbol stakes is **Sacré-Coeur**, the white marble wedding-cake basilica crowning the hill. When it was completed in 1910 (it took 35 years to build), its architect was heavily criticized for its Romanesque-Byzantine style, but no one realized how many millions would flood to see it. One good reason for its popularity is the view across Paris: on clear days it stretches a spectacular 18½ miles.

Presenting the past▶ To get a better idea of the history of this area, go to the **Musée de Montmartre** at 12 rue Cortot (*open*: Tuesday to Sunday, 11–6). This 17th-century house and its pretty garden once belonged to a member of Molière's theater troupe and was later inhabited by Renoir, Utrillo, and Dufy. Locally made porcelain, a reconstructed interior of a 19th-century bistro, caricatures of local eccentrics by Daumier, drawings by Toulouse-Lautrec… it is an interesting if not extensive collection.

Fruit of the vine Back in the land of the living, don't miss Montmartre's **vineyard** (opposite the historical cabaret) on the rue des Saules. Every October the grapes are harvested and 500 or so bottles of *Clos Montmartre* are filled. Lastly, whichever street you take, you can't miss the **place du Tertre**: at least you can truthfully say what a tourist trap it is.

Paris at dusk, from Montmartre—a romantic view of the capital from the steps of the Sacré-Coeur

Moulin de la Galette
The Moulin de la Galette, one of only three mills remaining at Montmartre, was built in 1622. During the 1814 siege of Paris, the mill owner, Debray, was crucified on its sails for trying to stop the invading Cossacks. In the late 19th century, the Debray family converted the mill into a popular open-air dance hall, providing inspiration for many artists, including Renoir and Van Gogh.

Walk **A circuit of Montmartre**

See map page 148.

Start at Abbesses metro station.
This station boasts one of the
original Guimard entrances dating
from the 1900s.

*Follow the rue des Abbesses, west
till the road branches. Turn right up
the rue Lepic.*
Van Gogh once lived at No. 54.

*Follow the curve until you see the
Moulin de la Galette on your left.*
The **Moulin de la Galette** was once
a dance hall frequented by Renoir.

*Turn left and left again onto the
avenue Junot.*
At No. 13 lived the artist Poulbot,
inventor of the ubiquitous wide-eyed
urchin image. Next door at No. 15 is
the Dadaist Tristan Tzara's house,
designed by Adolf Loos.

*Turn right along the rue S. Dereure
and onto the Allée des Brouillards.*
The Allée leads to an 18th-century
mansion, once a dance hall and
home to the poet Nerval.

*Follow the raised path beside the
gardens to the rue Girardon, where
you can either turn left down the
steps to visit the Cimetière St.-
Vincent or go along the rue de
l'Abreuvoir to the rue des Saules.*

The **Maison Rose** restaurant on the
corner was painted by Utrillo and
today provides an ideal terrace for
lunch. Opposite is Montmartre's
vineyard, harvested annually on the
first Saturday in October.

*Follow the rue St.-Vincent, passing
Au Lapin Agile. At the rue du Mont
Cenis, turn right and climb the steps.*
En route, pass Berlioz's former
apartment and the pretty **rue Cortot**.

*Continue straight ahead to the place
du Tertre.*
Patachon is a tearoom with a superb
view; walk around the back of it to
the **place du Calvaire.**

*Returning to the entrance to the
place du Tertre, follow the rue Azaïs
to the front of Sacré-Coeur.*
Here you can climb to the top of the
bell tower or take the Montmartre
funiculaire, which has been recently
modernized.

*At the bottom, go straight on down
the rue de Steinkerque, past a lively
string of shops selling cheap fabrics,
then turn right onto the rue d'Orsel.*
On your left you pass the charming
Théâtre de l'Atelier (1822).

Return to the place des Abbesses.

Place des Abbesses metro station

▶ Montsouris, Parc

metro: Porte d'Orleans RER: Cité Universitaire
Another of the Baron Haussmann's creations, the site of
the Parc Montsouris was once peppered with windmills,
relics of its granite quarry past. By the turn of the
century, this pocket of landscaped green had become a
favorite hideaway for artists and literati escaping the
intellectual overkill in nearby Montparnasse. The Belle
Epoque restaurant suitably called Jardin de la Paresse
(Garden of Laziness) on the rue Gazan is a superb
example of architecture of the period, and claims such
illustrious diners as Trotsky, Mata Hari, and Sartre. At
the top of the hill is a replica of the Tunisian palace of
Beys, built in 1867 and recently extensively restored.
Open: sunrise to sunset.

▶ Mosqué, La

place du Puits-de-l'Ermite, 75005
metro: Monge
One of the Left Bank's best surprises, the Paris Mosque
was built in 1926 with French funds as grateful thanks
for North African military support during World War I.
Strongly faithful to ornate Moorish architecture, its
roofs are green tiled, its fountains are pink marbled, its
doors are carved, and its walls are adorned with
mosaics, while the *salon de thé* whisks you to Cairo.
The worshiping area can be visited with a guided tour.
Open: Saturday to Thursday, 9–noon, 2–6.

▶▶ Mouffetard, Marché

metro: Monge
Thronging with tourists, the Marché Mouffetard is

African delights
The African section of the
Marché Mouffetard, near
the rue de l'Arbalète, has a
bright array of smoked fish,
handwoven baskets, and
sandals.

nevertheless one of Paris's most picturesque central
markets. This is the land of gastronomic fantasies,
where the products available probably outstrip any
mental invention. Go late morning, when shoppers
elbow past piles of vegetables and grocers' desire to sell
is peaking volubly. Stop for a coffee and succulent
homemade croissants at the **Café Mouffetard** at No.
116, and don't miss the colorful murals at the Italian
grocer **Chez Facchetti** (No. 134).
Open: Tuesday to Saturday, 8–1, 4–7; and Sunday
morning.

*Fruits de mer at the
Marché Mouffetard,
a colorful daily
market on one of
Paris's oldest streets*

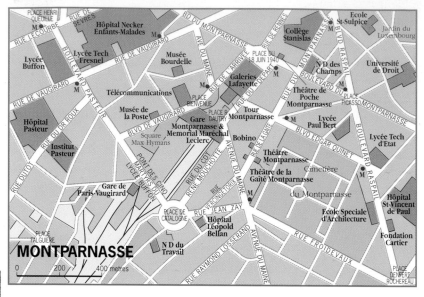

The cemetery at Montparnasse
Notable former residents of the area lie in the Montparnasse cemetery, accessible from the boulevard Edgar Quinet, where you can pay homage to Sartre, de Beauvoir, Baudelaire, Maupassant, Saint-Saëns and, car-lovers' hero, André Citroën.

The cemetery at Montmartre
This vast cemetery, laid out in 1795 and covering 25 acres, is one of the best known in Paris, including the graves of composers Delibes, Berlioz, and Offenbach (who wrote the famous can-can tune immortalized in Paris cabarets), painters Dégas and Fragonard, writers Heine, Dumas, Stendhal, and Zola, film director Truffaut, Russian dancer Nijinsky, and the playwright Sacha Guitry.

▶ Montparnasse

Although its sun set long ago, Montparnasse is so evocative of early 20th-century cultural history that it is hard to miss out. Legendary meeting places still exist, haunted by the shadows of the literary and artistic gurus of the 1920s and '30s, yet its main boulevards have lost much of their charm, sacrificed to the whims of latter-day consumerism.

Tour Montparnasse▶▶ Symbolic of this transformation, the heart of the area is towered over by the 690-foot **Montparnasse Tower**, an architectural faux pas erected in 1973 to crown a vast commercial center. It does, however, offer unbeatable panoramic views from its 59th floor. Across the windy esplanade is the modernized Gare Montparnasse, still confusing and badly designed despite the recent addition of the **TGV Atlantique** terminus. Behind this gigantic structure is a quartier that has undergone 20 years of hectic redevelopment, replacing atmospheric narrow streets with uninspired apartment buildings. Ricardo Bofill's neoclassical designs are perhaps the most interesting.

High points But despair not! Some corners are worth searching out, such as 16 rue Antoine Bourdelle, where you can visit the **Musée Bourdelle** (*open*: Tuesday to Sunday, 10–5:40); the picturesque garden, house, and overflowing studios of this sculptor, student of Rodin, are fascinating. Nearby, at 15 rue Falgère, stand the newly built offices of France's most respected daily newspaper, *Le Monde*, while farther south is another institutional landmark, the **Institut Pasteur**.

Pursuit of pleasure Back to the east of the Tower, follow the boulevard Edgar Quinet to the **rue de la Gaîté**, Montparnasse's answer to the rue St.-Denis. Its traditional pleasure-seeking character survives among

the sex shops and a number of small theaters and cabarets; here, too, floats the ghost of the modernist dancer Isadora Duncan, who performed at No. 26 and lived at No. 4.

Heart of the matter The pulse of Montparnasse remains centered along the stretch between the boulevard Raspail (reigned over by Rodin's statue of Balzac) and the rue du Montparnasse. Between fascinating specialty shops, restaurants, the architecture of the rue Vavin and, finally, Montparnasse's living symbol, **La Coupole**, visitors may at last experience something of the area's past ebullience.

Paris mapped out from the Tour Montparnasse, the tallest office building in the world

Cabarets and theaters can be found among the sex shops on the rue de la Gaîté

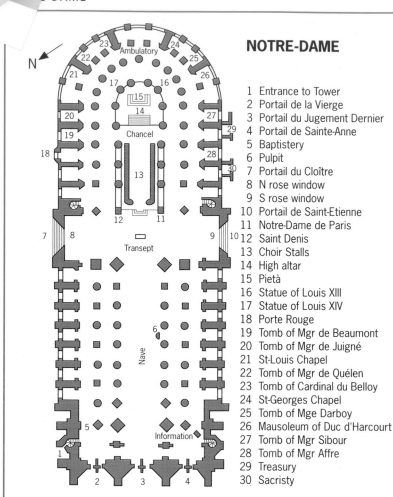

NOTRE-DAME

1 Entrance to Tower
2 Portail de la Vierge
3 Portail du Jugement Dernier
4 Portail de Sainte-Anne
5 Baptistery
6 Pulpit
7 Portail du Cloître
8 N rose window
9 S rose window
10 Portail de Saint-Etienne
11 Notre-Dame de Paris
12 Saint Denis
13 Choir Stalls
14 High altar
15 Pietà
16 Statue of Louis XIII
17 Statue of Louis XIV
18 Porte Rouge
19 Tomb of Mgr de Beaumont
20 Tomb of Mgr de Juigné
21 St-Louis Chapel
22 Tomb of Mgr de Quélen
23 Tomb of Cardinal du Belloy
24 St-Georges Chapel
25 Tomb of Mge Darboy
26 Mausoleum of Duc d'Harcourt
27 Tomb of Mgr Sibour
28 Tomb of Mgr Affre
29 Treasury
30 Sacristy

The place du Parvis Notre-Dame

A bronze star on the pavement in the place du Parvis marks the official geographical center of France, where all French national highways begin. The name Parvis is believed to originate from "paradisus" (heaven on earth), the name given to the view of the west front of a medieval cathedral, traditionally the most ornate side, from the open space fronting the building.

▶ ▶ ▶ **Notre-Dame**

metro: Cité

"Each side, each stone of the venerable monument is a page not only of the history of the country, but also of the history of science and of art." Victor Hugo's words—written in 1831 as part of his voluminous historical novel *Notre-Dame de Paris*, which introduced the famous hunchback Quasimodo—ring as true as the bells of this twin-towered cathedral. Notre-Dame occupies a site that goes back to early Roman times, when *Lutetia* was concentrated on the Ile de la Cité, the heart of the city. Further proof of Notre-Dame's importance is the fact that it is used as point zero for measuring distances from Paris.

Soon after the Romanesque abbey of St.-Denis, just north of Paris, was completed (1144), Bishop Maurice de Sully decided that Paris needed its own cathedral, and construction started in 1163 with foundations laid by Pope Alexander III. The choir was completed in 1182

and the west front and twin towers between 1200 and 1250. It was only in 1345 that the original plans were realized, thus making it an edifice of transition between the Romanesque and the Gothic.

As a work of the people, Notre-Dame was built by guilds of carpenters, stone carvers, iron forgers, and glass craftsmen, who all labored in the pure medieval spirit of a communal religious effort. For years it remained a meeting place for trade unions as well as a dormitory for the homeless. Its adjoining cathedral school was renowned throughout Europe and eventually gave birth to the Sorbonne.

Unfortunately, the structure of Notre-Dame suffered badly over the centuries, and by the time Napoleon came to crown himself emperor in 1804, it was in a very sorry state of disrepair. Victor Hugo's vehement criticism in 1831 finally goaded the government into action, led by the architects Lassus and Viollet-le-Duc, who enthusiastically set about remedying the damage of hundreds of years.

According to Hugo, the culprits were threefold: time, political and religious evolution, and, worst of all, the vagaries of fashion. He was virulent about the absence of countless statues from both the facade and the interior (many toppled during the Revolution), the clear

One of the classic views of Notre-Dame—seen at its best from the riverside promenade or from a bateau-mouche on the river

France's largest organ
The 7,000 or so pipes of the massive 1730 organ make it one of France's largest, fit to inspire the 6,500 music lovers who flock to free recitals held every Sunday at 5:45.

The impressive buttressed structure of Notre-Dame. Closer inspection reveals finely carved statues and gargoyles, many the work of Viollet-le-Duc

glass (Louis XV had decided that stained glass was out of date and replaced most rose windows), the replacement of the old Gothic altar with a heavy marble sarcophagus, and the amputation of the spire in 1787 by an architect of "good taste." Much of Hugo's ranting was well heeded: the Gallery of Kings was reproduced (some of the originals were excavated in 1977 and are now at the Cluny) and a 295-foot spire erected, but it was not until after World War II that the stained-glass windows were remade. Viollet-le-Duc also modestly added a statue of himself among the Apostles.

West facade Crowned by two 225-foot towers are three imposing, asymmetrical portals representing (left to right) the Virgin Mary, the Last Judgment, and Saint Anne, Mary's mother. In the Middle Ages when the statues were painted, these served as a Bible for the illiterate, and it is worth looking closely at each portal.

Apart from the lintels of the central portal, the sculptures of the tympanums and arches are all original. On the left the Coronation of the Virgin dominates the Resurrection and the Assumption, surrounded by kings, angels, prophets, and zodiac signs. The middle of the Last Judgment was much tampered with by Soufflot in 1771, and the statue of Christ is 19th-century. The sculptures of Saint Anne on the right that date mostly from 1165–75 are the oldest in the cathedral, showing scenes from her life, the childhood of Christ and, in the tympanum, Mary proffering Jesus to a kneeling King Louis VII (who consecrated the church), seen on the right and the founder, Bishop Sully, on the left.

The towers, originally intended to be surmounted by spires, make a strenuous climb (225 steps to the summit of the north tower, and another 125 to the top of the south tower). In the south tower hangs the famous 13-ton bell "Emmanuel," recast in 1686, evoking memories of a tormented Quasimodo. The fantastic range of gargoyles—grotesque stone figures of demons, birds, and weird beasts—are again the work of Viollet-le-Duc, serving to keep evil spirits at bay.

North and south facades These sides present three distinct, receding stories with bold flying buttresses. Look at the magnificent north porch, the *portail du cloître*, built in 1250 by Jean de Chelles. The statue of the Virgin is original, and the tympanum relates the story of Theophilius, a monk who, after signing a pact with the devil, was saved *in extremis* by the Virgin. Immediately to the east is the red door (*porte rouge*), a superb sculpted work by Pierre de Montreuil (1260). Here the tympanum shows the crowning of the Virgin, and the arches episodes from the Crucifixion and Resurrection of Christ.

Regally facing the Left Bank, the south porch is dedicated to Saint Stephen and was started by Jean de Chelles in 1258. Most of the arch statues are copies, but the tympanum relating the life of the saint and the medallions of student life are all original. The garden at the back of the cathedral was entirely filled with houses and chapels until the 1831 uprising, which destroyed most of this church property.

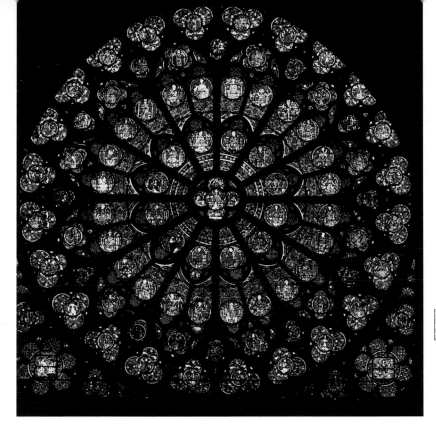

Interior Entering this awesome cathedral, note the difference in light between the nave, the transept, and the chancel—due to the gradual cleaning of the interior.

The traditional Gothic layout consists of a nave of 10 bays flanked by double aisles that continue around the choir. The walls are lined with 37 chapels altogether, added during the 13th and 14th centuries. Among the traditional annual offerings by the goldsmiths' guild are those adorning the first two chapels to the right, by Le Brun, and in the transept, by Le Sueur.

At the crossing of the transept you can admire the three rose windows, to the north depicting Old Testament figures surrounding Mary (almost totally original glass) and, to the south, Christ in a crowd of angels and saints. The choir, much altered under Louis XIV, also attracted Viollet-le-Duc's untiring attention: over half the original stalls remain, as well as some bronze angels (1711).

Numerous tombs of bishops lie below the choir and around the ambulatory. The sacristy, on the south side of the choir, houses the treasure of Notre-Dame (*open:* 9:30–6), which consists of medieval manuscripts, ecclesiastical plate, and reliquaries. The famous crown of thorns and piece of the True Cross are brought out on Good Friday.

Big ceremonial moments are, of course, at Easter and on Christmas Eve, but the cathedral, this "vast symphony in stone," radiates an extraordinary power at any time. The cathedral is closed over Saturday lunchtime.

The southern Rose Window, depicting Christ surrounded by saints and angels, is 69 feet high and still contains some of its original 13th-century stained glass

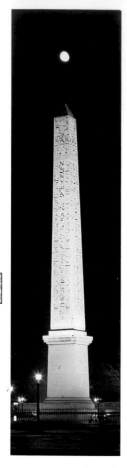

A 3,300-year-old needle: the Obelisk, in the place de la Concorde, was once used to measure the sun's shadow at the Temple of Thebes

► **Obelisk**
place de la Concorde, 75001
metro: Concorde
Like Cleopatra's Needle in London, the Obelisk is the city's oldest monument—about 3,300 years old. For once it is not a result of colonial grabbing, as it was actually donated in 1831 to King Louis-Philippe by Mohammed Ali Pasha, Viceroy of Egypt. The place de la Concorde has been a central symbol since the removal of Louis XV's equestrian statue during the Revolution, and the 230-ton pink granite Obelisk, after a lengthy journey from Luxor, ended the ongoing polemics.

Olympia
28 boulevard des Capucines, 75009
metro: Opéra
Still a favorite venue for solo performers of variety, old-time pop, or sometimes jazz since the days of Piaf, Aznavour, Charles Trenet, and Yves Montand, the Olympia possesses that rare quality in an old concert hall—comfort. Check out its varied schedule of attractions.

Opéra Bastille
120 rue de Lyon, 75012
metro: Bastille
This prestigious architectural operation, instigated by President Mitterrand, was a case of "watch the controversy grow." From day one, when a design by an unknown and relatively inexperienced architect (Carlos Ott) was inadvertently selected, all hell broke loose. Heavily criticized for its ungainly volume and exorbitant cost, the Opéra Bastille finally overcame most teething problems (including last-minute changes in its musical director) and by 1990 creaked into operatic action. Technically sophisticated and highly flexible, it has about 3,000 seats in the main auditorium and a smaller downstairs hall.

► **Opéra Comique**
5 rue Favart, 75002
metro: Richelieu-Drouot
This strangely oriented theater is tucked down a side street with its back firmly turned to the boulevard des Italiens. Originally built in 1780 (and rebuilt since after several major fires) to house the Comédie-Italienne, it was constructed in this way to distinguish it from the numerous "popular" theaters springing up along the boulevard. Often called the Salle Favart, the Opéra Comique long specialized in Italian opera and operetta and recently extended to classical music concerts and, occasionally, ballet.

►►► **Opéra de Paris**
place de l'Opéra, 75009 Paris
metro: Opéra
The sumptuous and prestigious Opéra Garnier was inaugurated in 1875, 15 years after the 35-year-old Charles Garnier's riotous design had been officially accepted. A fittingly lavish epitaph to the manic architectural activities of the Second Empire, it was once the largest theater in the world (13,156 square yards).

Since the opening of the Opéra Bastille, the Opéra Garnier has become exclusively devoted to ballet. Although the quality of the Ballet de l'Opéra de Paris is internationally renowned, its repertoire tends to remain on the traditional side of contemporary dance. Previously directed by the fiery Rudolf Nureyev, who walked out in 1990 in a cloud of controversy, the company is now enthusiastically run by the youthful *danseur étoile*, Patrick Dupond.

Even if you don't see a performance here, make sure you look at Garnier's breathtaking marble and gilt Grand Staircase and the equally baroque Grand Foyer. Outside, keep an eye open for Carrier-Belleuse's provocative lamp-bearing statue and the copy of Carpeaux's sculpted group *La Danse* to the right of the front arcade: the original is now at the Musée d'Orsay.

▶▶▶ L'Orangerie

place de la Concorde, 75001
metro: Concorde
Echoing the Second Empire architecture of the Jeu de Paume, its Tuileries twin, the Orangerie, was originally the greenhouse for the Tuileries Palace before becoming an exhibition center in the early 20th century. Home to the extensive Walter-Guillaume collection, which ranges from the Impressionists to the 1920s (Cézanne, Renoir, Sisley, Rousseau, Derain, Matisse, Soutine, Modigliani, Picasso, Van Dongen), it offers a pleasant, uncrowded art tour. Although airily displayed, the 144 works are patchy in quality and do not always represent the best of these masters. However, the high point is Monet's eight gigantic panels of *Water Lilies,* painted for the Orangerie's two oval basement rooms; the panels were presented to the museum in 1927, a year after his death. Go to Giverny to see his original inspiration, but make sure you see these glorious reflections and the depth of their multiple tones.
Open: Wednesday to Monday, 9:45–5:15.

Immense proportions
The Opéra de Paris's immense stage can accommodate 450 performers, watched by 2,200 spectators under a domed ceiling painted by Chagall (1964).

L'Orangerie, in the Tuileries Garden, was originally a greenhouse but now contains an important collection of Impressionist paintings

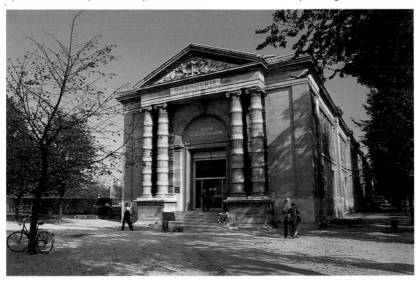

MUSEE D'ORSAY

GROUND FLOOR   UPPER LEVEL   MIDDLE LEVEL

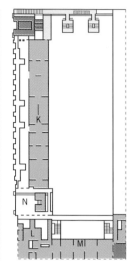

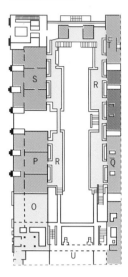

■	Painting	■	Art Nouveau
■	Sculpture	■	Photo and Cinema
■	Architecture	■	Special Exhibitions
■	Decorative Arts		

A Main Entrance
B Bookshop
C Impressionism before 1870
D Realism and the Barbizon School
E Symbolism before 1870
F Academism, Romanticism and
   Classicism 1848-1870
G Sculpture 1848-1870
H Salle de l'Opéra
I Architecture and Town Planning
   1850-1900
J Decorative Arts 1850-1880

K Galerie des Hauteurs-
   Impressionism after 1870
L Les Salles d'Angles-
   Neo-impressionism and
   Pastels
M Galerie Bellechasse-
   Pont-Aven school and
   the Nabis
N Café des Hau

O Painting and Sculpture
   of the Third Republic
P Symbolism and Naturalism
   1870-1914
Q Early 20th century painting
R Sculpture 1870-1914
S Art Nouveau in France
   and Belgium
T International Art Nouveau
U Restaurant

►►► Musée d'Orsay

1 rue de Bellechasse, 75007
metro: Solférino

Yet another example of Parisian metamorphosis, this building was originally a palace and subsequently a hotel and railway station. Now it is a rewarding, accessible museum of the fine and applied arts, 1848–1914.

Ground floor: to the right of a central sculpture passage are paintings by Ingres, Gérôme, Delacroix, and the academics of the period. Symbolism is represented by Puvis de Chavannes and Gustave Moreau, along with early works by Degas. The galleries on the other side present the pre-1870 teething days of Impressionism in Manet's superb *Olympia, Le Balcon,* and *Déjeuner sur l'Herbe,* Bazille, Renoir, Fantin Latour, Whistler's *La Mère,* and several seminal works by Monet. Toward the front of this floor are grouped realist works.

Top floor: to follow the collection chronologically, go straight to the top floor using the front escalators. Here you move into the Ecole de Pont-Aven (Gauguin, Emile Bernard, Sérusier), the Nabis (Maurice Denis, Bonnard, Vuillard, Vallotton), the mysterious world evoked in Odilon Redon's pastels, Toulouse-Lautrec, Henri Rousseau, and finally Seurat. Then starts the heart of the Impressionist collection, devoted to Cézanne, Van Gogh, Monet, Renoir, Degas, Sisley, and Pissarro.

Middle level: overlooking the entrance below, the middle level concentrates on the sculpture and painting of the late 19th century until 1914. In the superbly renovated ballroom are paintings by Bouguereau, *La naissance de Vénus,* and Gérôme's *Tanagra* alongside monumental sculptures. Through naturalism (Dalou, Cormon) discover more symbolist works with foreign parallels such as Burne-Jones and Böcklin. Most striking here are Rodin's sculptures (the powerful *Balzac,* busts, *The Thinker)* and those of his followers: Camille Claudel, Rosso, Bourdelle, Bernard, and the familiar rounded forms of Maillol. In the galleries to the right are the beginnings of modernism with the Fauves (Derain, Braque, Van Dongen) and Bonnard, Matisse, and Rousseau. This floor also displays some superb applied arts, concentrating on art-nouveau furniture and objects.
Open: Tuesday to Sunday, 9–6 (Thursday till 9:45); 10–6 in winter.

A remarkable railway station
The original hotel and railway station comprising what is now the Musée d'Orsay were erected in an astonishing two years to be completed for the Universal Exposition in 1900. Victor Laloux was the architect responsible for its soaring glass and iron roof, together with a wildly ornate Belle Epoque restaurant and ballroom, all still intact. Conversion into a museum came in the early 1980s, masterminded by Gae Aulenti, who created a structure of controversial imposing presence.

Café des Hauteurs
The striking Café des Hauteurs, on the top floor of the Musée d'Orsay, has an unusual view across Paris through the face of the enormous station clock.

Space and style in the Musée d'Orsay

Thankful recovery
The Panthéon was Louis XV's way of thanking Saint Geneviève, patron saint of Paris, for his recovery from gout.

A scientific experiment
The interior of the Panthéon's soaring dome was used in 1849 by the scientist Foucault to prove, with a pendulum, the rotative movement of the earth.

Musée Edith Piaf
Edith Piaf was brought up in the working-class east end of Paris, and began her career as a singer here in local bars and cafés before achieving international acclaim in the 1930s. A visit to the tiny museum in her honor at 5 rue Crespin du Gast, 11e, crammed with Piaf memorabilia, is worthwhile. Visits by appointment only (tel: 43 55 52 72).

▶   Panthéon

place du Panthéon, 75005
metro: Cardinal-Lemoine
Necropolis for the atheist citizens of France, the Panthéon shelters the remains of luminaries such as Voltaire, Rousseau, Victor Hugo, Zola, Louis Braille (inventor of braille), Jean Jaurès, and the Resistance martyr Jean Moulin, as well as a shrine containing the heart of left-wing hero Léon-Michel Gambetta. Originally commissioned by Louis XV in 1744, the Panthéon was only completed at the Revolution (1790).

By that time its architect, Soufflot, had died and his neoclassical edifice, based on the form of a Greek cross, was subsequently finished by one of his students 10 years after his death. In 1791, its windows were bricked up and its function changed from that of church to Temple of Fame. In 1885, it again changed to become the lay temple it remains today.

The austerity of this monument is slightly alleviated by late 19th-century paintings, the most famous being those by the Symbolist Puvis de Chavannes, depicting the life of Saint Geneviève.
Open: daily, 10–5:30.

▶▶   Pavillon de l'Arsenal

21 boulevard Morland, 75004
metro: Sully-Morland
Inaugurated in 1988 as a window on the city's architectural evolution, the Pavillon de l'Arsenal is proof of Paris's growing awareness of its museum-like role. A permanent exhibition on the ground floor, *Paris, la ville et ses projets*, retraces through drawings and photographs the historic projects that have etched the face of the city. These are arranged around a spectacular 60-square-yard, laser-activated scale model. Temporary exhibitions on the upper mezzanines of this luminous, skylit building cover architectural projects and competitions, often in an international context. All in all, it is well worth a detour.
Open: Tuesday to Saturday, 10:30–6:30; Sunday, 11–7.

▶▶   Père-Lachaise

boulevard de Ménilmontant, 75020
metro: Gambetta, Père-Lachaise
The strange fascination of this vast cemetery stems partly from its illustrious incumbents and partly from the fantastic variety of tomb designs. Laid out in 1803 on the slopes of a hill in Ménilmontant to echo a peaceful English-style garden, the cemetery is full of twisting paths, unexpected views, swaying trees and, above all, some ornate sculpture, altogether making it far from lugubrious.

Pay homage at the Mur des Fédérés to the 147 last defenders of the 1870 Commune, who were gunned down here and buried in a common grave, or to any number of political or cultural figures. An essential investment is the plan sold at both entrances, which will lead you to the tombs of Abélard and Héloïse, Chopin, Haussmann, Modigliani, Edith Piaf, Proust, Delacroix, Oscar Wilde, Alice B. Toklas, and Jim Morrison.
Open: daily, 8–5:30.

► **Petit Palais**

avenue Winston Churchill, 75008
metro: Champs-Elysées—Clémenceau
When you tire of the aggressive sights of the Champs-Elysées, this is where to take refuge. Rarely crowded, unless a popular exhibition is on, the museum offers an exceptional patchwork collection of mainly 19th-century French works: Delacroix, Ingres, Courbet, Carpeaux, the Impressionists, and Post-Impressionists. Examples of the Dutch school and two private donations of medieval art and 18th-century furniture complete this eclecticism.
Open: Tuesday to Sunday, 10–5:40.

► **Photographie, Centre National de la**

Hôtel Salomon de Rothschild, 11 rue Berryer, 75008
metro: Etoile
Situated just off the rue du Faubourg St.-Honoré, the Centre National de la Photographie has recently moved into the Hôtel Salomon, where it presents temporary exhibitions of photography, historical and contemporary, usually comprehensive and of a high quality. Extensive renovation currently underway will lead to the center's gradual mutation into the Palais de l'Image et du Son, thus centralizing under one generous roof a number of audio-visual organizations. An auditorium is already used for film projections, so it may be worth checking the schedule.
Open: Wednesday to Sunday, 9:45–5.

Twins
Like its twin, the Grand Palais, the Petit Palais' glass- and iron-domed building was constructed for the 1900 Universal Exhibition, not as a permanent fixture.

Nineteenth-century works are displayed in the Petit Palais. This smaller twin of the neighboring Grand Palais boasts an exquisitely presented permanent collection of French paintings and furniture

163

Jardin des Plantes
The Jardin des Plantes was set up in the 17th century to cultivate medicinal plants for Louis XIII.

Zoo food
When set up in 1795, the "people's democratic zoo" displayed survivors from the royal menagerie at Versailles. Although popular throughout the 19th century, with exotic animals donated from far afield, it was obvious prey for hungry citizens in the 1870-1 Prussian siege. For months, better connected Parisians regaled themselves with the equivalent of *éléphant bourguignon* or *blanquette de girafe*.

Buste d'une femme (1931), part of the excellent collection housed in the Musée Picasso

▶▶▶ **Picasso, Musée**
Hôtel Salé, 5 rue de Thorigny, 75003
metro: Chemin-Vert, St.-Paul
The grand opening of this museum in 1985 signaled the end of 11 years of legal wrangling over Picasso's potentially astronomical death duties. The difficulty for the French government lay in establishing just how much work he had hoarded away: he had an annoying habit of shutting one château and moving on to the next when it was full. Finally, one quarter of his collection was accepted from his heirs in lieu of death duties. Thus this superb, expensively renovated 17th-century mansion with fixtures designed by Diego Giacometti contains over 200 paintings, 158 sculptures, 1,500 drawings, and numerous other creations, as well as 60 or so works by mentors and contemporaries such as Cézanne, Miró, Braque, and Matisse.

A must for anyone remotely interested in 20th-century art, it is arranged chronologically, taking the visitor from Picasso's youthful turn-of-the-century classicism through years of Cubist experiments with Braque to the high points of the 1930s and beyond. The many women in his life figure strongly—including Dora Maar, Françoise Gilot, and Jacqueline, who survived him but eventually committed suicide. But above all, the collection gives a strong sense of the freshness and inventiveness that permeated every medium he touched—and they were many—throughout his long and creative life.
Open: Wednesday to Monday, 9:30–6, winter 9:30–5:30.

▶ **Pigalle**
metro: Pigalle
The mere name sets many a bell ringing. Renowned quartier of the lowlife since the last century, when local painters Renoir and Toulouse-Lautrec would scout around the place Pigalle looking for models among the dancers, it now flourishes in a blatant sex trade. Lining the boulevard Rochechouart and surrounding streets are sleazy bars, sex shops, peep shows, "live sex," and far more. Pimps, hookers, and transvestites all ply their trade here, and rows of tourist buses ensure the right balance of payments. But don't be put off by the sleaze, as the area also has some of the hippest nightclubs and bars in town, frequented by respectable trendies who enjoy the early-hour downhill crawl home (see pages 230–3).

▶ **Plantes, Jardin des**
metro: Gare d'Austerlitz, Jussieu, Monge
This spacious garden was set up in the 17th century; it runs down to the Seine from the Montagne Ste.-Geneviève, and is composed of a mosaic of carefully tended horticultural experiments. Presiding over this botanical paradise is the gigantic **Muséum d'Histoire Naturelle** (*open*: Wednesday to Monday, 10–5, 10–6 on summer weekends) and some aging tropical greenhouses.

On the Jussieu side, France's oldest public zoo still survives, although conditions for its animals are unfortunately rather pathetic.
Open: daily, 9–6 (9–5 in winter).

■ **Few other cities in the world have embraced the visual arts in the same way as Paris. The countless artists attracted to the city have left an unusual heritage of custom-built artists' studios and new ones are still being built. Although one of the most famous, Le Bateau Lavoir, went up in smoke, many other historic *ateliers* remain, peaceful islands in a city increasingly prone to gentrification and less and less accessible to "bohemians"** ...■

Even before the Revolution, artists were pandered to and some were given studios in the Louvre Palace; ironically, they were booted out so that the museum could be installed. The 19th century saw a rapid increase in the artist population, and many of Haussmann's boulevards in Montparnasse, Montmartre, and around Monceau incorporate studios, their high windows north-facing to benefit from the unchanging light.

Creation to conservation Some of the more bourgeois artists' studios have since become museums: the **Musée Henner** (43 avenue de Villiers, 17th); the **Musée Gustave Moreau** (14 rue de La Rochefoucauld, 9th); the **Musée Delacroix** (see page 112); **Musée Bourdelle** (see page 152); and the **Musée Bouchard** (25 rue de l'Yvette, 16th). Meanwhile, the likes of Rousseau, Degas, and Van Gogh moved from one miserable attic to the next, proof that creation is not dependent on comfort.

Working studios Most of the community studio complexes that flourished at the turn of the century are still inhabited, so if visiting them be discreet. Most famous is **La Rûche**, in the Passage Dantzig, south of Montparnasse, where Soutine, Chagall, Léger, and Diego Rivera gathered in the 1920s, heating themselves with vodka and using a communal waterpump in the garden. Conditions were rough, but from this emerged *l'Ecole de Paris*. Equally verdant, the **Cité Fleurie** on the boulevard Arago is the queen of

studio communities and recently only just escaped redevelopment.

❏ Celebrated paintings of the *atelier* include *Hommage à Manet* (Fantin-Latour, 1869), showing many of the artist's contemporaries, and *Atelier du peinture* (Courbet, 1858). ❏

Survivors At No. 31 rue Campagne Première in Montparnasse stands an exceptional block of *ateliers* built in 1911, while farther south around the Parc Montsouris, the creative hub of the 1920s survives in the **Villa Seurat**, adjoining rue Gauguet and rue Braque. Here struggled no lesser figures than Salvador Dalí, De Staël, Le Corbusier, Braque, Derain, Foujita and, recording it all for posterity, Henry Miller.

The Musée Delacroix is a former atelier in the place Furstenberg

165

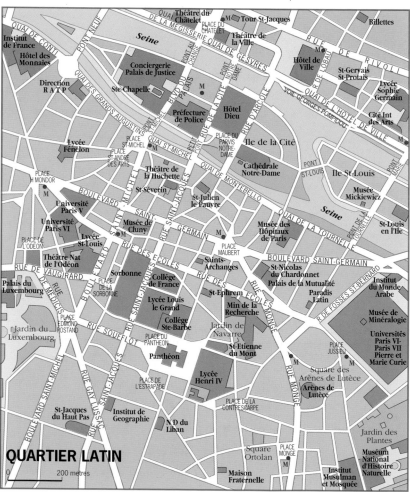

▶▶ **Quartier Latin**

For centuries Paris's intellectual heart, the Latin Quarter still thrives on its literary and artistic reputation. As you wander past Roman ruins (above all, the Cluny) along its boulevards and side streets, you will experience a distinctly relaxed and youthful atmosphere compared with the Right Bank's frenetic, business-oriented pace. Here the cliché of artists and students lingering for hours in cafés is actually true. No other area of Paris claims so many bookshops or schools, while historic churches, cinemas, jazz clubs, and narrow streets peppered with a cosmopolitan range of restaurants prevent any terminal tedium.

The university The founding of the university in 1253 (the Sorbonne) led to an animated influx of European students and professors; labeled "Latin" because students had to speak Latin, even outside classes, the area formed a Papal city within a city right up until the Revolution. In the 15th century, its intellectual life was

The Pont au Change
The Pont au Change, or "Money Changers Bridge," was set up near the Latin Quarter in the 9th century by King Charles the Bald—the only place in Paris where foreigners could change their money into French currency.

QUARTIER LATIN

0 — 200 metres

further extended by the proliferation of printing presses, which soon made the rue St.-Jacques France's publishing headquarters.

Wild reputation However, the area fast acquired a reputation for its undisciplined and bohemian inhabitants, making it fertile soil for the Revolution. Nearly 200 years later, the same characteristics of the Latin Quarter again hit the headlines in May 1968, when the students took to the streets, raised barricades, and gave the riot police hell. Demands for university reforms combined with a general rejection of consumer society values with such vehemence that the government was brought down and de Gaulle forced to resign.

Out with the old Unfortunately, much of the authentic Latin Quarter has disappeared behind the interchangeable facades and interiors of Greek restaurants, which have a particularly high profile between the **rue de la Huchette** and the **rue de la Harpe**. This is tourist land par excellence, although highlights such as the neighboring **Square René Viviani** with **St.-Julien-le-Pauvre**, one of the oldest churches in Paris, and **St.-Sévérin**, are not far. Keep heading east into the side streets off the quais and you'll discover a wonderland of small specialty shops along winding streets reeking pleasantly of the Middle Ages. Bookshops monopolize much of the trade that goes on here. Farther south, off the rue des Ecoles and within spitting distance of the **Sorbonne** and the **Collège de France**, you can plunge into the heart of academia and probably find a café once frequented by Latin Quarter intelligentsia such as Verlaine, Sartre, or Camus.

In the Latin Quarter people really do discuss life and the universe in cafés and brasseries

Map

CARREFOUR DE BUCI · RUE ST-ANDRÉ DES ARTS · QUAI DES GRANDS AUGUSTINS · PONT ST MICHEL · QUAI DU MARCHÉ NEUF · Pref de Police · PLACE DU PARVIS N D · 100 · 200 m · Ile de la Cité

RUE DE L'ANCIENNE COMEDIE · Cour de Rohan · PLACE ST-ANDRÉ · QUAI ST-MICHEL · MR DE LA HACHETTE · Cathédrale Notre-Dame

Café Procope · Lycée Fénelon · DES ARTS · Théâtre de la Huchette · QUAI DE MONTEBELLO · Seine

Statue du Danton · PLACE H MONDOR · St-Séverin · Square René Viviani · St-Julien le Pauvre

CARREFOUR DE L'ODÉON · SAINT-GERMAIN · RUE DE LA PARCHEMINERIE · RUE DANTE · RUE LA GRANGE

RUE DE CONDE · RUE DE MONSIEUR LE PRINCE · RUE A DUBOIS · Université René Descartes-Paris V · BOULEVARD SAINT-MICHEL · RUE DE LA HARPE · RUE DU HAUT

RUE DE L'ODÉON · Université Paris VI · RUE DE L'ECOLE DE MEDECINE · Musée M de Cluny · BOULEVARD SAINT-GERMAIN · RUE DE BIEVRE

PLACE DE L'ODÉON · RUE RACINE · RUE MONSIEUR LE PRINCE · PLACE MAUBERT

Palais du Luxembourg · Théâtre National de l'Odéon · Lycée St-Louis · RUE DES ECOLES · Sorbonne · Ecole Speciale des Travaux Publics · Saints-Archanges · St Nicholas de Chardonnet · RUE MONGE

PLACE PAUL CLAUDEL · Collège de France · Musée de la Pref de Police

Walk — Tracing the Latin Quarter's streets

Start at the place St.-Michel and turn down the rue de la Huchette. Cross the rue St.-Jacques and continue straight on to the square René Viviani. Honored by an acacia tree reputed to be the oldest in Paris, this square is the setting for the partly Gothic church of St.-Julien-le-Pauvre.

Circle back to the rue St.-Jacques, passing St.-Sévérin. Cut through the narrow rue de la Parcheminerie to reach the medieval rue de la Harpe, which, to the left, leads to the boulevard St.-Germain. Walk up the boulevard Saint-Michel to the rue de l'Ecole de Médecine on your right.

The radical Marat was stabbed in his bath by Charlotte Corday here.

Turn left up the rue André Dubois to reach the rue Monsieur le Prince. The rue **Monsieur le Prince** closely follows Philippe-Auguste's city wall; sections are embedded in Nos. 41 to 47. Today it is packed with cheap restaurants, including the historic Polidor at No. 41.

Continue uphill and turn onto the rue Racine leading to the place Paul Claudel. The 18th-century **Théâtre National de l'Odéon** dominates this area.

Meander down the rue de l'Odéon to reach Odéon metro. Across the boulevard St.-Germain is the rue de l'Ancienne Comédie. Pass Paris's oldest café, **Le Procope**, now a restaurant, on your right before you reach the Buci crossroads.

At the crossroads turn sharp right onto the rue St.-André-des-Arts. This street is thick with pizzerias, performers, and cafés.

This leads you back to St.-Michel.

The square René Viviani

Raynouard, Rue
This long street running parallel to the Seine takes you through the residential heart of Passy toward Auteuil. Apart from Balzac, who lived at No. 47 (see page 71), other illustrious inhabitants included the philosopher Jean-Jacques Rousseau, the poet Béranger, and Benjamin Franklin. Nos. 51 to 55 are the work of architect brothers Auguste and Gustave Perret who, after Le Corbusier had broken with their "classical" conceptions, designed this building for their agency and apartments (1929) before turning to the astonishing Musée des Travaux Publics, place d'Iéna.

► Rivoli, Rue de
It's easy to forget that Rivoli is an Italian town, scene of an almighty Napoleonic thrashing of the Austrians in 1797. In homage to this victory, the long, colonnaded street was designed by the emperor's official architects, Percier and Fontaine, in 1811, but only completed in 1835. Today its gracious arcades shelter rows of tourist shops interspersed with one or two classier joints such as the **Hôtel Meurice**, the *salon de thé* **Angélina**, and the bookshop **Galignani** (next door to each other). On its south side are the **Tuileries gardens**, the **Musée des**

Arts de la Mode, the **Musée des Arts Décoratifs**, and, finally, the **Louvre**.

►► Rohan, Hôtel de
87 rue Vieille-du-Temple, 75003
metro: Chemin-Vert, Rambuteau
Yet another Marais mansion enlisted to house the extensive Archives Nationales, the Hôtel de Rohan can only be seen during temporary exhibitions. Designed by Delamair in 1704 for the son of the Prince of Soubise, whose neighboring hôtel (see page 126) was built at the same time, it was inhabited by a string of fast-living cardinals. Their apartments are examples of the ornate yet delicate mid-18th-century style.

►►► Rodin, Musée
Hôtel Biron, 77 rue de Varenne, 75007
metro: Varenne
Even if you are not invited to the Elysée Palace or the

Elegant apartments in the heart of Passy. This was once just a simple village inhabited by wood-cutters, but is now one of Paris's most chic residential districts

Let there be light
The first lightning conductor ever seen in France was erected by Benjamin Franklin on the roof of his house in rue Raynouard.

A terrorist attack
Jo Goldenberg's, the most famous delicatessen and restaurant on the rue des Rosiers, was the tragic scene in 1982 of a terrorist attack, when gunmen killed six customers.

Hôtel Matignon, you can at least experience the pleasures of Paris's third-largest private garden, which surrounds the Hôtel Biron. Originally built for a prosperous wig maker in 1730, the harmonious mansion of columns and pediments was bought in 1753 by a dedicated horticulturalist, the Maréchal de Biron, who proceeded to indulge his gardening passion until he was dragged off to the guillotine.

Changing faces Subsequently a dance hall, convent, and school, the Hôtel Biron was, in 1908, yet again transformed, this time into artists' studios. In moved the redoubtable Rodin, who stayed until his death in 1917, paying his rent with works. His fellow inmates included Rainer Maria Rilke (working as Rodin's secretary), Isadora Duncan, Cocteau, and Matisse. On Rodin's death, the house became the Musée Rodin.

Musée Rodin: some of Rodin's finest works have spread beyond the mansion where he spent his last nine years, into the delightful rose gardens

The gardens The blissful rose gardens are one of Paris's greatest hidden treasures, containing several of Rodin's most important pieces: *Le Penseur*, permanently meditating, *la Porte de l'Enfer*, and *les Bourgeois de Calais*, eternally dragging their chains. A former chapel housing temporary sculpture exhibitions and an outdoor café, open during the summer months, complete its attractions.

The house Inside the elegant, airy house you can follow Rodin's evolution chronologically, from his early academic sketches and paintings to his vigorous watercolors. His lyrical power and technical breadth are as apparent in the passionate white-marble *Kiss*, the nude *John the Baptist*, the spiritual *Main de Dieu*, or *Eve* and *L'Age d'Airan*, each of which is displayed in the rotundas. Busts of contemporaries such as Puvis de Chavannes, Mahler, Carrier-Belleuse, Lady Sackville-West, or the suffragette Eve Fairfax reveal his penetrating approach to humanity, particularly evident in his paunchy nude studies of Balzac on the first floor. Works by contemporaries include his tragic model, muse, and mistress, Camille Claudel, Eugène Carrière, Munch, Renoir, Monet, and Van Gogh.
Open: Tuesday to Sunday, 10–5:45 (10–5 in winter).

▶▶   Rosiers, Rue des
This ancient street runs the length of Philippe-Auguste's famous city wall and some remnants remain, hidden behind recent facades. It was already known in 1230 under its present name, probably thanks to numerous rose gardens, but today street odors tend more toward Middle-Eastern falafel. Heart of the Jewish quarter, the street houses a noisy, animated community with numerous Mediterranean takeout specialties and Jewish shops.

▶▶▶   Royal, Palais
metro: Palais-Royal
From heaven to hell, the Palais-Royal has run the full gamut of social status. Designed by Lemercier for the wily Cardinal Richelieu, who died there in 1642, the palace became royal when the regent, Anne of Austria,

moved in with her young son Louis XIV. His horizons being wider, Louis XIV eventually settled into the more spacious Versailles, leaving the Palais-Royal to his brother, Philippe d'Orléans, who turned it into a lively meeting place for the wits and fashion victims of the day. The houses and galleries surrounding the gardens were added in the 1780s and soon sheltered gambling dens, cafés, and brothels; one visitor described it as possessing "every kind of luxury, dirt, and magnificence imaginable." Since the police were banned, its cafés became a fermenting ground for revolutionary ideas.

Current occupation Today the magnificent palace buildings are occupied by the Ministry of Culture and the Conseil d'Etat, while the shops display a bizarre but interesting mixture, from stamps and medals to contemporary design, antique porcelain, and books. The revamped garden offers clouds of brilliant color and its restaurants, tearooms, and benches are notorious summer crowd-pullers. A recent landmark is Buren's columns, which, in their black-and-white striped splendor, with underground waterways and nocturnal airport lighting, provide endless photo opportunities.

►   **Royale, Rue**
metro: Madeleine, Concorde
Haunt of luxury-goods hunters, the 18th-century rue Royale joins the Concorde to the Madeleine. Its most famous establishment is **Maxim's**, at No. 3, where high society flocked during the Belle Epoque, while at No. 21 once stood the famous literary café, the **Café Weber.**

►►►   **Sacré-Coeur**
metro: Abbesses, Anvers
It is often forgotten, but the Sacré-Coeur was commissioned as atonement for the 58,000 dead of the 1870–1 Franco-Prussian war. Even today, priests work in relays to keep the prayers going 24 hours a day. This extraordinary neo-Romanesque-Byzantine edifice has a strong tourist pull, mainly for its hilltop site overlooking Paris. Climb the dome (open: daily, 9–6; 9–7 in summer) at dawn or dusk for one of Paris's most spectacular views.

Sacré-Coeur—the highest point in Paris—affords 30-mile views from its dome

171

Auguste Rodin (1840–1917)
Rodin supported himself for years molding and chiseling before creating a scandal with *L'Age d'Airan*, in 1877. By 1900, he was established in the official cultural community and enjoyed a public fame greater than any of his contemporaries. His works often caused violent quarrels among the critics; he despised outward "finish" and was mistakenly categorized with the Impressionists.

Faith and generosity
A public subscription was opened to finance the Sacré-Coeur, a method that contributed to its lengthy construction—35 years.

Spectacular stained glass in Sainte-Chapelle creates a blaze of light and color beneath the ornate star-studded roof

Precious relics
During the Revolution, Saint Louis's ornate and valuable reliquary was melted down and the chapel itself narrowly escaped demolition, but the relics were saved and today they are kept in Notre-Dame, brought out only on Good Friday.

►►► **Sainte-Chapelle**
boulevard du Palais, 75004
metro: Cité, St.-Michel
Despite being one of Paris's oldest and most significant monuments, the Sainte-Chapelle is hidden in a courtyard behind the Palais de Justice, modestly holding back its charms. Built in under three years, its spire soars 245 feet above ground, unimpeded by flying buttresses—a daring architectural feat for the time. Proof of the intelligence of its design is that nothing has cracked over its 700-year existence, although there was a serious fire in 1630. But the most astonishing feature of this chapel is the ambitious range, color, and intricacy of its stained-glass windows; 1,134 biblical scenes are illustrated, so don't forget your binoculars.

Simple style Most of the castle chapels of the early Middle Ages were as architecturally straightforward as the fortifications themselves and were built on two floors, to accommodate the master and his family above, with retainers banished to the lower floor. In France, the real development of castle chapels came with Louis IX (later canonized), who employed Pierre de Montreuil to build the Sainte-Chapelle, his private chapel, that was completed in 1248. Saint Louis's aim was to have a shrine worthy of various relics acquired during the Crusades, including what was reputed to be the crown of thorns, pieces of the Cross, and drops of Christ's blood. These he had obtained, at an exorbitant cost, from the emperor of Constantinople.

The front of the chapel is given relief by two porches, above which rises an immense rose window, rebuilt under Charles VIII in 1485, surmounted by a *fleur de lys* balustrade. Entrance through the portal takes you into the somber lower chapel. The decorative paintwork here is a product of the mid-19th century, when attempts were made to reproduce the medieval style. It was badly damaged during the Revolution, when it was used as a flour warehouse, and Haussmann's medievalists (in particular Viollet-le-Duc) were only too happy to go to town on this exceptional monument.

The upper chapel A narrow spiral staircase leads to the upper royal chapel: here a visual shock awaits you. Instead of walls you have luminous, unmitigated color—the concentrated effect of 739 square yards of the oldest stained-glass windows in Paris. Surmounted by delicately sculpted gables, the structure of the vaults unfortunately recedes behind more 19th-century paint; however, the main interest lies in the windows. Starting immediately to your left, you can follow the biblical narrative from Genesis through the Crucifixion to the Apocalypse (the rose window), taking in Saint Louis himself on the way. Each window should be read left to right, bottom to top, apart from certain scenes in the choir apse.

The windows Starting with the first bay, these are the main themes:

1 Genesis, Adam and Eve, Noah, Jacob
2 Exodus, Moses on Mount Sinaï
3 Exodus, the Law of Moses
4 Deuteronomy, Joshua, Ruth and Boaz
5 The Judges, Gideon, Samson
6 Isaiah, the Tree of Jesse
7 Saint John, the Virgin, Christ's childhood
8 Christ's passion
9 Saint John the Baptist, Daniel
10 Ezekiel
11 Jeremiah, Tobias
12 Judith, Job
13 Esther
14 Kings, Samuel, David, Solomon
15 Saint Helena and the True Cross, Saint Louis and the Relics
16 The Apocalypse—a rose divided into 86 panels

Leaning against each pillar is a statue of an apostle, but few are originals, and all are heavily restored. Damaged originals are displayed at the Cluny.

In front of the altar stands a wooden canopied platform that once displayed the famous relics. The open spiral stairs leading to it (only the left-hand one is original) were often used by Saint Louis in a ceremonial inspection of his treasure.

Acoustic advantages Concerts are regularly held in the chapel, taking advantage of its fantastic acoustics, but as these are in the evening you will not have an opportunity to admire the stained-glass windows.
Open: daily, 10–5 in winter; 9:30–6:30 in summer.

Architectural highlights

Features to look for include 12 medieval wooden carvings of the Apostles, the niches reserved for the royal family on both sides of the chapel in the fourth bays, and Saint Louis oratory, which Louis XI added in the late 14th century so that he could watch Mass unobserved through a small angled grille near the door. His escape route back to the adjoining palace was via a gallery leading off from the second bay.

A spherical cinema
Across the moat outside the Cité des Sciences et de l'Industrie stands the spherical Géode cinema, which programs special wide-angle films in its hemispherical interior (reservations essential; tel: 40 05 70 00).

▶ St.-Denis, Rue

This idiosyncratic street was named after the martyr Saint Denis, who apparently accomplished the astonishing feat of staggering headless from where he was decapitated in Montmartre to the site of the future basilica of St.-Denis. The long Roman rue St.-Denis was once the processional route for French royalty arriving for coronation and departing for burial; today it presents a very different face, one of prostitutes, sex shops, and, at the Les Halles end, fast-food joints. Despite this sleazy appearance there are a few picturesque old-world bars squeezed between the new-world tack and a stroll north toward the ornamental 1672 **Porte St.-Denis** can be amusing.

St.-Germain see pages 176–7.

▶ St.-Honoré, Rue

Like the rue St.-Denis, it runs off the central area of Les Halles, yet the rue St.-Honoré is quite a different, well-mannered world. Lined with respectable clothes, food, and antiques shops, it is also one of Paris's oldest roads: Jeanne d'Arc was wounded here, Molière was born here, and Marie-Antoinette was transported to the guillotine along it. It takes in the baroque **Eglise St.-Roch**, skirts around the **Comédie Française**, and crosses the **place du Palais-Royal** behind the massive **Louvre des Antiquaires**, a costly antiques market. On the western side of the rue Royale it becomes the Faubourg St.-Honoré which, along with the avenue Montaigne, provides the greatest concentration of luxury clothing stores in the capital.

St.-Jacques, Rue

Apart from its status as Paris's oldest street (another Roman feat), the steep rue St.-Jacques makes clear the origin of the delicious *coquilles St.-Jacques* common in Parisian restaurants. With a street named after the crusader Saint Jacques, Paris became the starting point for pilgrims trekking south to his shrine in Spain, who set off attired in the saint's symbol, a scallop shell.

▶ St.-Jacques, Tour

metro: Châtelet
The Flamboyant Gothic tower still standing in this square dates from the early 16th century, once part of the church of St.-Jacques-La-Boucherie, which was demolished in 1797. It is now a meteorological station.

▶▶ St.-Sulpice, Eglise de

metro: St.-Sulpice
Apart from housing one of the world's largest organs, St.-Sulpice is a remarkable example of a public edifice that took 134 years to build and was left with two strangely asymmetrical towers. Don't miss Delacroix's murals in the first chapel on the right as you enter, and look for a bronze meridian line in the transept that, at winter solstice and equinoxes, reflects sunbeams onto an obelisk and then onto the cross—a true tribute to France's 19th-century scientific spirit.
Open: 7:30AM–7:30PM and during services on Sunday.

Cité des Sciences et de l'Industrie—a giant science and technology museum with over 7 acres of hands-on displays

▶▶ Sciences et de l'Industrie, Cité des

30 avenue Corentin Cariou, 75019
metro: Porte de la Villette
Set in the northeast of Paris in the expanding Parc de la Villette, the futuristic Cité des Sciences attracts young visitors to participate in its spectacular displays of science and technology. Life is never the same again after visiting their inventorium or Explora, which whisks you through 35,880 square yards, of "space, life, matter, and communication," the very spacey Planetarium, or the *Cité des Enfants*.
Open: Tuesday to Sunday, 10–6.

▶▶▶ Sens, Hôtel de

1 rue du Figuier, 75004
metro: Pont-Marie
It is well worth a special trip to see this mansion overlooking the Seine, Le Marais' greatest medieval building dating from 1475 to 1507. Built for the archbishops of Sens, it was later inhabited by Henri IV's first wife, Queen Margot. Her taste for young lovers created deadly rivalries, culminating in her ordering the beheading of one unfortunate victim on the mansion steps. Today, less dramatically, the building is used as an applied arts library, the Bibliothèque Forney, and sometimes organizes related exhibitions.
Open: Tuesday to Friday, 1:30–8:30; Saturday, 10–8:30.

Sèvres, Musée de la Céramique de

place de la Manufacture, 92310 Sèvres
metro: Pont de Sèvres
A leading name in world porcelain, this rich collection covers several centuries of Sèvres production, as well as European pottery of the Middle Ages, Islamic and Chinese ceramics, and Italian Majolica.
Open: Wednesday to Monday, 10–5.

A visit to the sewers
The Sewers (*égouts*), Pont de l'Alma, Quai d'Orsay (tel: 47 05 10 29) have, for some bizarre reason, become a popular tourist destination. One of Haussmann's greatest accomplishments, this vast 1,305-mile underground network—which also contains telephone wires and electricity cables—can be seen on a guided tour that includes a film and photographic display.
Open: Saturday to Wednesday, 11–5 (4PM in winter).

175

The bouquinistes
The history of these green
wooden bookstalls lining
the Seine dates back three
centuries to when second-
hand booksellers piled up
their wares on the river-
bank prior to taking them
across the river in wheel-
barrows.

▶ ▶ ▶ St.-Germain-des-Prés

Tranquilly cradled at the heart of Paris, St.-Germain
remains eternally magnetic for the visitor and resident
alike. Modern incursions are rare and the atmosphere
still has something of the Paris of history, literature, and
cinema. The pace seems more leisurely than on the
other side of the river, cafés still play their traditional
role, and backstreet bistros whisk diners back half a
century or so. Aproned waiters and waitresses scold as
they are reputed to, and the residents still include a fair
share of eccentrics and/or intelligentsia.

Origins Symbol of its genesis, the **Eglise St.-Germain-
des-Prés** dates from the late 10th century, when it was
part of a Benedictine monastery which replaced a 6th-
century abbey. By the 14th century it was surrounded by
a fortified wall, which disappeared with the Age of
Enlightenment to make way for housing — and the new
nobles of the Faubourg St.-Germain to the west. Badly

The church of St. Germain-des-Prés, the oldest church in Paris. Its eventful history dates back to a 6th-century abbey founded here by King Childebert

Boulevard St.-Germain
The lively cafés of Boulevard St.-Germain—the rendezvous of the literary elite—include the Café de Fiore, once frequented by Jean Paul Sartre, and Café les Deux Magots, former haunt of Ernest Hemingway. Brasserie Lipp was one of former President Mitterand's favorites.

damaged during the Revolution, only one of its original three towers remains, but the massive flying buttresses of the choir (12th-century), among the oldest in France, remain intact. As usual, the 19th century brought much retouching and both the nave and the choir contain murals by Flandrin from that period.

The living heart of St.-Germain is, of course, the **boulevard**, which runs west from the Latin Quarter to join the staid government buildings and bourgeois mansions of the 7th arrondissement. North of the boulevard, toward the Seine, remains an essentially arty district, crowded with small cinemas, galleries, antiques shops, the national art school (see page 79), and the Mint (see page 147). In the shadows of its narrow streets you can make your own discoveries of shops, restaurants, or hidden courtyards, all finished with a veneer of affluence. It's a quartier in limbo, which cannot decide whether it is part of the forward-looking new capital or clinging to its prewar intellectual days.

South of the boulevard the streets widen and the atmosphere changes. From the church of **St.-Sulpice** to the **Jardin du Luxembourg**, through the shopping streets of the **rue Bonaparte, rue de Sèvres**, and **rue de Grenelle**, this is the St.-Germain of fashion and publishing. Chic bars replace crowded cafés and furniture design shops line the **boulevard Raspail**, leading up to the crossroads of Sèvres-Babylone, which is dominated by the renovated art-deco **Hôtel Lutetia** and Paris's first department store, **Les Trois Quartiers**.

Seat of learning: La Sorbonne, the University of Paris, with its oldest building, the domed Church of Ste.-Ursule, dating from 1635

► La Sorbonne
45–7 rue des Ecoles, 75005
metro: Cluny-La Sorbonne

Symbol of France's great spirit of learning, the Sorbonne was founded in 1253 and for centuries maintained an independent attitude to the state, recognizing the English Henry V as king of France, condemning Joan of Arc, later fiercely opposing Protestants (Henri IV) and the 18th-century "philosophers." The student revolts in 1968 gave the state its first opportunity to allow police to enter these premises. Richelieu was responsible for the rebuilding of the dilapidated college in 1642, although Lemercier's domed chapel, where the cardinal lies in splendor, is all that remains: today's amphitheaters and endless corridors all date from the late 19th century. You can enter the imposing courtyard off the rue de la Sorbonne and ask for permission to see Puvis de Chavannes' mural in the Grand Amphitheater.

►► Sully, Hôtel de
62 rue St.-Antoine, 75004
metro: St.-Paul

All was not sweetness and light in the heyday of Le Marais, as the gambling owner of this superb 1630 mansion is said to have lost his fortune overnight. He left a richly decorated home that was soon bought by Henri IV's former minister, the Duc de Sully. The courtyard is a particularly impressive example of Louis XII, and the recently restored interior boasts some ornate ceilings and paneling. In the garden, an Orangerie is used for temporary exhibitions, and the bookshop of the Caisse Nationale des Monuments Historiques at the entrance has useful information on guided tours and monuments. The garden is open daily.
Open: By guided tour only (tel: 44 61 20 00 for times).

Synagogue
metro: St.-Paul

Although the architect Hector Guimard is best remembered for his fanlighted *Metropolitain* entrances, he was also prolific between 1895 and 1910. The synagogue in the heart of the Jewish quarter in Le Marais was one of his later designs, built in 1913. Distressed by the rise of fascism, Guimard later emigrated to the United States, where he died in 1942.

▶▶ Techniques, Musée National des
292 rue Saint-Martin, 75003
metro: Arts et Métiers
This extraordinary and much overlooked museum was set up under the revolutionary government of 1794, based on a farsighted idea of Descartes' who, a century earlier, had seen the need for conserving and exhibiting artisan machinery. Installed in a medieval priory, the museum encompasses a 13th-century church, and a section of wall is still crowned by two original towers of the same period.

Cars and curios The enlightening collection includes models and examples of early transportation—what other church nave accommodates parked Peugeots, Foucault's pendulum, and Blériot's first flying machines?—astronomical equipment, clocks (including a decimal example for the Revolutionary calendar), automats (mostly 18th-century rococo), energy, acoustics, glass (Daum, Lalique, Gallé, Murano), photography, and broadcasting. Modern inventions include an antiquated 1938 wooden washing machine and the first mass-manufactured car, made by Ford in 1908. Unfortunately, renovation is changing the museum's Victorian atmosphere.
Open: Tuesday to Sunday, 10–5:30.

Tristan Tzara, Maison
15 avenue Junot, 75018
metro: Abbesses
In one of Montmartre's select streets stands the only house in Paris designed by the Austrian architect Adolf Loos. Opponent of the "decorative" art nouveau and defender of a pure rationalist style, Loos settled in Paris in 1923 and soon designed this house for the monocled writer Tristan Tzara, at the time deeply involved in bringing about the death rattle of Dadaism.

▶▶ Trocadéro, Place du
metro: Trocadéro
Another landmark Parisian square, Trocadéro is actually laid out in a semicircle facing the wings of the **Palais de Chaillot** and beyond that, in a direct line, the **Eiffel Tower**. Named after an Andalusian fort occupied by the French in 1823, it was not given its present shape until 1858, when a first **Palais de Chaillot** was built. The 1937 Exposition Internationale replaced the palace with the present monumental buildings, which house several museums (see pages 91 and 94). Around the area are well-frequented cafés and restaurants, including the *salon de thé* **Carette**, a regular on the Passy agenda.

▶▶▶ Tuileries, Jardins des
metro: Tuileries
The famous Tuileries gardens were originally laid out Italian-style to complement the palace built for Catherine de Médicis in 1564. Corneille described them as "the land of the beautiful people and of gallantry," where balls, concerts, and fireworks provided constant animation. In 1649, Louis XIV stepped onto the scene with his minister Colbert and commissioned major

The Trocadéro Gardens, sloping down toward the Seine from the Palais de Chaillot, are dotted with unusual sculptures and fountains

179

Jardins des Tuileries—60 acres of beautifully landscaped gardens at the very heart of the city

Playing with boats in the Jardins des Tuileries

changes by his favorite landscape gardener, the prodigious André Le Nôtre (also responsible for the immaculate gardens at Versailles, Chantilly, and Vaux le Vicomte). Two lateral esplanades were built up and the central alley that led away from the château laid out. At the time, the garden was considered one of the best kept in Europe and was a fashionable promenading area. Although the royal residence went up in serious smoke at the hands of the Communards in 1871 and was never rebuilt, the gardens survived, changing their appearance little over the next century.

Mark of time Years of neglect and pollution have left their mark. Today the carefully aligned fountains, ponds, terraces, lawns, flower beds, and statues are undergoing renovation, as official light has been thrown on the sorry state of the vegetation and, particularly, the sick, badly pruned trees. A five-year plan has been drawn up to ensure that the Tuileries gardens will be as sparkling as the Louvre when its extension and renovations are completed by the end of 1996.

Regained role Opposite the pyramid, the Arc du Carrousel will regain its original role as a gate to the garden, a canal will be built and lined with Maillol's famous statues, which used to be dotted all over the lawns, and a terrace will be built up to improve the view looking across the gardens toward the Concorde. The main area will keep its basic form, but with numerous improved facilities (children's playgrounds, lawn bowling areas) and a vastly regenerated and replanted vegetation. Whatever immediate improvements are visible, a quarter-century is estimated as necessary for the full impact of the new plantings.

■ **If caught in Paris on one of its rare rainy days—March showers being the rule—head for the 2nd and 9th arrondissements, where a network of covered passages creates a sheltered itinerary full of surprises. Relics of pre-department store days, these passages were the fashionable shopping malls of early 19th-century Paris ...■**

Almost 30 survive out of the original 140 passages: many have been heavily restored, others are dusty, partly derelict reminders of an age past, but all have traders in the strangest of domains.

Start with one of the most picturesque, hardly touched since it was built in 1822, the **Galerie Véro-Dodat**, which runs between the rue Jean-Jacques Rousseau and the rue Croix des Petits Champs. Named after two butchers, it was one of Paris's first streets to be illuminated by gas. Today its black-and-white tiled floor, window boxes, and carved wood moldings make a shadowy, harmonious setting for an old-world restaurant, antiques shops, and galleries, including a wonderful antique doll shop.

High fashion A few streets away, beyond the place des Victoires, is the **Galerie Vivienne**, perhaps the most fashionable of these passages, built in 1828. Home to one of Paris's best wine merchants, Legrand; the now legendary enfant terrible of fashion, Jean-Paul Gaultier; an extraordinary toy shop; a unique bookstore, and a chic tearoom, whose tables spill out under the lofty skylights, the Galerie Vivienne should not be missed. Running parallel and off it is the overrestored **Galerie Colbert**, which houses some interesting shops and galleries, all belonging to the Bibliothèque Nationale, as well as a brasserie, the Grand Café Colbert.

Head north up the rue Vivienne past the Bourse and you will find a passage with a strange past: the **Passage des Panoramas**. It was built in 1800 by an American who came to France to propose various

The Galerie Vivienne

inventions to the new Directoire, among which were a torpedo and a submarine. To earn a few bucks while waiting, he built two towers containing panoramas at the boulevard end of his passage. Today the passage is a mass of specialty shops (look for the card engraver, Stern) with some unusual eating places, including a tearoom installed on the site of an old chocolate factory and an Italian trattoria that could be straight out of Rome.

Other options Across the boulevard Montmartre the passages continue (**Passages Jouffroy** and **Verdeau**), each one revealing its own unique character to the inquisitive visitor with time to explore them.

Frequented by the famous
Residents of the place Vendôme have included Chopin, who died at No. 12, and Anton Mesmer, the inventor of mesmerism, who held experiments at No. 16. The Ritz guest book includes Proust, Barbara Hutton, and Chanel.

Artist's exile
Juliette Drouet became Victor Hugo's devoted mistress and accompanied him on his self-imposed exile to Guernsey (in furious reaction to Napoleon III's coup d'état), where they remained from 1848 to 1870.

▶ Vendôme, Place

metro: Opéra, Tuileries

Supreme symbol of Parisian chic, the place Vendôme is densely populated by jewelry stores and anything else that can approach the same level of quality and price tags: the **Ritz Hotel**, for example. The square's facades were designed in 1685 by Hardouin-Mansart as an aptly gracious setting for an equestrian statue of Louis XIV by Girardon. This effigy did not outlast the energies of the mob during the Revolution and it was duly felled, to be replaced by the present bronze column. This was initially crowned by a figure of Napoleon; in 1814 a statue of Henri IV took over, but after several more changes, including the toppling of the column by the Communards, a copy of Napoleon's original statue resumed its post. The bronze itself came from canons captured at the Battle of Austerlitz.

▶ Vert-Galant, Square du

metro: Pont-Neuf

The pointed western tip of the Ile de la Cité is named after Henri IV, Paris's first regal town planner, who commissioned both the Pont-Neuf and the place Dauphine immediately across from his fine equestrian statue. This little garden has a wonderful view west along the Seine. Boat trips leave from the quay here.

Versailles see pages 210–3.

▶▶ Victor Hugo, Maison de

6 place des Vosges, 75004
metro: Bastille

This is one of Paris's most characteristic museums, giving a rounded view of the great writer's many talents and his changing residences, which included the second floor of this townhouse from 1832 to 1848. Displayed on the first floor are numerous pen and ink drawings by Victor Hugo, alongside occasional temporary exhibitions. Upstairs, the rooms are laid out to give the atmosphere of his diverse abodes and include a surprising *salon chinois* and furniture from actress Juliette Drouet's room in Guernsey, all carved and/or decorated by the writer himself. Other Hugo memorabilia include a bust of him by Rodin, portraits of his wife and mistress, photographs, and a few family souvenirs.

Open: Tuesday to Sunday, 10–5:40.

Maison de Victor Hugo: the Salle à Manger Chinoise from Hugo's villa in Guernsey has been reproduced here, with most of the oriental-style carving executed by Hugo himself

Vidéothèque de Paris

2 Grande Galerie, Forum des Halles, Porte St.-Eustache, 75001

metro: Les Halles

Another underground destination of Les Halles, the Vidéothèque is a must for anyone interested in both film and Paris. Since opening in 1988, this municipal video library has built up a stock of over 3,500 videotapes covering anything that has ever been put on celluloid concerning the capital—from the Lumière brothers in 1896 to the present—including TV documentaries, commercials, and feature films. You can either watch the excellent thematic programs shown daily on the large screen or use an individual monitor to view your own choice of film(s). Entrance costs less than a cinema seat. *Open*: Tuesday to Sunday, 1–9.

►► La Villette, Parc de

metro: Porte de la Villette, Porte de Pantin

Nearing completion, the multipurpose Parc de la Villette is one of Paris's most important cultural projects of the last decade. Stretching around the northeastern perimeter of the city, the 136-acre park has been developed since 1979 by architect Bernard Tschumi to offer a concentrated range of cultural and leisure activities on the grounds of an old slaughterhouse.

"Give me back my leg" High points in Vincennes' history include La Fayette heroically saving it from destruction by the mob in 1791, the Duc d'Enghien savoring his last dinner in the splendor of the Pavillon du Roi before facing Napoleon's firing squad at midnight, the peglegged General Daumesnil refusing to surrender the castle to the Allies in 1814 with the cry "First give me back my leg" (he had lost it at the Battle of Wagram), and the execution of the tantalizing spy Mata Hari in 1917.

Facilities and follies A major, integral part of the project, the **Cité des Sciences et de l'Industrie** (see page 175) sits in its moat beside the canal, faced by a spherical cinema, **La Géode►** (both designed by Fainsilber), but many of the surrounding walkway structures and red metal "follies" are cumbersome and apparently aimless. A survivor from 1867 is the original slaughterhouse, **La Grande Halle**, which in a renovated form now accommodates temporary events, from trade fairs to exhibitions to concerts. In front, dominating the Porte de Pantin park entrance, is the recently completed **Cité de la Musique**, designed by Portzamparc in a neo-1930s style, which gives music students modern facilities and a superb public concert hall. Another concert hall, **Le Zénith**, conceived specifically for rock concerts, stands on the northern edge of the park. Scattered between these landmarks are numerous children's facilities, cafés, gardens, a submarine, and the Inventorium, where anyone can "build" a house or program computers.

Parc de la Villette— the extensive urban park being developed in a previously run-down area, combining arts and sciences with nature, is nearing completion

VINCENNES

The Château de Vincennes' checkered history as a former royal residence, prison, porcelain factory, and arsenal makes a fascinating family day out

All the fun of the fair
The Bois de Vincennes plays host to the Foire du Trône, the largest funfair in France, from Palm Sunday until the end of May on the Reuilly lawns. The other main fair in Paris is held twice a year (summer and Christmas) in the Tuileries Gardens. Its big wheel affords spectacular views of central Paris. Near the Sacré-Coeur and at Forum Les Halles are old-fashioned carousels.

► **Vincennes, Château and Bois de**
metro: Château de Vincennes

Before its many reincarnations, the sturdy medieval castle commanding the east of Paris arose in the 14th century and was completed under Charles V. The symmetrical Pavillon du Roi and Pavillon de la Reine were added to the southern end by Le Vau while Cardinal Mazarin ruled the roost in 1652, but were badly damaged in 1944 when the Germans abandoned Paris.

Although Louis XIV spent his honeymoon here, Vincennes was soon supplanted by Versailles (completed in 1680) and thus started its string of transformations. Successively a prison, a porcelain factory (which then moved west to become the famous Manufacture de Sèvres), a military school, an arms factory, and, under Napoleon, an arsenal, Vincennes became a fortress under Louis-Philippe in the 1850s and an ammunition depot during the German Occupation. For over a century, starting with the fanatical medievalist Viollet-le-Duc in the reign of Napoleon III, intermittent restoration has been carried out.

Entrance to the château (*open*: daily, 10–4, 10–6 in summer) is through the Tour du Village, a powerful 138-foot tower that leads into the central courtyard. On your left is a strange museum, with even stranger opening hours (tel: 49 57 32 00), dedicated to the history of shoes. Entrance to the dungeons is with guided tours, commentary in French only.

The chapel The royal chapel dominating the courtyard, although in 14th-century Gothic style with a superb rose window, was completed in 1552 under Henri II, and its gracefully vaulted interior is well worth entering. The stained-glass windows in the choir are unusually toned Renaissance scenes of the Apocalypse, much restored in the late 19th century.

The dungeons Opposite the chapel, the dungeons are in a walled area surmounted by a square turreted tower, one of the finest in France. Inside, the ground floor once housed the kitchen and has now gained a door rescued from the Temple prison, where Louis XVI was imprisoned. A spiral staircase leads to the upper floors, where resident royalty, including Henry V of England and Charles IX, and later prisoners of state, enjoyed a panoramic view of Paris.

The royal courtyard, accessible through another gateway and closed at the southern end by the monumental Tour du Bois, is flanked by the royal pavilions, closed to the public apart from a small section containing yet another idiosyncratic museum, the Musée des Insignes. Le Vau's classical structure was inhabited by various minor royalty, as well as Cardinal Mazarin, who died there.

Bois Landscaped at the same time as the Bois de Boulogne by Baron Haussmann, the Bois de Vincennes traditionally served the working-class population of eastern Paris. It possesses no fewer than three lakes, the Parc Floral, a racecourse, a zoo, a tropical garden, a Buddhist center, a theater complex and, at the Porte Dorée entrance, the Musée des Arts Africains et Océaniens (see page 63). Like Boulogne, it, too, was once rich royal hunting ground, sectioned off by another of Philippe-Auguste's walls in the 12th century. By Louis XV's reign, it had become a popular promenading area and the woods were replanted.

The Zoo► Near the Lac Daumesnil, France's largest zoo (open: daily, 9–5) houses over 600 mammals and 200 species of birds in a fairly natural, spacious environment. The best time is had by mountain goats, careering up and down their 230-foot artificial rock. Avoid Wednesday afternoons and weekends, particularly in summer, when lines are long.

Nearer the château, the **Parc Floral** (open: 9:30–8 in summer, earlier closing in winter) provides an exceptional floral display renewed every season. Special sections exist for dahlias, water lilies, medicinal plants, iris, orchids, tulips, rhododendrons, and azaleas; there is also an exhibition hall and a children's playground. Rowboats and bicycles can be rented at the lakes. Vincennes also houses, adjacent to the Parc Floral, the famous collective theater, the **Théâtre du Soleil** at La Cartoucherie (a former munitions factory), founded by Ariane Mnouchkine in the late 1960s.

A boiled king
Macabre legend has it that on his death, Henry V's body, rotten with dysentery, was boiled in the château kitchens.

185

Contemplating life as residents of the Bois de Vincennes zoo

■ **Parisians seem to have an innate knack for staying chic. Even though 66 percent of French women now work full-time and often cope with children, too, they seem never to have a hair out of place or an unco-ordinated accessory. Not to speak of the men who swing along the boulevards or stub out their Gitanes with a flourish that is unmistakably Gallic ...■**

Fashion shows

Paris's fashion seasons start in January and July with the *haute couture* shows at the Cour Carrée du Louvre. Tickets are virtually impossible to obtain. However, to attend a private *couture* show, call the *haute couture* houses one month prior to the show to reserve a ticket.

Wine can be ordered and delivered from any of the Nicolas chain of shops

So what's their eternal and annoying secret? Self-respect (sometimes called egocentricity) is one good reason. And this means taking good care of oneself, pampering one's ego and one's outer shell.

Body beautiful Alexandre de Paris (3 avenue Matignon, 8e, tel: 42 25 57 90) is perhaps Paris's most famous hairdresser for men and women and also offers massages and facials. Service is suitably syco-phantic, and meals are also served during what can be time-consuming treatments. Carita (11 rue du Faubourg St.-Honoré, 8e, tel: 44 94 11 00) now specializes in both sexes, and their three floors of clinical-looking individual booths cater for manicures, pedicures, massages, facials, and (the specialty) hair treatments. Phones and snacks are all part of the service. Now you will understand how Catherine Deneuve remains eternally youthful.

For skin care only, it is hard to beat the time-honored Guerlain (68 Champs-Elysées, 8e, tel: 47 89 71 80; 29 rue de Sèvres, 6e, tel: 42 22 46 60). Elegant private salons in their original 1828 premises contrast with the frayed Champs-Elysées outside. In a similar vein, the Institut Payot (10 rue de Castiglione, 1e, tel: 42 60 32 87), founded by a Russian émigrée in 1919, has a timeless salon that specializes in body massages and, above all, facial care using its own excellent products. You can also buy the Institut's Pavlova perfume created for the great ballerina.

If the pores of your body really need liberating, head for the Hammam at the Mosquée, where the steam and dry baths will cure many ills (see page 125).

Clothes beautiful To be impeccable, turnout is another criterion for Parisian chicness. All Parisians make sure their clothes are clean and well-pressed before stepping out. For clothes alterations and more than perfect mending, go to **Mermoz Retouches** (21 rue Jean Mermoz, 8e, tel: 42 25 73 36); prices and quality are both high. Most dry cleaners also offer mending services. If you spill foie-gras or champagne on your *haute-couture* evening dress, opt for **Delaporte Star** (62 rue François I, 8e, tel: 43 59 82 11), much used by neighboring boutiques such as Dior and Balmain. Their prices are monstrous, but service is excellent. For really top-class, old-fashioned laundering, make for **Vendôme** (24 rue du Mont Thabor, 1e, tel: 42 60 74 38), which starches and irons collars for the presidential

minions of the Elysée Palace. Deliveries are part of the friendly service.

Down at the heel? Then make sure you see a *cordonnier*. There are plenty of old-fashioned cobblers in every neighborhood, but you can always rely on the delivery service of **Claraso** (34 rue Godot-de-Mauroy, 9e, tel: 47 42 49 79). Repairs take at least a week.

Missing a tuxedo or a chic cocktail dress for an occasion you didn't anticipate? Then go to **Beral** (2 rue Caulaincourt, 18e, tel: 43 87 72 37) for the former and **Latreille** for the latter (62 rue St-André-des-Arts, 6e, tel: 43 29 44 10).

Be chic to others How to thank your Parisian dinner hostess without arriving under a veritable forest of flowers? The answer is to have said forest delivered, and by the best. **Lachaume** (10 rue Royale, 8e, tel: 42 60 57 26) remains the incontestable king, established in 1845. Although prices are astronomical, your hostess will appreciate the label. **Les Jardins d'Anais** (52 rue Montorgueil, 2e, tel: 42 33 14 81), although a more modest establishment, creates the most imaginative, artistic bouquets.

Bottles clanking up the stairs never create a suave entrance, so why not have some of your chosen elixir delivered in advance? Any branch of the long-established (1822) wine shop chain **Nicolas** (tel: 42 27 22 07) will take phone orders and deliver; the minimum order is 200 francs.

Finally, a discreet box of fine chocolates never goes amiss, but again make sure it has the right label: choose from specialists **Christian Constant**, **Debauve et Gallais**, or **Dalloyau**.

Debauve et Gallais: chocolates with a chic label from the original 18th-century shop in St. Germain

Royal chocolates
Hot chocolate was served three times a week to the Sun King at Versailles. The first chocolate shop opened in Paris in 1659 and Voltaire was reported to drink 12 cups a day in his old age. In the early 19th century, Debauve et Gallais opened their shop, still in the rue des Saintes-Péres today, to promote chocolate's therapeutic qualities.

Itineraries

Week's Itinerary

Day one
St.-Germain-des-Prés. Besides the church, explore the art galleries, cafés, and antiques shops along the rue Jacob, rue Bonaparte, rue de Seine, and the **rue de Buci** street market.

Visit the church on the **place St.-Sulpice**; then continue to the **Jardin du Luxembourg**. By the river, go to the **Musée d'Orsay**. Cross the bridge and walk through the Tuileries to finish at the **Orangerie**.

Day two
Saint-Honoré. Start at the **Louvre**, not missing the **Cour Carrée**; cross to the **Palais-Royal**, entering the gardens beside the **Comédie Française**. Explore this area and see the **Bibliothèque Nationale** before continuing to the **Opéra**.

Walk through the **place Vendôme**, past the **Ritz**, to the **rue de Rivoli**. Visit the **Jeu de Paume** and walk around the **place de la Concorde** to the gardens of the **Champs-Elysées**.

Day three
Le Marais/Bastille. Start exploring the islands, **Notre-Dame** and **Sainte-Chapelle**. Pass the **Hôtel de Ville** and go to **Beaubourg**, then walk through **Le Marais**. Visit the **Hôtel de Soubise** and the **Musée Picasso**, then walk through the **place des Vosges** to the **Bastille**. Walk up the rue de la Roquette or take a bus to **Père-Lachaise** cemetery at the top.

Dine in **Belleville**.

Day four
Trocadéro. Start at the **Eiffel Tower**. Cross the bridge to the **Palais de Chaillot** and museums. Go to the Porte de la Muette, the **Jardin de Ranelagh**, and the **Musée Marmottan**, then head for the **Arc de Triomphe**. Take the RER to **La Défense** and visit **La Grande Arche**.

Day five
Spend the day in **Versailles**. Or drive to **Fontainebleau** and **Vaux-le-Vicomte**. Dine in **Montparnasse**.

Day six
Latin Quarter. Start at the **rue Mouffetard** market and nearby streets.

Have tea at the **Mosquée**, a stroll in the **Jardin des Plantes**, then go to the Roman **Arènes de Lutèce** and the **Institut du Monde Arabe**.

Follow the quais to **Saint-Séverin** and finish at the **Cluny** museum.

Day seven
Montmartre. If Saturday or Sunday, start at the **Marché aux Puces**, Porte de Clignancourt. Explore Montmartre, climb **Sacré-Coeur**. Take the metro from **Pigalle** to **Monceau**; stroll in the park and visit the **Musée Nissim de Camondo** for its collection of 18th-century decorative arts. (*Open:* Wednesday to Sunday, 10–12 noon, 2–5.)
Buy presents at **Galeries Lafayette**!

The sweeping views of the city from the north tower of Notre-Dame make the 387-step climb very worthwhile

Weekend's Itinerary

The following itinerary is designed for visitors on their first trip to Paris.

Day one

Start at the **Louvre** at 9AM. Don't miss the **Cour Carrée** behind the pyramid on your way out. Then stroll along the rue de Rivoli to **Angélina's** tearoom or the adjoining luxury **Hôtel Meurice** for a drink. Turn right along rue Castiglione to the **place Vendôme** and the **Ritz**, past the glitziest jewelers. At the place de l'Opéra, take the rue Auber past the **Opéra** to the RER express metro. Take line A to **La Défense**. From the roof of **La Grande Arche**, survey Paris.

Return by RER to **Les Halles** for lunch. Walk due east to the **Centre Pompidou (Beaubourg)**, then enter **Le Marais** following the rue des Francs-Bourgeois. A short detour takes you to the **Musée Picasso**; alternatively, go straight to the **Musée Victor Hugo** on the **place des Vosges**, a good spot for a coffee. Cross the rue St.-Antoine and take the rue St.-Paul through the antiques market, the **Village St.-Paul,** toward the **Hôtel de Sens**. Cross the Pont Marie, explore the lower quais, and spend your evening on the **Ile St.-Louis**.

Day two

Start in **Montmartre**, exploring the backstreets and **Sacré-Coeur**. Return to the boulevard below by taking the lively market street, the rue Lepic. The **Moulin Rouge** is to your right at the bottom. Take the metro from **place Clichy** to Varennes and the **Musée Rodin**, with its pleasant café and gardens. Walk or take a taxi past **Les Invalides** to the **Champ de Mars**, dominated by the **Eiffel Tower**.

Continue the afternoon in the **Latin Quarter**, going first to the **Cluny** museum. Explore the surrounding narrow streets before crossing to the **Ile de la Cité** to see the dazzling **Sainte-Chapelle**. Finish at **Notre-Dame** (free Sunday concerts at 5:45). Return to the Left Bank, following the quai to the **Hôtel de la Monnaie**. Turn into the mass of streets leading to the charming **place de Furstenberg,** past the church of **St.-Germain-des-Prés**, and start your evening at the elegant **Café de Flore**.

189

The geography of Paris
The Paris city boundary is roughly marked out by the ring road, or Périphérique. Within this area, Paris is divided into 20 districts or *arrondissements*, beginning at the center with the 1st *arrondissement*, then working outward in a clockwise spiral. When touring the city, use the main landmarks for instant orientation: Sacré-Coeur is to the north, Montparnasse Tower to the south, and the Eiffel Tower to the west.

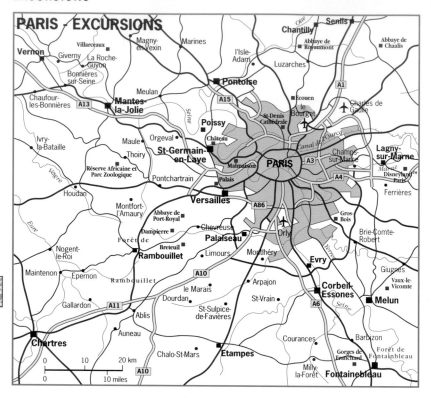

PARIS EXCURSIONS

▶▶▶▶▶ **EXCURSION HIGHLIGHTS**

FONTAINEBLEAU, CHATEAU DE
see pages 198–9

GIVERNY *see pages 200–1*

VAUX-LE-VICOMTE, DOMAINE DE *see pages 206–7*

VERSAILLES, CHATEAU DE
see pages 210–3

Opposite: the Horseshoe Staircase at Fontainebleau Palace

If the charms of one of the world's most romantic and historic capitals are occasionally overcome by the noise, the traffic and, in the height of summer, the heat, then the surrounding countryside of the Ile de France provides the perfect antidote to the city and some stimulating excursions.

A surfeit of the city's great cultural monuments and museums (or merely having children in tow) might result in a trip to the east of Paris to discover the fun of fantasy at Disneyland Paris or, alternatively, north to the popular Parc Astérix. France Miniature at Elancourt to the southwest offers a Gulliver's-eye view of the country, where you will find scaled-down monuments and typical village scenes.

Both history and the lush scenery of the Ile de France can be enjoyed on a trip to one of the great châteaus such as Rambouillet, Fontainebleau, Vaux-le-Vicomte, and Chantilly. A car (rental details on page 249) will enable you to take in some of the sights and small towns along the way: the Le Nôtre landscaped park of the Château de Courances is worth a detour on a journey to Fontainebleau, and so, too, is a stop at the well-preserved Abbaye de Royaumont, just south of Chantilly, or the nearby town of Senlis.

Closer to the center of Paris and therefore more convenient to reach by public transportation are the châteaus of Ecouen, Gros-Bois, Malmaison, St. Germain-en-Laye and, of course, the big brother of them all, glorious Versailles.

191

The 19th-century version of the Château de Chantilly

►► Chantilly

Musée Condé, 60500 Chantilly

By car: Autoroute du Nord, A1 to Survilliers exit.
By train: from Gare du Nord to Senlis, then bus shuttle to Chantilly.

Due north of Paris is the classy epicenter of French horses and riding fanatics. Over 3,000 trusty steeds are stabled in the forested area surrounding Chantilly, and anything horsey is a semipermanent talk of the town; both the local horse museum and the racecourse attract the relevant crowds. The 19th-century château contains a stunning art collection, and the surrounding canal-crossed park is a pleasure to explore.

Chantilly was originally founded by a Roman named Cantilius, but it was the famous head of the French army, the constable Anne de Montmorency, who in 1528 built a Renaissance château on the present site on his return from valiant battles in Italy. Montmorency brought in some of the greatest artists of the period: François Clouet, Bernard Palissy, and Jean Goujon all participated. Soon after, the architect Jean Bullant was commissioned to build a small neighboring château, the Capitainerie, which still survives today.

Change of hands After the Montmorencys, the château passed into the hands of the Condé family, powerful nobles who from 1643 to the 1830s made Chantilly their family seat. The prince, known as the Grand Condé, soon called in the great landscape designer Le Nôtre; he transformed the gardens and added lakes and canals, helping to make Chantilly one of the era's favorite partying places. Famous literati invited to the fashionable gatherings included La Fontaine, Fénélon, Bossuet, Racine, and Molière. It was also during this period that the resident chef invented *crème chantilly*.

During the 18th century, the magnificent stables were erected, intended to accommodate 240 horses and over 400 hounds for stag and boar hunts. (Today, these stables are devoted to a horse museum and dressage displays.) The Revolution, however, soon left its inevitable mark: most of the château was pillaged and demolished—except for the Capitainerie. Around 1840, the last of the Condé family bequeathed the property to the Duc d'Aumale. This was the man responsible for undertaking the rebuilding of the château (1876–83), which produced the Renaissance pastiche that we can visit today.

The main château On the ground floor, the Musée Condé displays some magnificent works and furnishings, from the Italian and French Renaissance through to the 19th century. The pièce de résistance is the illuminated medieval manuscript *Très Riches Heures du Duc de Berry* (only its reproduction is displayed). Look for works by Poussin, Delacroix, Raphael, Van Dyck, Corot, and the remarkable Cabinet Clouet, which displays 16th-century portraits painted by the Clouet brothers. The same fraternity designed the stained-glass windows in the nearby Galerie de Psyche, made in 1542 for the Château d'Ecouen. In Le Sanctuario are exhibited major works such as Raphael's *Trois Grâces*, Filippo Lippi's *Esther et Asséurus*, and Jean Fouquet's exquisite 1455 miniatures for a book of hours. The Cabinet des Gemmes exhibits further miniature portraits, porcelain, a rare collection of fans, and a copy of the famous *Diamant Rose*. A large octagonal room called the Tribune houses masterpieces by Watteau, Delacroix, Ingres, and Philippe de Champaigne.

A guided tour of the apartments leads to the Capitainerie, which, apart from its superb restaurant (tel: 44 57 15 89), contains some fascinating features such as panels painted by Huet in the main bedroom and the superb carved wood paneling of the music room. The balustrade of the main staircase leading to the chapel took 30 craftsmen a year to complete. Gobelins and Beauvais tapestries, inlaid furniture, a room entirely decorated with paintings of monkeys—Chantilly is not short of interest.

Park Allow an hour or so to wander around. Take in the Hameau, an aristocratic version of rustic living built in 1774, similar to that used by Marie-Antoinette at Versailles. Follow Le Nôtre's canals, in particular La Manche, which leads you to an amphitheater-shaped lawn, on either side of which are the *allées des philosophes*, where the thinkers of the day cogitated in bucolic surroundings. Finish your tour by going through the English-style garden, with its temple, island, and waterfall.
Open: Wednesday to Monday, 10:30–5 (10:30–6 in summer).

Musée Vivant du Cheval: Wednesday to Monday, 1–5 (open all day in summer).

Detail from the Château de Chantilly

Senlis
Combine a trip to Chantilly with a visit to the neighboring town of Senlis—a maze of picturesque, narrow streets dominated by the 12th-century Cathédrale de Notre-Dame, one of France's oldest cathedrals.

CHARTRES

The majestic cathedral of Notre-Dame de Chartres boasts world-famous stained-glass windows, as well as the widest nave and the largest crypt in France

Don't forget the town!
Take an organized trip to Chartres from central Paris with Cityrama (tel: 44 55 61 00) or Paris Vision (tel: 42 60 31 25), who arrange half-day excursions to Chartres including a guided tour of the cathedral.
If you have time, visit the Musée des Beaux Arts, a former bishop's palace, housing a fascinating collection of 17th- to 19th-century French furniture and paintings.

Druid connections
Even before the Christian era, Chartres was famous for its Druid temple, and many scholars believe it was actually the Druid capital of the Carnutes described in the famous Latin text, Caesar's "Gallic Wars."

▶▶ **Chartres**
By car: take the A10 from the Porte de St.-Cloud.
By train: from Montparnasse.
Rising above the wheat fields of Beauce are the two extraordinary mismatched spires of Chartres cathedral, "the very idea of the Middle Ages rendered visible" (Emile Male).

Notre-Dame de Chartres is the Virgin Mary's cathedral par excellence, built to house the precious relic of her *sacra camisia* (her tunic), still displayed in the Treasury in only slightly frayed form after 2,000 years. King Charles the Bald donated the valuable relic in the late 9th century, and it rapidly attracted streams of fervent pilgrims (many come on foot from Paris even today). Fires burned no fewer than five successive churches on the site, culminating in the devastating flames of 1194.

Miraculously, Mary's tunic survived unsinged, which led to a revival of religious fervor and a strong motivation for rebuilding. From the king to the lowliest farm worker, everyone offered money or physical labor, and the new cathedral was erected in a record 25 years.

Chartres today Centuries later, Chartres remains a remarkably homogeneous example of the transition from Gothic to Romanesque. The lower half of the cathedral's facade, surviving from the earlier church, is pure 11th-century Romanesque. Its main entrance, the *Portail Royal*, illustrates the life of Christ, and the central tympanum shows him surrounded by the Evangelists and the Apostles. The door seen to the right is dedicated to the

Virgin Mary. The left-hand door focuses on the Ascension.

The right-hand octagonal spire, which crowns the 345-foot south tower, is original, but the north tower was decapitated by lightning and rebuilt in the early 16th century. The latter can be climbed, but be prepared for 378 steps. From the outside, admire the flying buttresses, the two magnificently sculpted porches, and the 14th-century chapel in the garden at the back.

The 176 stained-glass windows cover an area of 2,990 square yards: the three crowning the facade escaped the 1194 fire, while most others are 13th-century. The three rose windows represent the Apocalypse, the Virgin Mary, and the Last Judgment; *Notre-Dame de la Belle Verrière*, in the south choir, is reputedly the oldest window.

The circular labyrinth on the nave floor is a unique medieval survivor symbolizing good and evil, with its center representing paradise. Pilgrims used to crawl around all 306 yards of its pattern on their knees. The choir, one of the widest in Europe, is surrounded by a magnificent lace-like wall of stone sculpture incorporating 200 statues. Behind the choir is the staircase leading to the Treasury in the Chapelle Saint-Piat. Below the cathedral is the impressive 9th-century crypt; guided tours start from the Maison des Clercs.

Chartres makes a charming spot for a day's wandering, as the lower part of the town has more historic churches. The river provides a picturesque backdrop for old public washhouses and drying lofts, while in Vieux Chartres some fabulous architectural features await discovery.

Ornamental residence
For a touching and astonishing spiritual monument, go to the Maison Picassiette (22 rue du Repos, tel: 37 36 41 39). In a nondescript suburb a local street sweeper, Raymond Isidore, spent his entire life decorating his house with fragments of china and glass, starting in 1938 on the interior and finishing his garden tomb in 1962. Not even his wife's sewing machine escaped his mania.

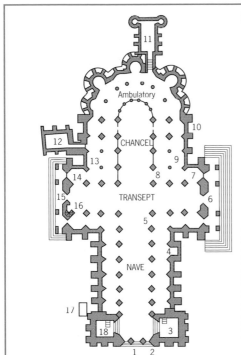

CHARTRES CATHEDRAL

1 Portail Royal
2 Stained glass windows
3 Old Bell Tower
4 Vendôme Chapel
5 Organ
6 Portail Sud
7 St-Fulberts window
8 Parclose screen
9 Notre-Dame de la Belle-Verrière
10 Crypt entrance
11 St-Piat Chapel
12 Sacristy
13 Vierge du Pilier
14 Window of Peace
15 Portail Nord
16 Access to New Bell Tower
17 Clock Pavilion
18 New Bell Tower

► **Disneyland Paris**
Central Reservations Office/BP 105, 77777 Marne-la-Vallée
By car: autoroute A4.
By train: RER line A.
Disneyland Paris, also known as Euro Disney Resort, a megaproject started in 1988, opened in April 1992 with a huge publicity campaign.

Situated 20 miles east of Paris in the bleak countryside of Marne-la-Vallée, Disney's fourth world resort (after California, Florida, and Tokyo) has, incredibly, been beset by financial problems. Not so surprising, perhaps, when you consider that the project budget was comparable to even the greatest of Louis XIV's extravagances at Versailles. For this vast operation to break even and be completed as planned, it would have to attract 11 million visitors annually—no mean crowd and a target it has yet to reach. The French, along with the rest of Europe, have not been overenthusiastic to experience the offerings of Disneyland Paris, with or without the generous price reductions.

Nevertheless, new attractions *are* being opened. As a concession to French culture, a modernistic area of the park called Discoveryland has been inspired by Jules Verne's visions of the future, and the summer of 1994 saw the inauguration of the Mystères de Nautilus underwater trip (based on *20,000 Leagues Under the Sea*) and, in June 1995, Space Mountain inspired by *From Earth to the Moon.*

Six hotels (five of them grouped around an artificial lake and each corresponding to a different American regional style and visitor's budget), together with a wooded camping site complete with log cabins (remember Davy Crockett?), make up the accommodations available. Many of the hotels have slashed their prices to attract more visitors; they now compare more favorably with their Parisian counterparts.

Numerous restaurants, shops, water sports, and a golf course offer alternatives to the seemingly endless round of rides and attractions; however, it might be difficult for the visitor to escape the beaming Disney smiles of the myriad "cast members." Originally numbering 12,000, employed from all over Europe to aid visitors and maintain the squeaky-clean image, their numbers have been reduced, but they are still to be found on every corner.

Magic Kingdom It is in the Magic Kingdom, of course, where your offspring can at last meet all of those characters that were previously reserved for the movies or television screen—Mickey, Minnie, Goofy, Pluto, and their diverse fairy-tale comrades are all here. Divided into five distinct areas or "lands," it has as its centerpiece the impressive and elaborately turreted Sleeping Beauty's Castle.

On entering the Kingdom, visitors find themselves projected into an idealized turn-of-the-century America on Main Street, with ragtime piano tunes, horse-drawn trolley cars, and "ye olde" shops and houses. Steam trains and boats leave here for a trip through Frontierland, with its fake canyons, gold mines, and rivers.

Sleeping Beauty Castle, Disneyland Paris

Disney restaurants
Disneyland Paris eateries range from snack bars and fast-food joints to waitress-service restaurants. Reservations are recommended for most sit-down restaurants, many of which have recently relaxed their no-alcohol policies. All six Disney hotels have restaurants open to the public. Alternatively, try the crab shack, steak house, or even the "Buffalo Bill" dinner-theater at Festival Disney, an enormous pleasure dome near the main Disney complex.

197

Fantasyland Inside the 15-story castle you enter Fantasyland, where Disney classics and European folklore are relived, with Sleeping Beauty the out-and-out winner. Make-believe becomes reality and young children squeal approval.

Adventureland This, on the other hand, is geared more to a slightly older age group, as here swashbuckling adventurers fight it out in a tropical setting. A 92-foot "tree" created to be climbed brings visitors to the rustic dwelling of the Robinsons, while the island of the hidden treasure is ferociously guarded by Long John Silver and Captain Hook look-alikes.

Discoveryland This final stopover is completely inspired by Jules Verne's and other visionaries' images of the future. It boasts the spectacular Space Mountain—where visitors are catapulted by rocket ship on a space journey from the barrel of a 72-foot-long Columbiad cannon—and the underworld adventure of The Mystery of the Nautilus. Star Tours, a flight simulator that whisks visitors onto an interplanetary journey, also projects a circular film, *Circle-Vision 360*, which draws visitors into themes of the future. Meanwhile, Starjets whiz above during the day and fireworks light up the sky at night.

You never know who might be joining you on a Disneyland Paris ride

*The Château de
Fontainebleau, once
a hunting lodge and
a palace, now draws
crowds of tourists.
Napoleon disliked
Versailles and there-
fore established his
imperial seat here.
The Napoleon
Museum, recently
opened in the Louis
XV wing, recounts
the story*

▶▶▶ **Fontainebleau, Château de**
77300 Fontainebleau
By car: take A6 or N7 from the Porte d'Orléans.
By train: from the Gare de Lyon.

A magnificent vast forest of 42,000 acres, once a royal
hunting ground, surrounds the marshy terrain of the
château, number two in the French royal domain stakes
after Versailles. Apart from touring the imposing palace,
visitors can indulge in horseback riding, cycling, rock-
climbing, or simply walking in the forest. Only a few
miles to the north lies Barbizon, famous for its mid-19th-
century school of landscape painters.

A former hunting lodge dating from the 12th century,
the château was transformed into a major royal
residence by François I in the 16th century; he brought
the best of Italy's Renaissance artists and craftsmen to
decorate its lofty interior and laid out the garden with
lakes and canals. Le Nôtre stepped in during the mid-
17th century to redesign the garden, and the palace

itself underwent numerous modifications and additions over the years before being finally adopted by Napoleon as a suitably majestic base.

The Château Entrance is through the famous Cour des Adieux, where the emperor bade farewell to his Imperial Guard in 1814 before being exiled on Elba. The famous horseshoe-shaped staircase was built by du Cerceau for Louis XIII in 1634. In the Galerie François I, the original Renaissance frescos painted by the Florentine Rosso remained hidden behind other paintings, only coming to light in the 19th century. More Renaissance glories decorate the staircase of honor.

The highlight of the interior, however, is the **Salle de Bal**, the ceremonial ballroom that hosted many a glittering occasion. Dazzlingly furnished and decorated with original frescoes and wood paneling, it was commenced under François I, the last elegant gilt touches being added under his successor, Henri II.

Napoleon's apartments occupy the second story of a wing built under Louis XVI, overlooking both the Jardin de Diane and the carp pond. His bedroom idiosyncratically contains a camp bed and some richly inlaid Boulle commodes. The **Salle du Trône**, created by Napoleon in 1808, is a decorative mixture of Louis XIII, XIV, and XV in the same way as the Queen's Apartments, the Chambre de la Reine, reveal the passage of every queen from Marie de Médicis to the Empress Eugénie. Adjoining this is the **Salon du Jeu de la Reine**, beautifully decorated thanks mainly to the luckless Marie-Antoinette, who commissioned Rousseau to paint its murals.

The most brilliant of 18th-century decoration can be seen in the **Salle du Conseil**, built under François I but entirely reworked under Louis XV, who commissioned the fabulous ceiling paintings by Boucher.

Further apartments can be toured but only with guides; inquire at the ticket desk. Otherwise, head outside to the gardens and the Tiber—the square central pond in Le Nôtre's formal Grand Jardin. Facing the Cour de la Fontaine is the fountain of Ulysees, which in its turn fronts the peaceful expanse of a carp pond. On the other side of this aquatic area, immediately to the right of the Cour des Adieux, stretches the English-style garden relandscaped by Hurtault in 1812.
Open: Wednesday to Monday, 9:30–12:30 and 2–6 (2–5 in winter). Gardens open sunrise to sunset.

Barbizon The illustrious village of Barbizon is now characterized by upscale restaurants and tourist galleries. Between 1825 and 1870, it attracted a group of painters who were the first to practice outdoor painting, thus creating their own movement, the Ecole de Barbizon, and paving the way for the Impressionists. Corot, Millet, Rousseau, and Daubigny all worked here, spending their days dabbling on canvas and their evenings at the Auberge du Père Ganne. The inn exhibits some touching memorabilia, as do the houses of Millet and Rousseau (both of which are situated on Grande Rue). Don't be surprised to encounter traffic jams made up of tourist buses here.

Sport in the forest
If the forest surrounding Fontainebleau is beckoning, go to the Office de Tourisme (31 place Napoléon Bonaparte, tel: 64 22 25 68) for information on horseback riding or bicycle rental. If you come by train, you can rent fairly basic bicycles at the station. If you have a car, then the 5½ miles to the village of Barbizon will be easy.

199

Barbizon, where art moved outdoors, away from the studio, paving the way for Impressionism

200

The magnificent garden provided Monet with constant inspiration during the last years of his life

Musée Americain
The building along the road from Monet's house is the Musée Americain, a privately owned museum showing the work of American artists who flocked to Giverny in the wake of Monet.

▶▶▶ **Giverny**
Fondation Claude Monet, 27620 Giverny
By car: autoroute A13, exit at Vernon, take D5 to Giverny.
By train: from St.-Lazare to Vernon, then taxi or bus.
Situated on the banks of the Seine as it flows northwest through Normandy, Giverny is famous for only one reason—Claude Monet. This charming village was where the painter lived from 1883 until his death in 1926, tending his famous garden, which became as important to him as the works it inspired. Each month is characterized by a dominant color, but the most striking is perhaps May/June, when apple trees blossom, rhododendrons flower around the lily pond, and the wisteria tumbles over the famous Japanese bridge. However, any of the summer months will provide a ravishing vision of a discreetly controlled, color-coordinated Nature.

Entrance is through the vast studio that Monet had built, which now unfortunately only houses reproductions of his works and a souvenir shop. Monet's simple two-story house dominates the gardens, which slope down to the Japanese section. The pink house with its green shutters is pure delight for the colors of its interior, which was thankfully extensively restored in the late 1970s after decades of neglect. Deep blue dominates the kitchen, brilliant yellow the dining room, while Monet's vast Japanese print collection is hung throughout the house exactly as it was in his time. Upstairs, his bedroom has a superb view extending across the garden and beyond to the valley.

Oriental influence The opening up of Japan to the West in the late 19th century stimulated artists' imaginations, and Monet was no exception: his Japanese garden stands as proof and memorial. When prospering finances allowed him to purchase this plot of land, Monet set about diverting the River Epte to create a pond. This was soon crossed by an arched bridge and surrounded by bamboo and other vegetation reminiscent of the Orient. Monet spent the rest of his life capturing on canvas the essence of its shadows and light, mottled tones, wisteria, and water lilies.
Open: April to October, Tuesday to Sunday, 10–6.

Claude Monet (1840–1926) Brought up in Normandy, the youthful Monet soon moved to Paris to study painting. Here he met Bazille, Lepic, Renoir, and Sisley, with whom he associated at the Brasserie des Martyrs. Monet and Bazille spent Easter near Barbizon, painting like Millet and Daubigny in that open air; the same year, Monet discovered Manet. By 1870, he was following the fate of a *peintre maudit*, with his work refused by the official Salon.

After a trip to London where he discovered the works of Turner, Monet returned to Paris and settled in Argenteuil, on the Seine just north of Paris. Here, like Daubigny, he installed his studio on a boat, capturing the changing light of the river as he traveled. Artistically, Monet always remained faithful to water, from his origins on the Channel coast to the banks of the Seine and eventually, of course, at Giverny. In 1874, the Impressionist group was finally able to exhibit together, and it was Monet's 1872 painting entitled *Impression: soleil levant* that gave the group its identity. Success, however, did not come easily, and Monet's dire financial straits were only alleviated by friends like Manet who bought his paintings.

In 1879, Monet's wife died, just a few years before he finally achieved recognition as the high priest of a radically new movement in painting. By 1882, critics were at last favorable, and the following year he moved to "Le Pressoir" in Giverny, together with his two sons, his mistress Alice Hoschedé (whom he later married), and her six children. Other Impressionists such as Renoir, Sisley, and Degas all visited him there over the years, and Cézanne even moved into the local inn for a period.

In 1897, with the maturing of the adjoining Japanese garden, Monet started on his water-lily series. He later had a studio built in the garden in order to accommodate his large-scale paintings. When Clémenceau asked him for a gift to the nation, Monet, by then in his 80s, set about painting a series of panels for the Orangerie, which he completed just before his death.

Monet's Japanese garden—a shimmering palette of changing colors— was the inspiration for his water-lily paintings, vast canvases that epitomize Monet's final period

201

Memorabilia
Right next door to Malmaison stands the late 17th-century Château de Bois-Préau, bought by Josephine in 1809 to house her doctor, ladies-in-waiting, and guests (avenue de l'Impératrice Joséphine, 92500 Rueil-Malmaison; tel: 47 49 20 07). Today, it is a memorial museum for Napoleon. Souvenirs include portraits of Napoleon on his deathbed in St.-Helena, his campaign bed, boots, hairbrushes, marble busts, and his death mask.
Open: Wednesday to Monday, 10–12 noon and 1:30–5 (4:30 in winter).

►► Malmaison, Château de

avenue du Château de Malmaison, 92500 Rueil-Malmaison
By car: N13 from La Défense.
By train: RER line A to La Défense. Bus 258.

This 17th-century manor with its unassuming front is the most elegant and luxurious surviving example of Napoleonic (Empire) decoration in France. Bought by the young general in 1799 as a present for his bride Josephine—Paris's most celebrated, though hardly most virtuous, beauty of the time—it was from the start more her domain than his. When Napoleon divorced Josephine in 1809 to marry Marie-Louise of Austria, he magnanimously allowed Josephine to keep the château, along with her imperial title and retinue.

Little was done to the exterior by Napoleon's architects, who merely added a canopied entrance in the form of a Roman tent, but the interior was entirely remodeled. The columned vestibule recalls a Roman atrium, its style perfectly reflecting Napoleon's love of grandeur and his imperial ambitions. Haughty busts of the Bonaparte family now line the walls. To the right are the billiard room, the *salon doré*, and the music room. The wall colors and hangings are a faithful re-creation of the original décor, while the furnishings and bronze candelabra are Empire originals from Malmaison itself or other imperial palaces. In the music room, which in Josephine's time had a picture gallery extension, were once displayed some of the greatest pictures in Europe, from Rembrandt to Rubens, many looted by Napoleon's armies in Italy.

On the left of the entrance hall is the dining room, which contains a remarkable 125-piece gilded silver service. The delicate wall paintings of muses and "Greek" motifs recall the decoration of ancient Pompeii. In Napoleon's council room next door, the walls and ceiling in striped silk create the illusion of a Roman military tent. The emperor's library boasts the most elaborate wall paintings as well as his famous

mechanical desk brimming with secret drawers.

Upstairs are the emperor's bedroom, dressing room, and sitting room decorated with portraits of the family. The central rooms are devoted to painting and memorabilia: David's celebrated *Napoleon Crossing the Alps*, Napoleon's toilet case, swords and captured weapons from the Egyptian campaign, and a rare Sèvres porcelain tea set with Egyptian motifs. An album of handpainted flower prints by Redouté evokes Josephine's passion for exotic flowers, once extended to the Malmaison greenhouses and gardens, the richest in Europe, which boasted plants and also animals specially imported from South America, Africa, and Asia.

Beyond lies Josephine's private apartment. In her "official" bedroom, the magnificent canopied bed decorated with gilded swans is the centerpiece of the room. This glamorous "imperial" style was installed the year of Josephine's divorce as a gesture of defiance to the new empress, Marie-Louise. Next door is Josephine's smaller, more modest real bedroom, painted in subtle colors. The exquisitely painted boudoir has a much lower ceiling and two fireplaces, making it the warmest room in Malmaison. This was where Josephine retreated in winter, her childhood in Martinique having left her with a lifelong aversion to cold weather.

In the attic rooms are Josephine's wardrobe and that of her daughter Hortense. Always coquettish, Josephine spent fortunes on clothes and jewelry and was easily the most luxuriously and best-dressed woman of her time. The dozens of pairs of shoes, parasols, day and court dresses with richly embroidered trains testify to this passion. Paintings and other memorabilia in these rooms illustrate the appearance of the Malmaison gardens and park under Josephine and trace the history of her descendants by Napoléon, including the future emperor, Napoléon's great-nephew, Napoléon III.

Open: Wednesday to Monday 10–12:30 and 1:30–5:30; guided tours only.

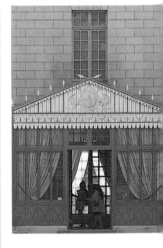

The Château de Malmaison— Napoleon's gift to Josephine. Her apartments exhibit bills for her extensive wardrobe. She died owing three million francs

Malmaison Park contains a replica of Josephine's rose garden, Napoleon's summer house cum study, and a coach house containing state carriages

Louis XIV's place of birth at St.-Germain-en-Laye—a fine Renaissance château that today houses the Musée des Antiquités Nationales, with exhibits dating from prehistory to the Middle Ages

► Saint-Germain-en-Laye

By car: Autoroute de l'Ouest (N13), exit at Versailles-Nord.

By train: take the RER line A1.

In under half an hour you can reach this rather chic suburb, once the home of kings of France, from François I to Louis XIV. Its popularity and clean air were such that in 1847 the Baron de Rothschild personally financed a connecting railway line with Paris. Often overlooked by tourists, St.-Germain-en-Laye is nevertheless a continuing favorite with Parisians. The atmosphere is unlikely to project you into provincial France, and on Sunday mornings most shops are open to accommodate the day-trippers—so be warned.

The main attraction remains the formidable fortress, originally erected in 1122 to protect the west of Paris but substantially rebuilt by François I in the 16th century. One of its splendors is the Sainte-Chapelle, a 13th-century Gothic masterpiece, 10 years older than its Parisian counterpart, although minus the stained glass, and with its rose window unfortunately obstructed by one of François I's constructions. Notice the sculpted heads crowning each arch, which are portraits of Saint Louis and his family.

Sun King's setting It was in this château that Louis XIV was born, took refuge during the popular uprising known as the Fronde (1648–53), and spent more time than at Versailles later in his life. Once Versailles was fit to move into, he graciously left the use of St.-Germain-en-Laye to the exiled James II of England, who died there in 1701 (his mausoleum stands in the church across the square from the château).

Le Nôtre created the impressive esplanade high above the Seine; a stroll along here and back to base covers 3 miles. The view from the terrace across the valley of the Seine inspired the Impressionist painter Sisley.

Since 1867, the château has housed the **Musée des Antiquités Nationales** (*open:* Wednesday to Monday, 9–5:15). This archeological collection ranges from prehistory to the Middle Ages. Superb examples of silver and gold Merovingian jewelry, weapons, and glass are displayed alongside Gallo-Roman ceramics, images of Celtic and Roman divinities, and funerary objects. The most astounding exhibit, going back 24,000 years, is the first known representation of a woman's face, **La Dame de Brassempouy.** Somewhat younger is the superb Bronze Age helmet with an engraved gold band from Amfreville. An entire room is devoted to a replica of the prehistoric wall paintings of bulls from Lascaux's caves in the Dordogne.

The other landmark to head for in St.-Germain-en-Laye, the **Musée du Prieuré,** is a short walk away (go past the church opposite the château and then turn left down the rue au Pain, until you reach the rue Maurice Denis). A former 17th-century hospital, this building is devoted to the painter Maurice Denis, who died in St.-Germain-en-Laye (*open:* Wednesday to Friday, 10:30–5:30; Saturday and Sunday, 10–6:30). Symbolism, the Nabis, and post-Impressionism are the movements represented in the posters, paintings, and sculpture of his contemporaries Bonnard, Vuillard, Vallotton, Maillol, and Paul Sérusier. Denis also tried to revive the tradition of sacred art; one example of his efforts is the chapel decorated by him, which adjoins the museum.

Maurice Denis (1870–1943) When he was still a precocious art student aged 18, Denis was already helping to form the group of Nabis. Sérusier, who had just spent the summer in the company of Gauguin at Pont-Aven in Brittany, shared the new theories with Denis and showed him the *Talisman,* an arrangement of pure colors on a wooden box lid painted under Gauguin's guidance. By 1890, Denis had published a manifesto of what he called neotraditionalism, outlining the formula that subsequently influenced much modern painting, with a vindication of pure and autonomous painting: "Remember that a picture, before becoming a warhorse, a nude woman, or any kind of anecdote, is essentially a flat surface covered with colors arranged in a certain order."

While borrowing certain elements from Impressionism, the Nabis were also interested in contemporary influences such as the newly popular Japanese print, equally visible in Gauguin's use of flat planes of color. Their art was intimate, an art of domestic interiors such as is seen in Vuillard's and Bonnard's works. Denis was the main exponent of its spiritual qualities, which he linked with nostalgia for the primitive and for nature.

Royal birthplace
Don't miss the Pavillon Henri IV in the gardens, where the Sun King was born and Alexandre Dumas wrote *Les Trois Mousquetaires.* It is now a rather exclusive hotel-restaurant and the only remaining element of the *château neuf.*

205

The Grande Terrace, Château de St.-Germain-en-Laye, designed by Le Nôtre with magnificent views across the Seine valley

Royal furnishings
A tapestry workshop was
set up in nearby Maincy to
produce the necessary
hangings for the château.
This later became the
celebrated Manufacture
des Gobelins. However,
Louis XIV took it over in
1662 and employed the best
craftsmen, including over
250 Flemish carpet
weavers, to furnish his new
palace at Versailles.
Traditional weaving
methods are used today at
the Gobelin factory, with
guided tours three times
a week.

A ruthless man
Nicolas Fouquet, the
ruthless, powerful Minister
of France, had quite a
widespread reputation. As
a result, the word
"squirrel" or "écureuil"
became known in local
dialect as "fouquet."
Throughout the château,
there are squirrels painted
by Le Brun, a cunning
reference to Vaux's
megalomaniac owner. The
castle also contains an
exhibition illustrating
Fouquet's rise and fall with
life-size wax figures.

▶▶▶ Vaux-le-Vicomte, Domaine de
77950 Maincy
By car: Autoroute A6, exit at Melun-Sénart.
By train: from Gare de Lyon to Melun, then bus or taxi.
Near Melun, 28½ miles southeast of Paris, lies Vaux-le-Vicomte, one of France's great baroque châteaus. Its colorful history, apart from its face, is so extraordinary that it needs to be known beforehand.

The land itself was bought in 1641 by Louis XIV's power-hungry minister of finance. Regent of France until Louis XIV came of age, Fouquet was also a great patron of the arts and passed on some of his immense fortune to the likes of Molière, La Fontaine, and Madame de Sévigné. His family motto, *Quo non ascendet?* (roughly, "the sky's the limit"), was particularly relevant to his tastes in decoration.

In 1656, he assembled the most talented artists and craftsmen of the time to create the ultimate symbol of his power and what was to become the first example of the Louis XIV style. Thus Louis Le Vau was appointed architect, the painter Le Brun brought in for the interiors, and André Le Nôtre for the landscaping of the enormous park. For five years an army of 18,000 workers slaved away to construct a château whose proportions were equaled only by the rate of embezzling Fouquet was reputed to have indulged in to pay his bills.

The party Finally, on a warm summer night in 1661, Fouquet threw a legendary housewarming party. The famous chef Vatel supervised the ovens, La Fontaine and Molière the cultural entertainment. Dishes of solid gold crowned dozens of buffet tables set out in the garden, while jewel-studded elephants lined the alleys of orange trees and Chinese fireworks were shot off from the ponds (there were over 1,000 fountains and water spouts). Never had Parisian society seen a social event quite so extravagant. Nor had the 23-year-old Louis XIV, who had recently come of age to rule in his own right. Two weeks later, Fouquet was arrested by the famous D'Artagnan. He was imprisoned, all his possessions confiscated, and at his trial he was found guilty of embezzlement. Thus his dream ended in a dank cell, where he remained until his death. Meanwhile, his talented craftsmen found new employment working on the king's new residence at Versailles—directly inspired by Vaux-le-Vicomte.

Although spared during the Revolution, the château nevertheless fell on hard times. Only seven paintings, six statues, and two tables remained when a wealthy industrialist, Alfred Sommier, bought it in 1875. Today the interior and the grounds have been magnificently restored by his descendants, while installed in the stables is a Musée des Equipages (horse-drawn carriages and accessories). Its historic collection includes the carriage Charles X used to escape from Paris in 1830.

The interior In the château itself, after entering through the hall with its 12 Doric columns, don't miss the Salon des Muses, with Le Brun's painted ceilings illustrating nine different muses. Here Molière and his troupe acted

L'Ecole des Maris for the first time, with Queen Henrietta-Maria of England and Fouquet as audience. The intimately scaled Cabinet des Jeux possesses another Le Brun masterpiece on its ceiling, this time *Le Sommeil*. It is hardly surprising that the artist spent two years closeted in the château accomplishing his marvels, which continue in the Salle des Buffets and upstairs in Fouquet's bedroom. Another highlight is the Chambre du Roi—which, of course, never hosted the king—used as a model for Versailles and subsequently imitated throughout Europe. Try to tour the château during one of its breathtaking candlelit evenings: more than 1,000 candles flicker away, conveying the atmosphere of Fouquet's time (every Saturday from May to September, 8:30–11).

The monumental gardens of Vaux-le-Vicomte are Le Nôtre's first masterpiece. A succession of terraces, lawns, fountains, and ponds, lined with statues and neatly sculpted bushes, lead away from the château down toward an impressive canal, hidden until your footsteps bring you to its edge. You can continue into the woods on the other side.

Open: April to October, 10–6 (11–5 in winter). Fountain displays April to October, second and last Saturday of the month, 3–6.

In the gardens
Le Nôtre's perfectly manicured gardens at Vaux-le-Vicomte make a pleasant afternoon's stroll. Within the grounds, the Musée des Equipages contains state carriages, saddles, and a smithy. Twice a month on Saturday afternoons there is a spectacular fountain display.

Vaux-le-Vicomte, built for finance minister Nicolas Fouquet, made Louis XIV so jealous that he built the palace at Versailles in response

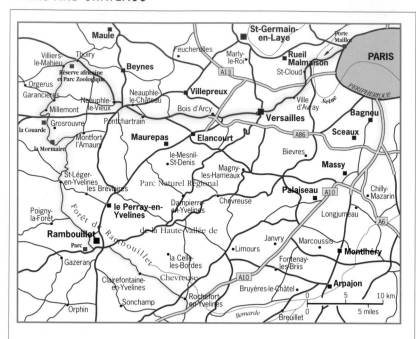

Drive **Parks and châteaus**

Leave Paris from the Porte Maillot, taking the N185 through the Bois de Boulogne and across the Seine towards Suresnes. Follow it through St.-Cloud and into the park.
A perfect combination of water and forest, the **Parc de St.-Cloud** was laid out by Le Nôtre, although the château was burned down during the 1870 Franco-Prussian War.

Continue along the N185 through Ville d'Avray to Versailles.
Stop to visit this remarkable architectural and landscaping feat. The town itself has some charm, particularly the small quartier of **St.-Louis**, near the royal kitchen garden.

Take the N10 and soon, at a rather complex series of intersections, turn onto the N12, leading to Neauphle-le-Château. Follow this road through a mixture of rolling countryside and far-flung suburban developments to the village of Pontchartrain.
Here there stands a pink and white 17th-century château, now a school

of agriculture, in a perfectly composed perspective. Although it is not open to the public, drive down through the curtain of trees to enjoy its setting. Continue through the village of **Neauphle-le-Vieux**, with its 13th-century church, once part of a Benedictine monastery.

Follow the D11 past the Forest of Beynes to Thoiry.
This is the perfect destination to appease restless young spirits, as the château (not open to the public), is set in a zoological park (*open: daily, 10–5*).

Immediately beyond the park on the D11 the road forks: turn left toward Villiers, where you pass another private château, and continue south to Garancières. At Millemont take the D197 and then the D199, turning right through Grosrouvre; a detour to the Château la Couarde is possible en route.
The **Château de la Mormaire** soon appears in this pretty agricultural

The president's retreat: the Château de Rambouillet, once a royal residence

landscape, where you join the D112 toward **Montfort-l'Amaury**, one of the most charming towns in the region. Once home to the powerful counts of Montfort (the 13th-century Simon de Montfort being the most notorious), the ruined castle remains at the top of the hill, as well as elements of former fortified walls. Don't miss the Gothic-Renaissance cemetery in the center of the village, which belongs to the church of St.-Pierre.

Leave Montfort by the D138 to St.-Léger-en-Yvelines, a village built up around a 12th-century church. Nearby stands an ancient menhir, a half-mile walk from the village.

Taking the D936, you soon come to the harmonious town of Rambouillet. The château of **Rambouillet**, once favored by kings and aristocrats, is now the president's official weekend and summer retreat. When he is not in residence it is open to the public. The *parc à l'anglaise,* with its follies, canals, and islands, was bought by Louis XVI for Marie-Antoinette and a dairy was built to keep her amused. The château was mainly rebuilt in the early 18th century, and its superb

woodwork is only rivaled by Versailles. The bulky Tour François I testifies to the Renaissance king's presence here; this is where he died.

Leave Rambouillet by the N306, turning immediately right along the D27, which takes you through the forested Vallée de Chevreuse to Rochefort-en-Yvelines and joins the A10 motorway leading back to Paris.

Stained-glass windows in St.-Pierre church, Montfort-l'Amaury

The Château de Versailles, seen from the south Parterre, the largest palace in Europe, capable of housing 20,000 people, and the crowning glory of the Sun King, Louis XIV

▶▶▶ **Versailles, Château de**

By car: take autoroute A13, then A12.

By train: RER line C to Versailles Rive-Gauche (closest) or main line from Saint Lazare to Versailles Rive Droite.

More than a palace, the Château of Versailles, Louis XIV's greatest creation, was conceived as a world unto itself. Seat of government, permanent residence of the royal family and the cream of French nobility, it also functioned as a permanent exhibition of French grandeur and sophistication. The endless grounds were tamed into a geometry so perfect that even nature seemed to obey the Sun King's commands. Surrounding the palace and its formal gardens were the largest kitchen gardens in the kingdom, the only zoo, the largest artificial lake, acres of game-filled forest, a new town catering to the needs of the court, and two weekend retreats with their own grounds, the Trianons.

The original château, built by Louis XIII in 1631, was a modest hunting lodge. In 1661, Louis XIV announced his intention of moving his court to this deserted swamp 10½ miles southwest of Paris, an astute way of isolating the nobility and his ministers while keeping an eye on his not-too-distant capital. Building hardly stopped until the king's death in 1715.

Three majestic avenues lined with trees and mansions converge on the great place d'Armes in front of the courtyard. Facing the square are the monumental stables built by Jules Hardouin Mansart, the second Versailles architect.

The first architect, Louis Le Vau, built around the original lodge on three sides, dressing up the old brick front in the center of the courtyard with urns, busts, and a wrought-iron balcony for the king's bedroom. Louis XIV's last addition to the palace was the magnificent baroque chapel behind the north courtyard block, finished in 1710.

Garden facade It is the garden facade that best epitomizes the Sun King's ambitions. Faced in stone, lined with Ionic columns, and capped by an ornamental balustrade and carved trophies, the central section is part of the original "envelope" designed by Le Vau. In 1678, Mansart filled in the terrace to create the Hall of Mirrors and added two lengthy blocks to the north and south, which make the garden front of Versailles the longest (624 yards) in Europe.

Royal apartments The central royal apartments are divided into two sections. Access to the Grands Appartements is from entrance A next to the chapel in the courtyard. The Petits Appartements (guided tour only) are reached from the south side of the courtyard. The Grands Appartements, laid out in the 1670s by the king's chief painter, Charles Le Brun, were the public rooms. Grand, luxurious, and draughty, they were used for official court assemblies and lavish entertainments.

Preceding the apartments is the king's private entrance to the chapel, laid out on two levels, the upper for the royal family and highest nobility, the ground floor for the rest of the court. The vaulted ceilings are painted in the illusionist Italian manner.

The **Grands Appartements** themselves are dominated by colored marble, gilded bronze, sculpture, illusionist painting, velvet, and silk. Each salon is dedicated to an Olympian deity symbolizing a royal virtue or duty. Apollo, closely linked to the cult of the Sun King, lends his name to the throne room.

What most visitors come to see is the Hall of Mirrors. Flanked on either side by the ornate salons of War and Peace, it is the largest, most magnificent, and last to be completed. It once boasted—apart from the 17 great mirrors—crystal chandeliers, precious furniture and vases, gilded candelabra, damask curtains, potted orange trees, and a silver throne. The painted ceilings, Le Brun's masterpiece, depict the king himself. It was here that Bismarck proclaimed the unification of Germany in 1871 and that the Treaty of Versailles, ending World War I, was signed in 1919.

Mob rule
On October 6, 1798, Versailles was invaded by a Parisian mob. They massacred the bodyguard and attempted to break into Marie-Antoinette's bedroom. She fled to the king's rooms, and they remained safe until morning, when they were removed forcibly to the Tuileries. The palace remained empty for over two years.

VERSAILLES, CHATEAU DE

Versailles was the ultimate symbol of royal grandeur, from the symmetry of its facade to the Apollo Fountain, a story of divinity for a king who believed in his own glory

From the Hall of Mirrors you enter the queen's official apartment. Hard to miss is the queen's bedroom, with the famous feather-canopied bed where all the royal babies were born in public view. Redecorated for Marie Leszinska, wife of Louis XV, the paneling is in the delicate rococo style, a welcome relief from the monumental grandeur of the Louis XIV salons.

Beyond the queen's apartment begin a series of dull picture galleries devoted "to the glories of France." Undoubtedly the greatest picture is David's huge *Distribution of the Eagle Standards* and a copy of his *Coronation of Josephine* (in the Louvre), both painted for Napoleon.

The **Petits Appartements** were the living quarters of the royal family and, of course, the king's mistresses. Built around dark inner courtyards, they aimed for privacy and an escape from court etiquette. They provide the finest and most priceless examples in France of 18th-century paneling and decoration.

The gardens The 247-acre Versailles grounds, the largest palace gardens in Europe, are the epitome of the French formal style. Laid out by Le Nôtre along a central axis leading to the great canal in the park, the severe symmetry is relieved by hundreds of statues, follies, and fountains. The most stunning are those of Latona and Apollo illustrating the story of the Sun King's favorite god. The monumental Orangerie south of the palace is by Mansart.

From the great Neptune fountain on the north side, stroll back to the center and past the Apollo fountain till

you reach the canal, where rowboats and bicycles can be rented and a pleasure boat or minitrain taken to the Trianons.

The Trianons The Grand Trianon was built for Louis XIV as a love nest and an escape from palace routine. Its delicate pink marbled architecture is a welcome contrast to the official grandeur of the palace. The garden, planted with flowers year-round (a million pots), was the most luxurious in France.

The Petit Trianon, built for Louis XV's mistress, Madame du Barry, was later presented to Marie-Antoinette by Louis XVI. Often described as the absolute jewel of French neoclassical architecture, its grounds were entirely transformed by her into a romantic "English" park with a make-believe village (Hameau), where the queen could lead the "simple" life away from the despised duties of the court.

Open: State apartments Tuesday to Sunday, 9–6:30 (5:30 in winter); Grand Trianon and Petit Trianon 10–6:30 (summer), 10–5:30 (winter). The park is open daily from 7AM to sunset. Every Sunday from May to September the fountains are on from 3:30–5.

Jam tasting at the Royal Kitchen Garden
Don't miss the gastronomic tour of the Potager du Roi (the royal kitchen garden). Open from May to mid-November, it can be toured with resident experts, culminating in vegetable and jam tasting. Tours start at 2:30 (daily except Tuesday) at the gate, 6 rue Hardy (tel: 39 50 36 22).

213

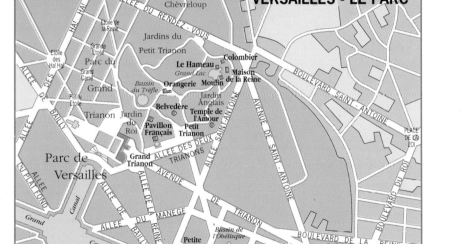

Shopping

Wine statistics
Wine was originally brought to the south of France by the Phoenicians and Greeks in the 6th century BC. In 1989, France produced over 6,081,800 tons and the French drank an average 74 liters a head, down from 117 liters per head in 1965.

Sales
It is not always easy to find a bargain in Paris with so many classy shops. However, some shops offer reduced goods just before Christmas, otherwise the best sales, called *soldes*, are held in January and July. Look for clothing marked *stock*, sold at stock price or *dégriffe*, meaning marked-down designer labels. Clothes marked *fripes* are secondhand.

Whether foie gras or shoes, Parisian goods just beckon customers, and totting up small fortunes on credit-card bills. But that is part of what this city is about, and nobody should leave with empty hands. Lovers of clothes and stylish accessories should window-shop in streets like rue des Francs-Bourgeois (affordable shoes, accessories, clothes), rue de Grenelle (designer clothes and shoes), rue Etienne-Marcel (the mecca of young designers), place des Victoires (successful designers), or Faubourg St.-Honoré (luxury). Both the rue de Rennes and boulevard St.-Germain are good stretches for reasonably priced boutiques. For gourmets the choice is similarly enticing, and for everything one of the greatest pleasures is the perfect packaging, making even a modest purchase look royal.

Accessories
Annick Goutal, 14 rue de Castiglione, 75001 (tel: 42 60 52 82), metro: Concorde. Delicate, sensuous scents, oils, and lotions, beautifully packaged, make a pleasant change from the usual mass-produced couture perfumes.

Charles Kammer, 14 rue de Grenelle, 75007 (tel: 42 22 91 19), metro: La Tour Maubourg. Branch off place des Victoires. Smart shoe designs with imaginative details and almost possible prices.

Fabrice, 33 and 54 rue Bonaparte, 75006 (tel: 43 26 57 95), metro: St.-Germain. Very Rive Gauche accessory shop: colorful jewelry, decorative headbands. Certainly not understated.

Lancel, 8 place de l'Opéra, 75009 (tel: 47 42 37 29), metro: Opéra. Branches all over Paris. Classic, good-quality bags, wallets, luggage.

Madeleine Gély, 218 boulevard St.-Germain, 75007 (tel: 42 22 63 35), metro: rue du Bac. Outstanding selection of more than 400 walking sticks (cigarette-holder canes, watch canes) and umbrellas of all shapes, designs, and sizes.

Marie Mercié, 56 rue Tiquetonne, 75002 (tel: 40 26 60 68), metro: Etienne-Marcel. Also at 23 rue Saint-Sulpice, 75006. Paris's wackiest hat designer also produces some seductive, very wearable designs. Look for the bargain bin in this tiny, very feminine boutique.

La Maroquinerie Parisienne, 30 rue Tronchet, 75009 (tel: 47 42 83 40), metro: Havre Conmartin. Vast choice of cut-price leather goods and luggage. Some top brands are available here.

Réciproque, 95 rue de la Pompe, 75016 (tel: 47 04 30 28), metro: Pompe, Victor-Hugo. Not strictly accessories but an excellent address for picking up secondhand couture and designer clothes abandoned by fickle ladies of the 16th arrondissement. Large accessory department stocks some real finds.

Sacha, 50 rue de Turbigo, 75002 (tel: 45 08 13 15), metro: Etienne-Marcel. Branches all over Paris. Young, fun shoes at accessible prices.

Stephane Kélian, 6 place des Victoires, 75002 (tel: 42 61 60 74), metro: Bourse. Branches in the Marais and Champs-Elysées. Some sensational designs (matched by prices) at one of Paris's top shoe designers. Beautifully made, could last forever.

Books, Records
Fnac, branches at Forum-des-Halles, rue de Rennes, and avenue Wagram. Chain of low-price book and record stores, also stocking camera, computer, and hi-fi equipment.

Galignani, 224 rue de Rivoli, 75001 (tel: 49 53 50 00), metro: Tuileries. Well-stocked, old-fashioned bookstore. Helpful bilingual service. Range of English-language books.

Virgin Megastore, 52 Champs-Elysées, 75008 (tel: 49 53 50 00), metro: Franklin-Roosevelt. The Parisian record shop. Track down records by French teeny-bopper hero Patrick Bruel or latest British groups.

Children
Agnès B Lolita, 10 rue du Jour, 75001 (tel: 45 08 49 89), metro: Les Halles. Ineffably Parisian, simple and stylish cotton-knit clothes that don't come particularly cheap.

Au Nain Bleu, 408/410 rue St.-Honoré, 75008 (tel: 42 60 39 01), metro: Concorde. The oldest toy store, illustrious, magical, unforgettable, with toy soldiers galore, puzzles, dolls and their houses, soft toys.

Le Ciel est à Tout le Monde, 10 rue Gay-Lussac 75005 (tel: 46 33 21 50), RER: Luxembourg. The sky may be for everyone, but this shop is especially delightful for children. Boomerangs, kites of all descriptions, puppets, and inexpensive toys.

Jouets & Cie, 11 boulevard de Sébastopol, 75001 (tel: 42 33 67 67), metro: Châtelet. Gigantic labyrinth stocking every toy and game currently available.

Pom d'Api, 13 rue du Jour, 75001 (tel: 42 36 08 87), metro: Les Halles. Also at 28 rue du Four. Adorable, hip miniature footwear—even Doc Martens for toddlers, made in France.

Si Tu Veux, 68 Galerie Vivienne, 75002 (tel: 42 60 59 97), metro: Bourse. Charming, affordable toy store with a teddy bear branch and a special party dressing-up/games department.

Department Stores
Au Bon Marché, 22 rue de Sèvres, 75007 (tel: 44 39 80 00), metro: Sèvres-Babylone. Founded in 1852, the oldest in Paris and the only Rive Gauche department store. Less crowded than the boulevard Haussmann stores, more genteel, more courteous. Good for household goods, lingerie, and children's wear. Basement bookstore is excellent.

Au Printemps, 64 boulevard Haussmann, 75009 (tel: 42 82 50 00), metro: Havre-Caumartin. An old classic. Wide-ranging clothes and accessories, good household and furniture departments—watch out for own-range Primavera. Quality not always up to its neighboring rival (Galeries Lafayette) but prices often lower. Own-label goods, Sélection Printemps, are good value.

BHV (Bazar de l'Hôtel de Ville), 52 rue de Rivoli, 75004 (tel: 42 74 90 00), metro: Hôtel de Ville. For kings and queens of do-it-yourself. The basement is a paradise of every imaginable tool, gadget, hardware, etc. Forget the fashion and stick to paint stripping; materials on 4th floor. Assistants are employed by brand names, so are supremely unhelpful.

Cheese statistics
France produces more varieties of cheese than any other country in the world. From Normandy to the Alps, cows', goats', and lambs' milk is siphoned off to create those miraculous odorous objects displayed in Parisian cheese stores—just a few kilos of the 160,000 tons produced annually. The French consume 46 pounds per year (the Americans a mere 22 pounds).

215

Au Bon Marché
Au Bon Marché was originally built in 1852 on the site of an asylum, located at the junction of rue du Bac and rue de Sèvres. It was expanded by Eiffel in 1867. Since then, it has maintained its chic image, and is particularly famous for its antiques and oriental rugs. It also houses an excellent food hall in the basement.

A treasure house of consumer goods: the Galeries Lafayette

Galeries Lafayette, 40 boulevard Haussmann, 75009 (tel: 42 82 34 56), metro: Chaussée d'Antin. Spectacular glass-domed store, luxurious, often pricey but also stocks more economical, own-label goods. Two floors devoted to fashion. Every top designer has an outlet here selling latest designs. Comparisons are easier and hours of window-shopping saved. Ground-floor accessory department is excellent for presents. There is a smaller branch of Galeries Lafayette at Montparnasse at the base of the tower.

La Samaritaine, 19 rue de la Monnaie, 75001 (tel: 40 41 20 20), metro: Pont-Neuf. Labyrinthine, multibuilding department store that sells everything if you can find it. Usually helpful service. Most useful is Magasin 2 for *perfumerie*, do-it-yourself, household goods, furnishings and, surprisingly, some designer clothes. La Samaritaine is not as crowded as BHV (see page 215). There is a rooftop tearoom.

Marks & Spencer, 35 boulevard Haussmann, 75009 (tel: 47 42 42 91), metro: Havre-Caumartin. British chain store, clothing and well-stocked quality food department, now a favorite with chic Parisians. No concessions to French taste. New branch on the rue de Rivoli, metro: Châtelet.

Food and wine
Cheese

Androuet, 41 rue d'Amsterdam, 75008 (tel: 48 74 26 90), metro: Liège. Encyclopedic range of aromatic French cheeses, perfectly ripened. Famous old restaurant and shop, delivery in Paris.

La Maison du Fromage, 62 rue de Sèvres, 75007 (tel: 47 34 33 45), metro: Sèvres-Babylone. This is where the five-star Lucas-Carton restaurant orders its cheeses. Sublime selection.

Tachon, 38 rue de Richelieu, 75001 (tel: 42 96 08 66),

metro: Palais-Royal. Fabulous range of cheeses, made from goats' and cows' milk, in an atmospheric old shop where the advice is friendly and professional.

Gourmet Groceries

A la Mère de Famille, 35 rue du Faubourg-Montmartre, 75009 (tel: 47 70 83 69), metro: Le Peletier. Superb 18th-century grocery with shelves full of ornate and colorful sweets, cookies, and jams. Friendly, old-fashioned service.

Fauchon, 26 place de la Madeleine, 75008 (tel: 47 42 60 11), metro: Madeleine. Over 20,000 exotic and luxury products from spices to fruit, tea, *charcuterie*, cakes. Too famous for good service. Outrageous prices.

Hédiard, 21 place de la Madeleine, 75008 (tel: 43 12 88 77), metro: Madeleine. Fauchon's main rival has branches all over Paris. Freshly roasted coffee, spices, expensive wines.

Izraël, 30 rue François Miron, 75004 (tel: 48 87 30 07), metro: St.-Paul. Colorful souk of North African and Asian products. Sacks of grains, bottles of spices, piles of African baskets.

La Maison du Miel, 24 rue Vignon, 75009 (tel: 47 42 26 70), metro: Madeleine. Offers countless types of honey (tasting possible) in pretty tiled interior. Established in 1908.

Legrand Filles et Fils, 1 rue de la Banque, 75002 (tel: 42 60 07 12), metro: Bourse. Renowned wine and fine grocery shop founded in 1890. Unbeatable range of wines, helpful service. Situated in the delightful Galerie Vivienne.

Maisonde de la Truffe, 19 place de la Madeleine, 75008 (tel: 42 65 53 22), métro: Madeleine. Unbeatable for luxurious truffles, caviar, and *foie gras*—the ultimate in gourmet delicacies.

Robert Labeyrie, 6 rue Montmartre, 75001 (tel: 45 08 95 26), metro: Les Halles. Famous shop selling products

A feast for the eyes and the taste buds: Fauchon, place de la Madeleine

SHOPPING

The best boulangerie
The most famous bakery in Paris is L'établisement Poilâne in the Montparnasse district, renowned for its wholewheat "Poîlane" bread. Indeed no other boulangerie can boast bread known by the name of its baker. There is often a line outside the shop at 29 rue de l'Ouest, 14e, especially at around 4PM when the fresh loaves come out of the oven.

from Landes. Raw goose and duck livers, truffles, dried cêpe mushrooms, foie gras.

Marché Biologique, Raspail market, boulevard Raspail, 75006, metro: Rennes. Only the freshest organically reared or grown produce is sold here every Sunday morning.

Pâtisseries and chocolates

Brocco, 180 rue du Temple, 75003 (tel: 42 72 19 81), metro: République. One of Paris's top pâtisserie shops and tearooms. Serves delicious *Cérisette* or Brazilian mocha cakes.

Christian Constant, 26 rue du Bac, 75007 (tel: 42 96 53 53), metro: rue du Bac. Tantalizing fruit tarts and rich cakes like Macao, Kalinka, or Pont Royal.

Debauve et Gallais, 30 rue des Saint-Pères, 75007 (tel: 45 48 54 67), metro: St.-Germain. Ask for Marie-Antoinette's chocolates! Original 18th-century shop selling tea, coffee, divine chocolates, and vanilla.

Dalloyau, 99/101 rue du Faubourg St.-Honoré, 75008 (tel: 43 59 18 10), metro: St.-Philippe-du-Roule. Pastry maker for Napoleon. Exquisite macaroons and Mogador cake. Branches in 6th and 15th.

Lenôtre, 44 rue du Bac, 75007 (tel: 42 22 39 39), metro: rue du Bac. World-famous desserts, cakes, chocolates, and ice creams. Try an *opéra* or a *concorde*. Main branch in 16th.

Fashion
Designer clothes (women's)

Agnès B, 6 rue du Jour, 75001 (tel: 45 08 56 56), metro: Les Halles. A young Parisian classic. Smart, sporty clothes at reasonable prices, with branches all over the world.

Anne-Marie Beretta, 24 rue St.-Sulpice, 75006 (tel: 43 26 99 30), metro: St.-Sulpice. Feminine, elegant clothes, often with original details.

Azzedine Alaïa, 7 rue du Moussy, 75004 (tel: 42 72 19 19), metro: St.-Paul. The inventor of the much-copied skintight dress. Follow Grace Jones's example if you can.

Barbara Bui, 23 rue Etienne Marcel, 75001 (tel: 40 26 43 65), metro: Etienne-Marcel. Gossamer silk fabrics, drapey designs. Up-to-the-minute femininity. Expensive.

Cacharel, 5 place des Victoires, 75001 (tel: 42 33 29 88), metro: Bourse. Good-quality designs for middle-of-the-road tastes. Last year's collection is sold at Stock, 114 rue d'Alésia, 75014 (tel: 45 42 53 04).

Chantal Thomass, 11 rue Madame, 75006 (tel: 45 44 60 11), metro: St.-Sulpice. Quality sexy designs from lingerie to gabardine suits. Romantic, imaginative, pricey.

Claudie Pierlot, 1 rue du Jour, 75001 (tel: 42 21 38 38), metro: Châtelet-Les Halles. Chic little dresses that are stunningly simple.

Emmanuelle Khanh, 2 rue de Tournon, 75006 (tel: 46 33 41 03), metro: Odéon. Very Rive Gauche style, sharp yet fluid cuts, superb blouses.

Irié, 8 rue du Pré-aux-Clercs, 75007 (tel: 42 61 18 28), metro: rue du Bac. Cheerful, brightly colored designs in supple, inventive fabrics. A former designer with Kenzo. Reasonable prices.

Issey Miyake, 3 place des Vosges, 75004 (tel: 48 87 01 86), metro: St.-Paul. Other boutiques on Left Bank, but this one is stunning. Now legendary sculptural designs beautifully displayed.

Jean-Paul Gaultier, 6 rue Vivienne, 75002 (tel: 47 03 85 71), metro: Bourse. Witty, irreverent clothes in a soaring futuristic boutique. Questionable prices.

Kenzo, 3 place des Victoires, 75001 (tel: 40 39 72 00), metro: Bourse. King of zappy, fun clothes. Huge boutique displays collection and accessories at high prices.

Scooter, 10 rue de Turbigo, 75001 (tel: 45 08 89 31), metro: Etienne Marcel. Wildly trendy, latest '60s revivals in clothes and accessories.

Tehen, 5 bis rue des Rosiers, 75004 (tel: 40 27 97 37), metro: St.-Paul. Stylish but comfortable jersey and knitwear coordinates in wide range of colors. Reasonable prices.

Un Après-Midi de Chien, 10 rue du Jour, 75001 (tel: 40 26 92 78), metro: Les Halles. Teeny-retro styles, embroidered cotton blouses, pastel colors. Reasonable.

Menswear

Autour du Monde, 12 rue des Francs-Bourgeois, 75003 (tel: 42 77 16 18), metro: St.-Paul. Safari image copied from surplus clothing. Timeless, ageless, good prices.

Daniel Hechter, 146 boulevard St.-Germain, 75006 (tel: 43 26 96 36), metro: Odéon, Mabillon. Branches all over Paris. Relaxed classicism, well cut, beautifully color-coordinated range. Not cheap, but not outrageous either. Women's range, too.

Façonnable, 9 rue Faubourg St.-Honoré, 75008 (tel: 47 42 72 60), metro: Madeleine. Parisian view of British style at astronomical prices, but you can always stick to the silk boxer shorts.

Island, 4 rue Vide Gousset, off place des Victoires, 75001 (tel: 42 61 77 77), metro: Bourse. Casual sportswear and accessories, well displayed, not overpriced.

Loft Design By, 12 rue du Faubourg St.-Honoré, 75008 (tel: 42 65 59 65), metro: Concorde. Revamped tweedy jackets, raincoats, and casual separates at very reasonable prices.

Household

Collection Orient Express, 15 rue Boissy-d'Anglas, 75008 (tel: 47 42 24 45), metro: Madeleine. For nostalgic travelers, an old-fashioned shop selling reproductions of crystal, china, tableware, etc. that were designed for the famous luxury train.

Dehillerin, 18 rue Coquillière, 75001 (tel: 42 36 53 13), metro: Les Halles. Gigantic copper pans, hundreds of sharp knives, *bain maries*, skewers, sieves, etc. The foodie's paradise, and where every self-respecting Parisian chef stocks up.

Etamine, 63 rue du Bac, 75007 (tel: 42 22 03 16), metro: rue du Bac. Vast home design shop, superb objects and fabrics imported from all over the world, but always with a Parisian stamp of taste. Own fabric range.

Souleiado, 78 rue de Seine, 75006 (tel: 43 54 62 25), metro: Mabillon, Odéon. Cheerful range of fabrics beaming out Provençal warmth. Traditional designs made into napkins, tablecloths, cushions, etc.

Mini couture
"Mini couture" is the name given to clothing produced by top Paris designers for children. For the best-dressed baby in town, shop at Baby Dior, Kenzo Bébé, Sonia Rykiel Enfant, or Caddie, which carries a wide range of designer labels.

219

Food and Drink

Although Napoleon apparently proudly claimed to complete his meals in under 18 minutes, you will rarely be able to do this in Paris and nor will you want to. Although trends toward more efficient eating have reduced traditionally endless lunches to more sprightly affairs, often wolfed down at the counters of bars and bistros, Parisians still enjoy their fodder, and still give it a lot of their time and money. Equally important is the liquid refreshment that over the last decade has given rise to a growing number of *bars à vins* (wine bars), where numerous nectars are served by the glass and accompanied by very reasonable plats du jour.

Restaurants In Paris lunch is generally served from noon to 2 or 2:30, after which you should head for a brasserie, which serves all day. Dinner is usually served from 7:30, although no self-respecting Parisian dines before at least 9, and orders usually stop between 10 and 11, after which diners will happily linger into the small hours. For avid post-midnight eaters, the area to head for is **Les Halles**, where old favorites such as **Au Pied du Cochon, Au Chien qui Fume,** or **La Poule au Pot** remain open very, very late (the first all night and the last till 6AM). Nearby, on the rue des Lombards, **Au Duc des Lombards** and **Le Sunset** continue the local tradition but with updated décors and music. Reservations are essential in more select restaurants, even if they are made in the afternoon for the evening.

Beware of Sundays, a favorite closing day, which leaves some quartiers deserted and recovering from the excesses of Saturday night. However, as Paris is Paris, you will not starve: head for one of the popular brasseries or the famous and chic **Café Drouant** near the Opéra, where the annual literary prize, the Prix Goncourt, is awarded. If in the 16th, go to the bustling **Brasserie Stella**; in the 7th, indulge in the rich specialties of the southwest at **Thoumieux**. Near the

Au Pied du Cochon
As the name suggests, this colorful, lively brasserie serves pigs trotters from 5AM onward, washed down by delicious onion soup. Formerly a popular haunt for high society, there to watch the workers in the market, today it is extremely popular with tourists and locals.

Food is a form of art in the French capital and almost as famous as Paris fashion

Arc de Triomphe? Walk downhill to **Le Boeuf sur le Toit** on the rue du Colisée and join the fun. On the islands? Go to **Nos Ancêtres les Gaulois**, which, despite being a favorite tourist haunt, makes a warm, boisterous retreat on a winter Sunday evening. Want a change from French cooking (unlikely)? **Darkoum** on the rue Ste.-Anne has a spectacular Moorish interior, impeccable service, and delectable couscous and tajines.

Budget eating Choosing where you eat in Paris depends very much on budget, and when this is relatively unimportant the city is at your feet. Without going to the ruinous top restaurants such as **Taill-event**, **Joël Robuchon**, or **Lucas-Carton**, you can still dine divinely in a growing number of serious restaurants that now propose a "menu" in the evening. Previously, this budgeting method (an all-in, three-course meal at a fixed price, wine excluded) was only available at lunchtime, but in these budget-conscious times, many chic destinations are now using this method to drum up more evening business.

Even if your pocket does not stretch to haute cuisine, you can try the more affordable bistros of top chefs Michel Rostang (**Le Bistrot d'à Côté**) or Guy Savoy (**Bistrot de l'Etoile**), both of whom opened these more affordable establishments as an alternative to their renowned temples of gastronomy nearby. The 17th arrondissement running into the 8th is the heart of Parisian gastronomy, with a heavy concentration of celebrated chefs and their restaurants. Reservations sometimes have to be made months in advance, but if you want to spend anything approaching 1,000 francs for just one admittedly divine dinner, it is well worth thinking ahead.

If you are looking for a more intimate tête-à-tête at a price that will allow you a taxi back afterward, then head for **Le Marais**, whose backstreets are full of wonderful surprises. The rue des Rosiers, the Jewish quarter, specializes in both North African and Eastern European restaurants, while surrounding streets such as the **rue des Ecouffes** (try the chic yet relaxed **Myrtho**), rue des Francs-Bourgeois, rue Vieille-du-Temple, and the rue Ste.-Croix-de-la-Brétonnerie all harbor an interesting selection. The junction of the latter two streets specializes in gay bars.

For more classic cuisine, go to the place des Vosges, where **Ma Bourgogne** reigns supreme on summer nights with tables spilling out under the arcades. Although there is nothing special about its basic dishes, prices are reasonable and the setting is unique. As this quartier thrives, the number of restaurants grows, and it is worth investigating the nearby **rue des Tournelles** (try the intimate **Gaspard de la Nuit**) and the **rue de Birague**, without forgetting a charming little square, the place du **Marché Ste.-Catherine**, which has several reasonably priced restaurants. Back toward St.-Paul, the **rue François Miron** has some old favorites, while the **rue du Pont Louis-Philippe** will take you down to a string of interesting restaurants lining the quai by the Seine. Here **Le Trumilou** serves basic fish dishes in a provincial-style atmosphere.

Regal restaurants
Many restaurants offer palatial settings that make the food seem irrelevant. Le Grand Véfour, in the Palais-Royal, is a magnificent example of sumptuous decoration from the 1820s, although the establishment itself dates from before the Revolution. On the rue de Rivoli, the *salon de thé* Angélina is unrivaled for its early 1900s classical style, complete with Mediterranean landscape murals. Art deco reaches its zenith at La Coupole in Montparnasse; and the most over-the-top example of turn-of-the-century opulence is to be found in the extraordinary restaurant at the Gare de Lyon overlooking the platforms, Le Train Bleu.

221

FOOD AND DRINK

Le Pub Renault, on the Champs-Elysées, adds French style to a British institution

Couscous
Couscous restaurants can be found in every quartier. The word "couscous" refers to the cornmeal grain (semolina) that, ideally, is heaped in a moist, buttery pile and mixed with a fresh vegetable stew. Completing the dish is the meat you have chosen; the best bet is nearly always *brochettes d'agneau* (lamb kebabs) or *méchoui* (a piece of roast lamb). The other mainstay of Moroccan, Algerian, and Tunisian cuisine is the tajine. Baked in a clay dish, tajine is basically a meat stew but with a combination of exotic ingredients—olives, almonds, prunes, conserved lemons—and cooked slowly to create a delicious sauce.

St.-Germain Similar in style and budget are the numerous restaurants crowded into the narrow side streets of **St.-Germain**. Streets leading south from the metro Mabillon toward St.-Sulpice are packed with intriguing places, whether **Le Charpentier**, an old classic full of carpenter's models, or **Guy**, where you munch to live samba, or family-run pizzerias, or haunts papered with old film posters. Perfect for budgeting, too, St.-Germain claims old favorites along the **rue Monsieur-le-Prince (Le Polidor)** or tiny little places lining the very narrow **rue de l'Echaude**. This is not the haunt of high gastronomy (although **L'Echaude St.-Germain** comes high in the candlelit-dinner stakes), but you will emerge well fed without feeling totally fleeced. Continuing in the same direction, the **rue Dauphine** claims some reasonably priced, reliable restaurants, culminating at the bottom in one of Paris's best Indian restaurants, **Yugaraj**.

In the summer months, this area is a delight to wander around. Try **Le Bistrot de Paris**, a sign of a return to traditional bourgeois cuisine. One of the city's best Vietnamese restaurants, **Tan Dinh**, is beyond the rue du Bac toward the Musée d'Orsay, and has a particularly impressive wine list. Finally, the ultimate in conditions for a *dîner à deux* can be found at **Laperouse**, which still has ornately mirrored, turn-of-the-century private rooms upstairs—although its cuisine is not what it used to be.

Le Sandwich An unexpected craze has begun to sweep Paris at lunchtimes. The "English sandwich," white sliced bread and all, is now in such demand that Marks and Spencer are importing the bread daily from the U.K. and feverishly filling and packing sandwiches at the boulevard Haussman, ready for the lunchtime rush. Now even French department stores are getting in on the act.

Wine bars *Bars à vins* are increasingly popular as relaxed lunchtime spots where quality wine accompanies a basic hot dish or even more copious "menu." Friendly, bustling places where some clients eat at the counter and others squeeze around small tables, they epitomize the Parisian character: fast, no frills, and with a quick patter. Those that come closer in style to bistros are open in the evenings, but the purist *bar à vin* usually closes around 9PM. The 1st and 2nd arrondissements, where businessmen are thick on the ground, have a wide choice, but try and go either before 12:30 or just after 2PM if you want to get a table. An old favorite is **Le Rubis**, where plates of charcuterie or cheese help absorb varying amounts of wine. **Willie's Wine Bar**, opened and run by an Englishman, and its brother, **Juveniles**, both serve thirsty stockbrokers from the nearby Bourse. In the same quartier, **La Côte** is becoming justifiably popular, while **Aux Bons Crus**, overlooking the Palais-Royal at the back, is packed with ravenous bankers and business people.

In Le Marais, don't miss **Le Coude-Fou**, a narrow bistro often peopled by local eccentrics. **La Tartine** on the rue de Rivoli is yet another old-timer, where nothing seems to have changed for at least 40 years. Beyond the Bastille, near the place d'Aligre market, is the traditional old favorite, **Le Baron Rouge**, where locals fill their bottles from the wine barrels. The atmosphere is particularly lively on a Sunday morning. Another Parisian monument, even further afield, is **Jacques Mélac's** famous wine bar. The jovial, mustachioed owner produces his own Parisian vintage, resulting in a rowdy wine-picking festival every September. During the rest of the year, his bistro overflows with enthusiasts of the heavier end of French cuisine.

St.-Germain has its famous **Chai de l'Abbaye**, a popular but rather soulless wine bar near the rue de Buci market, but is better represented by **Chez Georges** on the rue des Canettes. Popular with the local fashion crowd is **Au Sauvignon**, which has a terrace for improving summer tans. The chain of **L'Ecluse** wine bars (on the Quai des Grands Augustins, in Les Halles, or at the Madeleine) is excellent for sampling smooth Bordeaux, although their dishes are mainly cold platters.

Bastille Outside the tourist center, wine bars gain even more character, generally because of a faithful crowd of regular customers. Near the Bastille, go to **Au Limonaire** or finish your long day or evening in style at **La Nuit des Rois**, which specializes in champagne.

The spread of trendiness is only a recent phenomenon around the Bastille. Squeezed between the latest "in" places are numerous local restaurants serving basic fare, and many of the hotspots serve ethnic food. Here you can dine on Thai cuisine among low-flying parrots at the **Blue Elephant**, or dive into a mountain of couscous at the reputable **Chez Léon**. A favorite with young trendies is the **China Club**, a vast red-laquered restaurant and bar, more recommended for its cocktails than its fairly standard Chinese dishes.

On the same street, the rue de Charenton, but nearer the Opéra Bastille, is a theatrical Italian restaurant serving regional specialties, **Sipario,** while between the two is a variety of young and friendly eating places. Slip down a side street here and you can try out a longstanding classic bistro, **Fin de Siècle**. Across the

Parisian wine bars offer the chance to sample a wide range of wines

Wine tasting
Most wine bars offer wine by the glass; however, it is cheaper to order it by the carafe. Different sizes are referred to as a *quart* (25cl), a *demi* (50cl) or a *pichet* (equivalent to a 75cl bottle).

FOOD AND DRINK

The legendary Jules Verne
Perhaps the hardest dinner reservation to get in Paris, and certainly the highest at 400 feet, is the exclusive Jules Verne Restaurant on the second level of the Eiffel Tower. Book two months in advance for a window table!

There is still plenty of scope for serious foodies, despite the increase of fast-food eateries

place de la Bastille, go to **La Mousson** if you really like people-watching: the cuisine is so-so exotico-colonial, as is the décor, but it can be a good place for an early evening cocktail.

Chic eating Further east of the Bastille, toward Faidherbe, is a new epicenter for trendy eating. Go to the fashionable and chic Moroccan **Le Mansouria** or, in the rue Chanzy, a decidedly camp, operatic Italian bistro, **La Magnani**. Visitors determined to remain firmly within the limits of Gallic cuisine should go a few steps further to **Chardenoux**, an unpretentious Belle Epoque restaurant serving the best of traditional bistro food.

Back in the heart of the Bastille on the rue de Charonne is a firm favorite with locals and visitors alike: **Chez Paul**, where booking is necessary despite its relaxed appearance.

Still in the Gallic home-cooking mood, but situated in the uninspiring district around the Gare de Lyon, is a justifiably famous bistro, the elegant **Au Trou Gascon**, where fish is treated in unusually full-flavored ways and hot foie gras is dished up with asparagus.

If you find yourself up at **La Villette**, don't hesitate to

stay there for lunch or dinner. On the main avenue, Jean-Jaurès, is a traditional Parisian restaurant, complete with red benches and lace curtains, **Au Cochon d'Or,** where generous portions of grilled meat dishes are served—at a price. For those more interested in fish, the next-door restaurant, **Dagorno,** is a local institution and its decorative Belle Epoque setting creates an elegant background.

Eating with a view Finally, for lunching or dining in bucolic splendor, the **Parc Montsouris,** the **Parc des Buttes-Chaumont,** and the **Bois de Boulogne** all oblige, each with reputable, chic, and rather costly establishments. The greenhouse-styled **Pavillon Montsouris** now has an affordable menu and the view over the park will make up for any frustrations over service. **Au Pavillon Puebla** is, in fact, a Napoleon III pavilion, and its decorative style is suitably theatrical: here the cuisine is an astute mixture of traditional and new, served in a vast room overlooking the hillocky park. Queen of them all is **Le Pré Catalan,** housed in a small palace hidden in the verdant Bois de Boulogne. Here you can sample exquisite lobster, crab, or tender young

Le Train Bleu restaurant in the Gare de Lyon

225

Salons de thé
Tea shops in Paris are extremely popular, opening from noon until early evening. Laduré at 16 rue Royale is particularly grand, with Louis XIV décor and delicious pâtisseries. Angélina, near the Louvre, is famous for its hot chocolate with whipped cream. Alternatively, the Café de la Mosquée near the Jardin des Plantes serves refreshing mint tea.

Parisian delicatessens are in a class of their own. Most serve delicious pâtés and quiches—ideal for a picnic

rabbit, followed by divine desserts. If the weather is fine, few pleasures are greater than eating in this peaceful, romantic setting.

Ethnic eating Increasingly cosmopolitan, Paris now offers a vast selection of ethnic restaurants. Although **St.-Germain** is traditionally strong, and the streets near the Opéra such as the rue **Ste.-Anne** now cater almost exclusively to a growing Japanese business community, much enjoyment can be had by venturing out of the center to farther-flung arrondissements. Home to communities of French Asiatics, North Africans, or West Indians, quartiers such as **Belleville** or the 13th (**Chinatown**) offer a wide spectrum. Good for tight budgets, too, many of the Chinese/Vietnamese restaurants are excellent value, proof being the custom generated by Asiatic families. **The Royal Belleville**, an enormous establishment, and **Le Nioullaville** all have endless menus, satisfying specialties, and rapid service. Around the crossroads of the boulevard de Belleville and the Faubourg du Temple, you cannot go wrong. Venture further up the rue de Belleville and you will find **Tai Yien**, another canteen, this time featuring an enormous carp aquarium. But Paris is immense, so it should not be too hard to track down your own favorites.

Fish and seafood vocabulary

anguille	eel
bar	sea bass
bouillabaisse	fish and seafood soup
brandade de morue	creamed salted cod
brochet	pike
cabillaud	fresh cod
crabe	crab

coquilles St.-Jacques	scallops
crevettes	shrimps
daurade	sea bream
écrevisses	crayfish/prawns
hareng	herring
homard	lobster
huîtres	oysters
langouste	spiny lobster
loup	catfish
lotte	angler
maquereau	mackerel
merlan	whiting
morue	cod
moules	mussels
raie	skate
rouget	red mullet
saumon	salmon
sole	sole
thon	tuna
truite	trout

Meat and poultry vocabulary

agneau	lamb
andouillette	blood sausage
bœuf	beef
brochette	kebab
caille	quail
canard/caneton	duck/duckling
cassoulet	meat and bean casserole
chevreuil	venison
choucroute	sauerkraut
contrefilet	loin steak
côte de bœuf	T-bone steak
côtelettes	chops
dinde	turkey
dindonneau	young turkey
foie	liver
gigot	roast leg of lamb
langue	tongue
lapin /lapereau	rabbit
lièvre	hare
oie	goose
perdrix	partridge
pintade	guinea fowl
porc	pork
poulet	chicken
poussin	spring chicken
saucisses	sausages
steak tartare	raw minced beef
veau	veal

Paris is a paradise for anyone who has a sweet tooth

Cooking methods

Remember that the French love undercooking meat, so if you want what is considered "rare" in an Anglo-Saxon country, it is safer to say *à point*.

bleu	very rare
saignant	rare
à point	medium rare
bien cuit	well done (relatively)

See also pages 276–81.

Sports

Spectator sports
Highlights of the Parisian sporting calendar include the Roland Garros International Tennis Grand Slam tournament from mid-May to late-June, the Prix de l'Arc de Triomphe horserace in October, and the climax of the annual Tour de France bicycle race in July, along with numerous rugby and football internationals. The 24-hour car race at Le Mans every June is only 115 miles southwest of Paris.

228

Paris's best jogging circuits are in the Champs de Mars, the Bois de Boulogne, and the Bois de Vincennes

If you're dying to sweat off some of the extra foie gras and Sauternes that your poor body has been assailed with, you can turn to the gymnasiums and swimming pools of the capital. But practicing sport in Paris is not easy. Although there are officially 97 gyms, 36 pools, and 57 tennis stadiums, the real picture is a different one, with inconvenient opening hours, far-flung locations, members-only policies, and overcrowding the norm. Don't forget the big peripheral parks of Boulogne and Vincennes: both have good cycling and boating facilities as well as endless jogging potential. For information on municipal facilities and sporting events, contact **Allo-Sports** (tel: 42 76 54 54).

Cycling The excellent SNCF system of "Train + vélo" combines a train journey with renting a bike from the station at your destination, a perfect way to discover forests, châteaus, and villages. A list of stations is available at any mainline SNCF station. Otherwise, you can rent them in Paris for confronting the merciless city traffic.
La Maison du Vélo: 11 rue Fénélon, 75010 (tel: 42 81 24 72).
Paris-Vélo: 2 rue du Fer-à-Moulin, 75005 (tel: 43 37 59 22).
Calf muscles fading? Then rent a scooter.
Location Scooter Voiturette, 14 rue St.-Maur, 75011 (tel: 43 48 16 73).

Gymnasiums Private chains have taken the lead over municipal gyms, which remain dusty, underequipped affairs in comparison. However, it is usually possible to get a day pass or a book of 10 passes at a reasonable rate.
Gymnase Club is the biggest on the market and, ever expanding, it has now even taken over the Garden Gym chain. The best-equipped Gymnase Club gym is at 17 rue du Débarcadère; 8e. Call for details (tel: 40 20 03 03).
Vitatop has two more exclusive, sophisticated gyms on the outskirts (tel: 40 68 00 21). The branch on the roof of the Sofitel Hotel offers a spectacular Parisian skyline from your Jacuzzi.
Lastly, for those who have really overdone it in the restaurants, a vast and extravagant new multisports complex could be the answer.
Aquaboulevard, 4 rue Louis-Armand, 75015 (tel: 40 60 10 00). Artificial nature brought to the *périphérique* of Paris. As well as a gym, there are indoor putting greens, a wave pool, tennis and squash courts, and water sports. *Open*: late and day pass available.

Swimming Most of the 30-odd swimming pools in Paris are municipal, therefore affordable. But avoid, if you can, Wednesdays and weekends, when local kids take over. Opening times are complicated, so phone direct or check *Pariscope* for current details. Listed below are the more central pools.
Piscine des Amiraux, 13 rue des Amiraux, 75018 (tel: 46 06 46 47). This architectural landmark in the north of Paris was built in 1924. Renovated recently; 36-yard pool.

Piscine Buttes-aux-Cailles, 5 place Paul-Verlaine, 75013 (tel: 45 89 60 05). A tiled art-deco gem of a 36-yard pool, another one outdoors, open in summer.

Piscine des Halles, Porte du Jour, Forum-des-Halles, 75001 (tel: 42 36 98 44). 55-yard underground pool, clean and bright with "tropical" garden.

Piscine Jean Taris, 16 rue Thouin, 75005 (tel: 43 25 54 03). Two 27-yard pools, favorites with local students, and one toddler pool. Built in 1978; water cleaned electronically, so no chlorine!

Piscine du Marché Saint-Germain, 7 rue Clément, 75006 (tel: 43 29 08 15). Hidden beneath the St.-Germain market complex is a 27-yard pool with special diving section.

Piscine Quartier Latin, 19 rue de Pontoise, 75005 (tel: 43 54 06 23). A 36-yard pool with a distinct 1930s air. Solarium, squash courts, and sauna.

Piscine Saint-Merri, 18 rue du Renard, 75004 (tel: 42 72 29 45). Right next to Beaubourg, small indoor 27-yard pool with solarium.

Tennis Your best bet for a game of tennis is in the Bois de Vincennes, where 24 courts huddle in the Plaine de la Faluère, a gigantic sports complex. The desirable, much-coveted public courts in the Jardin du Luxembourg are more central but require advance booking through a municipal club.

For details on joining local clubs, contact **Allo-Sports** (tel: 42 76 54 54). Numerous private clubs exist, mainly at the portes of Paris (exits from the périphérique), but membership is costly and is probably only worthwhile if you are staying for a long period of time.

Boules or pétanque is a less strenuous sporting option, but it's taken just as seriously as any other

Parisian pastimes
Typically Parisian sports include afternoon boating or horse riding in the Bois de Boulogne or the Bois de Vincennes, and pétanque—which Parisians claim to be their most popular sport—played on any shady stretch of gravel or earth in the parks. Golf is also becoming increasingly popular, with many clubs developing on the outskirts.

Nightlife

ndies go:
, Parisian
 gged in, hip)
float from one club to the next, making and breaking the fortunes of barmen. Pigalle neon and fun tackiness remains a favorite: try Le Moloko for drinks, La Locomotive for a dance floor twirl, or La Cigale for a rock concert. The Bastille is now firmly established, and the rue de Lappe never sleeps. Revel in the kitsch splendor of Le Balajo or join the crowd at La Casbah. Other streets like rue de Charenton or rue de Charonne are burgeoning with bars, too. Les Halles and in particular the rue des Lombards are good for late drinks and music, but to really rub shoulders with Paris jetsetters, head for Les Bains.

The boulevard de Clichy, similar to London's Soho with its fast-food joints, cinemas, sex shops, and "live" shows, is always a crowded nightspot

Parisian nightlife changes fashion as the proverbial snake does its skin. Old favorites are few and far between, often handed over to the destiny of tourist buses, while others sink in the wake of youth's fickleness. But a vast choice remains, and you will never find yourself at a loss for a drink or a swing around the dance floor in the wee hours.

One warning: prices of drinks in clubs can be astronomical, so if quantities of alcohol are essential, stick to regular bars (though after 10PM prices are uncontrolled everywhere).

Opening hours Action starts in the nightclubs well after midnight, continuing till 5AM or so, while some of the jazz bars also carry on late. All clubs are closed on Mondays, and jazz is unusual, though not impossible, on both Sundays and Mondays.

Check the listings published in the weekly *Pariscope, 7 à Paris,* or *L'Officiel des Spectacles* for detailed schedules and hours.

Feather Clubs

Many visitors come to Paris for just that: the renowned cabaret shows that seem straight out of a time-warped Hollywood. All are virtually monopolized by ogling tourist parties. You can unload a small fortune on exorbitantly priced drinks.

If this is the kind of evening out you're looking for, the following selection might be useful.

Crazy Horse Saloon, 12 avenue George V, 75008 (tel: 47 23 32 32), metro: George V. Bare-breasted girls strut

The famous Folies-Bergère, once considered to be the naughtiest cabaret in Paris, with striptease introduced as part of the show in 1894

Jazz
All styles of jazz from Free-form to Dixieland can be heard in this jazz-crazy city, with venues ranging from pubs to concert halls. New Morning is one of the most popular clubs, along with Au Duc des Lombards and Le Petit Opportun. The Grande Halle de la Villette hosts a huge international jazz festival in July and the Paris Jazz Festival takes place every October.

231

through their erotic routines, assuming seemingly impossible postures. Reputed to be the most professional show.

Folies-Bergère, 32 rue Richer, 75009 (tel: 44 79 98 98), metro: Cadet, rue Montmartre. Renowned for diamanté, feathers, more breasts, and glitter. Not what it used to be, but the vast setting is historic and admission relatively reasonable.

Le Lido, 116 Champs-Elysées, 75008 (tel: 40 76 56 10), metro: George V. Fantastic special effects alleviate an otherwise predictable show. The Bluebell Girls dance to a sea of regimented tourists.

Moulin Rouge, 82 boulevard de Clichy, 75018 (tel: 46 06 00 19), metro: Blanche. A thousand costumes, 100 girls, singers and acrobats, an aquarium, crocodiles. What is this? Just the delirium of a spectacular show in the classic venue.

Paradis Latin, 28 rue Cardinal-Lemoine, 75005 (tel: 43 29 07 07), metro: Cardinal-Lemoine. Not in the same league as the above, but a shimmering floor show.

Jazz Bars

Au Duc des Lombards, 42 rue des Lombards, 75001 (tel: 42 33 22 88), metro: Châtelet. Comfortable, dark jazz lounge with average to good musicians. Nightly.

Baiser Salé, 58 rue des Lombards, 75001 (tel: 42 33 37 71), metro: Châtelet. Blues, funky or jazz, with cocktails till 4AM.

Les Bouchons, 19 rue des Halles, 75001 (tel: 42 33 28 73), metro: Châtelet. Relaxed American-style bar in restaurant basement with live groups.

Café de la Plage, 59 rue de Charonne, 75011 (tel: 47 00 91 60), metro: Ledru-Rollin, Bastille. Till early, a Bastille hot spot for mixed fauna. Good soul, rap, salsa.

Café Rive Droite, 2 rue Berger, 75001 (tel: 42 33 81 62). High-decibel sounds by local musicians till dawn.

Caveau de la Huchette, 5 rue de la Huchette, 75005 (tel: 43 26 65 05), metro: St.-Michel. An old classic.

Harry's Bar

This cozy, wood-paneled bar is the original Harry's Bar, named after its first bartender, Harry MacElkone. Harry bought the bar in 1923 and it soon became a regular haunt for Ernest Hemingway and F. Scott Fitzgerald. Today it is run by Harry's son.

American in Paris: Harry's Bar opened in 1911 by American jockey Tod Sloane on the rue Daunou

Smoky, crowded basement bar and dancing for students and tourists.

Meridien, 81 boulevard Gouvion St.-Cyr, 75017 (tel: 40 68 30 88), metro: Porte Maillot. Rather staid hotel bar, but good jazz classics play here.

Montana, 28 rue St.-Benoît, 75006 (tel: 45 48 93 08), metro: St.-Germain. Upscale American-style jazz bar and restaurant for local tourists.

New Morning, 7–9 rue des Petites Ecuries, 75010 (tel: 45 23 51 41), metro: Château d'Eau. Paris's best. Excellent program of international jazz concerts.

Passage du Nord-Ouest, 13 rue du Faubourg Montmartre, 75009 (tel: 47 70 81 47). The latest on the scene with a nightly program of live jazz, world music, or blues.

Petit Journal St.-Michel, 71 boulevard St.-Michel, 75005 (tel: 43 26 28 59), metro: Luxembourg. New Orleans–style jazz till 2AM in this favorite, though cramped, old venue. Restaurant and bar.

Le Petit Opportun, 15 rue des Lavandières-Ste.-Opportun, 75001 (tel: 42 36 01 36). Well-established bar, good French jazz program in crowded basement.

Le Sunset, 60 rue des Lombards, 75001 (tel: 40 26 46 60), metro: Châtelet. Funky jazz cellar for Les Halles late-nighters. Restaurant and bar.

La Villa, 29 rue Jacob, 75006 (tel: 43 26 60 00), metro: St.-Germain. Chic jazz bar in designer hotel.

Late-Night Bars

Ascot, 66 rue Pierre-Charron, 75008 (tel: 43 59 28 15), metro: Franklin-Roosevelt. Established piano bar for smart set off Champs-Elysées.

Bar Romain, 6 rue Caumartin, 75009 (tel: 47 42 98 04), metro: Havre-Caumartin. Original 1905 décor of neo-Pompeii frescoes makes background for choice of over 200 cocktails. Popular with showbiz crowd.

Bilboquet, 13 rue Saint-Benoît, 75006 (tel: 45 48 81 84), metro: St.-Germain. Classic, straitlaced atmosphere. Restaurant and bar with live jazz.

Birdland Club, 20 rue Princesse, 75006 (tel: 43 26 97 59), metro: Mabillon. Friendly, late. Golden oldie jazz records set the laid-back tone.

La Casbah, 18/20 rue de la Forge-Royal, 75011 (tel: 43 71 71 89), metro: Faidherbe-Chaligny. Vast, imaginative mauresque-art deco cocktail bar with dancing down-stairs. Video screen and a team of fancy barstaff.

China Club, 50 rue de Charenton, 75012 (tel: 43 43 82 02), metro: Ledru-Rollin. Vast, shady, red-laquered bar/restaurant with discreet upstairs cocktail lounge. Hip, crowded, buzzy. Near Bastille.

L'Entrepôts, 14 rue de Charonne, 75011 (tel: 48 06 57 04), metro: Bastille. Cheerful, popular cocktail bar guarded by bouncer. Smoky billiard room downstairs.

Harry's Bar, 5 rue Daunou, 75002 (tel: 42 61 71 14), metro: Opéra. Old favorite. Pub atmosphere stimulating enough for Gershwin to compose *American in Paris*. Mature, tanked-up crowd.

Kitty O'Shea's, 10 rue des Capucines, 75002 (tel: 42 96 02 99), metro: Opéra. Warm, pub atmosphere frequented by sonorous Irish expatriates and business people revving up.

La Luna, 28 rue Keller, 75011 (tel: 40 21 90 91), metro: Bastille, Ledru-Rollin. Two lively, high-tech floors for Bastille troopers.

Mayflower, 49 rue Descartes, 75005 (tel: 43 54 56 47), metro:·Cardinal-Lemoine. Lively all-night pub. Stagger out at dawn for breakfast on the place de la Contrescarpe.

Moloko, 26 rue Fontaine, 75009, (tel: 48 74 50 26) metro: Blanche. Newly "in" late-night bar for Pigalle clubbers and party crowd.

Rosebud, 11 bis rue Delambre, 75014 (tel: 43 35 38 54), metro: Vavin. Shady Montparnasse bar, intimate atmosphere for tête-à-têtes.

Nightclubs/Discos

Les Bains, 7 rue du Bourg-l'Abbé, 75003 (tel: 48 87 01 80), metro: Etienne-Marcel. Still top, still selective at the door, but a nocturnal landmark for fashion, showbiz and media personalities. Go late. Restaurant.

Le Balajo, 9 rue de Lappe, 75011 (tel: 47 00 07 87), metro: Bastille. A survivor of the 1930s, ritzy décor for hip young things. Monday and Thursday nights are best.

Bobino, 20 rue de la Gaîté, 75014 (tel: 43 27 24 24). A top disco spread over two floors of a converted variety theater. Good DJs.

Castel's, 15 rue Princesse, 75006 (tel: 43 26 90 22), metro: Odéon. Members' club for monied, older generation. Bar upstairs and dance floor downstairs. Twinkle a diamond cufflink and you may get in.

La Chapelle des Lombards, 19 rue de Lappe, 75011 (tel: 43 57 24 24), metro: Bastille. Swinging rhythms from Latin America, Africa, and the Caribbean. Friendly.

La Locomotive, 90 boulevard de Clichy, 75018 (tel: 42 57 37 37), metro: Blanche. Ambitiously scaled, three-tiered basement club below Moulin Rouge. Latest hip sounds mixed with 1960s nostalgia.

Nouvelle Eve, 25 rue Fontaine, 75009 (tel: 45 26 68 18), metro: Pigalle. Gilded theater changes from cabaret to nightclub on stroke of midnight. Good DJs.

Olivia Valère, 40 rue du Colisée, 75008 (tel: 42 25 11 68). You don't come here by metro. Very upscale, more mature business/glamour crowd. Restaurant.

Le Palace, 3 cité Bergère, 75009 (tel: 42 46 10 87), metro: rue Montmartre. Once unique in Paris; opened in 1977 in a barely renovated 19th-century theater. Now lost its eccentric decadence and style to rough bikers. Restaurant in Le Privilège downstairs.

Régine, 49 rue de Ponthieu, 75008 (tel: 43 59 21 13). Careful grooming necessary to get in. Flashy, mature crowd similar to Castel's bops night away.

Rex Club, 5 boulevard Poissonière, 75002 (tel: 42 36 83 98), metro: Bonne Nouvelle. Part of gigantic art-deco concert hall and cinema. Different DJ every night from house to rap, rock, disco, salsa. Good concerts.

Sheherazade, 3 rue de Liège, 75009 (tel: 42 85 53 78), metro: Liège. 1,001 nights oriento-exotico décor. Changing nightly style of rap, house, rock, etc.

Le Tango, 11 rue au Maire, 75003 (tel: 42 72 17 78), metro: Arts-et-Métiers. Hot-blooded Afro-Latin rhythms, tango, salsa, and reggae keep this unpretentious club boogeying.

Rubbing shoulders with the rich and famous
Where the rich and famous go: the Champs-Elysées area still attracts those with true glitter, so try Olivia Valère or Les Bains, where you might trip over the toes of French showbiz personalities or just plain rich folk. Everything is a question of generation, so you are more likely to find youthful successes (media, photographers, designers etc.) at Les Bains, whose reputation never wanes. Finally, the longstanding Castel's, theoretically a members-only club, is where you're most likely to sit next to mature French film stars accompanied by their latest blonde girlfriends.

Eating out on the Champs-Elysées

Watch where you park your car
In 1990, Paris police handed out 7,994,846 tickets; 7,506,419 of these were parking tickets.

Booking agencies
Looking for accommodations? Two agencies, Paris-Séjour-Reservation at 50 avenue des Champs-Elysées, 8e (tel: 42 56 30 00) or Ely 12 12 at 9 rue d'Artois, 8e (tel: 43 59 12 12) will book accommodations on your behalf.

234

Following in the footsteps of the famous
Paris is famous for its luxurious hotels, frequented by the rich and famous. The Hôtel de Crillon was built for Louis XV and Le Grand for Napoleon III, and patronized by many distinguished guests including Winston Churchill. L'Hôtel was the last home of Oscar Wilde, and Lutétia was decorated by top designer Sonia Rykiel. The Ritz, former haunt of the Duke of Windsor and Ernest Hemingway, is now Madonna's favorite Paris hotel.

With 1,500 or so hotels and an annual average of 18 million tourists spread among them, Parisian accommodations cater to all tastes and budgets. This is one of the rare European capitals that offers quite acceptable and affordable accommodations in central areas, often family-run in idiosyncratic fashion.

At the top end of the spectrum are the luxury hotels, straight out of another epoch, that cater to countless well-heeled travelers or business people. Their prices for short stays are very high, but some hotels make discount arrangements with travel agents abroad, so it is worth inquiring at home well in advance of your trip.

The season The Paris "season" is a strange one and is worth bearing in mind if you want good value. May, June, September, and October are the hardest months to find rooms, and prices often go down in July and August, particularly in the 3-star establishments, which are sorely missing their business clientèle at that time.

Remember that checkout time is midday. On arrival, make sure you check in before 6PM as after this time the hotel has the right to give the room to someone else, even if they hold a deposit from you. Breakfasts are always Continental-style (coffee or tea and rolls or croissants plus a fruit juice if you are lucky). Only 3-star hotels upward are obliged to offer service in the rooms, otherwise you will have to head for the dining room. Not all 1-star hotels offer breakfast. No hotel can charge you for breakfast unless you have ordered it, and you may prefer to join in the city bustle outside for better coffee at a lower price.

If you come to Paris by car, remember that you will undoubtedly encounter parking problems. Hotels that have parking are generally the uninspiring modern buildings to be found outside the center: many are, however, located close to public parking areas.

Finding a base Choosing your base quartier is tricky. Every part of Paris has its advantages and disadvantages, its charms and its horrors. For the heart of luxury, go straight to the 8th arrondissement (Champs-Elysées, avenue George V, avenue Montaigne, Faubourg St.-Honoré and surrounding streets). Here is the highest concentration of luxury and 4-star establishments, and this is where to stay if you need to pop out for a fitting at Dior's, pick up some presents at Hermès, or impress your business acquaintances. Even if your budget does not stretch to these palaces of refinement, at least drop in for a drink at the bar to soak up some of its features—call girls included. Although everyone has heard of the Ritz, the Crillon, the Bristol, the Plaza-Athénée, or the George V, not everyone knows the less monumental establishments such as the **Hôtel de la Trémoille**, the **Raphaël**, or the **San Régis**, favorites with the more discreet variety of wealthy travelers.

Following closely in the luxury stakes is the 1st arrondissement (Tuileries, Louvre, place Vendôme), convenient for high-class jewelry and culture, yet whose side streets have a good sprinkling of 2- and 3-star hotels. Preening themselves in old-world splendor here are the **Ritz** and the **Meurice**, both of which have remarkable interiors and are wonderful for an early evening drink. Closer to most people's budgets are places such as **Le Molière**, the **Hôtel des Tuileries**, or the **Hôtel Saint-Roch**. Immediately north is the 2nd arrondissement, which, despite its small size, has a large number of 2- and 3-star hotels, catering mainly to the business community centered on the area's banks and the Bourse. **Timhotel La Bourse** is one of a chain of fairly reasonable hotels, which are usually extremely well situated, and in this case it is particularly convenient for doing raids on all the designer boutiques in and around the place des Victoires.

Budget choice The adjacent 9th arrondissement (Opéra, Grands Boulevards, Faubourg Montmartre) has the densest concentration of hotels of any Parisian arrondissement, and over half of them are budget 2-star establishments. The Faubourg Montmartre and its side street claim the majority; many of these hotels are used by tour operators, giving a rather un-Parisian feel to this otherwise interesting neighborhood. One of Paris's most popular nightclubs, Le Palace, is situated here, and the Folies-Bergère is just around the corner in an area full of ethnic restaurants (kosher, Turkish, North African). Try the **Corona**, a 1930s establishment on an interesting backstreet lined with hotels, or the **Bergère**, now completely modernized and part of the Best Western chain.

If you do decide to give these places a wide berth, then head further north toward Pigalle and Montmartre, where a number of characteristic family-run hotels can be tracked down. Near the delightful place St.-Georges, try the **Hôtel de la Tour d'Auvergne**, an atmospheric, renovated 3-star place, which boasts fourposters in every room.

Paris atmosphere The area most visitors head for with alacrity is the Rive Gauche, the 5th, 6th, and even 7th, arrondissements. Less business-oriented in atmosphere and more *vieux Paris*, the Quartier Latin and St.-Germain-des-Prés provide all the ingredients for a classic vacation in Paris. Throughout this district is a host of reasonably priced 1-, 2-, and 3-star hotels whose prices are generally lower than their equivalents across the Seine. In the same area you can find fairly basic student hotels and restaurants, gathered around the rue Mouffetard, the place de la Contrescarpe, and the rue des Ecoles, and the slightly more upscale **Hôtel du Collège de France**. Here, in a quiet side street, simple but pleasant rooms rise up to the sixth floor, from where you can glimpse the spires of Notre-Dame. Similarly quaint in spirit is **Le Jardin des Plantes**, whose freshly decorated rooms, all with a floral theme, look out over the park of the same name. Rock-bottom prices can be had at the tiny **Hôtel des Carmes**, situated in an atmospheric side street off the boulevard St.-Germain. With its strong student population, due to the proximity of the university, this lively part of the Rive Gauche is particularly recommended for those with a limited budget. Within easy reach of numerous monuments and

235

Linguistic help
In the more upmarket establishments, receptionists are usually bilingual, and any hotel with two or more stars must by law have a receptionist speaking a second language.

Cheap chain hotels
More and more chain hotels are springing up on the outskirts of Paris, including Ibis (tel: 43 42 91 91), Mercure (tel: 43 35 28 28), and Formule I. Although they lack Parisian character and are often located on a busy road, they offer a cheap, clean, practical solution for budget travelers in Paris.

ACCOMMODATIONS

A tight fit

France has the smallest minimum legal size in Europe for hotel bedrooms and bathrooms, and in Paris, where real estate does not 0come cheap, many hoteliers exploit this to the full. Thus the so-called bathroom is more than likely to be chopped out of the corner of the bedroom. When booking a room, make sure you distinguish between a *salle d'eau* (shower room) and a *salle de bain* (bathroom).

museums, it has an easygoing atmosphere and caters well to young travelers.

Higher prices St.-Germain harbors a wide selection of good 3-star hotels, but prices can rocket here. The **Hôtel de l'Abbaye** is justifiably expensive within its category, but service is impeccable and the rooms are perfectly appointed, if limited in size (this is medieval Paris, after all). The delightful **Hôtel des Marroniers** is tucked away in its pretty courtyard in the heart of the antiques district, and here the prices are more reasonable if you can get a room. The area of the rue Jacob, the rue de l'Université, and the rue de Seine is thick with small family-run hotels, and it is a chic and pleasant part of town. If you must overlook the river, try the **Hôtel du Quai Voltaire**, a rambling old place where Baudelaire once stayed. A sure favorite for its location and price is the **Hôtel Michelet-Odéon**, on the place de l'Odéon, just a few steps from the Luxembourg Gardens.

Montparnasse makes a good base: transportation is easy, and the bars of the boulevard stay open late. Here you could try squeezing into the tiny **Hôtel Danemark**, renovated from a charming old flowery-wallpaper establishment into a more chic and elegant place. Nearby, in the arty rue de la Grande-Chaumière, is a small family-run hotel, excellent for low budgets: the **Hôtel des Académies**. Farther east and across the

The place de l'Opéra, set in the 9th arron-dissement, where hotels are plentiful, often inexpensive, and within easy reach of the many theaters, bars, and restaurants in the area

boulevard is the **Hôtel Istria**, part of the Montparnasse cultural legend, and reasonable value. Still following the artists' trail, go as far south as you can in Paris—almost—to the **Hôtel du Parc Montsouris**, a simple establishment but with all the necessary comforts and straight across the road from the park. In this charming, peaceful neighborhood are many of the artists' custom-built studios from the 1920s.

Le Marais This is a quartier not to be forgotten if you want up-to-the-minute Parisian life. Numerous hotels, old and new, pepper this animated district and you are more likely to find peace and quiet here than anywhere else on the Rive Droite. Although these are mainly 2- and 3-star establishments, the occasional budget hotel can still be found, such as the fun **Hotel du 7^e Art** or the **Grand Hôtel Malher**. In the middle category, try the **Hôtel de la place des Vosges** or the **Jeanne d'Arc**, deservedly popular. Once for low budgets, now rising with an extra star, is the characteristic **Hôtel Saint-Merry**, perfectly located for avid visitors to Beaubourg. And for those seeking discreet refinement, the **Pavillon de la Reine** is the *crème de la crème*, modestly set back from the place des Vosges behind a pretty little garden. All in all, this is a good place to be.

See also pages 274–6.

237

■ **It's hard to generalize about 2 million people, but as a rule, the best way to communicate with Parisians is by using their language. The tourist who relentlessly speaks loud English is much less welcome than the visitor who squeaks out** *s'il vous plaît*, **however poorly pronounced** ...■

Could it be that old devil flattery at work? Whatever, once you have initiated contact, you then run the risk of hearing in return a slew of unintelligible noises, impossible to decipher. To this you simply reply, *Parlez-vous anglais*? If the answer is a brusque *non*, do not despair. An increasing proportion of the younger generation (officially 59 percent of all age groups and 89 percent of the 15- to 19-year-olds) speak a foreign language and willingly help foreign visitors. So keep your eyes open for some bright-eyed teenager.

Forms of address For those who speak some remnants of French, it is worth bearing in mind other practical rules. Addressing people with a *Madame* or *Monsieur* tacked on the end is a sign of politeness that is appropriate no matter what the person's social status. It can work wonders in persuasive tactics. With strangers always stick to *vous*, and with acquaintances only use *tu* once they do. The younger generation is less rigid about this now, but the best rule is to play it safe.

As in many Latin countries, you will be pigeonholed according to the way you dress. Keep in mind that a certain sober elegance will break through most barriers and what seems to an Anglo-Saxon to be "dressing up" is actually normal daily wear for a Parisian. It is almost impossible to overdress unless you go completely overboard, whereas a sloppy appearance will definitely lose you precious points.

Talking as tourists Because of its incredible popularity among visitors (16 to 20 million annually), Paris has its fair share of locals who believe that tourists equal money, and that is the end of it. Yet they love to hear foreigners praise their city, and waiters and waitresses are only too pleased to hear that the food and/or wine they are serving is good. Humor will also take you a long way—contrary to general belief, the Parisians are actually blessed with a subtle sense of irony and love to share it. Waiters will change from surly monsters to cheerful fellow human beings if your French is up to this kind of exchange. Otherwise, a friendly smile never goes amiss.

Although there is no traditional drinking hour in French cafés to facilitate striking up conversations, curiously enough, the restaurants can oblige. Bistros and brasseries—those bustling, old-fashioned dining halls where tables are squeezed in and customers barely have enough room to raise their forks—are ideal meeting places. Mealtimes are the moment when the French at last drop their guard and relax, and many a

A Parisian vineyard
The French are passionate about wine. Indeed, it is a way of life and even in Paris, wine is produced. Wine-growing is one of the most ancient traditions of Montmartre, the slopes of the Butte de Montmartre formerly covered in vineyards. Nowadays, the only remaining vineyards are at the corner of the rue St.-Vincent and rue des Saules, with an annual wine festival celebrated in October.

conversation has been started over the label of a bottle of wine or the relative merits of an unusual dish.

Points of etiquette If you manage to break down the barriers and get to know a French person, a number of rules should be remembered. Two men always shake hands when greeting each other and on leaving, even when they know each other. Members of the opposite sex kiss each other on the cheek, usually twice, though suburbanites and people from the provinces actually go through this procedure four times. The "Continental Kiss" may seem strange, but it is truly commonplace for ordinary, nonprofessional encounters, even when you've only met the person an hour earlier.

When entering a room full of strangers, it is usual practice to do the rounds of each person, shaking hands and giving your name, as they do theirs. When you leave, you have to go through the same ritual as you say *au revoir*, shaking hands or giving the *bise* (kiss), depending how much communication has taken place.

Lastly, a universal piece of advice holds equally true for Parisians: if you are invited to someone's home for dinner, make an effort to take flowers, chocolates, or a good bottle of wine. It always works wonders.

Protecting the French language
The French are so protective about their language that there is a special society within the Académie Française whose job it is to prevent English words from becoming part of daily French vocabulary. Some words like *le weekend* and *le goal* seem to have slipped through the net, though.

239

Striking up a conversation over a drink or a meal is an ideal way of breaking the ice

PARIS METRO

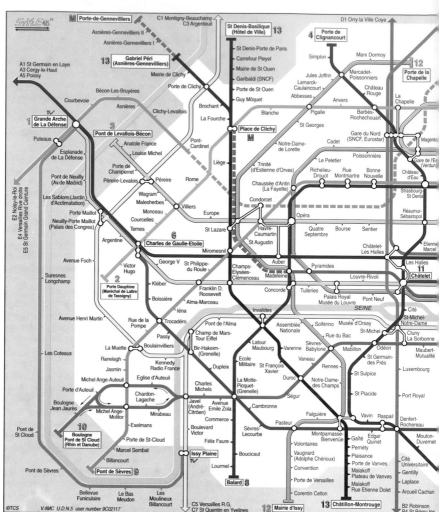

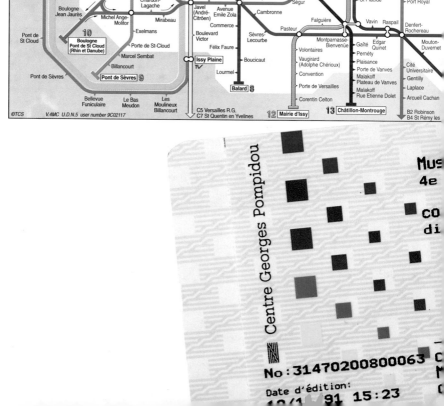

Centre Georges Pompidou

Mus
4e

co
di

No:31470200800063

Date d'édition:
...91 15:23

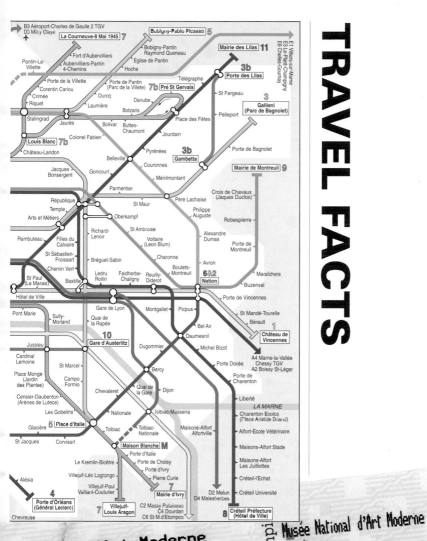

Arriving
U.S. citizens need a valid passport to enter France for stays of up to 90 days. First-timers should apply in person at least five weeks before departure to one of the 13 U.S. Passport Agency offices. Also, local county courthouses, many state and probate courts, and some post offices accept applications. Necessary documents are: (1) a completed passport application (Form DSP-11); (2) proof of citizenship (certified birth certificate issued by the Hall of Records of your state of birth, or naturalization papers); (3) proof of identity (valid driver's license or state, military, or student I.D. card with your photograph and signature); (4) two recent, identical, two-square-inch photographs (black-and-white or color head shot with white or off-white background); and (5) $65 for a 10-year passport (those under 18 pay $40 for a five-year passport). Check, money order, or cash (exact change) are accepted. Passports are sent in 10 to 15 business days.

You may renew in person or by mail. Send a complete Form DSP-82; two recent, identical passport photographs; your current passport

The Gare de Lyon: trains leave here for southeast France and Italy

(if it's less than 12 years old and issued after your 16th birthday); and a check or money order for $55.

Air Paris is served by two airports: Orly in the south and Roissy (Charles-de-Gaulle) in the north. Most American flights now arrive at the expanding Roissy Airport. Orly-Ouest terminal is monopolized by internal French flights. There are no airport taxes to be paid on arrival or departure.

Both Orly and Roissy have extensive international airline facilities, including car rental, duty-free shops, restaurants, post offices, hotels in the proximity, and ground transportation into the city center. Air France and airport staff are, on the whole, helpful, and they always speak English.

Transportation to and from Roissy: Two possibilities exist apart from a rather costly taxi ride (200 francs) covering the 14 miles. The easiest is the Air France airport bus, which leaves every 15 minutes, 6AM–11PM) and in 40 minutes whisks you straight into the central Arc de Triomphe (Etoile) or the nearby Porte Maillot. Taxis usually await the bus, and the metro station is a few yards away. On leaving, pick it up again at Etoile, avenue Carnot. A new alternative is Roissy-Bus, an airport bus serving all terminals that heads

for Opéra in central Paris. It runs every 15 minutes.

The budget transportation system is the RATP shuttle, which links with Roissy-Rail (RER line B). If you have a lot of baggage, it's not so easy heaving cases on and off the bus and then down escalators to the RER express train, but it will take you directly into the Gare du Nord or Châtelet-Les Halles. Allow 30–40 minutes. Trains run from 5:30AM to 11PM, every 15 minutes.

Transportation to and from Orly: Only 10 miles from the center, Orly is more feasible by taxi, but it also has more transportation possibilities. The Air France bus (departures every 12 minutes) goes to Invalides but will drop you off, if requested, at Porte d'Orléans or Duroc metro. Allow 30 minutes. Much cheaper but less plush is the Orlybus, which arrives at the RER and metro station of Denfert-Rochereau in south Paris. You can also take the RER line C, called Orly-Rail, from St.-Michel, but the shuttle connection is not as well organized as at Roissy. Orly-Val connects a shuttle with the RER line B.

Passenger information is available at both airports (Roissy tel: 48 62 22 80; Orly tel: 49 75 15 15).

Camping

There are altogether about 90 campsites scattered throughout the Ile-de-France, many of which are in or near the forests. Rating, as it is with hotels, ranges from 1-star to 4-star; those at the top end usually have a swimming pool or are close to a swimmable lake or river.

Useful guidebooks can be obtained from the **Fédération Française de Camping Caravaning** (a campers' association), 78 rue de Rivoli, 75004 (tel: 42 72 84 08) or the **Comité Régional du Tourisme d'Ile de France**, 73-75 rue Cambronne, 75015 (tel: 43 71 82 35), which also has a free guide to the campsites in the Paris area.

Many Parisians park their camping vans year-round on a site just outside Paris and use it as a weekend retreat. This is why, although the high season runs from April to September, it is not too difficult to find space in July or August when the Parisians have taken off. It also explains why the 3-star campsite in the **Bois de Boulogne** (between Longchamp racecourse and the Seine) is strictly reserved for non-Parisians (tel: 45 24 30 00). Otherwise, head for **Versailles** (tel: 39 51 23 61), **Rambouillet** (tel: 30 41 07 34) or **St.-Quentin-en-Yvelines** (tel: 30 58 56 20)—three countrified sites that have excellent transportation connections into Paris. Always beware of school holidays (Easter, Pentecost). For on-site rental, check the guidebook published by the Federation: each campsite offers different facilities.

As a general rule, municipal campsites, though up to reasonable standards, are not particularly dynamic in their upkeep and equipment. However, if you aim for 4-star sites such as at **L'Isle-Adam**, situated beside the biggest river beach in France (tel: 34 69 08 80), or **Ormoy-la-Rivière** (tel: 64 94 21 39), you should be well installed.

The best shop for camping equipment in Paris is **Au Vieux Campeur**, 48 rue des Ecoles, 75005 (tel: 43 29 12 32).

243

Children

Children can fit in well with visiting Paris. Restaurant staff do not generally turn up their noses at the sight of a stroller, and Parisians are generally tolerant of the presence of children. Hotels obviously vary in terms of the services they provide, but all will provide extra beds or sometimes cribs in a double room at little more than the usual room price. The Novotel chain even allows up to two children under 15 to stay free in their parents' room. Other chains offer good deals, particularly in July and August when there are no business customers. Squares and parks all have specific areas with slides, sandboxes, and more set aside for children. River trips, science museums, and certain parks (see pages 26–7) are always favorites.

English-speaking babysitters can be found through **Ababa**, a private service that also arranges day trips and tea parties. *Open*: daily (tel: 45 49 46 46). Qualified babysitters or

Paris has plenty to offer young people and children

nannies can also be hired through **Kid's Services** (tel: 47 66 00 52). **Inter-Service Parents** (tel: 44 93 44 93) is a free advisory service giving details of babysitting agencies and children's activities all over Paris.

When dining out with children, aim for family-style bistros where staff are more helpful. Elegant, upscale restaurants are less enthusiastic about strollers and juvenile voices.

Climate
Cool but gloriously sunny days often surprise the population in October

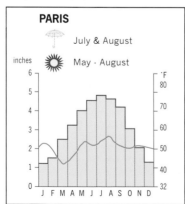

Weather Chart Conversion
25.4mm = 1inch
°F = 1.8 x °C + 32

and late February, whereas the old cliché of "Paris in the spring" does not usually apply until well into May. Rarely stifling in midsummer, Paris tends to get very muggy after a few consecutive days of sun. This is when much of the population heads down to the *quais* beside the Seine for a fresher breeze and a chance to sunbathe. Blessed with a fairly low rainfall overall, Paris nevertheless commonly sees showers, above all during March and April as well as November (possibly the least inspiring month climatically, along with chilly January).

Crime
Street crime varies from arrondissement to arrondissement. Generally speaking, if you stick to the more touristy inner areas you are safe—except for pickpockets. Followers of this pursuit are particularly prevalent on public transportation. *Never* keep your wallet in a back pocket, and ladies should make sure their bags are firmly closed and held on to. Be careful, too, in crowded cafés, flea markets, restaurants, and movie

theaters. If you lose something, the first step is to make a declaration at the local police station, which you will need to do if you are claiming insurance. Ask for the nearest *commissariat*. Stolen credit cards should be reported immediately to any of the following 24-hour services: American Express (tel: 47 77 72 00); Diners Club (tel: 47 62 75 00); Visa (tel: 42 77 11 90); MasterCard (tel: 45 67 53 53). You will need to follow this up with written confirmation and a copy of your police declaration. If you are using traveler's checks, make sure you keep a separate note of their numbers, along with the relevant phone number to contact in case of theft.

If your car is stolen (unlikely) or broken into (more likely), you will need to follow the same procedure at the commissariat and should contact your insurance office as soon as possible.

The police lost-property office does not deal with phone inquiries but is open Monday to Friday, 8–5, at 36 rue des Morillons, 75015, metro: Convention. It is worth checking here several days after any theft, as most thieves are only interested in cash and credit cards and so dump the rest. In fact, there is a notable rise in "gentlemen thieves" who actually return the unwanted contents of wallets to owners' addresses.

Victims of more serious crimes should call S.O.S. Help, an English crisis hotline that offers advice and counseling. *Open*: daily (tel: 47 23 80 80).

❑ Serious crime (armed robbery, muggings) in Paris dropped between 1990 and 1991, but burglaries and car thefts are on the increase, as are fake identity papers, bounced checks, and graffiti. ❑

Customs Regulations
You may bring home up to $400 of foreign goods duty-free, provided you've been out of the country for at least 48 hours and you haven't made an international trip in the past 30 days. Each member of the family, regardless of age, is entitled to the same exemption; exemptions may be pooled. For the next $1,000 of goods, a flat 10 percent rate is assessed; above $1,400, duties vary with merchandise. Travelers 21 or older are allowed one liter of alcohol, 100 cigars (non-Cuban), and 200 cigarettes, and one bottle of perfume trademarked in the United States. Antiques and works of art over 100 years old are duty-free. Exceed these limits, and you'll be taxed at the port of entry and additionally in your home state. Gifts under $50 may be mailed duty-free to stateside friends or relatives, with a limit of one package per day per addressee. Perfumes over $5, tobacco, and liquor are prohibited. For "Know Before You Go," a free brochure detailing what you may and may not bring back to this country, contact the U.S. Customs Service (1301 Constitution Ave., Washington, DC 20029, tel. 202/927–6724).

Disabled Travelers
The national organization for the disabled is **CNFLRH**, 38 boulevard Raspail, 75007 (tel: 53 80 66 66). The offices are open Monday to Friday, 9–noon and 2–6; they will provide advice on all relevant matters. **The Centre Information et de Documentation Jeunesse**, 101 Quai Branly, 75015 (tel: 44 49 12 00) also helps with information for young disabled people and they publish a booklet called *Vacances pour personnes handicapées*.

Buses are not suitable for wheelchairs, but certain metros and the express RER have access. A leaflet listing stations equipped with elevators, and showing which connections are feasible, is published by the Paris transportation system, the **RATP**, 53 ter, Quai des Grands Augustins, 75006 (tel: 43 46 14 14). The RER express train, being more modern, is better equipped for wheelchairs, and certain SNCF trains are now specifically designed for them, but you should inquire with the information service in advance (tel: 45 65 60 00). All Parisian

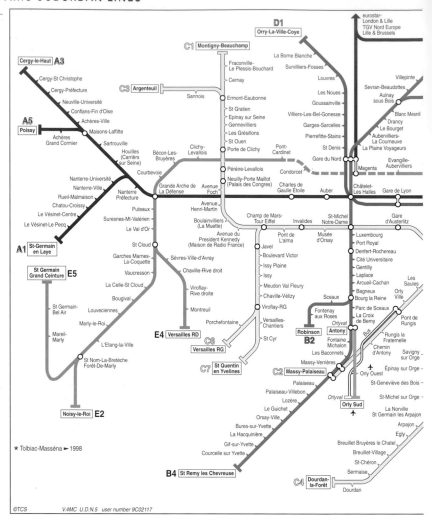

©TCS   V.4MC U.D.N.5 user number 9C02117

mainline stations have wheelchair access, special toilets, and phones; assistance can be asked for at the *accueil* in each station.

Both Orly and Roissy airports are well equipped for disabled people. For more specific information, contact the Service Image et Communication, Aéroports de Paris, 291 boulevard Raspail, 75014 (tel: 43 35 70 00). It publishes a brochure, *Guide des personnes handicapées,* describing facilities available. A specially equipped shuttle transports passengers between the terminals at Roissy, but there is nothing between Orly and Roissy. For getting to Orly Sud or Ouest, contact **Serval** (tel: 47 26 45 00).

Parisian taxis must by law accept disabled clients. There is no longer a specific service for the disabled, but it is possible to rent minibuses through a number of nonprofit organizations. Try **Valem** (tel: 42 64 48 60). For renting wheelchairs (free for a few days), the very central **Pharmacie Canonne**, 88–90 boulevard Sébastopol, 75003 (tel: 42 72 83 08) will oblige, while specially equipped cars can be rented from **Inter Touring Service**, 117 boulevard Auguste Blanqui, 75013 (tel: 45 88 52 37).

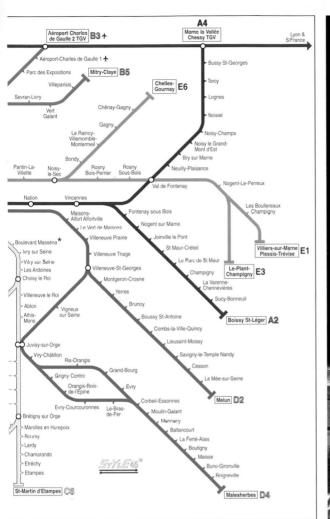

Aéroport Charles de Gaulle 2 TGV **B3** ✈

A4 Marne la Vallée Chessy TGV

Lyon & S/France

Aéroport-Charles de Gaulle 1 ✈

Parc des Expositions

Mitry-Claye **B5**

Bussy St-Georges

Villeparisis

Chelles-Gournay **E6**

Torcy

Sevran-Livry

Lognes

Vert Galant

Chênay-Gagny

Noisiel

Gagny

Noisy-Champs

Le Raincy-Villemomble-Montermeil

Noisy le Grand-Mont d'Est

Bondy

Bry sur Marne

Pantin-La-Villette

Noisy-le-Sec

Rosny Bois-Perrier

Rosny Sous-Bois

Neuilly-Plaisance

Val de Fontenay

Nogent-Le-Perreux

Nation

Vincennes

Les Boullereaux Champigny

Maisons-Alfort Alfortville

Fontenay sous Bois

Nogent sur Marne

Le Vert de Maisons

Villeneuve Prairie

Joinville le Pont

Boulevard Masséna ★

Villeneuve Triage

St Maur-Créteil

Villiers-sur-Marne Plessis-Trévise **E1**

Ivry sur Seine

Vitry sur Seine

Villeneuve-St-Georges

Le Parc de St Maur

Le-Plant-Champigny **E3**

Les Ardoines

Choisy le Roi

Montgeron-Crosne

Champigny

La Varenne-Chennevières

Villeneuve le Roi

Yerres

Sucy-Bonneuil

Ablon

Brunoy

Athis-Mons

Vigneux sur Seine

Boussy St-Antoine

Boissy St-Léger **A2**

Combs-la-Ville-Quincy

Juvisy-sur-Orge

Lieusaint-Moissy

Viry-Châtillon

Savigny-le-Temple Nandy

Ris-Orangis

Cesson

Grand-Bourg

Le Mée-sur-Seine

Grigny Centre

Orangis-Bois-de-l'Epine

Evry

Evry-Courcouronnes

Le-Bras-de-Fér

Corbeil-Essonnes

Melun **D2**

Moulin-Galant

Brétigny sur Orge

Mennecy

Marolles en Hurepoix

Ballancourt

Bouray

La Ferté-Alais

Lardy

Boutigny

Chamarande

Maisse

Etréchy

Buno-Gironville

Etampes

Boigneville

St-Martin d'Etampes **C6**

Malesherbes **D4**

Hotels (particularly in the budget category) are not always easily accessible, but the red Michelin hotel and restaurant guide shows which ones are, as does the list published by the Office de Tourisme de Paris. The Paris branch of the **Association des Paralysés de France**, 17 boulevard Auguste Blanqui, 75013 (tel: 40 78 69 00) publishes *Où ferons-nous étape?*, a guide listing specially equipped hotels and motels in France.

Although Paris is not an easy city for disabled people (curbs are high, ramps are few, and elevators sometimes too small), facilities are

The Arc de Triomphe and the Champs-Elysées

improving and awareness of needs is growing. All renovated and newly constructed buildings are now well equipped.

The **Information Center for Individuals with Disabilities**, 20 Park Plaza, Room 330, Boston, MA 02116 (tel. 617/727–5540, TDD tel. 617/727-5236) provides information and a referral service. The center also publishes two fact sheets, "Tips on Planning a Vacation" and "Tour Operators and Travel Agencies." There is no charge for the fact sheets, but donations are always appreciated.

Moss Rehabilitation Hospital Travel Information Service, a telephone information resource center (tel. 215/456–9603, TDD tel. 215/456–9602), provides information on tourist sights, transportation, and accommodations in destinations around the world for a small fee. They also provide toll-free telephone numbers for airlines, with special lines for the hearing impaired.

The **Society for the Advancement** of Travel for the Handicapped (SATH, 347 5th Avenue, Suite 610, New York, NY 10016, tel. 212/447–7284, fax 212/725–8253) provides information on and lists of tour operators specializing in travel for the disabled. Annual membership is $45, $25 for students and senior citizens. Send $3 and a SASE for information on specific destinations.

Driving

Drivers in Paris must be 18 or over, have valid car registration papers, a driver's license and car insurance.

France follows international road signs and regulations. All road signs are those of the international code except one: *Vous n'avez pas la priority* (you do not have priority).

Parisian streets are regularly resurfaced. August is the peak month for any kind of road works; it's also when driving is most pleasurable, as the capital is

Driving up the avenue: a bird's-eye view of the Champs-Elysées

relatively empty. For the rest of the year, you will find a car more of a hindrance than a help, and Parisian traffic manners need getting used to. Nobody waits or watches out for anyone else, cars move fast when possible, pedestrians dive across streets risking life and limb. However dangerous all this may seem, drivers do have fast reactions and are used to getting out of unexpected situations. Several main north–south and east–west axes have now been declared *axes rouges*, which means parking or even stopping is absolutely forbidden. If you are traveling through France, call 47 05 90 01 for highway information.

Accidents/Breakdown 24-hour breakdown service can be obtained through the garages listed below. Others are listed in the yellow pages under *Dépannages et remorquages:*
Aleveque, 180 rue de la Convention, 15e (tel: 48 28 12 00).
Allô-Assistance, 129 rue de Vaugirard, 15e (tel: 43 06 39 16).
Alfauto, 132 rue Abbé Groult, 15e (tel: 44 19 73 55).
S.O.S. Dépannage, (official breakdown number, tel: 47 07 99 99).

Car/Motorcycle/Camper rental
Most major car rental companies are represented in France, and visitors are advised that it is usually best to make a reservation in advance. Usually, you must be over 21 (25 in some cases) to rent a car, and restrictions may apply to drivers over 60. Your current driver's license is usually acceptable, but some require an International Driver's Permit, available through an Automobile Club (AAA or CAA) office.
   For reservations call:
Avis (tel. 800/331–1212);
Budget (tel. 800/527–0700);
Dollar (tel. 800/800–4000);
Hertz (tel. 800/654–3131);
National (800/328–4567).

Fuel Super, *sans plomb* (lead-free), and diesel are the three types of fuel available. Fuel pumps are located above ground as well as in parking garages. There are several 24-hour pumps:

Motorcycles are available for rent at several outlets—and can be the object of admiration.

corner Champs-Elysées/avenue Georges V, 8e;
1 boulevard de la Chapelle, 10e;
avenue de la Porte de Chatillon, 14e;
6 avenue de la Porte de Clichy, 17e;
avenue de la Porte de Saint-Ouen, 18e.

249

Parking This is Paris's perennial problem. Most central streets are now metered, a system that costs residents considerably less than it does visitors. Meters are situated at intervals along streets: put in the coins corresponding to the length of time you want to park, press the button, collect the ticket, and put it inside your car so that it is visible on the dashboard.
   More and more underground parking garages are being constructed to meet the growing demand, and these can be spotted

> ❑ Of all major European cities, Paris has the highest rates of lead and carbon-monoxide pollution. Cars are responsible for 75 percent of city pollution, and 59 percent of Parisians favor a limitation of traffic in the center. ❑

by their blue signs marked with a large P. If you decide to park your car for a few days and visit Paris in a more leisurely fashion, the cheapest 24-hour parking facilities are situated on the perimeter (Porte de Saint-Ouen, Porte de Clignancourt, Porte d'Italie). Otherwise, central underground parking costs considerably more.

Boots and car pounds (*fourrière*): Although boots are uncommon, they do appear, so avoid parking illegally (pedestrian crossings, loading zones, bus lanes, *axes rouges*, etc.). You may be towed away to one of the six Parisian car pounds that cover all Parisian arrondissements. Contact the local police station to find out where you have to go. It is a costly business, in any case.

Speed limits 50 kmh. (31 mph) in cities; 90 kmh (56 mph) outside cities; 80 kmh (50 mph) on the *périphérique* (ring road); 110 kmh (81 mph) on two-lane highways; 130 kmh (68 mph) on four-lane highways).

> ❏ 1,300,000 vehicles circulate in Paris daily—four times as many as 20 years ago. About 85 percent of traffic jams in France occur in and around Paris. ❏

Electricity
Voltage is 220 V, and sockets take two round pins. Americans will need to purchase an adapter.

Embassies and Consulates
Always check opening hours by phone in advance: many consulates are only open in the morning and close for both French public holidays and those of their own country. In general, the consulate deals with day-to-day problems facing their citizens or travelers to the country, whereas the embassy is for more official business. Other embassies are in the phone book under *Ambassades*.
U.S. Embassy: 2 avenue Gabriel, 75008 (tel: 43 12 22 22), metro: Champs-Elysées—Clémenceau. Consulate/visas: 2 rue St.-Florentin, 75001 (tel: 36 70 14 88), metro: Concorde.

Emergency Phone Numbers
Ambulance (Samu) tel:15 (or 45 67 50 50).

Fire tel:18
Police tel:17
Anti-poison tel: 40 37 04 04.
Doctor (S.O.S. Médecins), tel: 47 07 77 77. Emergency house calls only. Ask for an English-speaking doctor, or contact **The American Hospital**, 63 boulevard Victor-Hugo, Neuilly (tel: 46 41 25 25), which has a 24-hour emergency service—at a price. **The Hertford British Hospital**, 3 rue Barbes, Levallois-Perret (tel: 46 39 22 22) provides a similar emergency service.

For burns go to the **Hôpital St.-Antoine**, 184 rue du Faubourg St.-Antoine, 75012 (tel: 49 28 20 00). Emergency treatment for children can be obtained at the **Hôpital Necker**, 149 rue de Sèvres, 75015 (tel: 44 49 40 00).
Dentist (S.O.S. Dentistes), tel: 43 37 51 00. Emergency house calls only.
Motorway and road information tel: 48 94 33 33.
S.O.S. Help (tel: 47 23 80 80) is an emergency crisis line for English speakers.

Etiquette
French etiquette is a bit more formal than the variety most Americans are familiar with, although that is disappearing with the younger

The Panthéon

generations. Handshaking is prevalent when meeting someone, even when you have already been introduced. You can feel justifiably proud when the local barman or restaurant owner proffers his hand on your arrival. This is a sign of respect and acceptance. Do not use Christian names unless you yourself have been addressed in this way.

Smoking is widespread but is completely banned in movie theaters and inside Parisian buses and metros. Taxis will display a no-smoking sign when drivers are averse to it; but if you find yourself with a smoking taxi driver, there is little you can do. Cafés and restaurants are now required by law to provide a no-smoking section.

Health

There are no inoculations necessary to enter France, but if you plan on staying more than three months, a medical checkup is required for non-E.C. nationals.

France offers no more health risks than any other European country (apart from the effects of overeating and drinking, so bring a stock of Alka-Seltzer with you). Tap water in Paris is perfectly drinkable, though you may prefer the taste of mineral water.

If you need to buy prescription drugs, have your doctor write a prescription using the drug's generic name; brand names vary from country to country. The International Association for Medical Assistance to Travelers (in the U.S.: 417 Center St., Lewiston, NY 14092, tel. 716/754–4883) offers a free worldwide list of approved physicians and clinics whose training meets British and American standards.

Hospitals Public hospitals are found all over Paris (listed in the phone book under *Hôpitaux*), the most central being the Hôtel Dieu, right outside Nôtre-Dame. All have a 24-hour emergency service *(urgences)*, as well as specialist doctors in every field.

Payment is made on the spot for any kind of consultation, but if for any reason you are hospitalized, ask to see the *assistante sociale* to arrange reimbursement directly through your own insurance. By law, any emergency case must be treated and, once out of danger, foreign

Making contact in a restaurant on the Left Bank

patients are flown home.

Private hospitals are a lot more expensive, and treatment is not necessarily better, but for linguistic reasons you may prefer one of the following:

American Hospital: 63 boulevard Victor-Hugo, Neuilly (tel: 46 41 25 25).

Hertford British Hospital: 3 rue Barbes, Levallois-Perret (tel: 46 39 22 22).

Local doctors can be found by asking at a nearby *pharmacie.*

Appointments are usually made in advance, but very few will refuse to see an emergency case. House calls can be arranged by calling **S.O.S. Médecins** (tel: 47 07 77 77). A similar dental service exists (tel: 43 37 51 00).

Specific problems AIDS advice (in English): **FAACTS** (Free Anglo American Counseling Treatment Support), The American Church, 65 Quai d'Orsay, 75007 (tel: 45 50 26 49).

AIDES (AIDS information center) tel: 44 52 00 00. *Open:* Monday to Friday, 10–7.

Poison center tel: 40 37 04 04.

Burns center tel: 42 34 17 58.
Centre de Soins MST (Center for sexually transmitted diseases), **Institut A. Fournier**, 25 boulevard Saint Jacques, 75014 (tel: 40 78 26 00), metro: St.-Jacques.
S.O.S. Help English Hotline tel: 47 23 80 80.
S.O.S. legal services tel: 43 29 33 00.

Hitchhiking

Hitchhiking in France is legal except on highways. As in any city, hitchhiking inside Paris will get you nowhere unless there is a general transportation strike. However, if you are heading out of the capital to the rest of France, the best places are at the relevant portes leading to the main highways—but do not stand where traffic is already traveling at speed. Firstly, it is dangerous and, secondly, nobody will stop.

At the Porte d'Orléans there is usually a line of hopeful hitchhikers on the slip road leading down to the southbound Autoroute du Soleil, and a similar crowd of optimists gathers at the Porte de la Chapelle for the Autoroute du Nord. For those heading west, go to the Porte d'Auteuil, while for eastern destinations go to the Porte de Bercy. It is a good idea to have a sign declaring your destination, but do make sure you are standing where cars can pull in safely without stopping the traffic flow, otherwise the local *gendarmes* will pick you up instead.

A much safer and surer method is to contact a hitchhiking service. They link up drivers with potential passengers, who contribute to fuel costs: **Allostop**, 84 Passage Brady, 75010 (tel: 42 46 00 66), metro: Strasbourg-St.-Denis. It has been in existence for over 15 years and is reliable.

Insurance

Travel insurance should be taken out before you leave home. Travel agents can usually provide information, and certain credit cards also provide cardholders' insurance if the tickets are purchased with their card.

Language
Numbers

1	un/une
2	deux
3	trois
4	quatre
5	cinq
6	six
7	sept
8	huit
9	neuf
10	dix
11	onze
12	douze
13	treize
14	quatorze
15	quinze
16	seize
17	dix-sept
18	dix-huit
19	dix-neuf
20	vingt
30	trente
40	quarante
50	cinquante
60	soixante
70	soixante-dix
80	quatre-vingt
90	quatre-vingt-dix
100	cent
1000	mille

Days of the Week

Monday	lundi
Tuesday	mardi
Wednesday	mercredi
Thursday	jeudi
Friday	vendredi
Saturday	samedi
Sunday	dimanche

Basic Phrases

yes/no	oui/non
please	s'il vous plaît
thank you	merci
excuse me	excusez-moi
I'm sorry	Je suis désolé
hello	bonjour
goodbye	au revoir
how are you?	Comment allez-vous?
Very well, thanks	Très bien, merci
Do you speak English?	Parlez-vous anglais?
I don't understand	Je ne comprends pas
why?	pourquoi?
who?	qui?
what?	quel?
when?	quand?
how?	comment?
how much?	combien?
today	aujourd'hui
yesterday	hier
tomorrow	demain
this morning	ce matin
this afternoon	cet après-midi
tonight	ce soir

Directions

where is...	Où est...
the nearest metro	le métro le plus proche
the telephone	le téléphone
the bus stop	l'arrêt de bus
the bank	la banque
the bookshop	la librairie
where are the toilets?	Où sont les toilettes?
in the basement	au sous-sol
on the ground floor	au rez-de-chaussée
on the second floor	au premier étage
turn right/left	tournez à droite/gauche
go straight on	allez tout droit

253

the first street	la première rue
before the intersection	avant le carrefour
after the rotary	après le rondpoint
at the traffic lights	aux feux rouges

Hotels

Do you have...?	Avez-vous...?
a double room	une chambre double
with bathroom	avec salle de bains
with shower room	avec salle d'eau
a single room	une chambre simple
We need an extra bed	Nous avons besoin d'un lit supplé - mentaire
What time is breakfast?	Qquelle heure est le petit déjeuner?
Do you accept credit cards?	Prenez-vous les cartes de crédit?
we leave tomorrow	nous partons demain
please prepare our bill	s'il vous plaît préparez la note

Restaurants

waiter! waitress!	Monsieur! Madame!
We want to book a table for 9 o'clock	Nous voulons réserver une table pour neuf heures.
Do you have a fixed price menu?	Avez-vous un menu?
I am a vegetarian	Je suis végétarien
a bottle of ...	une bouteille de ...
a glass of ...	un verre de...
Can I have the menu please?	Donnez-moi la carte, s'il vous plaît

the bill	l'addition
breakfast	le petit déjeuner
lunch	le déjeuner
dinner	le dîner

Lost Property

The central lost property office for anything handed to the police is at 36 rue des Morillons, 75015, metro: Convention. No information is given over the phone.
Open: Monday, Wednesday, Friday, 8:30–5; Tuesday and Thursday, 8:30–8.

Maps

The Office du Tourisme—at 127 avenue des Champs-Elysées, 75008 (tel: 49 52 53 54), metro: George V—is open daily, 9–8, and provides extensive free information. City maps can also be found free in most hotels, while metro stations and some buses have free transportation maps. If you are staying for a longer period, it is worth investing 40 francs or so in a *Paris par Arrondissement*, a small publication with road index and arrondissement maps.

Media

Parisian Press Reading habits in France are very different from those in the United States. Parisians do not spend their Sundays perusing bulky supplements to catch up on the week's news. This role is filled by weekly magazines (similar to *Time* or *Newsweek*), all published on Thursdays. Covering the political spectrum, they range from *Le Nouvel Observateur* and *L'Evénement du Jeudi* (broadly left-wing) to *L'Express* (center) and *Le Point* (center-right). *Paris-Match* still deals in society gossip or disaster-related scoops, while political scandals are dug up in the investigative satirical weekly newspaper, *Le Canard Enchaîné*.

Numerous monthly magazines exist, one of the most interesting being *Actuel*, a young glossy, sociocultural magazine.

There are seven main daily newspapers, none of which has an enormous circulation. Most respected intellectually, although sometimes tough to read, is *Le Monde*, which goes on sale at 2:30PM daily except Sunday. Its entertainment supplement, published on Wednesday afternoon, gives a useful overview of the best current shows and exhibitions. The other afternoon newspaper, *France Soir*, is lightweight, concentrating more on consumer affairs, sports, and entertainment. *Info Matin* is a new daily, also lightweight with brief easy-to-read articles for people who are short on time.

The Parisian daily par excellence is *Libération*, a young, witty paper carrying on much of the 1968 radical thought, although many of its readers are now affluent and middle-aged. Its coverage of the arts is excellent.

Le Figaro, historically the most established (since 1866), veers from being ultraconservative to providing a useful antigovernment voice, while its classified ads constitute the bible of property and job seekers.

On the far right of the political spectrum stands *Le Quotidien de Paris*, while swimming along beside it is *Le Parisien*, a tabloid that only seems to be read free of charge in the cafés.

L'Humanité, the anachronistic Communist Party newspaper, creaks along with a faithful hardcore readership.

Foreign press Central newspaper stands usually carry a fairly reasonable selection of European dailies, and you can always pick up the European edition of the *International Herald Tribune*, which is published in Paris.

For a wide range of European and American press and magazines, go to one of the NMPP bookshops (52 rue Jacques Hillairet, 75012, or 87 rue Charolais, 75012). This is the central distribution organization for all press in France and so carries the gamut of the extensive French regional press, too.

Entertainment magazines Both come out on Wednesday, the day new films are released. Take your pick from the old mainstay *Pariscope*, or *L'Officiel des*

CONVERSION CHARTS

FROM	TO	MULTIPLY BY
Inches	Centimeters	2.54
Centimeters	Inches	0.3937
Feet	Meters	0.3048
Meters	Feet	3.2810
Yards	Meters	0.9144
Meters	Yards	1.0940
Miles	Kilometers	1.6090
Kilometers	Miles	0.6214
Acres	Hectares	0.4047
Hectares	Acres	2.4710
U.S. Gallons	Liters	3.7854
Liters	U.S. Gallons	0.2642
Ounces	Grams	28.35
Grams	Ounces	0.0353
Pounds	Grams	453.6
Grams	Pounds	0.0022
Pounds	Kilograms	0.4536
Kilograms	Pounds	2.205
U.S. Tons	Tonnes	0.9072
Tonnes	U.S. Tons	1.1023

MEN'S SUITS

U.K.	36	38	40	42	44	46	48
Rest of Europe	46	48	50	52	54	56	58
U.S.	36	38	40	42	44	46	48

DRESS SIZES

U.K.	8	10	12	14	16	18
France	36	38	40	42	44	46
Italy	38	40	42	44	46	48
Rest of Europe	34	36	38	40	42	44
U.S.	6	8	10	12	14	16

MEN'S SHIRTS

U.K.	14	14.5	15	15.5	16	16.5	17
Rest of Europe	36	37	38	39/40	41	42	43
U.S.	14	14.5	15	15.5	16	16.5	17

MEN'S SHOES

U.K.	7	7.5	8.5	9.5	10.5	11
Rest of Europe	41	42	43	44	45	46
U.S.	8	8.5	9.5	10.5	11.5	12

WOMEN'S SHOES

U.K.	4.5	5	5.5	6	6.5	7
Rest of Europe	38	38	39	39	40	41
U.S.	6	6.5	7	7.5	8	8.5

255

Spectacles (less easy to follow the latter's classifications, but pocket-size like *Pariscope*). *Le Figaro* also enters the fray on Wednesdays with a well-listed entertainments supplement, *Figaroscope*.

Radio If you tune in to FM in Paris, you will be amazed by what bounces off the crowded and varied airwaves. No longer the bonanza that it was in the early 1980s, when anybody and everybody jumped on the free-radio bandwagon, the number of stations is now—thankfully—controlled.

Minority tastes are catered to, from **Judaïque FM** (94.8 MHz) to **Radio Notre-Dame** (100.7 MHz) for Christians, or **Beur FM** (106.7 MHz) for the North African community. **Media Tropical** (92.6 MHz) takes you even farther, specializing in African and Caribbean sounds. The quaint-sounding **Chérie FM** broadcasts on 91.3 MHz. News is broadcast around the clock on **France Infos** (105.5 MHz), while the latest update on Parisian traffic jams interjects a mixed music program on **FIP** (105.1 MHz).

Classical music fans should tune in to **France Musique** (91.7 and 92.1 MHz), though presenters tend to chat, whereas **Radio Classique**

(101.1 MHz) provides virtually nonstop music. Not as influential as they were, but still powerful, are current affairs and variety stations such as **France Inter** (87.8 MHz), **RTL** (104.3 MHz), **Radio Monte Carlo** (103.1 MHz), and **Europe 1** (104.7 MHz).

For unadulterated rap/rock/House/world music, your best bet is to tune in to **Radio Nova** (101.5 MHz) or **NRJ** (100.3 MHz).

The **BBC World Service** can be found on medium wave, 648 KHz.

Television The two main state channels, FR2 and FR3, still have a long way to go in the quality of their programs, but the recently privatized **TF1** is even worse. Addicted to trite panel discussions, variety shows, reruns of "family" films, and dubbed American police shows, none of the channels has a clear identity. France 2 occasionally rises out of mediocrity with a good documentary and, like FR3, gives cultural events reasonable coverage.

Canal Plus, a private subscribers' channel launched in 1983, has been very successful in its rotation of recent films, good documentaries, sports events, and children's programs. It starts the day at 7 with

the CBS Evening News. When Berlusconi's **Le Cinq** finally disappeared, its slot was taken by the French/German Cultural Channel **Arte**. The sixth channel (M6), created in 1987, is increasingly popular. Mixing music videos with movies, it also schedules some excellent BBC documentaries and TV films (dubbed). Arte, whose programs are all coproduced with Germany, provides an interesting alternative to mainstream channels, devoting much of its coverage to cultural and minority interests. Satellite TV can be picked up easily, and most big hotels are linked up.

Money Matters

The French currency is the franc (symbolized by FF), which is divided into 100 centimes. Coins come as 5, 10, 20, and 50 centimes; 1, 2, 5, 10, and 20 francs. Banknotes start at 20 francs, continue with 50 francs, 100 francs, 200 francs, and end at 500 francs. The latter are hard to change in taxis and small shops, so avoid being given them when you change money. Foreigners can bring in currency up to the generous limit of 50,000 francs, in any form: cash, travelers' checks, Eurocheques, etc.

Banks Most Parisian banks are open 9–4:30, Monday to Friday, but shut at noon the day before any public holiday (see below). They usually have a foreign exchange counter, which charges a small commission on any operation. If you are confronted with a choice, BNP is likely to offer the best rates and lowest commission. Banks that display credit card symbols outside will also advance cash on the basis of your card. Remember to have your passport on you for any transaction. Bureaux de change outside any bank take Visa, sometimes Diners Club and MasterCard, and often give instructions in English.

For emergency exchange on weekends, go to the Champs-Elysées, where the CCF (115 Champs-Elysées, metro: George V) remains open daily except Sunday till 8PM. There is also a 24-hour exchange cash dispenser at this address, and another at 2 Carrefour de l'Odéon, 75006. If you have large amounts of cash to change, it may be worthwhile going to the rue Vivienne near the Stock Exchange (metro: Bourse), where numerous private bureaux de change give good rates and charge no commission. Some are open till 7PM.

If you're desperate, it's 8:30PM, the exchange machine on the Champs-Elysées has run out of notes and you have no credit cards—well then, you have no other choice than to go to a bureau de change at one of the main stations (*open*: 8AM–9PM daily at the Gare du Nord and the Gare de Lyon; Monday to Saturday at the Gare St.-Lazare and Austerlitz). The exchange bureaus at Orly and Roissy airports are open 7AM–11PM daily.

Foreign banks American Express is at 11 rue Scribe, 75009 (tel: 47 14 50 00), metro: Opéra. Here you can cash personal checks if you are a cardholder, as well as having funds rapidly transferred from the United States but with a high commission.

Barclays, (main branch), 21 rue Laffitte, 75009 (tel: 44 79 79 79), metro: Richelieu-Drouot. Many other branches throughout Paris.

Citibank, 17 avenue Montaigne, 75008 (tel: 49 06 10 10), metro: Franklin-D.-Roosevelt.

Lloyds, 15 avenue d'Iéna, 75016 (tel: 44 43 42 41), metro: Opéra.

National Westminster no longer has any branches open to the public.

Credit cards are now widely accepted anywhere from supermarkets to restaurants. Top of the popularity list is any card linked to the Visa network, including MasterCard, but always check before making assumptions. American Express is less popular due to the relatively high percentage the trader loses on any transaction.

Bring a combination of cash, traveler's checks (in French called simply *travellers'* with a heavy Chevalier accent) and credit cards, and you can't go wrong. Traveler's checks are not accepted in place of

❑ Although central Paris represents only 0.022 percent of the total French territory with 4 percent of its population, it possesses 96 percent of bank head offices, 70 percent of insurance company head offices, 39 percent of all professional people, and furnishes 45 percent of income tax revenue. ❑

currency and need to be changed at banks. Avoid changing large amounts in hotels, as their rates are considerably worse.

National Holidays
The many public and religious holidays in France are known as *jours fériés*. Transportation timetables change; banks, most museums, and shops close; even newspapers do not come out. So bear this in mind when booking your holiday. Parisians make a habit of stretching a public holiday to bridge with a weekend, commonly known as *le pont*, which gives them a four- or five-day holiday. This is particularly visible in May, when there are no fewer than three public holidays. The following are the official one-day *jours fériés*:

January 1	New Year's Day
March/April	Easter Monday
May 1	Fête du Travail (Labor Day)
May 8	Armistice (WWII)
Last week in May	
	Ascension
Early June	Whit Monday
July 14	Bastille Day
August 15	Assumption
November 1	Toussaint (All Saints)
November 11	Armistice (WWI)
December 25	Christmas

The most steadfastly respected of the above are January 1, May 1, November 1, November 11, and December 25, when nearly everything is closed. Always check with museums and monuments to see if they remain open on the public holidays. Some smaller ones even shut up shop for all of August.

Whatever the cultural potential, you will, however, never starve. Restaurants do a good trade on these days, as do certain local grocery stores, but public transportation slows down considerably, so do not try to venture far afield.

Hotels are notoriously difficult to book in May, June, September, and October, when trade fairs and fashion shows abound, attracting thousands of business visitors. July and August are, surprisingly, not particularly booked up, as no self-respecting Frenchman would be seen in the capital at this time of year.

Opening Hours
Banks respect to the letter every public holiday and close on the preceding afternoon, so beware! Otherwise, their hours are generally 9–4:30, although smaller branches may close for lunch and remain open an hour longer.

Shops Most shops open at 9 and close at 7, although many fashion boutiques wait till 10 or even later. Few large food stores in central Paris close for the lunch hour, although small specialist traders may take a one- or two-hour break. Department stores, supermarkets, —and central boutiques all remain open. Saturday is a major trading day. Sunday—apart from food markets and the odd local grocer (who often remains open daily till 10)—is definitively closed, while Monday provides a balance between the two.

Museums These, too, vary. On the whole, the larger the museum, the less likely it is to close for lunch, but watch out for the common closing days of Monday and Tuesday. National museums close on Tuesdays (except the Musée d'Orsay, which opts for Monday), while municipally financed museums close on Mondays. Most museums remain open on Sunday, when entrance fees are reduced or, in some places, waived.

258

Opening hours vary. The more traditional museums stick to about 9:30–5, while certain avant-garde art museums (Centre Pompidou, Jeu de Paume, Arts Décoratifs, Arts de la Mode) don't open their doors till past noon. The important museums usually have a late-night opening (*nocturne*), and this is often a good opportunity to avoid lines (for example, the Musée d'Art Moderne de la Ville de Paris and the Grand Palais both remain open late on Wednesdays). Always check small museums in advance; they can be idiosyncratic, and the renovation craze has not helped matters.

Organized Tours
Bicycle tours
Paris á Velo, c'est Sympa, 9 rue Jacques Coeus, 75004 (tel: 48 87 60 01) organizes tours of Paris by bike.

Boat trips
One of Paris's greatest pleasures is the Seine, so make sure you see some of the monuments from this perspective.

The enormous glass-roofed bateaux-mouches leave every half-hour from the Pont de l'Alma (Right Bank), take you east to beyond the Ile Saint-Louis, then circle back. The entire trip takes over an hour and commentaries are given in six languages.

In summer, trips start at 10 and the last one at night leaves at 11. In winter (mid-November to mid-March) departures are every hour starting at 10. Try the extra-long lunch trip or even longer dinner trip—a spectacular way to see the monuments (leaving at 1 and 8:30 respectively). Reductions for children under 14 (tel: 42 25 96 10).

Very similar, but more central and easier to get to, is the flotilla of Vedettes du Pont-Neuf (tel: 46 33 98 38), which leave from the tip of the Ile de la Cité at Pont-Neuf. These boats accomplish a one-hour

Galeries Lafayette, queen of department stores

trip around the islands and down to the Eiffel Tower but have the advantage of dropping you back in central Paris. In French and English, the slightly more expensive summer departures start at 10, running almost every half-hour through to the last boat at 10:30. The evening tours do not include dinner. The winter service runs every hour starting at 10. Reductions for children under 10. The **Bateaux Parisiens-Tour Eiffel** leave from the Left Bank side of the Pont d'Iéna and provide an almost identical service to the Bateaux-Mouches (tel: 44 11 33 44).

Canal St.-Martin
Paris Canal Croisières organizes three-hour boat trips that take you along the Seine from the Musée d'Orsay to the Canal St.-Martin and north to the Parc de la Villette. Commentaries are in French and English. This is an unusual trip, perfect for a sunny afternoon, and it will take you through parts of Paris you may not have seen. Departures are at 9:30 and 2:25 from the Musée d'Orsay and 2:30 from La Villette (10 weekends only). Booking by phone is essential (tel: 42 40 96 97). Prices are reasonable

considering the length of the trip; children under 11 and young people under 25 get a reduction.

Trips along the Canal St.-Martin with **Canauxrama** between the Bastille and La Villette leave at 9:30 from 5 bis Quai de la Loire, 75019 (metro: Jean-Jaurès) or 9:45 from the Port de l'Arsenal, opposite 50 boulevard de la Bastille (metro: Bastille). Departures in the other direction leave at 2:45 and 2:30, respectively. The same company organizes a delightful one-day trip through canals out into very pretty countryside. Commentaries are in French and English. Reductions are available for children under 6. Booking is essential (tel: 42 39 15 00).

Bus tours
For first-time visitors without much time, a bus trip is ideal to orient yourself if you don't mind the group-style travel. All these tours are in comfortable double-decker buses, with a live or recorded commentary (in whatever language you want) and

A detail from the Grand Palais— one of the museums open late on Wednesdays

One of the great riverside sights of Paris: the Louvre

last 2 to 3½ hours.

Two companies, **Paris Vision** and **Cityrama**, monopolize the field; their services are virtually identical, although **Cityrama** is slightly cheaper. Both organize thematic tours (Paris by Night, Artistic Paris, Erotic Paris, Cabarets) as well as excursions to Versailles, Fontainebleau, Chartres, and the Loire Valley.

Brochures are available and bookings can be made through the Office du Tourisme, 127 Champs-Elysées (tel: 49 52 53 54), metro: George V.

Paris Vision (terminus), 214 rue de Rivoli, 75001 (tel: 42 60 31 25), metro: Tuileries. Tours start at 9:30 and leave hourly till 2:30. Arrive at least 15 minutes in advance.

Cityrama (terminus), 4 place des Pyramides, 75001 (tel: 44 55 60 00), metro: Pyramides, Palais-Royal. The same conditions apply as for Paris Vision.

A third company, **Parisbus** (tel: 42 30 55 50), entered the field a few years ago sporting red double-decker buses and a system leaving you free to get on and off their buses at any of the nine stops. Buses leave from the place du Trocadéro at 9:30 and the Eiffel Tower at 9:55. There are now nine departures a day with a bus arriving every 50 minutes at each stop (in theory), so waiting time is not long. Your ticket is valid for two consecutive days and commentaries are in French and English on all the buses.

Walking tours

An excellent daily schedule of walking tours of Paris covering specific areas or themes (often with entrance to monuments closed to the general public) is organized by the **Caisse Nationale des Monuments Historiques**, Hôtel de Sully, 62 rue St.-Antoine, 75004 (tel: 44 61 20 00). Many walking tours are listed in the weekly entertainment magazines (under *Conférences*), and you can simply turn up at the appointed time and place. The only problem is that many of the guides speak only French, but the accessibility of unusual sites may outweigh this.

Pharmacies

The hundreds of pharmacies in Paris are identified by large illuminated

261

Inside-out architecture at the Centre Georges Pompidou

green crosses in front of their entrances. Most are open Monday to Saturday, 9–7 or 9–8. When closed, they provide on the door a list of other local pharmacies that are open.

Authorized to supply medication under prescriptions, they also have a monopoly on the sale of certain beauty and health products.

Generally helpful, pharmacists also give immediate first aid (bad cuts, etc.), and you will probably find that there is at least one who speaks English. They can also direct you to local doctors and specialists. For ordinary items (soap, toothbrushes, razors, etc.), it is cheaper to go to a supermarket. All health needs are available in pharmacies, from aspirin to condoms to tampons or baby requisites.

Late-night pharmacies:

Caillaud has become **Pharmacie Opéra**, 6 boulevard des Capucines, 75009 (tel: 42 65 88 29), metro: Opéra.

Open: Monday to Saturday, 8AM–12:30AM; Sunday, 8PM–12:30AM.

Cariglioli, 10 boulevard Sébastopol, 75004 (tel: 42 72 03 23), metro: Châtelet.

Open : Monday to Saturday,

9–midnight, Sunday noon–midnight.

Drugstore St.-Germain, 149 boulevard St.-Germain, 75006 (tel: 42 22 80 00), metro: St.-Germain.

Open: 8.30AM–2AM daily.

Dhéry, 84 avenue des Champs-Elysées, 75008 (tel: 45 62 02 41), metro: George V.

Open : 24 hours daily.

Places of Worship

Worshipers of any religion should be able to find the appropriate church or temple in Paris, although Catholics obviously get the best choice. Below is a selection.

Anglican Protestant

American Cathedral, 23 avenue George V, 75008 (tel: 47 20 17 92), metro: Alma-Marceau.

American Church, 65 Quai d'Orsay, 75007 (tel: 47 05 07 99), metro: Invalides.

Church of Scotland, 17 rue Bayard, 75008 (tel: 48 78 47 94), metro: Franklin-Roosevelt.

St. George's English Church, 7 rue Auguste Vacquerie, 75016 (tel: 47 20 22 51), metro: Etoile.

St. Michael's Church of England, 5 rue d'Aguesseau, 75008 (tel: 47 42 70 88), metro: Madeleine.

International Center for Religious Information, 8 rue Massillon, 75004 (tel: 46 33 01 01). Helpful people at the end of the phone offer information on times of services, nearest churches, etc, for Catholic, Protestant, and Orthodox churches. English spoken.

Catholic
See pages 140–1.
Every arrondissement has at least four or five.

Jewish
Synagogue, 10 rue Pavée, 75004 (tel: 42 77 81 51), metro: St.-Paul.

> ❏ Only about 50 of the 300 churches that stood in 18th-century Paris remain today. A further 150 have been built since World War II. ❏

Synagogue Nazareth, 15 rue Notre-Dame-de-Nazareth, 75003 (tel: 42 78 00 30), metro: République.
Synagogue, 44 rue de la Victoire, 75009 (tel: 45 26 95 36), metro: Notre-Dame-de-Lorette.

Orthodox
Eglise Grecque Orthodoxe, 2 bis rue Laferrière, 75009 (tel: 42 81 42 67), metro: St.-Georges.
Saint Alexandre de la Néva (Russian Orthodox), 12 rue Daru, 75008 (tel: 42 27 37 34), metro: Courcelles.

Police
No longer those familiar figures sporting *képis*, Parisian police now look like any other national police force and wear flat caps.

There are over 16,000 uniformed police officers scattered around the police stations and streets of central Paris. The fire department is loosely related and will deal with immediate first aid, lost cats, victims of accidents, gas leaks, etc, apart from dealing with fires.

Each arrondissement has several police stations, including a main one open 24 hours a day that is often integrated into the arrondissement town hall. They will be able to help with most problems (finding a

263

The Eglise St.-Germain-des-Prés dates back to the 10th century

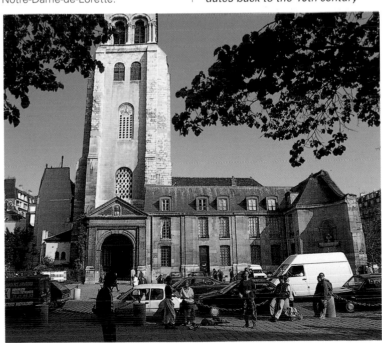

plumber, local vet, doctor, etc.) as well as administrative matters, drug problems and, of course, crime.

1e place du Marché St.-Honoré (tel: 42 61 09 19)
2e 5 place des Petits Pères (tel: 42 60 96 87)
3e 5 rue Perrée (tel: 42 78 40 00)
4e 2 place Baudoyer (tel: 42 77 67 21)
5e 4 rue de la Montagne Ste.-Geneviève (tel: 44 41 51 00)
6e 78 rue Bonaparte (tel: 43 29 76 10)
7e 9 rue Fabert (tel: 44 18 69 07)
8e 1 avenue du Général Eisenhower (tel: 42 25 88 80)
9e 14 bis rue Chauchat (tel: 44 83 80 80)

Sacré-Coeur has hourly services every morning, and also evening mass

10e 26 rue Louis-Blanc (tel: 44 18 60 10)
11e place Léon-Blum (tel: 43 79 39 51)
12e 78 avenue Daumesnil (tel: 44 87 50 12)
13e 144 boulevard de l'Hôpital (tel: 40 79 03 22)
14e 112–116 avenue du Maine (tel: 53 74 14 06)
15e 250 rue de Vaugirard (tel: 53 68 81 81)
16e 58 avenue Mozart (tel: 45 27 03 78)
17e 19 rue Truffaut (tel: 44 90 37 17)
18e 79 rue Clignancourt (tel: 53 73 63 00)
19e 2 rue André Dubois (tel: 48 03 82 00)
20e 6 place Gambetta (tel: 40 33 34 00)

The central Préfecture de Police on the Ile de la Cité deals with driver's licenses, residence and work permits, licenses for various activities, etc. (tel: 53 71 53 36). Another section of the police force is the river police, which controls crime and administrative matters on the River Seine. Parking fines are usually dished out by a separate section, whose officers are generally female and dressed in cornflower-blue uniforms. The CRS are the military-looking, shield-bearing riot police who hang around in vans near any demonstration, ready for action.

Emergency calls
Police: 17
Fire Department *(pompiers)*: 18
SAMU (24-hour ambulance): 15

Post Offices
A French post office is known as *la poste*, officially the PTT, and in Paris each is signposted in the street. Many have outside cash machines that accept Visa cards.

Opening hours are: Monday to Friday, 8–7; Saturday, 8–noon. Avoid lunch hours and late afternoon when office workers dealing with business mail create endless lines. Most post offices have phone booths, photocopiers, fax (*télécopieur*), and free access to the Minitel directory

service. Express post facilities (called *Chronopost)* for within France and abroad are also available.

Stamps can also be bought at *tabacs* (tobacco shops), and yellow postboxes are situated immediately outside.

The central post and sorting office of the Louvre is open 24 hours a day, but at night this is only for sending mail and *poste restante* (general delivery). PTT, 52 rue du Louvre, 75001 (tel: 40 28 20 00), metro: Louvre.

Poste Restante Use the Louvre post office for convenience; it is central and you can pick up mail at any time. Otherwise, every post office provides this service as long as the full address is given. American Express (see Banks) also has a poste restante service.

Other central post offices
PTT Paris Archives, 67 rue des Archives, 75003.
PTT Hôtel de Ville, 9 place de l'Hôtel de Ville, 75004.
PTT Paris Bastille, 1 rue Castex, 75004.

PTT Paris Sorbonne, 13 rue Cujas, 75005.
PTT Paris St.-Germain-des-Prés, 53 rue de Rennes, 75006.
PTT Paris Pigalle, 47 boulevard de Clichy, 75009.
PTT Paris Champs-Elysées, 75008.

Public Transportation
Parisian public transportation is one of the best systems in the world. Metro/RER and bus maps are available free from any metro station and from some hotels. Bus routes are clearly marked at every bus stop and again inside the bus, so don't be afraid to use this as an excellent and cheap sightseeing service. As in every big city, avoid the morning and evening rush hours, when travel can become unbearable (roughly 8:30–9:30AM and 5–7PM).

Buses Buses should be hailed from bus stops. Use one or more metro tickets (depending on length of journey), which you punch in a machine beside the driver. It is possible to buy a single ticket on the bus, but it costs more this way. Most routes operate from 6:30AM–8:30PM, with a few exceptions carrying on till midnight. Night buses (*noctambus*) radiate hourly from Châtelet between 1 and 5AM.

Metros Identified by a large M in a circle, metro stations are easily spotted. The network of lines covers central Paris, and every station has clear indications, so you are unlikely to need help. Lines are identified by their end station; only two have branches, which means you have to check the destination on the front of the train.

Doors open easily: lift the handle or press the button, and they shut automatically. Connections are called *correspondances*, and an orange sign on the platform indicates directions to your connecting line. Blue signs marked *sortie* indicate the exits.

One ticket is valid for every uninterrupted journey. After braving the automatic barriers, keep the ticket on you until you end your journey in case of inspectors. There is no longer a first-class carriage service.

First metros start at 5:30AM, last around 12:30AM.

Radio taxis

Alpha-taxis:	45 85 85 85
Taxis Bleu:	49 36 10 10
Taxi Etoile:	42 70 41 41
G7:	47 39 47 39

All the above take advance bookings for travel to airports.

RER This express train system runs underground in the city center and stretches far out into the suburbs. It can be a good time-saver if you are going from one side of Paris to the other, but access to platforms is often long and complicated, so it is not often worth it for a short trip. Metro tickets can be used for trips in central Paris; otherwise buy a ticket from a machine. Keep it with you, as you have to slot it into a ticket machine when you exit and enter the train.

Taxis These can be hailed in the street (when the roof light is switched on completely), picked up

The metro: a convenient means of transportation and a work of art

from taxi ranks, or ordered by phone. Not the most openminded of species, some taxi drivers are also accompanied by a faithful, slavering hound. Few accept more than three passengers. Fares (displayed on a meter) are reasonable, and it is normal to add a 15 percent tip.

Tickets/Travel passes Various formulas exist for travel passes, but even if you don't use one of them, make sure you buy a *carnet* of 10 tickets (metro/RER/bus) rather than the more costly individual tickets.

A special tourist pass called *Paris Visite* gives you unlimited travel for three or five days. You can choose how many travel zones it covers (from two to four, plus the suburbs and airports). Formule I is a one-day pass, also valid on metro, RER, and

❑ Opened in 1900, the metro's 15 lines measure 123 miles placed end to end and have 366 stations. The RER has added a further 63 miles. ❑

bus, with a similar choice of zones. Parisians themselves rely on monthly passes (*carte orange*) or weekly passes (*coupon hebdomadaire*), but for both of these you need a photo to have a special pass made on the spot. They are valid from the first day of the month or, for weekly passes, from Monday.

Senior Citizens

If you can prove that you are over 60, you will be given discounts for entry to museums and monuments and sometimes other attractions. It is always worth checking. There is, however, no reduction on Parisian public transportation, although Air Inter and SNCF do have special deals. **The American Association of Retired Persons** (AARP, 601 E Street, NW, Washington, DC 20049, tel: 202/434–2277) has two programs for independent travelers: the Purchase Privilege Program, which

offers discounts on hotels, car rentals, and sightseeing; and the AARP Motoring Plan, provided by Amoco, which furnishes emergency road-service aid and trip-routing information for an annual fee of $39.95 per person or couple. AARP members are age 50 or older; annual dues are $8 per person or couple. AARP advises that all members can now purchase tours and cruises and pay for them with a credit card.

When using an AARP or other senior-citizen identification card for reduced hotel rates, mention it when booking, not when checking out. At participating restaurants, show your card before you're seated; discounts may be limited to certain menus, days, or hours. When renting a car, ask about promotional rates that might be cheaper than the senior-citizen discount.

The Gare de Lyon

Elderhostel (75 Federal St., 3rd floor, Boston, MA 02110–1941, tel. 617/426–7788) is an innovative educational program for people 60 and older. Participants live in dorms on over 1,200 campuses worldwide. Mornings are devoted to lectures and seminars; afternoons to sightseeing and field trips. Fees for two- to three-week trips—including room, board, tuition, and round-trip transportation—range from $1,800 to $4,500.

Sports

Unless you are staying for a lengthy period in Paris, this is probably not what brought you to the City of Light. However, if you are desperate, there are some possibilities, notably swimming pools, gyms, and bicycle paths in parks (see pages 228–9).

Check the weekly entertainment magazine *Pariscope* in the *Sports et Loisirs* section for a list of bowling alleys, skating rinks, and squash and tennis clubs. For more specific information, contact the Hôtel de Ville phoneline, which specializes in municipal sports facilities and sporting events in the Paris area: **Allô-Sports**, 25 boulevard de Bourdon, 75004 (tel: 42 76 54 54), metro: Bastille.

Golf enthusiasts who want to keep their wrists supple should contact: **Fédération Française de Golf**, 69 avenue Victor-Hugo, 75016 (tel: 44 17 63 00), metro: Victor-Hugo. The Federation provides a list of golf courses in France, but remember that most of them are out in the suburbs.

□ Over 45 billion francs are spent annually among the national lottery, Loto, horseracing, and casino gambling. This represents 12 billion francs in revenue for the government. □

Spectator Sports

Palais Omnisport, Paris-Bercy 8 boulevard de Bercy, 75012 (tel: 43 46 12 21), metro: Bercy. A vast, modern structure holding up to 17,000 spectators for cycling races, horse jumping, motocross, and hockey championships.

Parc des Princes, 24 rue du Commandant-Guilbaud, 75016 (tel: 42 88 02 76), metro: Porte de St.-Cloud. The king of Parisian stadiums holds 50,000 spectators and is home to two Parisian soccer teams: Paris St.-Germain and Racing Paris 1. It also hosts major and international rugby matches.

Roland-Garros, 2 avenue Gordon-Bennett, 75016 (tel: 47 43 48 00), metro: Porte d'Auteuil. Home to the French Tennis Open held in late May, Roland-Garros is increasingly popular, but many of the tickets are in the hands of black marketeers who ask exorbitant prices at the gates.

Book seats in advance, asking for a reservation form (by February)—contact: **FFT Service Réservation**, BP 333-16, 75767 Paris Cedex 16 (tel: 47 43 48 00).

Racecourses

Hippodrome d'Auteuil, Bois de Boulogne, 75016 (tel: 45 27 12 25), metro: Porte d'Auteuil. Closed July and August. Mainly hurdle racing.

Hippodrome de Longchamp, Bois de Boulogne, 75016 (tel: 44 30 75 00), metro: Porte Maillot or Porte d'Auteuil, then shuttle bus. It is closed for part of summer. One of the world's most famous flat races, the Prix de l'Arc de Triomphe, is held here.

Hippodrome de Vincennes, Bois de Vincennes, 75012 (tel. 49 77 17 17), RER: Joinville-le-Pont. Mainly sulky racing, a colorful treat to watch. The big race is the Prix d'Amérique.

Student and Youth Travel

If you have a valid International Student Identity Card, it will earn you numerous reductions (museums, movies, air and rail travel). Being a student city, Paris has endless facilities aimed specifically at the student population. The following organizations will set you in the right direction.

AJF (Accueil des Jeunes en France), 119 rue St.-Martin, 75004 (tel: 42 77 87 80), metro: Châtelet, Rambuteau. *Open*: Monday to Saturday, 9–5:30. Help and information for accommodations, discount train tickets, etc., for foreign students. It also runs some centrally located youth hostels. Another branch is at 139 boulevard St.-Michel, 75005 (tel: 43 54 95 86).

CIDJ (Centre d'Information et de Documentation Jeunesse), 101 Quai Branly, 75015 (tel: 44 49 12 00), metro: Bir-Hakeim. *Open*: Monday to Saturday, 10–6. Excellent information center for young people looking for jobs, courses, sports, etc.

CROUS, 39 avenue Georges Bernanos, 75005 (tel: 40 51 36 00), metro: Port-Royal. *Open:* Monday to Friday, 9–5. A useful student organization that runs university restaurants, organizes sporting and cultural events, and can provide information on jobs and accommodations.

Youth Hostels

Cité Universitaire, 19 boulevard Jourdan, 75014 (tel: 45 89 68 52), RER: Cité Universitaire. During the summer months, rooms are available in the student dormitories for anyone with an International Student Card.

UCRIF, 72 rue Rambuteau, 75001 (tel: 40 26 57 64), metro: Les Halles/Etienne Marcel. Open: Monday to Friday, 9–6. Operates several cheap hostels in Paris as well as social events and language courses for foreigners.

Student travel agencies

Council Travel, 16 rue de Vaugirard, 75006 (tel: 46 34 02 90), or 22 rue des Pyramides, 75001 (tel: 44 55 55 44) specializes in cheap air fares, tours and charters to the U.S.

Jeunes Sans Frontières (Wasteels), 5 rue de la Banque, 75002 (tel: 42 61 53 21). Cheap flights and train fares.

Club Français du Tourisme de Jeunes, 8 avenue de l'Opéra, 75001 (tel: 42 96 10 23). Information about traveling throughout France specifically for young people.

SNCF

SNCF's Carissimo card is available to people aged from 12 to 25 and gives discounts of up to 50 percent. Students under 26 can buy BIGE

The Latin Quarter

tickets and cut the cost of traveling around France by up to 20 percent. For going further afield, use Eurodomino. Ask at your local French Tourist or French Railway office.

Telephones

Prior to 18 October 1996

Repairs: 13

Directory inquiries
national: 12; international: 19 33 12 + country prefix

Telegrams
national: 36 55; international: 05 33 44 11.

French numbers currently have eight digits.

For calling a number in the Ile de France, (i.e., Paris and its environs), you do not need any prefix. For numbers outside the region but within France, you need to first dial 16, await the tone, then dial the main number. For phoning Paris from the provinces, dial 16+1, then the eight-digit number.

International calling If you are phoning France from abroad, dial the international code, then 33 (for the provinces), then the eight-digit number; for Paris, dial 133. For phoning abroad from France, dial 19, then the country code, then dial the number (omitting the area code's initial 0).

From 18 October 1996

As of October 18, 1996, new ten-digit numbers will replace eight-digit numbers by adding two figures before existing numbers as follows:

01   Paris and Paris outskirts
02   North west France
03   North east France
04   South east France
05   South west France

To dial Paris to the provinces and the provinces to Paris, dial 01. To dial abroad from France dial 00 followed by the country dialling code: ie for the UK, dial 0044.

Public phones Nearly all Parisian public phones now function with phone cards (*télécartes*). These can be bought at post offices or tobacconists for 50 or 120 units. Public phones in cafés and restaurants use either phone cards or coins, or they have to be switched on by staff, in which case you pay after the call (ask which system it is beforehand). For coin phones lift the receiver, insert a 1, 2, 5, or 10 franc piece, await the dial tone, then dial.

Avoid using hotel phones for long-distance calls, as they are usually far more expensive.

Reduced rates For calls within France, the cheapest times are at night, 10:30PM–6AM. Next cheapest rate is after 9:30PM on weekdays, after 1:30PM on Saturday, and all day Sunday. Lunchtime (12:30–1:30) and early evening (6–9:30) periods are 30 percent cheaper than peak daytime rates.

International off-peak rates depend on the destination but are generally 30 percent or so less than normal rates.

U.S. and Canada: Cheapest is daily, 2AM–noon. Medium rate is noon–2 and 8PM Sunday.

Any public holiday has the same rates as Sunday.

Time

As the world has not yet agreed on a mutual start and finish of winter time and summer time, there is often a period in spring and autumn when the winter time differences given below are incorrect for a week or so.

However, for most of the year these differences apply. France changes her clocks in late September (back one hour) and late March (forward one hour). Her winter time is the same as that of Western Europe (except Portugal, which goes along with the U.K.).

Australia	
Perth	+ 7 hours
Sydney/Melbourne	+ 9 hours
Canada	
Montreal	– 6 hours
Vancouver	– 9 hours
Ireland	– 1 hour
New Zealand	+ 11 hours
U.K.	– 1 hour
U.S.	
New York	– 6 hours
Los Angeles	– 9 hours

Tipping

Tipping in France is a complex affair, varying from service to service. In hotels, restaurants, and cafés, service is included (up to 15 percent), but it is usual to leave a small extra tip if you are satisfied, ranging from 50 centimes for a coffee to 10 or 20 francs at a restaurant.

Theater ushers look for tips (5 or 10 francs) and movie theater attendants depend on them for a living, so slip them 2 francs when they tear your ticket. Taxi drivers expect 10 to 15 percent, as do hairdressers.

Hotel porters and bellboys should be given 10 francs or so per bag (going up with class of hotel) and chambermaids a banknote at the end of your stay. Room service also appreciates at least 10 francs. If the hotel concierge has achieved the impossible for you, he, too, will appreciate a solid tip.

Any tour guide should be tipped roughly 10 to 15 percent.

Toilets

Public toilets can be found all around the city. Large off-white plastic affairs, they cost 1 franc to use, have automatic flushing and disinfecting systems, and are usually well maintained. Every café has a toilet, ranging from the old smelly squatters to pristine affairs reeking of chlorine. These are for customers only, so don't tempt fate by marching in off the street to use one without first ordering a drink. They are nearly always in the basement. A small number are coin-operated. Some metro stations still house relics from the old days of public toilets, those at Madeleine being particularly characterful.

Tour Groups

Apart from fending for yourself and making your own trip around Paris, there is also the option of a package tour. Creative itineraries abound, offering access to places you may not be able to get to on your own, as well as the more traditional spots. They also tend to save you money on airfare and hotels. If group outings are not your style, check into independent packages; somewhat more expensive than package tours, they are also more flexible.

When considering a tour, be sure to find out exactly what expenses are included (particularly tips, fares, side trips, additional meals, and entertainment); governmental ratings of all hotels on the itinerary and the facilities they offer; cancellation policies for both you and the tour operator; and, if you are traveling alone, the price of the single supplement. Most tour operators ask that bookings be made through a travel agent (there is no extra charge for doing so). Initially, you should contact your travel agent or the French Government Tourist Office.

Tourist Offices

L'Office de Tourisme de Paris, 127 avenue des Champs-Elysées, 75008 (tel: 49 52 53 54), metro: George V. *Open*: daily, 9–8. Drop by here to pick up free maps and leaflets about museums, tours, and châteaus in and around Paris. Tourist offices will find you accommodations and are generally extremely helpful.

Other smaller tourist offices are situated in the main railway stations (Gare du Nord, de l'Est, Austerlitz, de Lyon), and in the summer the Eiffel Tower claims its own branch. The station offices can be very

useful in getting last-minute accommodations; in summer they open till 9.

Each French region has its own tourist office in Paris and can be a useful source of information if you are traveling around the rest of the country. The Maison de la France, 8 avenue de l'Opéra, 75001 (tel: 42 96 10 23) regroups information from all of them but in less detail. Below is a selection of regional tourist offices.

Maison Alpes Dauphiné, 2 place André Malraux, 75001 (tel: 42 96 08 43).

Maison d'Alsace, 39 avenue des Champs-Elysées, 75008 (tel: 42 25 93 42).

Maison de la Bretagne, 17 rue de l'Arrivée, 75015 (tel: 45 38 73 15).

Maison des Hautes Alpes, 4 avenue de l'Opéra, 75001 (tel: 42 96 05 08).

Maison du Nord-Pas de Calais, 25 rue Bleue, 75009 (tel: 48 00 59 62).

Maison du Périgord, 6 rue Gomboust, 75001 (tel: 42 60 38 77).

Maison de Poitou-Charentes, 68 rue du Cherche-Midi, 75006 (tel: 42 22 83 74).

Maison des Pyrénées, 15 rue St.-Augustin, 75002 (tel: 42 86 51 86).

Maison de Savoie, 31 avenue de l'Opéra, 75001 (tel: 42 61 74 73).

Local French Tourist Offices

The French Government Tourist Office (FGTO) publishes a great deal of literature in English, available from the following addresses:
U.S.: 444 Madison Avenue, 16th Floor, New York, NY 10022 (tel: 212/838-7800, fax: 212/838-7855). 676 North Michigan Avenue, 3360 Chicago, IL 60611-2819 (tel: 312/751-7800, fax: 312/337-6339). 9454 Wilshire Boulevard, Beverly Hills, CA 90912–2967 (tel: 310/271-7838, fax: 310/276-2835).

Valeting/Laundry

For general laundry go to a launderette *laverie automatique*, although these are not as common as dry cleaners. Dry cleaners *(pressing)* can be found all around Paris but are not cheap. Some have an economy service, not recommended for your best silk jacket.

HOTELS AND RESTAURANTS

Accommodations

Expensive

L'Hôtel 13 rue des Beaux-Arts, 75006 (tel: 43 25 27 22). A Parisian legend that doesn't come cheap. Antiques galore, elegance, and memories of Oscar Wilde. Much-frequented basement restaurant and piano bar.

Hôtel Lutetia 45 boulevard Raspail, 75006 (tel: 49 54 46 46). Huge, historic, a masterpiece of art-deco architecture. Renovated and restyled by Sonia Rykiel in 1989. Elegant, well located between St.-Germain and Montparnasse. Good brasserie.

Hôtel le Ste.-Beuve 9 rue Ste.-Beuve, 75006 (tel: 45 48 20 07). High style to be had in this pricey but exquisite bed and breakfast establishment a short walk from the boulevard St.-Germain. Hosts occasional stylish theme weekends and art exhibitions.

Hôtel San-Régis 12 rue Jean Goujon, 75008 (tel: 44 95 16 16). Elaborately redecorated a few years ago, a favorite with American film stars.

Personalized style for each room. All top 4-star facilities.

Hôtel de la Trémoille 14 rue de la Trémoille, 75008 (tel: 47 23 34 20). Down a chic side street off the fashion hub of the avenue Montaigne, a discreet luxury hotel with all the comforts and consequently high prices.

Pavillon de la Reine 28 place des Vosges, 75003 (tel: 42 77 96 40). A historic setting for a discreetly luxurious hotel. Flowery courtyard, and tasteful period decoration.

Regent's Garden 6 rue Pierre-Demours, 75017 (tel: 45 74 07 30). Elegant townhouse with magnificent garden, huge rooms decorated in period or provincial style. Excellent amenities, though no restaurant.

Le Warwick 5 rue de Berri, 75008 (tel: 45 63 14 11). Suitable for incognito VIPs, a modern luxury hotel off the Champs-Elysées.

Moderate

Hôtel de l'Abbaye 10 rue Cassette, 75006 (tel: 45 44 38 11). A very upscale but affordable hotel in a former monastery. Flowery, cobbled courtyard, elegant salons, terraced duplex rooms, smiling staff.

Hôtel Agora 7 rue de la Cossonnerie, 75001 (tel: 42 33 46 02). Smack in the middle of Les Halles in a 12th-century street. Part modern, part provincial in atmosphere; reasonable value. Branch in St.-Germain.

Hôtel Banville 166 boulevard Berthier, 75017 (tel: 42 67 70 16). Elegant, well-decorated, small hotel. Not central, but excellent value.

Hôtel Bergère Best Western 34 rue Bergère, 75009 (tel: 47 70 34 34). Reliable service and comforts in this chain-owned hotel. Close to the Grands Boulevards. Some rather tacky haunts surround the neighboring nightclub, Le Palace.

Hôtel Bradford 10 rue St.-Philippe-du-Roule, 75008 (tel: 45 63 20 20). Old-fashioned chic, period furnishings. Impeccable service, large rooms. Consequently expensive, but worth it.

Hôtel Chopin 46 passage Jouffroy, 75009 (tel: 47 70 58 10). A remarkable setting in a 19th-century shopping arcade for this modest 2-star hotel.

Hôtel du Collège de France 7 rue Thénard, 75005 (tel: 43 26 78 36). Simple, quiet bed-and-breakfast establishment in a tiny street off boulevard St.-Germain.

Hôtel Corona 8 Cité Bergère, 75009 (tel: 47 70 52 96). A large, well-appointed hotel favored by tour operators. Comfortable rooms, a quartier that stays awake late. Parking available.

Hôtel Danemark 21 rue Vavin, 75006 (tel: 43 26 93 78). A small, friendly, spruced up, family-run hotel near the high spots of Montparnasse.

Hôtel des Deux Iles 59 rue St.-Louis-en-l'Isle, 75004 (tel: 43 26 13 35). Chintz-covered comfort, at the hub of the island. A charming patio and vaulted breakfast room add to its attraction.

Hôtel Esmeralda 4 rue St.-Julien-le-Pauvre, 75005 (tel: 43 54 19 20). Opposite Notre-Dame, so some rooms have great views. Dollhouse atmosphere and scale with characteristic 19th-century furniture and objets d'art.

Hôtel des Grandes Ecoles 75 rue du Cardinal-Lemoine, 75005 (tel: 43 26 79 23). Well-kept rooms overlooking the garden of this picturesque country-house hotel in a verdant corner of the Latin Quarter. Advisable to book well ahead.

Hôtel Istria 29 rue Campagne Première, 75014 (tel: 43 20 91 82). Follow Montparnasse legends such as Rilke, Duchamp, Man Ray, and Aragon to this friendly, comfortable hotel.

Hôtel Lenox 9 rue de l'Université, 75007 (tel: 42 96 10 95). A favorite with the design and fashion world. Chase T.S. Ellot's ghost and enjoy the restored, stylish 1930s bar. Make sure you book well ahead. **Hôtel des Marronniers** 21 rue Jacob, 75006 (tel: 43 25 30 60). Its fame has spread. Book well in advance to enjoy this gracious country-house atmosphere (see page 147). **Hôtel Mayflower** 3 rue de Châteaubriand, 75008 (tel: 45 62 57 46). Near the Etoile, a well-run, relaxed English-style hotel with pretty, peaceful bedrooms. Prices vary according to size of room. **Hôtel Michelet-Odéon** 6 place de l'Odéon, 75006 (tel: 46 34 27 80). Extremely reasonable rates for superb, quiet location near the Luxembourg Gardens. Modernized interior, no frills. **Hôtel Opal** 19 rue Tronchet, 75008 (tel: 42 65 77 97). Tiny rooms but well located behind the Madeleine. Convenient for forays into the nearby department stores. **Hôtel du Parc Montsouris** 4 rue du Parc Montsouris, 75014 (tel: 45 89 09 72) Very reasonable 2-star establishment outside the center and located across the road from a delightful park. **Hôtel de la place des Vosges** 12 rue de Birague, 75004 (tel: 42 72 60 46). Charming 17th-century townhouse with modernized rooms. Quiet, well maintained, a few steps from the place des Vosges. **Hôtel du Quai Voltaire** 19 quai Voltaire, 75007 (tel: 42 61 50 91). Dusty 18th-century setting, but unbeatable location overlooking Seine opposite Louvre. Baudelaire and Wagner stayed here in their day. **Hôtel Riboutté-Lafayette** 5 rue Riboutté, 75009 (tel: 47 70 62 36). Close to Opéra and Grands Boulevards. Peaceful, small place, very reasonably priced. **Hôtel Saint-Louis** 75 rue St.-Louis-en-l'Isle, 75004 (tel: 46 34 04 80). Tasteful,

comfortable hotel with well-equipped, though small, rooms right in center of Ile St.-Louis. **Hôtel Saint-Merry** 78 rue de la Verrerie, 75004 (tel: 42 78 14 15). Eccentric, neo-Gothic style, attached to a church. Rather boxy rooms but extremely central and quiet. **Hôtel Saint-Roch** 25 rue Saint-Roch, 75001 (tel: 42 60 17 91). Good-value, 2-star hotel near the Tuileries on an interesting street. Disregard the entrance. **Hôtel Spéria** 1 rue de la Bastille, 75004 (tel: 42 72 04 01). Convenient for Bastille nights and Marais days. Reasonable value; unpretentious renovated interior. **Hôtel de la Tour d'Auvergne** 10 rue de la Tour d'Auvergne, 75009 (tel: 48 78 61 60). A small, well-maintained 3-star hotel in a relatively undiscovered area between the Grands Boulevards and Pigalle. **Hôtel des Tuileries** 10 rue St.-Hyacinthe, 75001 (tel: 42 61 04 17). Renovated 18th-century style, comfortable and quiet but with small rooms. **Hôtel du Vieux Marais** 8 rue du Plâtre, 75004 (tel: 42 78 47 22). Floral wallpaper territory in heart of Marais. Friendly hotel and reasonably priced. **Le Jardin des Plantes** 5 rue Linne, 75005 (tel: 47 07 06 20). Still reasonably priced for the facilities it offers—including a sun terrace and views over the botanical gardens. **Le Molière** 21 rue Molière, 75001 (tel: 42 96 22 01). Convenient for central monuments, on a quiet street that is near the Louvre and Opéra. Reasonable rates and well-equipped rooms. **Terrass Hôtel** 12 rue Joseph-de-Maistre, 75018 (tel: 46 06 72 85). Splendid views over the rooftops of Paris. Some rooms retain original art-deco work. **Timhotel La Bourse** 3 rue de la Banque, 75002 (tel: 42 61 53 90). Small, friendly chain hotel with billiards room.

Well located near the place des Victoires.

Budget
Grand Hôtel des Arts et Métiers 4 rue Borda, 75003 (tel: 48 87 73 89). Tucked away just north of Marais. Small, friendly hotel, very reasonable rates. **Grand Hôtel Malher** 5 rue Malher, 75004 (tel: 42 72 60 92). In a quiet side street near St.-Paul, a tiny nine-room hotel for very thin wallets: no credit cards taken. **Hôtel des Académies** 15 rue de la Grande-Chaumière, 75006 (tel: 43 26 66 44). A historic street for artists in Montparnasse. Family-run hotel with some basic 1950s-style attics. Good value. **Hôtel Andréa** 3 rue Saint-Bon, 75004 (tel: 42 78 43 93). Friendly, well-maintained hotel in quiet street behind rue de Rivoli. Good value, so popular. **Hôtel André Gill** 4 rue André Gill, 75018 (tel: 42 62 48 48). Very reasonable, pleasant rooms and charming courtyard setting, around the corner from less picturesque Pigalle.

HOTELS AND RESTAURANTS

Hôtel des Carmes 5 rue des Carmes, 75005 (tel: 43 29 78 40). In a narrow street of the Latin Quarter, a very reasonable 2-star hotel. Limited facilities.

Hôtel les Degrés de Notre-Dame 10 rue des Grands-Degrés, 75005 (tel: 43 25 88 38). Choose between view of Notre-Dame at the front or tranquility at the back in a very pleasant, well-kept hotel.

Hôtel Esmeralda 4 rue St.-Julien-le-Pauvre, 75005 (tel: 43 54 19 20). Dollhouse hotel in one of the most hectic parts of the Latin Quarter. Charmingly furnished, reasonable rates.

Hôtel Henri IV 25 place Dauphine, 75001 (tel: 43 54 44 53). Extremely basic. One communal bathroom per floor, but a rare old-world atmosphere on one of Paris's most delightful squares. Advance booking essential.

Hôtel le Home Latin 15/17 rue Sommerard, 75005 (tel: 43 26 25 21). Basic but clean and at heart of Latin Quarter. Some rooms have showers, others not, but all are quiet.

Hôtel Jeanne d'Arc 3 rue Jarente, 75004 (tel: 48 87 62 11). Charming, provincial-style hotel in heart of Marais, clean and quiet, so well booked up.

Hôtel du Lion d'Or 5 rue de la Sourdière, 75001 (tel: 42 60 79 04). Excellent location near Louvre, modernized but fairly basic amenities.

Hôtel Lescot 26 rue Pierre Lescot, 75001 (tel: 42 33 68 76). Conveniently situated above a café, this hotel is pretty simple but clean and central. No pretentions but the staff are helpful.

Hôtel Montpensier 12 rue de Richelieu, 75001 (tel: 42 96 28 50). Once the residence of one of Louis XV's mistresses, a hotel with a difference and remarkably cheap. Next to the Palais-Royal.

Hôtel de la Nouvelle France 23 rue des Messageries, 75010 (tel: 48 24 70 74). Good value, roomy and

clean, although in a rather uninspiring neighborhood.

Hôtel Prima Lepic 29 rue Lepic, 75018 (tel: 46 06 44 64). In bustling Montmartre; an airy, light hotel with well decorated if smallish bedrooms and a courtyard-style reception area.

Hôtel de Rouen 42 rue Croix-des-Petits-Champs, 75001 (tel: 42 61 38 21). Small, basic hotel. Well situated for Louvre and Les Halles.

Hôtel St.-André-des-Arts 66 rue St.-André-des Arts, 75006 (tel: 43 26 96 16). A 17th-century Latin Quarter classic, usually packed. Lively but noisy.

Hôtel du 7e Art 20 rue Saint-Paul, 75004 (tel: 42 77 04 03). Nothing if not fun, this hotel has a good line in film posters and movie memorabilia, plus it's in the budget-hotel starved Marais.

Hôtel Sévigné 2 rue Malher, 75004 (tel: 42 72 76 17). Near the Jewish quarter in the Marais, a pleasant, relaxed, well-run place, excellent value.

Hotel de la Sorbonne 6 rue Victor-Cousin, 75005 (tel: 43 54 58 08). Unsurprisingly located near the famous university. Small but comfortable rooms.

Hôtel du Vieux Paris 9 rue Gît-le-Coeur, 75006 (tel: 43 54 41 66). Near action of St.-Michel, the original "beat" hotel frequented by Burroughs, Ginsberg, and the like. Relaxed atmosphere, tiny rooms.

Tim Hôtel 11 rue Ravignan, 75018 (tel: 42 55 74 79). Near the famous Bateau Lavoir in Montmartre, a chain hotel, well maintained and friendly.

Restaurants

Expensive

L'Ambroisie 9 place des Vosges, 75004 (tel: 42 78 51 45). Set in a restored jeweler's shop, book one month ahead for this romantic, intimate restaurant, one of Paris's best.

Au Chien qui Fume 33 rue du Pont-Neuf, 75001 (tel: 42

36 07 42). Classic seafood brasserie from way back.

Au Cochon d'Or 192 avenue Jean-Jaurès, 75019 (tel: 42 45 46 46). A worldly Parisian crowd pours in here for its famed grilled meat dishes and gigantic steaks.

Le Pavillon Puebla Parc des Buttes-Chaumont, 75019 (tel: 42 08 92 62). In the incomparable setting of this landscaped park, an elegant restaurant serving imaginative cuisine influenced by its Catalan owner.

Au Quai des Ormes 72 quai de l'Hôtel-de-Ville, 75004 (tel: 42 74 72 22). Inimitable architecture and setting facing Ile Saint-Louis. Fresh dishes culminating in delicious desserts. Terrace in summer.

Au Trou Gascon 40 rue Taine, 75012 (tel: 43 44 34 26). Lost in the 12th, a monument to the rich cooking of southwest France. Divine cassoulets, imaginative fish preparations, and emphatic cheeses.

Beauvilliers 52 rue Lamarck, 75018 (tel: 42 54 54 42). Elegant 19th-century setting. Delicious nouvelle cuisine dishes, menu changes weekly.

Le Bélier l'Hôtel, 13 rue des Beaux-Arts, 75006 (tel: 43 25 27 22). Romantic restaurant in basement of elegant hotel. Fountain, flowers, and sophisticated cuisine.

Café Drouant 18 rue Gaillon, 75002 (tel: 42 65 15 16). Illustrious old literary sanctuary, superb décor. Expensive specialties but reasonable menu offered in evenings.

Chez Pauline 5 rue Villedo, 75001 (tel: 42 96 20 70). One of Paris's prettiest bistros. Successful combination of traditional and modern dishes. Pricey.

Chez Georges 1 rue du Mail, 75002 (tel: 42 60 07 11). Thronging with clients day and night, ruled by brusque matrons. Character and classic French cuisine.

L'Escargot 38 rue Montorgueil, 75001 (tel: 42 36 83 51). Famous old restaurant, elegant setting.

Sophisticated cuisine and prices.

La Fermette du Sud-Ouest 31 rue Coquillière, 75001 (tel: 42 36 73 55). Famous for homemade southwest France specialties, meaty fare.

La Fermette Marbeuf 5 rue Marbeuf, 75008 (tel: 47 23 31 31). Stunning setting. Imaginative, seasonal dishes. Elegant, stylish clientèle.

Joël Robuchon 59 avenue Raymond Poincaré, 75016 (tel: 47 27 12 27). Undoubtedly one of France's great chefs in a beautiful art-nouveau mansion.

Jules Verne Tour Eiffel, 75007 (tel: 45 55 61 44). For a spectacular, memorable treat overlooking Paris. Book several weeks (if not months) in advance.

Lapérouse 51 quai des Grands-Augustins, 75006 (tel: 43 26 90 14). No longer renowned for its cuisine, but remains a typical *fin de siècle* setting.

Lucas-Carton 9 place de la Madeleine, 75008 (tel: 42 65 22 90). Extremely pricey and chic. Beautiful Belle Epoque architecture combined with inventive cuisine.

Le Grand Véfour 17 rue de Beaujolais, 75001 (tel: 42 96 56 27). For a memorable dinner in historic splendor next to the ghosts of Colette, Cocteau, Sartre, and Napoleon.

La Marlotte 55 rue du Cherche-Midi, 75006 (tel: 45 48 86 79). Exquisite cuisine in sophisticated, candlelit setting. Not excessive prices but the restaurant is closed on weekends.

Pavillon Montsouris 20 rue Gazan, 75014 (tel: 45 88 38 52). Paris's most deliciously bucolic setting in the Parc Montsouris. Go for a discreet summer lunch if you want to enjoy adventurous dishes in this 1900 pavilion.

Au Petit Riche 25 rue le Peletier, 75009 (tel: 47 70 68 68). Superb, ornate 1880s interior. Delicious bourgeois cuisine, impeccable service. Favorite for business lunches.

Le Pré Catalan route de Suresnes, Bois de Boulogne, 75016 (tel: 45 24 55 58). Very expensive, but if you must dine in a Parisian rose garden, this is it. Don't skip Lenôtre's desserts.

Le Procope 13 rue de l'Ancienne Comédie, 75006 (tel: 43 26 99 20). Claims to be Paris's first café, dating from 1686. Touristy but spectacular, renovated décor, and good seafood dishes.

Taillevent 15 rue Lamennais, 75008 (tel: 44 95 15 01). Book months ahead, save years in advance. One of Paris's top gourment restaurants.

Tan Dinh 60 rue de Verneuil, 75007 (tel: 45 44 04 84). Exquisite personalized Vietnamese cuisine served with equal delicacy. Renowned wine list. Chic oriental décor.

Le Train Bleu Gare de Lyon, 75012 (tel: 43 43 09 06). A stunning Belle Epoque décor overpowers the Lyonnais cuisine; choose simple dishes and revel in the setting.

Yugaraj 14 rue Dauphine, 75006 (tel: 43 26 44 91). One of Paris's best Indian restaurants. Charming and friendly Sri Lankan service, in a very discreet atmosphere.

Moderate
Altitude 95 Tour Eiffel, 75007 (tel: 45 55 20 04). Belle Epoque setting, unique views, very fair fare, considering.

Androuet 41 rue d'Amsterdam, 75008 (tel: 48 74 26 93). Famous old cheese restaurant, over 200 varieties. Recently renovated.

Angélina 226 rue de Rivoli, 75001 (tel: 42 60 82 00). One of Paris's classic *salons de thé*, on the tourist trail. Proustian setting, delectable cakes, light lunches. Daytime only.

Astier 44 rue Jean-Pierre Timbaud, 75011 (tel: 43 57 16 35). No hidden surprises in Astier's copious, reasonable menu, fantastic cheeses. Friendly, unpretentious local spot.

L'Auberge Nicolas Flamel 51 rue Montmorency, 75003 (tel: 42 71 77 78). Trendy showbiz crowd attracted to contemporary cuisine in one of the oldest houses in Paris.

Au Pied du Cochon 6 rue Coquillière, 75001 (tel: 42 36 11 75). An old classic from market days of Les Halles. Open nonstop, it is a good place for pig's trotters at 5AM.

Aux Lyonnais 32 rue Saint-Marc, 75002 (tel: 42 96 65 04). Old-fashioned, straitlaced bistro serving classic dishes, a favorite for after the opera. Very reasonable.

Baalbeck 16 rue de Mazagran, 75010 (tel: 47 70 70 02). Popular with Paris's Lebanese community. Delicious Middle Eastern cuisine, with belly dancers after 10PM.

Le Balzar 49 rue des Ecoles, 75005 (tel: 43 54 13 67). Fashionable brasserie near the Sorbonne. Classic fare

and service, but quite pricey.

Bar des Théâtres 6 avenue Montaigne, 75008 (tel: 47 23 34 63). Sophisticated, animated bar/restaurant opposite famous theater. Actors and chic audience mix in here for reliable dishes.

Bilboquet 13 rue St.-Benoît, 75006 (tel: 45 48 81 84). Favorite with jazz enthusiasts, good atmosphere.

Bistro d'à Côté 10 rue Gustave Flaubert, 75017 (tel: 42 67 05 81). For those who can't afford chef Michel Rostang's 5-star affair, his bistro fare is excellent. Not cheap. Three other branches.

Bistrot de l'Etoile 75 avenue Niel, 75017 (tel: 42 27 88 44). Top chef Guy Savoy has also opened this middle-market branch down the road. Succulent and chic dishes.

Le Bistrot de Paris 33 rue de Lille, 75007 (tel: 42 61 15 84). Bourgeois cuisine at its best in a sleek, very Parisian setting.

Bistrot sur le Toit 34 rue du Colisée, 75008 (tel: 43 59 83 80). Not the original but a huge, glittery replacement. Open late for seafood and classic brasserie fare.

Blue Elephant 43 rue de la Roquette, 75011 (tel: 47 00 42 00). Over-the-top décor for a trendy Thai restaurant serving spicy specialties.

Le Boeuf sur le Toit 34 rue du Colisée, 75008 (tel: 43 59 83 80). Part of Paris's famous chain of brasseries, reopened in 1985. Spectacular 1920s setting for a good sprinkling of rich and famous. Fabulous seafood and foie gras.

Bofinger 5 rue de la Bastille, 75004 (tel: 42 72 87 82). One of the most beautiful Belle Epoque brasseries in the city. Good food, too.

Brasserie dè l'Ile Saint-Louis 55 quai de Bourbon, 75004 (tel: 43 54 02 59). Noisy, crowded, fun brasserie on tip of island. Sunny terrace, reasonable prices.

Brasserie Stella 133 avenue Victor-Hugo, 75016 (tel: 47

27 60 54). Original 1950s décor. Large, animated, upscale brasserie with classic seafood.

La Butte Chaillot 110 bis avenue Kléber, 75116 (tel: 47 27 88 88). Guy Savoy's latest venue is currently one of the chicest places in Paris.

Café Max 7 avenue de la Motte-Piquet, 75007 (tel: 47 05 57 66). Popular with local yuppies. Typical old bistro proposes reliable classic dishes.

Chardenoux 1 rue Jules-Vallès, 75011 (tel: 43 71 49 52). Charming 1900s bistro setting. Adventurous, dependable cuisine. Pricey.

La Chaumière en l'Ile 4 rue Jean-Bellay, 75004 (tel: 43 54 27 34). Pleasant, atmospheric 19th-century setting on Ile Saint-Louis. Rich specialties from southwest.

Chez André 12 rue Marbeuf, 75008 (tel: 47 20 59 57). Chic lady shoppers and businessmen congregate here for lunch: game, seafood, or bistro cuisine.

Chez Léon 11 boulevard Beaumarchais, 75011 (tel: 42 78 42 55). Classic couscous. Rather plasticized interior but popular.

Chez Maître Paul 12 rue Monsieur-le-Prince, 75006 (tel: 43 54 74 59). Friendly little bistro, delicious specialties from eastern France.

Chez Paul 13 rue de Charonne, 75011 (tel: 47 00 34 57). Favorite with local gallery owners, artists, and clients. Revamped old bistro with traditional dishes. Booking essential.

Chez Ribe 15 avenue de Suffren, 75007 (tel: 45 66 53 79). In shadow of Eiffel Tower, a plush, discreet bistro amiably serving reliable fare. Terrace in summer.

Chez Toutoune 5 rue de Pontoise, 75005 (tel: 43 26 56 81). Fashionable, busy restaurant with fresh, hearty cooking. Service slow, quite expensive.

La Closerie des Lilas 171 boulevard du Mont-parnasse, 75006 (tel: 43 26

70 50). Famous old Montparnasse bar/ brasserie/restaurant. Piano tinkles in background; sophisticated, bustling atmosphere.
Coup de Coeur 19 rue St.-Augustin, 75002 (tel: 47 03 45 70). Slick and sleek interior, delicate inventive cuisine. Reasonable menu.
La Coupole 102 boulevard du Montparnasse, 75014 (tel: 43 20 14 20). A Montparnasse institution. Restored art-deco interior, still magnificent. Vast, noisy, trendy. Tourists and regulars. Classic seafood and brasserie fare.
Dagorno 190 avenue Jean-Jaurès, 75019 (tel: 40 40 09 39). Another spectacular 1900 setting for a variety of seafood and traditional meat dishes in La Villette, an area once dominated by the abattoirs.
Da Graziano 83 rue Lepic, 75018 (tel: 46 06 84 77). Topped by one of Montmartre's last windmills. Copious Italian cuisine in bright, theatrical surroundings.
Darkoum 44 rue Ste.-Anne, 75002 (tel: 42 96 83 70). Spectacular Moorish interior for delectable couscous, tajine, and pastilla.
L'Echaudé St.-Germain 21 rue de l'Echaudé, 75006 (tel: 43 54 79 02). Romantic St.-Germain ambience; reliable cuisine.
L'Ecluse 15 place de la Madeleine, 75008 (tel: 42 65 34 69). One of a small chain of wine bars. Bordeaux by the glass, cold snacks. Fashionable clientèle.
Fin de Siècle rue Saint-Nicolas, 75012 (tel: 43 43 49 40). Charming, old-fashioned bistro with a faithful clientèle keen on Beaujolais. Closes early.
Le Flamboyant 11 rue Boyer-Barret, 75014 (tel: 45 41 00 22). Reasonable value for one of Paris's best *antillais* restaurants. Spicy *accras*, stuffed crab, turtle kebab.
La Fontaine de Mars 129 rue Saint-Dominique, 75007 (tel: 47 05 46 44). Closed

weekends. Friendly local bistro offering tasty, simple cuisine.
La Galoche 41 rue de Lappe, 75011 (tel: 47 00 77 15). Rare survivor in hub of trendiness. Robust, central France in old-fashioned clog-lined setting.
Gaspard de la Nuit 6 rue des Tournelles, 75004 (tel: 42 77 90 53). Calm, comfortable atmosphere for classic bourgeois cuisine.
Au Grain de Folie 24 rue de la Vieuville, 75018 (tel: 42 58 15 57). Generous portions of vegetarian food; organic wine available. Extremely good value.
Le Grand Colbert 2 rue Vivienne, 75002 (tel: 42 86 87 88). Recently restored Belle Epoque brasserie serving classic dishes and seafood till late.
Le Grizzli 7 rue Saint-Martin, 75004 (tel: 48 87 77 56). Traditional Auvergne cooking served in a pretty dining room. Specialties include grilled meat and fish.
Jacques Mélac 42 rue Léon-Frot, 75011 (tel: 43 70 59 27). An exuberant patron keeps the bistro overflowing with clients and wine. Good for daytime sustenance and Tuesday and Thursday evenings only!
Joe Allen 30 rue Pierre-Lescot, 75001 (tel: 42 36 70 13). Faithful hamburger branch for more mature crowd. Predictable but enjoyable classic.
La Magnani 21 rue Chanzy, 75011 (tel: 43 71 27 48). Theatrical Italians feed satisfied locals with a wide range of their specialties.
Le Mansouria 11 rue Faidherbe, 75011 (tel: 43 71 00 16). Fashionable Moroccan restaurant with elegant décor and delicate tajines.
Mexico Café 1 place de Mexico, 75016 (tel: 47 27 96 98). Fashionable haunt. International cuisine, quite chic.
La Mousson 9 rue de la Bastille, 75004 (tel: 42 71 85 20). One of the Bastille's first trendsetters, now a little past it. Cocktail bar

downstairs and neo-ethnic cuisine upstairs.
Ma Bourgogne 19 place des Vosges, 75004 (tel: 42 78 44 64). Tables spill out onto the pavement in one of Paris's most lovely squares. Unpretentious food; steaks, salads.
Myrtho 10 rue des Ecouffes, 75004 (tel: 42 77 00 36). Relaxed elegance, smartly designed interior, inventive French cuisine.
Natacha 17 bis rue Campagne Première, 75014 (tel: 43 20 79 27). For showbiz stargazing, not cuisine. Copious bourgeois cooking in elegant setting. Pretentious, very Parisian.
Nioullaville 32/34 rue de l'Orillon, 75011 (tel: 43 38 30 44). Hong Kong comes to Paris, or Belleville. Vast kitsch Chinese restaurant with endless menu and passing trolleys for sampling.
Nos Ancêtres les Gaulois 39 rue St.-Louis-en-l'Isle, 75004 (tel: 46 33 66 07). Unlimited wine, rowdy, fun atmosphere in pseudo-medieval setting.
La Nuit des Rois 3 rue des Pactour-Wagner, 75011 (tel: 48 07 15 22). Comfortable, quite elegant retreat for sipping champagne late into the night.
Le Petit Plat 3 rue des Grands-Degrés, 75005 (tel: 40 46 85 34). Good rustic-style cooking (rabbit terrine) in popular setting.
Pharamond 24 rue de la Grande Truanderie, 75001 (tel: 42 33 06 72). Pretty, ceramic-tiled old bistro. Increasingly trendy clientèle. Quite pricey classic dishes.
La Potée des Halles 3 rue Etienne-Marcel, 75001 (tel: 42 36 18 68). Robust regional cooking served up in superb Belle Epoque tiled setting.
La Poule au Pot 9 rue Vauvilliers, 75001 (tel: 42 36 32 96). Open till 6AM. Spend all night here sampling traditional dishes in a very animated atmosphere.
404 69 rue des Gravilliers, 75003 (tel: 42 74 57 81). Low seats, low lighting, high

ceilings. Popular Moroccan restaurant with lively young crowd.

Restaurant Curieux 14 rue Saint-Merri, 75004 (tel: 42 72 75 97). Curiouser and curiouser. Eccentric baroque interior, clients regimented by strict, buttoned-up waitresses, but excellent choice of classic cuisine.

Sipario 69 rue de Charenton, 75011 (tel: 43 45 70 26). Classy Italian cuisine and theatrical restaurant. Near Bastille Opera.

Thoumieux 79 rue Saint-Dominique, 75007 (tel: 47 05 49 75). Part bistro, part brasserie, a fashionable, friendly, animated place serving southwest specialties.

Vagenende 142 boulevard St.-Germain, 75006 (tel: 43 26 68 18). Art-nouveau setting and classic cuisine.

Willi's Wine Bar 13 rue des Petit-Champs, 75001 (tel: 42 61 05 09). Cheerful, British-run restaurant/wine bar. Stylish with good, fresh cuisine.

Budget

A la Cloche des Halles 28 rue Coquillière, 75001 (tel: 42 36 93 89). Typical animated local wine bar. Good for lunch; closes at 9 and on weekends.

L'As du Fallafel 34 rue des Rosiers, 75004 (tel: 48 87 63 60). Good kosher food shop with delicious falafels to eat on the spot or take away.

Au Bistrot de la Sorbonne 4 rue Toullier, 75005 (tel: 43 54 41 49). Crowded with students, noisy, friendly. Very basic dishes and prices.

Au Limonaire 18 Cité Bergère, 75009 (tel: 45 23 33 33). Classic, friendly bistro specializing in Côtes-du-Rhône. Local crowd comes for plats du jour and occasional spontaneous live music.

Au Petit Prince 3 rue Monsieur-le-Prince, 75006 (tel: 43 29 74 92). Gothic shadows reign. Attentive service and imaginative, seasonal dishes. Slightly upscale.

Au Sauvignon 80 rue des Saints-Pères, 75007 (tel: 45 48 49 02). Good for a quick snack if shopping in St.-Germain. Small, popular wine bar with much frequented terrace in summer.

Aux Artistes 63 rue Falguière, 75015 (tel: 43 22 05 39). Rock-bottom prices, but avoid the carafe wine. Otherwise copious, hearty menu. Crowded, not for tête-à-têtes.

Aux Bons Crus 7 rue des Petits-Champs, 75001 (tel: 42 60 06 45). Popular wine bar serving hot lunches. Barrels tower over tiny tables packed with locals.

La Baracane 38 rue des Tournelles, 75004 (tel: 42 71 43 33). Cooking from Gascony (duck) in small bistro. Very reasonable for the quality.

Le Baron Rouge 1 rue Théophile-Roussel, 75012 (tel: 43 42 54 65). A classic bistro selling wine from its barrels and serving delicious little platters. Closes early.

Batifol 14 rue Mondétour, 75001 (tel: 42 36 85 50). Part of chain but lively, friendly café-bistro attracting gregarious youth.

Bhai Bhai Sweets 77 Passage Brady, 75010 (tel: 42 46 77 29). One of numerous Indian and Pakistani restaurants in this atmospheric old passage. Excellent tandooris, lassis, and more.

Bistro de la Gare 59 boulevard du Montparnasse, 75006 (tel: 42 22 55). Also part of a chain but good value meat dishes, superb turn-of-the-century décor.

Le Bistrot d'Asie 16 rue de Belleville, 75020 (tel: 46 36 23 97). In a row of comparable Asian restaurants. Thai, Laotian, and Chinese specialties.

Casa Miguel 48 rue St.-Georges, 75009 (tel: 42 81 09 61). World-famous soup kitchen. Rock-bottom prices; lines are endless: noon–1 and 7–8 only.

Chai de l'Abbaye 26 rue de Buci, 75006 (tel: 43 26 68 26). Good lunchtime spot. Wine by the glass, reasonable salads, and plats du jour in heart of market street.

Chartier 7 rue du Faubourg-Montmartre, 75009 (tel: 47 70 86 29). Famous food institution, popular with tourists but still a must. 1900s setting, shared tables, speedy waiters.

Chez Georges 11 rue des Canettes, 75006 (tel: 43 26 79 15). A rowdy Left Bank institution, much loved by intellectual drinkers. Open till 2AM.

Chez Pépita 21 rue Bayard, 75008 (tel: 47 23 58 49). A rarity in this area: traditional cuisine in provincial-style bistro.

Le Citoyen 22 rue Daguerre, 75014 (tel: 43 22 53 53). Fresh dishes and home-made desserts, delightful summer terrace in animated market street.

Le Cochon à l'Oreille 15 rue Montmartre, 75001 (tel: 42 36 07 56). Open 4AM–3PM. Old-time Les Halles classic bar, good for early risers and late-nighters. Delicious hot dishes at lunchtime. Crowded.

La Côte 77 rue de Richelieu, 75002 (tel: 42 97 40 68). Quick, bustling wine bar, a favorite with local businessmen at lunchtime.

Dîlan 13 rue Mandar, 75002 (tel: 42 21 46 38). Friendly, large tables, basic setting. Kurdish and Turkish specialties.

Le Drouot 103 rue de Richelieu, 75002 (tel: 42 96 68 23). Large canteen style similar to Chartier but less fancy. Basic cuisine, cheap and cheerful.

Au Duc des Lombards 42 rue des Lombards, 75001 (tel: 42 33 22 88). Reasonably priced menu in young, friendly setting with jazz bar on first floor.

L'Ecluse 15 quai des Grands-Augustins, 75006 (tel: 46 33 58 74). Bordeaux by the glass, cold platters, small relaxed wine bar.

La Ferme 40 rue de la Montagne-Ste.-Geneviève, 75005 (tel: 43 54 49 85).

HOTELS AND RESTAURANTS

Relaxed, rustic atmosphere. Good value, popular with local students.
La Frégate 1 rue du Bac, 75007 (tel: 42 61 23 77). Unbelievable value for a chic quartier beside Musée d'Orsay. Old-fashioned, stilted brasserie (quite cheap) and restaurant (pricier).
Le Frog et Rosbif 116 rue St.-Denis, 75002 (tel: 42 36 34 73). English "pub grub" at lunchtimes only; English pub atmosphere.
Le Grand Bistrot 7 rue Saint-Séverin, 75005 (tel: 43 25 94 21). Serves late. Noisy, friendly atmosphere with reasonably priced menus. Make sure you try the snails.
La Gueuze 19 rue Soufflot, 75005 (tel: 43 54 63 00). A beer-lovers' paradise. Belgian specialties, lengthy list of beers.
Hawaï 87 avenue d'Ivry, 75013 (tel: 45 86 91 90). Huge, animated canteen-style restaurant in Chinatown. Generous soups and Vietnamese specialties on offer.
L'Incroyable 26 rue de Richelieu, 75001 (tel: 42 96 24 64). Tiny, friendly, tucked away in atmospheric passage. Closes early.
Juveniles 47 rue de Richelieu, 75001 (tel: 42 97 46 49). Tapas-style snacks and salads served with wine by glass. Small, crowded, hard to squeeze in. Go early!
Osteria del Passepartout 20 rue de l'Hirondelle, 75006 (tel: 46 34 14 54). Simple Italian restaurant down minuscule alley. Inventive pasta dishes for reasonable prices.
Le Petit Saint-Benoît 4 rue Saint-Benoît, 75006 (tel: 42 60 27 92). A favorite cheap restaurant, its waitreses and décor unchanged since the 1930s.
La Petite Chaise 36 rue de Grenelle, 75007 (tel: 42 22 13 35). Founded in 1680. Copious all-in menu. Smart, popular, fun place.
Polidor 41 rue Monsieur-le-Prince, 75006 (tel: 43 26 95 34). In every guidebook but

still good value. Cheerful, open late, and tasty basic dishes. Service can be brusque.
Relais de la Butte 12 rue Ravignan, 75018 (tel: 42 23 94 64). Heavily laid-on Montmartre atmosphere, but excellent value nevertheless.
Le Relais Savoyard 13 rue Rodier, 75009 (tel: 45 26 17 48). Family-run neighborhood bistro. Good bourgeois fare.
Restaurant des Beaux-Arts 11 rue Bonaparte, 75006 (tel: 43 26 92 64). Popular meeting place for art students and impoverished philosophers. Inspiring décor and classic family cuisine.
Rose de Kashmire 66 Passage Brady, 75010 (tel: 42 46 23 75). Indian and Pakistani dishes in dilapidated covered passage, monopolized by Asian restaurants.
Le Royal Belleville 19 rue Louis-Bonnet, 75011 (tel: 43 38 22 72). Vast, canteen-like Chinese restaurant with endless menu of fine specialties. On the first floor with a different entrance is Le Président, which is slightly more upscale.
Le Rubis 10 rue du Marché St.-Honoré, 75001 (tel: 42 61 03 34). Time-honored wine by the glass and platters of cheese or charcuterie in jovial atmosphere.
Le Sunset 60 rue des Lombards, 75001 (tel: 40 26 46 60). Open till early hours, for jazz fanatics only. Traditional French food on the menu.
Tai Yien 5 rue de Belleville, 75019 (tel: 42 41 44 16). Another Belleville institution, popular with the local Asiatic community. You can enjoy wonderful soups and dim-sum specialties.
La Tartine 24 rue de Rivoli, 75004 (tel: 42 72 76 85). Popular old wine bar, good for lunchtime snacks, a glass of wine, and smoky atmosphere.
La Taverne Henri IV 13 place du Pont Neuf, 75001 (tel: 43 54 27 90). Ideal for a

quick snack, especially the open sandwiches on Poîlane bread.
Le Temps des Cérises 31 rue de la Cérisaie, 75004 (tel: 42 72 08 63). Closed in the evening. Popular 1900s bistro. Excellent value lunches.
Thuy Huong 15 avenue de Choisy, 75013 (tel: 45 86 87 07). Extraordinary concrete jungle environment for pavilion restaurants. Delicious Cambodian and Vietnamese specialties on the menu.
La Tourelle 5 rue Hautefeuille, 75006 (tel: 46 33 12 47). Unpretentious restaurant in historic building. Local favorite offering fast service and a choice of reliable dishes.
Le Troumilou 84 quai de l'Hôtel-de-Ville, 75004 (tel: 42 77 63 98). A range of very reasonably priced menus. Generous helpings, provincial atmosphere.
Le Volcan 10 rue Thouin, 75005 (tel: 46 33 38 33). Dependable old favorite with a choice of menus; international dishes are available.

Index

INDEX

INDEX

Acknowledgments

The Automobile Association would like to thank the following photographers, libraries, and associations for their assistance in the preparation of this book.

JAMES DAVIS TRAVEL PHOTOGRAPHY (front cover)

PICTOR INTERNATIONAL LONDON (inside back cover)

ALL SPORT (UK) LTD 95a (Gerard Vandy Stadt)

FULTON PICTURE LIBRARY 14, 46/7

MARY EVANS PICTURE LIBRARY 30b, 31a, 33, 36a, 37a, 37b, 38a, 38b, 39a, 40, 42b, 43a, 48b, 49, 112

MUSEE BACCARAL 79

MUSEE DE CLUNY 105a, 140a

PHILIPPE COVETTE 84

POPPOFOTO 115

TOPHAM PICTURE SOURCE 19

ZEFA PICTURE LIBRARY 82, 83
The following photographs were taken by **BERTRAND RIEGER** and from the Automobile Association's picture library (© AA Photo Library).

P ENTICNAP 3, 56b, 114, 134/5, 137a, 137b, 171

E MEACHER 24c, 181b

D NOBLE 29a, 35, 61a, 191, 192a, 193, 194, 198, 199, 202/3, 204, 205, 209a, 209b, 210, 211, 212a, 212b

K PATERSON 5, 6, 12, 13, 16, 20a, 21, 23, 26/7, 41, 46a, 52, 55a, 56, 69b, 71b, 76a, 87a, 88a, 89b, 91a, 93a, 94a, 98a, 101a, 101b, 106, 110a, 116a, 120b, 122a, 139, 140b, 166, 172, 177a, 177b, 184, 185, 186a, 186b, 187, 216, 226, 227, 232, 238, 244, 248, 249, 250/1, 256, 262, 263, 268/9, 270, 273, 277

B RIEGER 4, 7, 9, 14, 20b, 22, 26, 29, 30, 32, 34, 44a, 48a, 54, 58a, 59a, 59b, 60a, 63, 66, 66/7, 68, 69a, 70, 71a, 73a, 73b, 75a, 75b, 76b, 77, 81, 87b, 88b, 89a, 92a, 92b, 93b, 95b, 96a, 96b, 97a, 97b, 98b, 99a, 102, 107a, 107b, 109a, 109b, 111a, 113a, 113b, 117a, 118, 119a, 119b, 120a, 123a, 124, 125, 126, 127, 128a, 128b, 130a, 130b, 134, 136, 143, 144a, 144b, 146, 148, 149a, 149b, 150, 151a, 158, 163, 165b, 170, 173, 178a, 180a, 181a, 182a, 188, 189, 192b, 203, 207, 217, 218, 219, 220, 222, 223, 225, 228, 236/7, 239b, 242, 247, 260a, 261, 264, 267, 274, 275, 278, 281

C SAWYER 200, 201

B SMITH 237

A SOUTER 8, 17, 18, 24a, 36b, 42a, 45a, 61b, 64, 82a, 85b, 100a, 121a, 132a, 138a, 145, 156, 159, 161, 164, 165a, 168, 169, 174, 175, 179a, 179b, 224, 229, 230, 231, 233, 239, 252, 259, 265, 266

Contributors

Revision copy editors: Donna Dailey, Colin Follett
Original copy editor: Nia Williams